AWKINS
XLII-S 60
RDS 7/17/85
ROCK
odger
A&M RECORDS
xtra extra
ity
ONE RED CENT
P JR. &
HE CRIMINAL ELEMENT
S RADIO SPECIAL
D-C60
T.E.V.I.N.
Scotch XS II 60
maxell
BELIEVE?
UB UP THUGS
IC : V 2324
9/85
NING
LIMERICK
(212) 664-1000
New York, N.Y. 10019
ONES
ty Girl

CRIMINAL RECORDS SAMP
Jimmy Somerville/
ARTIST. NONA HENDRYX
PAUL McCARTNEY "NO MORE LONELY NIGHTS"
ARTIST. JENNIFER HOLLIDAY
BRUCE SPRINGSTEEN #2
TDK SA60 Tears for Fears "Shout"
'til tuesday 1
JET VEGAS 23.1.89
ARTIST Gwen Dickey
BILLY CRYSTAL: "YOU LOOK MARVELOUS!"
NEW ORDER 5 tracks
chappell music Ltd
TDK SA60 SOULSONIC - RENEGADES
Planet Patrol (rough)
SONY Ruffin/Kendrik UCX-S 90
MCA Sheena Easton "What Comes Naturally" (REMIXES)
Tina Turner "Whatever You Want"
TDK SA60 SOMETHING WILD
NEW ORDER - THIEVES LIKE US
TDK D30 The ABANDON Party Scene 1/12/84
POLYGRAM RECORDS NEW MUSIC SEMINAR SAMPLER
TDK

CW01020336

AKER
TDK SA60 Freeze Planet Patrol
FREEEZ ASSORTED
Confusion / Planet Patrol
(213) 938-3377 "QUINCY JONES PLAYS HIP HOP"
PRODUCED by Maurice STARR + michael Jonzun
TDK SA-X 60 ART: Debbie Harry Prod: Arthur Baker
H+O RUFFS w/BV's 8/1/8
PETER WOLF
DEBORAH HARRY Album Compilation
TDK "THE SAINT" NYC 10/83 DJ John Buchanan
TDK SA60 THE DANCE
WALLY JUMP JUNIOR
TDK SA60 CIRCUIT II (VERY ROUGH
BMG MUSIC PUBLISHING 2 SONGS GUY CHAMBE
UPFRONT 1 VARIOUS ARTISTS.
soundtrack
songs for Al Green
"TROUBLE" - Big Troub
TDK AV-D30
JVC
PETE WYLIE

LOOKING FOR THE PERFECT BEAT

This book is dedicated to my parents, Irving and Marilyn Baker, who gave me the freedom to follow my own path and taught me to treat all people the same; to my grandparents, Jennie Levicheska and Arthur H. Baker, and Jacob Kaplan and Jeanette Salamoff, immigrants who made their way to this country and did the best for their children; to my aunt, Dorothy Levine, the matriarch of our family, for always being there for me; to Owen Epstein, Mark Kamins, Gabby Mejia and Greg Sutton, amazing friends who left us way too soon; and especially to my wife Annette and my daughter Amarone for their constant love, understanding, support and faith.

ARTHUR BAKER

LOOKING FOR THE PERFECT BEAT

• REMIXING & RESHAPING •
HIP-HOP, ROCK & RHYTHMS

faber

First published in 2025
by Faber & Faber Ltd
The Bindery, 51 Hatton Garden
London EC1N 8HN

First published in the USA in 2025

Typeset by Faber & Faber Limited
Printed and bound in the UK by CPI Group (UK) Ltd,
Croydon CR0 4YY

All rights reserved
Copyright © Arthur Baker, 2025

The right of Arthur Baker to be identified as author of this work has been asserted in accordance with Section 77 of the Copyright, Designs and Patents Act 1988

Every effort has been made to trace copyright holders and to obtain permission for the use of copyright material. The publisher would be pleased to rectify any omissions that are brought to its attention at the earliest opportunity.

A CIP record for this book
is available from the British Library

ISBN 978–0–571–38742–7

Printed and bound in the UK on FSC® certified paper in line with our continuing commitment to ethical business practices, sustainability and the environment.
For further information see faber.co.uk/environmental-policy

Our authorised representative in the EU for product safety is
Easy Access System Europe, Mustamäe tee 50, 10621 Tallinn, Estonia
gpsr.requests@easproject.com

10 9 8 7 6 5 4 3 2 1

CONTENTS

INTRO

FIFTY YEARS OF LOOKING FOR THE PERFECT BEAT

Over the years I've been asked many times what a record producer does. It's a job most music fans have heard of and have a basic understanding of, but it's rarely explained. My take is based on my five decades in the music business. It is specific to me but may shed some light on this complex role.

When I first started reading the credits on record sleeves as a young music fan, I realised numerous people were involved in the making of the records I loved. I noticed that on my favourite labels – Philly International, Stax and Motown – the acts typically weren't writing their own songs. There were guys like Norman Whitfield, Gamble and Huff, Porter and Hayes who were creating the music – record producers. Other names popped up on rock records – Glyn Johns for the Stones, George Martin for The Beatles, Tom Wilson for Dylan – but they were producers, not writers, since most rock bands wrote their own songs.

While I loved rock, I was really drawn to black music. But I couldn't sing and had neither the focus to master an instrument nor a performer's personality. All I wanted to do was write songs like Gamble and Huff, find great vocalists to sing them and make people dance (OK, I had irrational confidence).

I first started working in a record shop, then tried my hand at DJing, before taking an engineering course, which got me into a studio. And as luck would have it, I was able to convince the owner to let me produce a disco record, totally on a blag . . . and that's how I started my career as a producer.

What does a record producer do? In film and theatre, producing is a business function, while in music it's creative, akin to the work of a film director. A record producer's job description? First, you must be an excellent listener, not only of the act's music but also their deeper thoughts and desires. You need to know what you like – be an arbiter of good taste – while staying focused on helping the artist achieve their own unique goals. You must direct and inspire this creative process, while keeping your own instincts secondary to those of the artist. Good communication skills are a must, along with being a great leader – part headteacher, part therapist, part blagger and part salesman. Finally, you need full focus on your ultimate goal: to facilitate the timely completion of the record to the satisfaction of the artist and the record label. Not an easy job, and not one, amazingly, I have ever felt very comfortable in.

From day one, I just wanted to make my own music, more in the Mark Ronson style than that of my old friend Rick Rubin (who claims he knows nothing about music or technology). I may be a hybrid of the two, tech not being my strength and having never mastered an instrument, but I love songwriting. Collaborating on compositions with bands like New Order and Freeez was always my dream gig; it was really the only way to keep me fully engaged in a project. However, remixing is my perfect job because you are left on your own to finish the track.

I constantly hear the 1980s sound I was known for referenced in the pop music of today, be it the 808-like beats of Taylor Swift or the arrangement style of Olivia Rodrigo. The programming, FX and innovations developed with 'Planet Rock' have become part of a pop template that has survived all these years. I hear them all over tracks by The Weeknd, Kendrick Lamar and Drake. These artists probably have no clue where that sound came from, and maybe even their producers don't know the original source. These elements are now just part of the musical lexicon.

Trying to organise my life story hasn't been an easy experience. Researching a life spent carelessly going for it, at least in my early days, while combating ADHD has been, let's say, somewhat challenging. When I first attempted to decipher a timeline of my life's work, I was often saved by the engineer's notes carefully transcribed on forty-year-old track sheets stashed in my boxes of two-inch tape and cassette cases from the numerous studios I worked in all over the world. Having seen how they have finally come in useful, my wife Annette has finally stopped calling me a hoarder!

It was my incredibly understanding wife who convinced me to sit down and write this book. She thought it was important that I leave a coherent story of my life for my daughter, Amarone, so that she would have access to it once she was old enough to understand and appreciate it. So, of course, I gave it a go.

As I watch my daughter grow, it's crazy how much of myself I see in her. She is creative and loves to sing, dance and make up songs (and also has my lack of focus!). She's ten now, and she doesn't listen and thinks she knows better than me! It's always a discussion, which was how I was with my own dad. I was fortunate to be able to give my father, in his later years, some precious time with Amarone, having moved to Miami when she was about six months old. When they immediately bonded, I really appreciated the fact that I had finally given him a grandchild to enjoy. I think he had given up hope. Unfortunately, he was on dialysis the entire time and sadly passed away three days before her second birthday. He was an extremely loving, open and liberal person to the very end, which absolutely influenced me in a big way. He gave me the opportunity to follow my dreams and taught me how to treat all people the same, which, surprisingly, wasn't that common among my friends' parents. But one thing that my dad attempted to instil in me as a child was how crucial it is to keep your things organised. He was a Leo, and an anal one at that. His mantra was, 'Put your bike away.' For some reason, I was totally incapable of doing it. I'd stuff papers in my desk drawer as opposed to filing them – something I do to this very day. This inability to focus (no one mentioned ADHD back then) showed up in another way: my decision-making process, or lack of it.

What I'd love to communicate to my daughter, first and foremost, is that artistic creation should be motivated by joy, not by fame and financial gain. The other day, the words 'Put your heart into your art' came out as I watched her make some jewellery. I told her that when I first set off on this journey in music, it wasn't about celebrity or money; it was about moving people, both physically (as in dancing) and spiritually/intellectually (as in getting my message across).

Fifty years later, that hasn't changed. I'm still driven by the joy of seeing people in a club jumping to that first play of a track I've written . . . and yes, I'm still looking for the perfect beat.

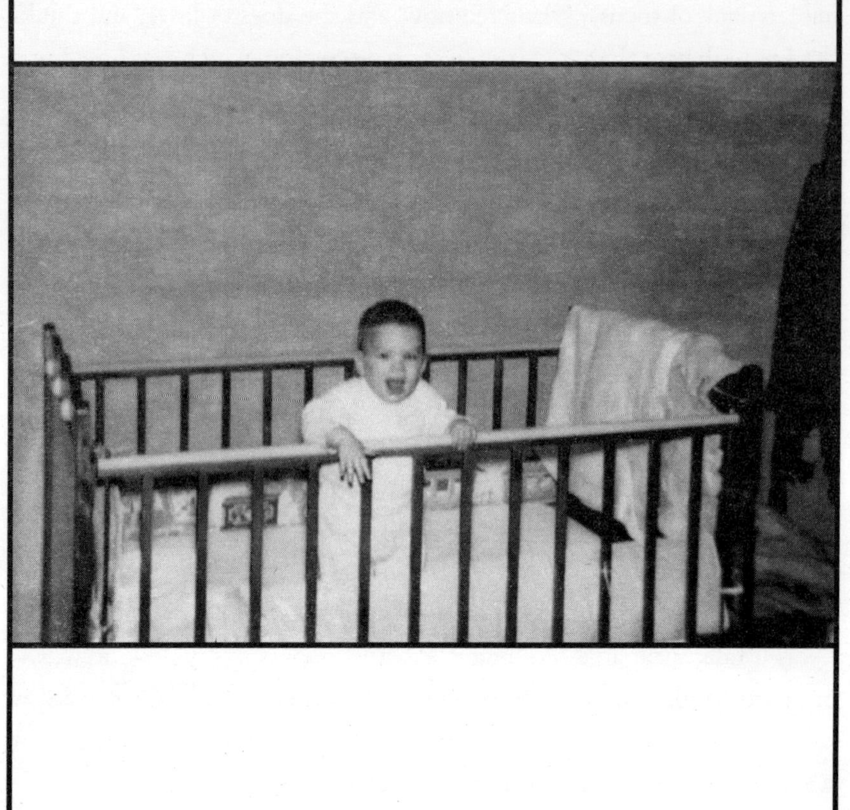

1.

SCHOOL DAZED

1955–69

From the first time I heard the mournful psalm 'Avinu Malkeinu' during a 'Kol Nidre' service at temple as a small child, to my parents playing me the *Fiddler on the Roof* soundtrack on the new hi-fidelity record player they were so proud of, to hearing The Beatles on *The Ed Sullivan Show* blaring out of the small speaker on my cousin Marcia's television, music has been a constant for me.

My mother, Marilyn Kaplan, loved to sing and came from a musical family. Her first cousin was Sidney Ramin, Leonard Bernstein's lifelong friend and arranger, who won an Oscar for his arrangement of *West Side Story*. He also wrote the theme tunes for *The Patty Duke Show* and *Candid Camera*, as well as 'Music to Watch Girls By', which was used in a 1960s commercial for Pepsi. His accomplishments were a source of great pride for my family.

My mother's brother, my uncle Arnie, always bought *Billboard* and *Cashbox*, followed the charts and loved acts like Johnny Mathis, Perry Como, Tony Bennett and, strangely, British vibist Victor Feldman. But, alas, my father, Irving, a real Nat King Cole fan (he met him when he worked for a florist and delivered flowers to him – and I have the autographed picture to prove it), was totally tone deaf, a fact that would always embarrass me and my sister Linda when he sang loudly and proudly, yet tunelessly, in temple.

My first exposure to pop came from tuning in to the station WMEX, either with my ear stuck to the speaker of my little transistor radio (which I also used to listen to the games played my beloved Red Sox and Celtics – what kid in Boston didn't?), cruising with my parents in their Chevrolet or combing the beach, girl-watching with my father and his friends and usually listening to Arnie 'Woo Woo' Ginsburg, a Jewish DJ who grew up near my dad in Roxbury.

Arnie was supposedly buddies with The Beatles, and he was the quintessential early-1960s DJ, with all the bells and whistles. He shilled for the local burger joint, Adventure Car Hop, and would give away records if you could get to the joint quickly enough with the answer to his quiz. Which is how I got my first-ever record, 'My Bonnie' by The Beatles

My sister Linda and I walking the Freedom Trail, Boston, Massachusetts, 1964.

(featuring Tony Sheridan). We were driving out to Winthrop to visit my grandmother when Arnie announced the contest, followed by his trademark 'woo woo' horn. My father sped over to the Adventure Car Hop in Revere, and I ran to the counter to collect my 45 and a greasy burger. I was nine years old and became hooked on music right there and then.

My parents spent a lot of time driving in that new white Chevy, with my sister and I in the back seat. They would educate us, frequently taking us to museums and historically significant Boston activities, such as the Freedom Trail. Linda was a few years younger, and I was that big brother who loved to tease. One time my dad, pissed off at me for annoying her, pulled the car over, kicked me out and then sped off. I was saved by Linda, who started to cry, and my dad, who I assumed had planned to return for me after a while anyway, drove back and picked me up.

As a toddler I was very hyperactive and would, incredibly, run off to Nantasket Beach whenever I could. When I started school, I had issues. I was regularly sent home and was once given a week off to think things through. I had a lot of energy, which I burnt off via sport, which was my other love besides music. I played them all, but I was only really good at basketball. I was on my high-school team, until I had a run-in with our right-wing coach, who wanted me to cut my hair! I was obsessed by the

My friend Donnie Merowitz, Marques Haynes of the Harlem Globetrotters, me and my cousin Arthur Levine, Boston Garden, 1966.

Celtics, the Red Sox and the Patriots. As was my dad, luckily enough. He had missed having a father who took him to sporting events, so he really enjoyed taking me to see the local teams, often with the entire family, which might have been uncommon back then. But sometimes it would be just me and him, and he would often let me stay late afterwards to get autographs. We met the legendary Marques Haynes of the Harlem Globetrotters after one game and even got a photo with him. But another night really stands out, when the Celtics played the Baltimore Bullets, who had this amazing rookie named Earl 'The Pearl' Monroe. He was the flashiest new player in the league. I really wanted his autograph, so Dad and I waited and waited after the game. After most of the players had left and I'd got a few of their autographs, we decided that I must have missed Monroe. But just as we were ready to leave, the Pearl appeared. I approached him nervously and asked for his autograph, and he signed my magazine. But he seemed a bit disturbed, like he was looking for someone. My dad asked him if there was anything wrong. It turned out that he had been inside doing an interview, and the team bus had left without him. He didn't know Boston, nor where he was going. Being helpful, my dad asked if we could drop him off somewhere. It seemed like a dream to me when the Pearl said, 'Yes, if you could drop me off at my hotel, that would be great.'

The Pearl squeezed into the passenger seat, moving it as far back as it could go. I got in the back. We stopped at a payphone and called the hotel for directions. It took a bit of a search, as the team was staying outside the city, but we finally found the place. The Pearl got out and thanked us a lot.

Years later, when I was living in New York, I ran into the Pearl right by my apartment on the Upper West Side. At the time, he had a record label called Pretty Pearl Records, which had a bit of a hit with 'I Want You (All Tonight)' by Curtis Hairston. I introduced myself and congratulated him on the record. I then told him the story of that night, knowing he wouldn't remember. He didn't, but I always thought it was cool of my dad to have done it.

If you had cool parents, like I did, you could actually listen to WMEX with them. We'd hear songs like Roy Orbison's 'Oh, Pretty Woman', the Beach Boys' 'Fun, Fun, Fun', The Supremes' 'Baby Love' and The Beatles' 'Michelle'. We'd listen to Tom Jones, Engelbert Humperdinck and the Four Seasons at our house or lounging by the beach, and all ages would dance to their songs, along with 'Hully Gully', 'Wooly Bully' and 'The Twist', at the bar mitzvahs I would attend until 1968. That was the cut-off point, when my musical tastes and political positions started to depart from those of my parents.

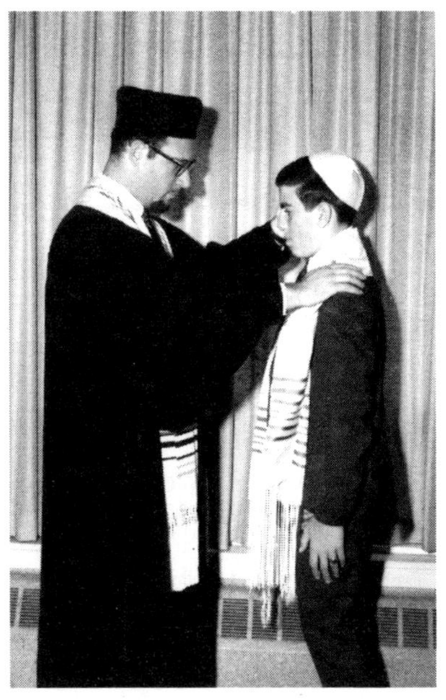

My bar mitzvah, 1968.

MARCO
POLO

2.

CHANGE THE TRACKS

1969–71

In the summer of 1968 I was thirteen, and in typical teenage fashion, ready to move on from sharing the car radio with my parents. I was looking for something different, and growing up in Boston in the late 1960s and early '70s, I was damn lucky. We had one of the first commercial alternative radio stations ever, WBCN, a station that was really a way of life for someone coming of age in those radicalised times. Man, what a time to grow up. The excitement was non-stop, electrifying. Everything felt new because everything *was* new. Bands didn't have to throw away the rulebook as there were no rulebooks written yet. Every day there was a new discovery to be made, and WBCN was your guide – in both politics and music.

There was a fight to wage, and win, with authority. They were the days of the Vietnam War, Richard Nixon, the Black Panthers, Yippies, Students for a Democratic Society (SDS) and the battle for civil rights. Believe what you've seen and read about these times. The music and WBCN – with its line-up of DJs, such as Charles Laquidara (fired after speaking out against the Polaroid Corporation for supplying lenses to the army for bombers, but reinstated after protests), Peter Wolf (who would become lead singer of the J. Geils Band) and radical newsman Danny Schechter, the 'news dissector' (who would later help me with the Sun City project) – spoke to us and for us. These guys were my teachers. Spurred on by them, my crew and I would participate in the anti-war protests in Boston. I was suspended from junior high for skipping class, heading up to the high school and inciting the students there to leave their lessons to protest the war.

The music they played on WBCN? From English medieval folk to west coast acid rock to acoustic jazz to psychedelic soul – there were no boundaries. I grew up listening to everything. Bands like Jefferson Airplane, Quicksilver Messenger Service, the Steve Miller Blues Band, Big Brother with Janis Joplin. Al Green and the Mahavishnu Orchestra would merge with Miles Davis, Jimi Hendrix, Led Zeppelin, Charles Mingus, Horace Silver and Muddy Waters. Sly and the Family Stone, the Allman Brothers, James Taylor, Joe Simon. Pentangle and Fleetwood

Mac would battle it out with Bob Marley, Bob Dylan, The Temptations, Jethro Tull and the Mothers of Invention.

Boston was the last stop on the concert tour route that most groups would take before hitting New York City, so I was lucky enough to see many of these bands perform in my home town. And when they played Boston, they typically played the 'Gahden': Boston Garden, where the Celtics played and I happened to have a great connection. Or my dad did. One of his business colleagues, Holly Holiver, a hat-maker, had a season ticket for the Celtics games. Holly introduced my dad to *the* guy at the box office, Ed Mullaney. This was the box office that handled the tickets for all the concerts at the Garden, so my dad had five great seats on hold for every gig. We had to pay, but . . .

While I couldn't convince my parents to let me go to Woodstock with my older cousin Marcia, they were comfortable with me going to the Garden, where I saw my first concert: Led Zeppelin, Johnny Winter and the MC-fucking-5 on 25 October 1969. I was fourteen, and I was going for it with my crew – Wade, Ralph, Bill and Jackie. We were a unique group. Wade was already a decent guitarist and

My friend Ralph Robinson and I on the Newman Junior High School football field, 1971.

had a lot of freedom, seeing as his bohemian parents owned the local record shop, and he was able to stay up late watching Johnny Carson. Ralph, Bill and I had somewhat stricter parents. Bill ran cross-country and loved the Mothers of Invention. Jackie was the ladies' man and the crew's tough guy. Ralph, who I'm still in touch with, was always messing around with his cameras, loved Miles Davis and had a waterbed. We all shared a love of rock music and marijuana. We came to that first concert with a bag of popcorn and a pocket full of joints. It was an unbelievable gig, with the MC5 kicking off with their proto-punk anthem 'Kick Out the Jams'. The sound wasn't great, but the energy was everything. I loved Johnny Winter, and his version of Dylan's 'Highway 61 Revisited' was unbelievable, probably my favourite cover ever. While Johnny was playing a rocking B. B. King track, a fight broke out in the crowd between two warring motorcycle gangs. As the lights came on, I'll never forget seeing blood spurting into the air as one biker hit another over the head with a crutch. To the fourteen-year-old me, this was rock'n'roll!

Zeppelin came on next, rocking their entire debut album (and sounding pretty much just like the record), as well as tracks from their yet-to-be-released second LP. One life-defining moment for me was closing my eyes while stoned as Robert Plant's voice decayed into eternity, singing the words 'Woman you need me . . .' Not bad for a first gig.

My second, a month later, wasn't bad either: Terry Reid, B. B. King, Ike and Tina Turner and the Rolling Stones. Besides the fact that the first live female rocker I got to see was the amazing Tina Turner, the headlining Stones were at their peak, playing lots of tracks from *Beggars Banquet*, with Mick Taylor on guitar on his first US tour.

While Ike and Tina Turner could share the stage with the Rolling Stones – in my new world, black and white bands would gladly appear together – racism and anti-Semitism were sadly still in the air in Boston. The Celtics were coached by a Jew, Arnold 'Red' Auerbach, and led by a black man, William 'Bill' Russell. The team would be the first NBA side to have an all-black starting squad and a black coach, but Boston itself was known throughout the league as a racist town, and with good reason. When most Americans of a certain age think of the city, they remember the racism shown by the citizens of South Boston during desegregation in 1974–5. Bused-in black children were jeered at, menaced and attacked by white kids and their parents. It was something reminiscent of the Deep South, and it featured on the national TV news every night. My parents were outraged.

My grandmother Jennie Levicheska Baker, 1971.

I had been born and raised in the city of Boston, proper, where my Ashkenazi grandparents had settled after leaving their homelands. My dad's mother, Jennie Levicheska, had made her way, alone, on a freighter from Chernobyl, Ukraine, to Boston, where she met my grandfather, Arthur Henry Baker (his name was actually Artur Beker, but whoever took the information at immigration anglicised it), who was from Augustów, Poland. My mother's parents, Jacob and Jeanette (Salamoff) Kaplan were also of Polish and Ukrainian descent. We were a small, close-knit family. My dad had two sisters, Edith and Dorothy, who had three kids between them – my only first cousins. We spent lots of time together, especially when celebrating the Jewish holidays with my grandmother Jennie, who cooked a great brisket and amazing sweets, which I'd pocket any time I could.

My parents, sister and I lived in the city of Boston until I was ten, when we moved out to the suburb of Needham, to our own house, complete with a backyard. Little did we know we were moving to a part of town that wasn't very tolerant of people of the black or Jewish persuasion, of which I was one. I was called a 'kike' for the first time by my Irish 'friend' John, who, I assume, hadn't learnt the word on a game show. There were not many Jews in Needham, but *no* black kids in our school or anywhere else, as far as I could tell. When the first black family moved in, it was big news in our 'hood, and the welcome wagon was not waiting for them. Apart from, I can proudly say, my dad. Being Jewish, he'd experienced anti-Semitism and wouldn't stand for the racism of some of our neighbours. I'll never forget that long walk down our street to knock on the door of the Evanses, welcoming them to the neighbourhood. They were very nice and accepted our hospitality.

There weren't any black kids in my school until 1971, when a programme called METCO started to bus in from Boston black and Latino kids who wanted to get a better education. It was great for me because I could finally expand my horizons a bit. I had always loved black music and respected black athletes but had no black friends. It took a while before the new kids became comfortable with their surroundings, and it was sports and music that helped break down the walls. I became friends with a METCO kid named Taweh Baysolow, from Nigeria. He played soccer and ended up being a star on the high-school team, and we were both into Isaac Hayes. Then my sax-playing friend Tom Nutile joined a band that one of the METCO kids was in called the Concessions. They ended up gigging at our school, playing convincing versions of Sly and the Family Stone songs. Everyone in the band was black, apart from Tom (who ended up with a black girlfriend).

As I was navigating and growing up in these crazy times, my heroes, both political and musical, seemed to be dropping like flies: JFK, RFK, MLK, Malcolm, Fred, Jimi, Janis, Duane, Otis, Brian. I clearly remember losing each one. One political hero I did get to meet was a local kid gone 'bad'. When Abbie Hoffman was young, he had been the head of the same Jewish youth group, NFTY, that I later belonged to, but had gone on to become a leader of the radical Yippie movement and one of the legendary Chicago 7. How I met Abbie was typical of me as a kid. I was getting ready for school – this was in my last year of high school – and had the local TV station on (and I do mean local – it was a five-minute walk away from my house), when the host said, 'Next on, Abbie Hoffman.' As the show broke for commercials, I grabbed an already-rolled joint (I kept them prepped in a cassette case) and was out the door. I ran all the way to the station, managing to catch my breath and appear somewhat chilled just as Hoffman strolled out of the door. There was a limo waiting for him. I greeted him, pulled out a joint and fired it up. He motioned me to the car, and we started hitting the joint. He asked me where I was going. I told him I lived close by, so we took a ride around my neighbourhood, getting stoned. As we pulled up to my house, he handed me an aluminium wrap and said, 'Here, kid. Good meeting you.' And he was gone.

I ran into the house, unwrapped the tin and found a greyish powder in it. My first opiate, courtesy of Abbie Hoffman!

My family home, 28 David Road, Needham, Massachusetts.

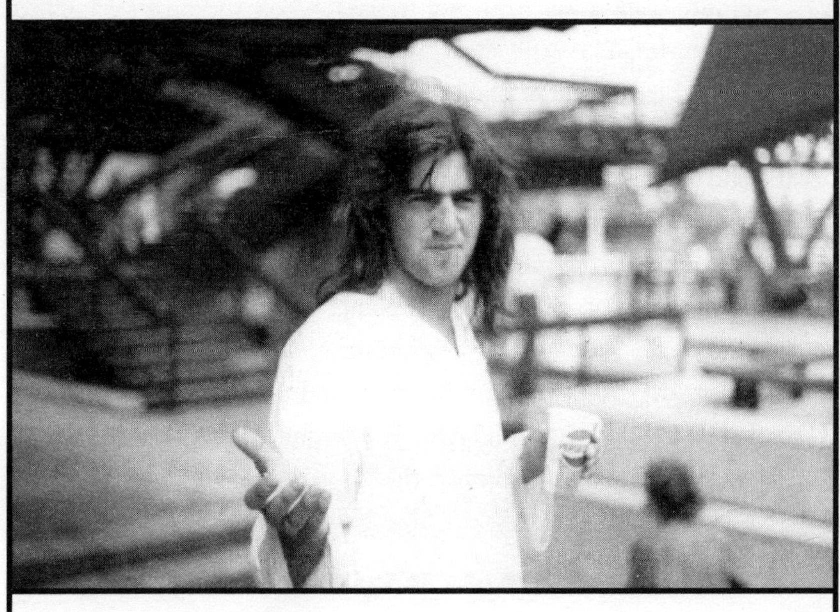

3.

STREETS OF LAREDO

1972–3

In the summer of 1972, right before senior year at high school, I somehow convinced my parents to let me go on a road trip to . . . Mexico! My friend Steven and I, in his VW bug, travelled in a convoy with his older brother, Neil, who had his own car. He was moving down to Laredo, Texas, and Steven was helping him with his move. I didn't know till a bit later that he was going there to enter a Jews for Jesus seminary.

As a student in Needham's Alternative High School, I was able to make this trip part of my senior curriculum, borrowing a video camera to document our travels. My English teacher, Phil Wallace, had helped me convince my parents that it would be a great learning experience. I remember how angry my grandfather, Jacob Kaplan, was that my parents were letting me go. He was pretty much a full-blown bigot, much like the Archie Bunker character in the TV sitcom *All in the Family*. Crazy thing was, he was friends with many 'coloureds', whom he would play pool and go to the horses and dogs with. Also, he had run away at twelve to go on a whaling ship, despite not knowing how to swim at all. His parents had thought he was dead, until he just showed up a few years later. So the idea that he didn't think I should be able to hit the road at seventeen was pretty funny. What's more, at the end of World War II my dad had tricked his mother into signing a waiver so that he could enlist in the Coast Guard at the age of sixteen and serve with his older friends! My road trip seemed quite tame in comparison.

Steven and I would follow Neil to Laredo and then make our way to Mexico. We decided to make a stop in New Orleans. This was summer 1972, and we were totally immersed in rock'n'roll. I had

My grandfather Jacob Kaplan.

made plenty of cassettes for the trip, and The Who, The Kinks and the Stones were heavily represented on the playlist.

We had some weed with us and were driving stoned fairly frequently. At one point we picked up a hitchhiker named Larry, an ex-Marine who played a pretty mean blues harp. He also had a bag of so-called crossroad speed, which we started popping. Since there were now four of us travelling in two cars, we'd swap driving companions to alleviate the boredom. Neil was a relatively straight dude, and I don't remember him doing any drugs.

The action really started when we got to New Orleans. Steven and I were at a stop light, and a car pulled up next to us. The two brothers inside it asked if we wanted to buy some weed, which by coincidence we did. So we stopped the car, and before you knew it, one of the guys had pulled a knife and grabbed my camera.

We drove away after that.

Ex-Marine Larry was in the other car, unfortunately. He and Neil pulled up, and we told them our sad story. We were in New Orleans, so we decided to walk around and try to have some fun. We started drinking, which you could do on the street. Larry got a bit messy, and one thing led to another, and he ended up giving a cop shit. Not a good idea. The cop grabbed him and threw him in his police car. Busted. Larry's pills were in our car. Should we wait or should we stay? My memory of this is a bit vague, but next thing I remember is heading out of the Big Easy without Larry and popping the pills.

We got to Laredo and the Jews for Jesus compound. I was weirded out by the place and told Steven I'd like to get the fuck out. He said he wanted to check out what his bro was getting into, so we went in and sat in this big circle, while people gave testimonies about their Jewish relationship with Jesus. I looked at Steven and saw he was sort of getting into it, as was Neil. Remember, the car was Steven's. I sort of shook him a bit, trying to wake him up from his Jesus slumber. Which worked. We hightailed it out of there, leaving Neil in the circle.

Steven Wolfson.

So we were off to Mexico. The first night, we ended up crashing on a strip of grass next to a road in Laredo, in the middle of a residential area. We were woken up the next morning by a dog. We were both hungry, so we ended up going to a diner, where we met a mother and a daughter who invited us back to their home. I'll leave the rest to the imagination.

When we finally made it to the border, we were told by a Mexican border guard to 'Get a fucking haircut, you hippie scum. You ain't getting into Mexico with all that hair!'

Steven and I looked at each other, and then at him, and said in unison, 'Fuck you, asshole. I will never come to your fucking country.' And I didn't, until decades later.

We'd had enough and got in the bug, popping pills all the way home. Tripping, but not on acid. The most insane spiritual moment of the trip happened when we finished singing The Who's 'I Can See for Miles' at the top of our lungs in the middle of the night, and I turned on the radio and that very same song was playing.

We luckily made it back in one piece, and I readied myself for my last year in high school. The Alternative High School saved my life back then. Without it, I would never have graduated. We were allowed to make up our own curriculum, and work experience counted. So during that last year I got a job at a record store, Strawberry Records, on Boylston Street in Boston. It was co-owned by a man who would become a business partner with me in New York about ten years later: the legendary Morris Levy. Working at Strawberry Records allowed me to expand my record collection and experience stuff outside of my small-town surroundings. The main thing was, it got me free entrance to gigs at the two best live music venues in Boston, the linked basement clubs Paul's Mall and the Jazz Workshop, where I got to see some incredible shows. I was in the house for Bob Marley and the Wailers' first US concert performance, in 1973. Full original band in a 300-capacity bar! I also saw Little Feat's Dixie Chicken tour, when Bonnie Raitt performed with them too.

Mike Connors, Wade Daniels, Judy Daniels, unknown and me, alone at home, summer 1973.

But probably my most magical experience happened when I got to see the man himself, Muddy Waters, right before my eighteenth birthday on 13 April 1973. I went on my own, as most of my friends' parents wouldn't let them sneak into bars underage. Somehow, I convinced my parents it was important. Paul's Mall wasn't the typical juke joint that Muddy might have played in Chicago or Memphis, but it would do. It was a snug basement bar, with a low ceiling and old-school wooden walls. Muddy was touring to promote his Chess Records *Fathers and Sons* album and had 'Mojo' Buford with him on harp. The show was rocking. I mean, c'mon, man, Muddy fucking Waters in a basement bar – of course it was rocking! Afterwards, I tried to get backstage as usual. Often, I didn't manage it, but this time – BAM! I walked through a half-opened door, and there was the man, Muddy Waters. I had a million questions for him, but I forgot them all in that moment. I ended up blabbing on about what a fan I was, how I loved the blues and was trying to play harmonica. Muddy was kind and listened to me, until he suddenly realised that we were there alone and the rest of the band had left. So I asked him if he needed a ride, much like my dad had with Earl the Pearl years before. He explained that he wasn't staying in Boston but crashing at his agent's home, in a suburb called Newton. Amazingly, it was the next town over from Needham. I could drive Muddy Waters home!

Not wanting to miss the opportunity to get his new album signed, I took a detour via my house so I could grab my copy. We then continued to the suburban apartment house and met up with the rest of the band. They were already in the midst of some hardcore whisky drinking and had a few laughs about me driving Muddy to my house first. I had a few shots of Jack Daniel's, got my record signed and made it home before sunrise.

Then there was my meeting with the wicked one, Wilson Pickett. He was in town for one of his legendary Sugar Shack gigs. The Sugar Shack was *the* place for black music in Boston in the 1960s and '70s. Mr Pickett needed a reel-to-reel tape deck to listen to something (never really knew what, probably some Memphis demos) in his hotel suite. My job was to bring the deck in, set it up and then leave. I didn't expect Wilson himself to open the door and let me in. Picture it: me, a seventeen-year-old, ripped-jeans-wearing hippie kid, walking into the penthouse of this sharkskin-suit-wearing, baddest dude around (he had quite a rep). I turned the corner into the grand suite, and there was an actual pool table in the centre of the room. In the decades since, I've been in thousands of hotel rooms all over the world, and I've only ever seen a pool table in one other room: Chris Blackwell's suite at the Marlin Hotel in Miami, and Chris owns that hotel. Wilson's suite also had a bar, where three ladies were hanging out. They looked like they were ready for evening work, despite the fact it was only mid-afternoon. My throat tightened up a bit. There was a bottle of whisky on the bar and some glasses filled with rocks.

'Hey, kid, set it up over here!' Wilson ordered, pointing to the back bar. The ladies giggled. I probably looked a bit nervous. 'You wanna drink?' Wilson queried, with a look of what could be considered mock concern.

'Um, well, ah, OK.'

It went something like that. Whisky on the rocks it was, no mixer in sight, and still no music.

In a dream state, I hooked up the deck, got some music playing and started planning my escape. But before I could make my excuses, Wilson slammed a few balls around the pool table with a whack. 'Hey, kid, you play pool?' he drawled, as he reached inside his sharkskin-suit coat pocket, pulled out some sort of revolver and smacked it onto the bar. My heart dropped into my belly. I loved pool, but playing against Wilson Pickett? Panic must have painted my face. At this point I mumbled something about double parking and a traffic ticket and left Wilson, his ladies, his bemused 'Thank you' and my five-dollar tip in the dust.

I was clearly not destined to become a pool hustler, although years later I would end up co-owning a chain of pool bars. But I was destined to do something connected with the music I loved and the characters who made it.

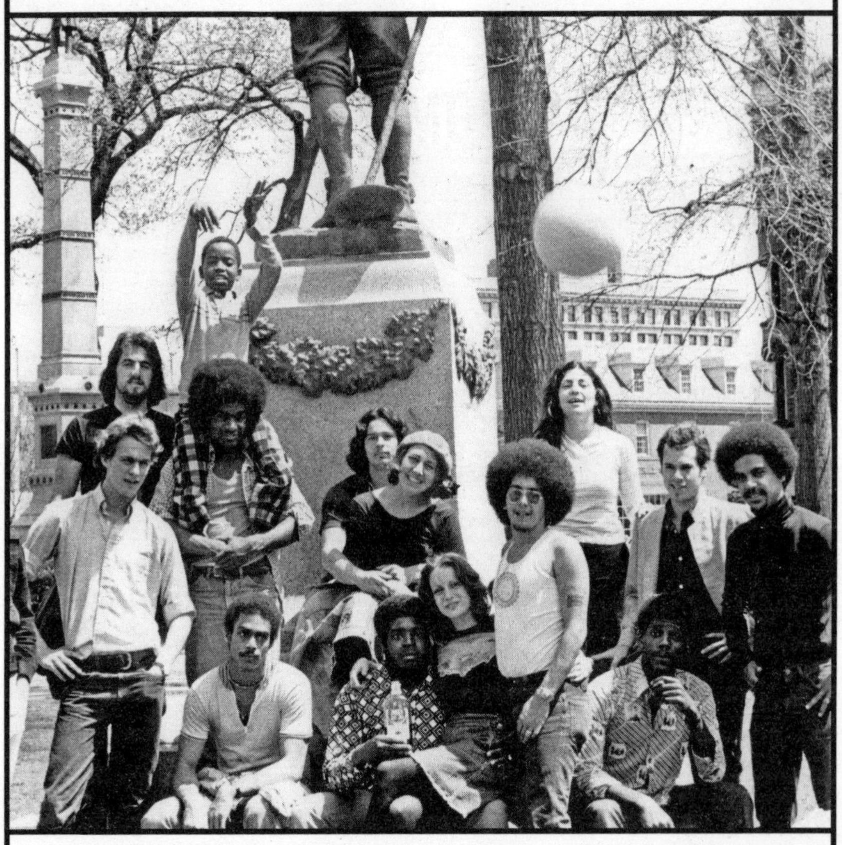

4.

'BOOM BOOM' BAKER

1973–5

I'm not sure where I first heard the word 'disco', but I know I first discovered soul music at thirteen, when I heard Sly and the Family Stone, Motown, Otis Redding and Sam & Dave on the radio. Then, a few years later, in 1972, I remember being stopped in my tracks by a song: Norman Whitfield's production of 'Papa Was a Rolling Stone' by The Temptations. I was driving to school one morning, pumping the radio on WILD in my mother's Plymouth Sport Fury, when I heard that bass intro, layered with symphonic strings. I immediately pulled over, mesmerised, and listened to the full ten-minute-plus version. I was transfixed. Yeah, I was late for school, but who cared? That song was a total game-changer for me, and Whitfield, along with the Philly International mighty three of Gamble, Huff and Bell, were the guiding lights I referenced when I eventually decided to try my hand at making music.

My love of danceable music has been a constant since those days. I loved the funk of Stevie Wonder, James Brown, the Average White Band and Earth, Wind and Fire, along with all those great classic Philly acts. But the concept that an individual could make a living playing this music in a club, as a DJ, was foreign to me in the early 1970s, and if you'd told me that DJs would take over the world some years later and become bigger than most musicians, I'd have asked what you were smoking.

I guess I *thought* I could be a DJ, as I had already built up a good enough record collection thanks to working at the record shop, with plenty of tracks that could make people dance. But the possibility that I could actually *make* that kind of music? Be a producer like my heroes Norman Whitfield or Gamble and Huff? Write and arrange songs, with no training and the lack of patience even to learn an instrument? That seemed woefully unrealistic and delusional. At the time, things appeared to move slowly, but looking back now, it seems that in a pretty short time I went from being a record-store clerk to an audio-engineering student to producing my own records to making tracks that got played at major clubs like Paradise Garage. I have to admit now that was an impressive trajectory.

So in 1973, when I graduated from high school, left my suburban home and took off for the wilds of Amherst, Massachusetts, and Hampshire College, it was with my growing collection of records in hand. I easily pegged into college life, smoking dope, playing basketball and blasting my James Brown jams out into the quad at very high volume. I met most of my new friends that way, including Tina Klein, who would go on to be my girlfriend.

Doc Rucks, going up for a jam, watched by Apache Ramos, José Aponte and me, Hampshire College, 1974.

Tina was a cute girl from Brooklyn with great hair and smile, and she was really clever. She loved the music I played and lived on the same floor as I did. We didn't become boyfriend and girlfriend right away, as I first messed around a bit – this was my first year at college, after all – but we ended up bonding that first year, during the famous arsonist semester at Hampshire. We had a crazy kid burning dorm rooms on a regular basis. Not a good look for an expensive hippie school. I had an idea on how us students could patrol the place, on the lookout for the culprit, without having to walk around for hours. The co-ed bathrooms were on the corners of the long hallways. We'd keep the bathroom doors open and have one student there, scanning the corner, and two other students, one at each end of the hallway. Tina and I patrolled on the same shifts. Never caught the kid, but the fires ended and one student disappeared, so . . .

Amherst was less than two hours from NYC, so I'd often head down to New York on weekends to check out the clubs and grab some hot tunes at Downstairs Records. I purchased a GLi Disco 3500 mixer and a Cat synthesizer on one trip, making my first jaunt over to Brooklyn to get them. The mixer gave me some cred and helped me throw money-making parties at Hampshire, in our own version of *Animal House*.

In my second semester, I moved into the House 3 modules, which were five-bedroom standalone condos, as opposed to the typical dorm room I had lived in earlier. My housemates included a crazy crew of Puerto Ricans from NYC and brothers from assorted east coast urban centres. Our crib was the place to be.

Me and Tina Klein at Hampshire College, 1975.

I was dubbed 'Boom Boom' Baker by my boy Apache Ramos (a short Puerto Rican with a huge afro and a great sense of humour), thanks to the volume and bass of my DJ sets. We shared a love of Santana, and he introduced me to salsa music. By early 1975 my growing reputation helped me blag a DJing gig at the only disco in town, Rachids. I had all the great jams of the day, like Donna Summer's new track, 'Love to Love You Baby', and I also had my crew, who'd come down to the club to hear me play records. I was never a great DJ. In fact, I was dreadful, lacking both technical proficiency and patience. If I played a track and people didn't dance, I might smash the record and throw it on the floor. I couldn't beat match or mix in general, my only plus being that I had decent taste.

Me DJing at Rachids disco, Amherst, Massachusetts.

I really didn't do much studying at Hampshire, but I did take an electronic-music class, which was cool and way ahead of its time. The professor was named Everett Hafner, and it was a one-of-a-kind class. They had one of the first ARP synthesizers and a bunch of reel-to-reel tape recorders. I don't think a studio like that existed anywhere else at the time. My friend Garth and I took the course, and there were two other strange dudes: a guy whom I played ball with called Rob Manning, and his friend, a nerdy guy named Chris Hanley, who went to Amherst College. They would both reappear in my life in the early 1980s, as owners of Intergalactic Studios in NYC.

Hampshire sort of emptied out for winter break, and in early 1974 my old travelling buddy Steven called me again, this time inviting me to take a road trip to Miami with him. His parents had a condo stocked with filet mignons, and it was empty for a few weeks. Sounded great, but little did I know what was in store for me. 1974 was a great year for American soul music. Between the sound of Philly and Motown, amazing tracks were dropping daily. But the South was also the stronghold of a new soulful sound, and riding through there listening to regional radio gave me an amazing education. Songs like Latimore's 'Let's Straighten It Out', Little Beaver's 'Party Down' and Betty Wright's 'Secretary' all hit me like a brick, even when they were coming out of Steven's little VW speakers.

Black Mail!

Send your letters to: Black Mail!, Black Music, Dorset House, Stamford Street, London SE1 9LU. Most interesting wins an album token, and the writers of all letters published will get BM T-shirts . . .

Top Notch Import

I have been reading Black Music for a year now, having stumbled upon it in an import magazine shop in Cambridge, Massachusetts. I find it definitely the most interesting journal on the subject of black music to be found, in the USA or elsewhere. Since a good deal of the music you cover in your magazine originates from America, you would probably assume that there would be top notch magazines dealing with such an important American art form. Not so! There are plenty of pre-teen picture book soul star mags, but nothing which covers the music with the intelligence and in-depthness of Black Music. It is a shame, since there is so much to be learned from and about the artists who are now entertaining such a great cross-section of my country and the rest of the world. Whether it be a form of institutional racism or a lack of the profit incentive that rules most facets of the music business everywhere, something is denying America a much needed journal. I consider myself lucky to have found Black Music. I am a disco DJ in a club on the outskirts of Boston, Massachusetts, and I find it very interesting to be able to observe British trends in soul/danceable music and also seeing outside observations of my own culture and trends. The articles in your magazine stimulate my thinking often. For example, I see that some of your writers have more purist leanings than I myself do. I try to view all music, whether it be jazz, rock, folk or soul on a musical continuum. I see so-called sophistisoul as a part of that popular music continuum; which may or may not be here for a long while, but will definitely be outlived by pure soul music. People like Van McCoy, Biddu, Hugo and Luigi, Jacques Morali, Harold Wheeler and the multitude of TSOP geniuses will definitely influence soul music, now and in the future, but eventually a good deal of the groups now churning out highly orchestrated disco material will revert to a more soulful sound. As for now, it may be commercial, but you sure can get down with it. I would really like to be able to correspond with Black Music readers; perhaps swapping the new releases in both of our countries and trading stories of our good times with our favourite music. **Arthur "Boom Boom" Baker, Apartment 39, Mt. Sugarloaf apts., Sunderland, Mass., USA.**—*LP winner.*

Keep On Keepin' On

Firstly I would like to thank you sincerely for "Black Music" throughout 1975 and for your exciting presentation, both educational and entertaining. Your writers are undoubtedly the best in the music papers of this country. I believe that it is no coincidence that black music has increased in popularity in this country since the face of Stevie attracted my attention back in November 1974. There is no doubt in my mind that BM has been, and shall continue to be, greatly instrumental in exposing true black music in Britain. Your variety is our mag, i.e. via an extended Black Mail, more crosswords, competitions and the like. The Disco Roadshow was a great idea for meeting the readers in the flesh and I can only hope that you will visit Merseyside next time around. We scouse brothers and sisters are lucky to have two fine soul radio programmes on Radio City and BBC Radio Merseyside presented by Phil Easton and Terry Lennaire, respectively. In many discos one can find a mixture of both fast "Northern" sounds and the latest funky records from the heart of Black America. Although certain people have criticised you for it, I am glad to observe that BM is concerned not only with the music but also with the people who make it. One must have an idea of the environment in which our music is made. You give us that. **Mike Allen, Monk Road, Wallasey, Merseyside.**

Reviewed Review

Nice to see the Originals in February's Black Music, but not so nice to read the comments on page 24 (singles reviews) regarding Tamiko Jones' "I'M SPELLBOUND". If you would like to rectify the implications, here are a few facts: The "A & R guy" was in fact "on the case" in August 1975 when Motown Los Angeles were first asked to provide the tape. It transpired after a month of searching, that America simply could not find it. Naturally the next step was to find an as near to mint copy of the original single, Now, no one needs to tell you, of all people, the difficulty in getting superstar disc jockeys to part with their precious exclusives, even for the few weeks needed to dub a disc. The result was, and still is, no Tamiko Jones original. If, however, any of your readers do possess a clean copy and are prepared to loan it, then the said record may appear. The same applies to any other suggestions that Black Music readers may have for oldie re-issues. Tamla Motown '76 is not Tamla Motown '75 and we are now open to all suggestions. **Bob Fisher, Press Officer, Tamla Motown.**

OHMS Out Deh . . .

I am one of your many FORCES readers and would like to thank the publishers of BM for a great mag. My interest in music is reggae, so I would like to say a special thanks to CARL GAYLE who did the article on BOB MARLEY which included "Dem Dread Out Deh", "Confessions Of A Rasta Man" and more recently "Straight to the Nation's Head". I find the pre-release charts good as I have to rely on the mag for info on the latest sounds and dubs, I would like to see more letters sent from the people who read BM—can you also encourage more younger readers to write in to the Black Mail spot in the mag. The mag has come a long way since the first edition, so keep up the high standards which make it the Nation's best mag for a long time. Hail to all the Brothers of the forces—come forward and let us unite through the powers of the most high. Jah can set us free. MARCUS GARVEY meets the ROCKERS uptown. What sheer brilliance dread out here . . . **Dexter B. H. White, CAD Bramley, Nr Basingstoke, Hants.**

well performed by Jimmy Helms and the delicious Kelle Patterson. Yes, thank you BBC for stirring. Now how about a new "Colour My Soul" series, or the showing of your recording of the Supremes' concert which you have left to be buried under inches of dust in your archives? I don't think the BBC (or ITV for that matter who seem to be totally unaware of the soul boom) have yet fully realised that soul is the music of the people and that the people want much more soul on television. COME ON TELEVISION COMPANIES LISTEN TO US!! **B. D. Thompson, Hardie Green, Blackfords, Cannock, Staffordshire.**

Swedish Opportunist

I absolutely agree with Charlie Gillett regarding your magazine, although I've said it before you started to quote him on your cover. It's one of the few magazines I find worth buying and reading. But can you please write something about the best of them all. The man who started all the jazz funk. MILES DAVIS! It will also make me happy if you would like to mention something about what Sly is doing nowadays, and something about that wonderful group called Parliament. I really enjoyed seeing and 'hearing' the Blackbyrds at Barbarellas in Birmingham. They were great! It's a fantastic opportunity I have this year when I'm staying in England, as no soul groups ever tour Sweden, where I usually live. All my answers to your Blackbyrds quiz are correct, and I think your questions are a little bit too simple. I'm looking forward to winning that album. Have you heard the resemblance on the track "Happy Music" between Ronald Byrd and Miles Davis?—**Mr Matz Borgstrom, 4 Gagdon Court, Gaydon Road, Solihull, West Midlands.**

Disco Mum

I am a newcomer to the disco scene—but I was lucky to choose a fabulous one in Bournemouth as an introduction. I may be relatively advanced in years but I discovered that age is not important—it is how you feel for music of today. I am sure that there are hundreds of "girls" in their thirties, like me, who have been out of action because of rearing families, who would love to return to the scene. Believe me, they will feel as right now as any teenager or twenty year old. The reason I chose the disco was the appearance there of George McCrae in concert. I was right among all the kids at the stage, and that fantastic man made it a night to remember—by holding MY hand, saying a few words to ME—and caressing MY face. Thank you for a wonderful magazine that encouraged me to get back into my music again. **Mrs Janette Nugent, Stone Lane, Yeovil, Somerset.**

Northern Soul-less . . .

All I want to say is that I agree entirely with Mrs. J. Anderson of Derby about the so-called Northern Soul Scene. Nothing is special about it all and it doesn't sound soulful to my ears either. Mind you, those who appreciate Northern Soul will probably say the same about good funk and reggae.

My award-winning letter to *Black Music* magazine, 1976.

Once we made it to Miami, I headed directly to a record shop and discovered that a lot of the records I was loving, be they on the Glades or the Cat labels, were coming from one source: TK Records. I also found out about a place where some of the best music was being cut: Criteria Studios. So Steven and I went over there on a whim, and I told the receptionist that I was a DJ from Boston. After a few minutes we were let in! I got all the way to the control room, where I met the producer of that day's session, Cory Wade, and watched the band, a new group called T-Connection, jam. They were rocking, and of particular interest to me was that the band and the mixing board were all set up in the one room.

So the trip was an amazing one, and besides discovering a whole new sound, we got to eat tasty filet mignon daily and drink gallons of fresh grapefruit juice. I lost 25 pounds during that winter break, without even trying. But when I got back to Hampshire, I didn't last too long at school. I really had no interest in anything other than music, sports and drugs. So when Tina graduated and got into law school back in Boston, it was a no-brainer for me to get out of Hampshire and head back there with her.

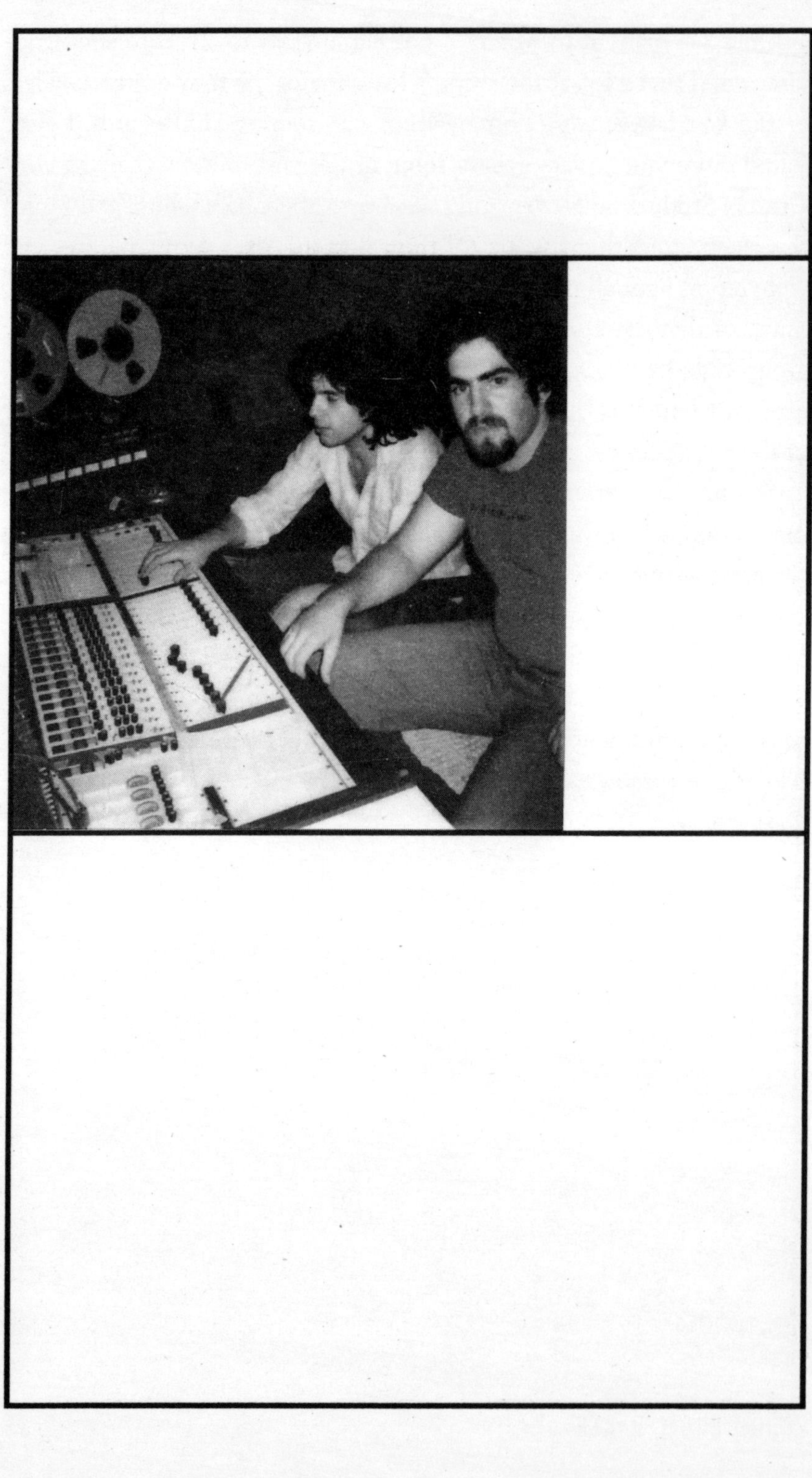

5.

THE COMBAT ZONE

1975–7

When Tina and I hit Boston, she started classes at Boston University law school. Actually, it was me who convinced Tina to be a lawyer. I once had vague dreams of being a lawyer myself but knew I didn't have the scholastic chops or focus to make it, so her being one would be the next best thing.

Following my typical pattern, I was back working in a record store, this time in downtown Boston. Discount Records was smack dab in the middle of an area called the 'Combat Zone', which was known for the Orpheum Theatre, strippers, hookers, pimps, porn-movie theatres and numerous all-night Chinese restaurants, where we often got an after-gig plate of decent Chinese for 99 cents. Discount was part of a chain, but although it was a nondescript corporate record store, it was full of characters, both employees and customers, who came right out of a 1970s flick. The manager's name was Reggie, and we clashed from day one, because I thought I knew more about black music than he did (he was black), and of course I did. I eventually gained his trust, and we became friends. He had this one great side hustle that really impressed me: he was way ahead of the curve, making and selling mix tapes ('Marvelous' Marvin Hagler, the champion boxer, was one of his regular customers), along with less legal stuff, from under the counter.

Around this time I took a trip down to NYC to attend the first *Billboard* Disco Forum. I drove down with Alan Schivek, another Jewish kid from Boston who was trying to hustle his way into the record business. I'd met Alan through the Boston Record Pool, which I had just joined. The Pool, a distribution centre/DJ clubhouse that record labels used to reach DJs with their new releases, was headed by a very impressive DJ named John 'TC' Luongo.

TC spun at a black club called Rhinoceros, where he would rock the crowd by extending the breaks of the funky 45s he'd play by going between two copies, much like Grandmaster Flash and other hip-hop pioneers would later do. John also published a music/lifestyle magazine called *Nightfall* and had already produced his own *Nightfall* disco awards show. John Luongo pretty much *was* the disco industry in Boston.

So hitting NYC with Luongo's name in my pocket and my Record Pool membership to open doors, I was able to make some great record-label hook-ups. Disco was just about to peak. Alan and I would do the official events and then hit some of the labels, getting records from Tony G, disco promo man par excellence at CTI Records, and legendary label owner Florence Greenberg of Scepter Records. We also somehow talked our way into the infamous Latin music imprint Fania Records and got to hang out with its owners, the legendary Masucci brothers, Alex and Jerry, picking up promo 45s and talking absolute shit.

'Yeah, Jerry, *really*. I'm the only DJ playing salsa in western Massachusetts.'

It worked, and I still have those early Fania discs.

Going to the Disco Forums helped me make connections with labels from Paris, Montreal and Tokyo, and also with the heads of the disco departments (yes, back then record labels had whole departments dedicated to the genre) of the New York labels, guys like Doug Riddick from Atlantic and David Todd from RCA. David was a DJ from Philly who had scored the disco promo gig at RCA, and I became friendly with him. A lot of local DJs would hang out at his office on Avenue of the Americas and 43rd Street, right by Downstairs Records. We'd rap about records and mess around, using the full DJ set-up he had in his office. There I met other jocks, like Richie Rivera and Larry Patterson.

Early one evening we headed over to a club called Galaxy 21, where David's friend, Walter Gibbons, was spinning. The club was pretty empty, and we were sitting on a banquette, listening to Walter play. At one point my head snapped up upon hearing this rapid-fire horn riff that kept repeating, on and on. At first, I thought that Gibbons had to be going back and forth between two 45s to extend the riff, just like I had seen Luongo do. But this kept going and building, until it broke into a great drum groove. David and I both got up and ran to the booth, only to find that Walter was playing a 12-inch unlabelled record. We were both blown away. We asked him, 'What the fuck is that?' He smiled and said it was his remix of 'Ten Percent' by Double

Exposure, and that it was going to be the first commercially available 12-inch record. We had just experienced the future of disco!

It felt like magic looking down at the decks and seeing this one 12-inch record doing the work we had assumed Walter was doing live. I knew immediately that the idea of extending a track, as we had done through the manipulation of two 45s, would become a thing of the past, once more of these extended versions were made and released.

When it came to disco, I was way ahead of Roger at Discount, thanks to my NYC connections, so I'd sometimes suggest European imports to him for his black-market tapes. He occasionally listened to me and would let me sell those imports from under the counter, splitting my small profit with him. One evening I was just locking up the store when a girl and two guys knocked on the door. I was about to tell them that we were shut, but the woman looked a bit familiar, and I realised it was Donna Summer, who was a Boston girl, with her hair tied back under a po-boy hat. The guys turned out to be Brooklyn Dreams, another act on Casablanca. So I let them in, and we hung out for an hour, them blasting and buying records, and me trying to pick their brains. Donna was very low-key and happy to listen to me go on about my love of disco and her music, and she signed one of her albums for me. I told them about my aspirations, and Donna was sweet and positive, saying that if she had made it out of Boston, I could too.

Everyone who worked at the shop had other stuff that they *really* did. A cashier named Barry Marshall had a band with his brother and sister called The Marshalls, who gigged around Boston. He mentioned a studio, Intermedia Sound, where he had been hanging out. I vaguely knew about Intermedia, as both Jonathan Edwards ('Sunshine') and Aerosmith ('Dream On') had recorded their recent hits there. So I went down to check it out, and finding that they offered engineering courses, decided to take one.

We needed a band to record for the engineering course, so I volunteered The Marshalls, and we ended up cutting their song 'In My Car'. Their Beach Boys-esque sound wasn't really my style. I wanted to cut a disco track, but I stuck with the course and finished it, getting my diploma that September.

I still wanted to DJ. The money was decent and being part of the Pool helped me get a regular gig at a chain of discos called Sadie's, located within the cocktail lounges of the Chateau De Ville supper clubs, which were as cheesy as the name suggests. I usually played the Sadie's in Framingham, close to Needham. This was in the early heyday of disco, right before *Saturday Night Fever*. Besides Sadie's, I occasionally scored gigs in some way seedier spots. One night I was playing in a random disco in Fall River, when I ran into a real character named Chico Walker. He was a singer who claimed he had been in the Motown group the Hearts of Stone. He now had a new group that was called, naturally, the New Hearts of Stone. He looked like a character from a blaxploitation flick. Chico made it clear to me that he ran girls in Providence, Rhode Island, and had plenty of cash money to make a record. I somehow convinced him that I was a record producer. Well, I had already produced The Marshalls' 'In My Car', and by then a ballad I had cut with C. L. Smith and the Fabulous Trends called 'Touch Me' was out and playing on the radio.

I had met Carl Smith at the Sugar Shack one night, when I went to see Blue Magic. The Trends had been the opening act, and I was impressed by Carl's falsetto. We got into a discussion about soul music, and I told him that I was a producer. We ended up going into a studio, using the Trends' back-up band for the session, and cut a cover of the Harold Melvin & the Blue Notes song 'You Know How to Make Me Feel So Good'. Carl decided to retitle it 'Touch Me'. It was a ballad and got played on WILD and my friend Rod 'The Hitman' Knight's soul show *For Lovers Only*.

Chico had heard it and was impressed, so we arranged for me to drive down to Providence to meet the rest of his band. I somehow found my way to Chico's spot, a seedy bar with music, dancing girls and flashing lights. He was sitting there when I arrived, with a few of his ladies in tow. He got up and introduced me to David Lawrence, his co-lead singer. They were both suited up, while I was wearing my

The Hearts of Stone, featuring David Lawrence (left) and Chico Walker (second from right), 1978.

standard sweatpants. We sat at the bar and had a few shots of whatever brandy a Providence dive bar was serving back in 1976. They were excited by a song they had written called 'Losing You' and quickly sang it to me a cappella. It sounded pretty good: Chico had a falsetto like Ted Mills from Blue Magic, while David had more of a Teddy Pendergrass-style gruff baritone. Together their voices worked well. I thought the song could be whipped into shape and we might have something. And Chico had some cash to invest.

I went back to Intermedia and met with the studio owner, Dan Cole. By then we had already chatted about music quite a few times. He was pretty cool, probably in his thirties, a hippie music guy. I had already hyped him up about disco, and when I told him about this group from Rhode Island that I had discovered, he seemed interested, so I asked the guys to come up and meet him at the studio. Still in suits (Chico didn't do casual), they stood and sang and showed some moves. Dan decided he'd front me some studio time and help me produce the recording. I was about to produce my first disco record!

I figured out what a producer did pretty much on the fly. It helped that I knew what I wanted the track to sound like. Dr. Buzzard's Original Savannah Band was hot at the time. I had met them at the *Nightfall* disco awards, and I liked their sound and the arrangements on their album. I thought their leader, August Darnell, was extremely hip, reminding me of my Puerto Rican boys from the Bronx. When Dan hired an arranger, John West, to do the charts for the various parts, I had him check out the Savannah album for inspiration. I mentioned I'd like a tom-tom break and described the type of drum pattern I was looking for. He went away for a few days to write up the arrangement and came back with the string, horn and rhythm charts all written. All super-professional. We ended up cutting the track at Intermedia on 7 April 1977. I was not even twenty-two yet, and I was in a studio producing a record with horns and strings. I couldn't believe my luck!

The track was cooking. John nailed that catchy tom-tom part, the horns were retro in the Savannah style and the vocals were hooky, especially the backgrounds. I thought we had recorded something really nice. I decided to bring in my now-mentor, John Luongo, to help me out with the mix. He was a creative DJ, but only had one remix under his belt, a Leon Collins record from back in 1974. This was his first 12-inch remix. I also had our two close friends, DJs Joey Carvello and Cosmo Wyatt, come in as disco-mix consultants. Cosmo and Joey both had the credibility of playing in Henry Vera's Kenmore Square discos: K-K-K-Katy's and Yesterdays (where I met my doppelgänger,

Wolfman Jack, in Joey's DJ booth!). Henry was already a legend and supposedly part of the Boston underworld. He was considered the Don of Boston's discos.

Me and Wolfman Jack at K-K-K-Katy's disco, Boston, 1978.

Joey, Cosmo, TC and I went into the studio to mix 'Losing You', working the cheap all-night slot. As we mixed, mapping out the structure of the song, I found inspiration in Walter's 12-inch mix of 'Ten Percent' by Walter Gibbons. We noted elements that we thought might work for disco breaks – sections where some of the music would be muted and other parts highlighted. We soloed vocals against driving drum and extended percussion sections. By the end of the night, we had an extended disco mix and a shorter version for radio. Next step, check it out in a club. Then try to get a record deal.

Since I had three of Boston's top DJs involved, I got an acetate cut so they could test the track out at their clubs. The response was pretty good, but I still ran into a problem in getting a deal for the record. Dan was no help; he was a rocker and had no disco connections. Luongo, who I thought would have some juice, helped me put a list of potential labels together, but that led nowhere. Cosmo had lots of contacts too, so we sent out cassettes and press releases and waited. One label, Vanguard, sent me a rejection letter, but there was pretty much nothing else.

As one last punt, I decided to try outside the States. Canada was a disco hotbed, and I had met some Canadian record guys at the Disco Forums. I had also been importing singles from Canada to sell under the counter at Discount Records, so I had a good list of Canadian labels. I tried quite a few of them, finally getting a response letter from Pat Deserio of Disco 1 records. I had met him recently at the third Disco Forum at the end of August 1977. Pat offered me my first record deal. It was a shit one, $300. But it *was* a deal, and it was a guarantee that the record would be released.

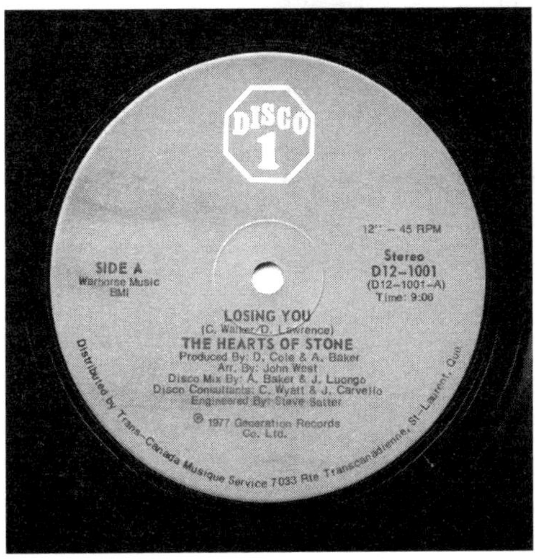

'Losing You' by the Hearts of Stone made it out in 1977, right at the end of December. The song made it onto the *Discotheken* 26 December chart at #48. *Discotheken* was the first standalone monthly disco magazine, run by DJs in NYC. 'Losing You' also charted on the *Billboard* Disco Action page at #13 in Boston and #9 in Montreal. DJ Richie Rivera, from New York's famous Flamingo, listed it in his top ten in *Record World*. So it was getting played in clubs in Boston, New York and Montreal. It felt like a great start.

6.

MAKE ME DANCE

1977–8

After the release of 'Losing You' I gained some credibility, as I was now actually a charted record producer. Didn't really matter to me what chart it was. Back then it was uncommon for a DJ to make the jump to producing, especially a no-name DJ like me. It was a start, but the recording scene in Boston wasn't like being in NYC, so I just had to keep hustling.

I met a French-African guy named Jo Bisso, at Music Designers Studio, who was making disco records. He was pitching himself as the French Barry White, which meant he did a lot of talking and a bit of singing. Not great, but his tracks did groove. To be honest, at this point I would have said yes to anything to get in the studio working with musicians, so I convinced Jo to let me advise him on the arrangement of a new track he was working on called 'Love Somebody'. For free, of course.

Jo Bisso's *Love Somebody*.

It was the summer of 1977, a famously hot one, and Tina and I were living temporarily in Brooklyn, as she had a summer internship at the Marshall, Bratter law firm (made famous by *The Wolf of Wall Street*). We were in a second-floor walk-up across from her parents' house by Kings Highway. This was also the summer of the Son of Sam murders, so everyone was really jittery. Which meant I was very happy as we hopped on a train back to Boston, trying to make it there in time for the Bisso session. Tina was going to sing backgrounds, and she was a bit nervous. I remember catching a cab from the train station straight to the studio and the excitement of walking in and hearing the musicians running through the song.

It was an epic thirteen-minute disco/afro-funk opus that went through three distinctly different sections. Tina was able to jump right in, joining the other two girls, Sharon and Linda, who were already there. She blended in well on the 'Love somebody, don't fight the feeling' background part, with the girls sounding very much like the Three Degrees. There was also some spoken word by Jo and talking and moaning (similar to Cerrone's 'Love in C Minor'). I was impressed by what I was hearing: the music was rocking and the bass player, Jeff Anderson, was super-funky, poppin' his bass like Larry Graham from the Family Stone. I took his number for future reference. Besides making a couple of random suggestions for breakdowns to Jo, I told him I thought the track was great and that I might be able to help him get a deal. He was going back to Paris to mix it but promised to stay in touch.

When summer ended, we moved back to Boston. I heard from Jo about four months later, saying he had released the track on Mercury in France, and he sent me some copies. It was, coincidentally, right around the time of Luongo's third annual *Nightfall* disco awards at Boston's Park Plaza Hotel. By then, I was a real member of the *Nightfall* family, having just written an article called 'The Rise and Triumph of Euro-Disco' for their April 1978 issue. The artists and producers who performed and attended that night were the crème de la crème of the disco world: the Village People, Chic, Loleatta Holloway, The Trammps, Peter Brown and Odyssey. Lots of national record-industry people were also in the house, so I figured this might be just the place to get Jo a deal.

There was a brunch at the disco/restaurant Jason's the morning after the awards, and I somehow managed to get 'Love Somebody' on the turntable to soundtrack the meal, bringing it to the attention of Howard Smiley, the vice president of TK Records. He loved it right away, saying he'd be interested in signing it to TK's new Marlin imprint. I connected him with Jo, and a few months later the album was released. My credit was a simple 'Thanks for strong personal support'. Better than no mention, I guess.

Right around this time, my mother fell ill. She was found to have cancer of the liver, a very aggressive form of the disease. She fought her hardest, and I focused a lot of my energy on her, spending time in the hospital and bringing family members over to see her. Of course, it really shook all of us. My sister came back from Ithaca, where she was at school, and transferred to Boston University, where Tina was finishing her law studies. Tina was very supportive towards the entire family and was always there for me. We fast-forwarded our plans and decided to get married while my mother was still with us, but she was too ill to attend, which made the wedding rather a sad event, with very few friends and family. Tina and I went over to the hospital after the ceremony to show my mother some Polaroids we had taken, so at least we were able to share the moment with her in some way. Recently, Tina mentioned that my mother told her that she thought I was going to be successful in whatever I did. I had no idea she had said this. Sadly, she didn't make it to see my career flourish, passing away shortly after the wedding day. This obviously threw the family for a loop. I gained a lot of weight, drank and rediscovered cocaine, which I sold to DJ friends in order to pay for my own stash. I threw myself into whatever work I could find.

I was introduced to a great lady named Kay Bourne by a writer at *Nightfall*, Mike Freedberg. Kay was the editor at the *Bay State Banner*, Boston's premier black newspaper. She happened to be white, but she seemed to be beloved by the black community. For some reason, she took a liking to me and offered me a music column called 'Breakdown'. No money was offered, but I jumped at the chance, as it gave me something to focus on. She promised that she'd get me into any soul/funk/jazz gigs that I'd like to review.

One of the first shows I attended as a journalist was by James Brown. And since I was on assignment, I got a photo of my meeting with the Godfather. I was somewhat speechless and just told him how

DISCO MUSIC:

The Rise and Triumph of Euro-disco

Dancing to the beat of a different drum.

By Arthur Baker

First there was *Love To Love You Baby*. Then there was *Love in C Minor*. Then there was more of Donna Summer, again and again; then there was no stopping it: a veritable flood of imported dance records blew disco dancers away and finally entered radio play-lists. We began to hear a host of new names: Bellotte, Moroder and Baldursson; and Cerrone, Costandinos and Ray. When Kraftwerk, an austere German combo whose fans were equally untrendy rockers, found themselves with an R&B hit, *Trans-Europe Express*, it also surprised their record company, the question had to be asked: why were Americans going wild about synthesizers and mechanical rhythms and love fantasies in foreign accents? Why were all manner of people entranced by this slinky fragrant music, which came to be known as Euro-disco?

Giorgio Moroder had been an itinerant, bass-playing, pop writer/producer. He teamed with Pete Bellotte, a vagabond guitarist who also wrote, produced and arranged, in early 1972; their sensibilities were nothing memorable, simply pop fluff, and rock critics didn't exactly take notice of their few European hits; or *Son Of My Father*, which seems to have made some American Top 20 charts. Eventually they settled down in Germany and came across transplanted Bostonian Donna Summer. Again nothing earth-shattering was produced; Summer enjoyed a few pop European hits from their pens, including a rather tactless song which made a joke out of being a hostage, but something in Moroder and Bellotte's bouncy bubblegum appealed to Casablanca Record's Neil Bogart, who agreed to distribute Moroder's Oasis label in America.

Shortly thereafter, Moroder and Bellotte went into the studio with Summer and recorded *Love To Love You Baby*, a record that bombed in all markets previously favorable to Summer's music except for disco conscious France.

Willa Heider

European Music wasn't hung up on skin color; it was a people's dance.

It started as a moan, ended as a sigh, and breathed sixteen minutes of erotic mystery in between. Birkin and Gainsbourg's *Je T'aime* was the model as Bellotte and Moroder draped Donna's love ode in a sentimental lush of strings, twitchy bass and heaving drums. Guitar, keyboards and horns punctuated the rhythmic humping; a snare drum sustained its pulse while the body of the music caught its breath. Continually edging up on musical climax but never coming, breaking down again and again to a bare bass, a single drum or a moan, *Love To Love You Baby* teased dancers into thinking their exertions done; but over and over the music arose, as elastic as a woman. Summer was the superhuman lover — alluring, evasive, but willing to push and pull till satisfied. She was an actress playing the lead role in our fantasy — and if nothing else, this music illustrated to what lengths the disco lover imagined going.

The stereotyped sexy European image fit snugly and begged to be incorporated into this Euro-music. Summer became, according to *Time*, the "Queen of sex rock." Imitators followed: true porn queens (Andrea True), fashion models (Grace Jones), and direct copies (Michele and Claudja Barry), but none would fit so easily to Donna's role and none would lure the public away from Donna.

Less obviously, however, this wasn't strictly a performer's music, like rock and roll. Although Summer became a star quickly, it was more because of the stage directions she was given. Any number of background moaners might have taken the role; the irreplaceables in *Love To Love You Baby* were Moroder and Bellotte. In the same way as European classicists before them, these men were creating music that was its own image, that didn't serve the star personality of its performer. Controlling the music, the producers controlled the image; and Moroder and Bellotte were also successful with projects that lacked a star front person. Giorgio stepped out of the studio's shadows with his own solo album, Bellotte formed his own group Trax, and their studio musicians, known as The Munich Machine, recorded two albums. And this music, as well as Summer's would develop through several stages.

The success of *LTLYB* guaranteed Casablanca Records a market for disco-directed, passion-responding music from

Arthur Baker is a disco producer and freelance writer.

22 NIGHTFALL: APRIL

My first published article, for *Nightfall* magazine, 1978.

much I liked the gig. A few years later, when we met again, I'd have more to say.

I continued working with Jo and his background girls, whom he dubbed 'Venise', writing 'Mystery with Me', 'Love Is the Real Thing' and 'My Man' for them, which were my first recorded compositions. I co-wrote 'My Man' with a quirky Londoner, my first British acquaintance, Keith Maynard, whom Jo used for arrangements.

Having produced and released a record that was being played by major DJs, I was feeling optimistic about this music thing. Then getting an artist signed to TK, one of the top disco labels, and having three of my songs recorded and released in France pushed my confidence even higher. So at this point I decided to jump all the way in and try my hand at writing and producing. I wanted to create an entire disco album, à la my Philly heroes Gamble and Huff. Makes sense, right? First, I needed something to record. I needed some songs.

The most important connection I made through Keith was a keyboardist and singer named Tony Carbone. We would become friends and collaborators. We sat in a diner with Keith and discussed music over breakfast, finding that we had lots of musical influences in common, including blue-eyed soul acts like Hall & Oates, Todd Rundgren and disco. Immediately hitting it off, Tony and I started writing together for my album project. Looking back, the confidence I had in my songwriting talent was totally unfounded. I had absolutely no training at all, but I had ideas in my head, and I'd tape myself singing them into my little cassette recorder. And Tony had all the keyboard skills that were necessary. Plus, he had a great voice. The first song we wrote was 'Storm Warning', which had a Trammps-like vibe to it. I remember Tony riffing a piano bass line as we stomped a beat on the floor.

So the songs were coming. Now . . . the cash. Money was required to hire musicians and arrangers and to book a studio. Dan and Chico had been helpful with the finances for 'Losing You', but even though it got released, we hadn't made a cent on it, other than the $300 advance. I'd need access to some money.

I still had some bar mitzvah money saved, but that alone wouldn't do it. I somehow convinced my dad that since I was serious about making a career out of music, he should help me raise some capital. He probably felt bad for me having lost my mom. We decided to approach his friends and our relatives, asking them to invest $1,200 each to become partners in Prince Arthur Productions (Tina and I lived on Prince Street in Brookline). Tina wrote up the agreement (which had no date on it!), listing two songs, 'Small Circle of Friends' and 'Sparkling Burgundy'. My grandmother, aunt, parents and a group of friends and business associates of my dad all ponied up. With that $12k and the $5k I had from my bar mitzvah, I was in business. I was going to make an album the correct way.

Introducing Boston's finest new independent production company...

Take One Productions, Inc.

...making music to keep you hot...

Arthur Baker
President & Chief Producer
617-277-9834

59 Prince St.
Suite 2
Brookline, Mass., 02146

My first production company, Take One Productions, Inc.

Tony and I were doing well on the song front, but vocalists were an issue. The pickings were slim in Boston, as far as I could tell, but there was this group called The Ambitions that was making some noise. Their lead singer was a soul shouter in the vein of Eddie Levert from The O'Jays. His name was Larry Wedgeworth, aka Larry Woo. I tracked him down, and we met up. It turned out that he was a very good songwriter, along with being a great singer, so Tony and I took him in as part of our writing team. Larry helped us finish 'Storm Warning', and we also knocked out another concept I had, 'I Don't Need No Music'. I felt very optimistic about that track from day one.

Then, through Larry, I connected with a keyboardist/arranger named Terry Gholson. Terry was a real fan of Thom Bell, one of my favourite Philly producer/arrangers, who had produced The Delfonics, The Spinners and The Stylistics. So we also started writing as a team, coming up with 'Am I Dreaming' and 'Thank You for Being My Girl'. I then reached out to Jonathan Klein, an arranger and keyboardist I had met through Jo, and along with Larry and Tina, we knocked out the song 'Small Circle of Friends'.

Me in a Montreal record shop with DJ Dominique Zagra, 1978.

I had my songs, a team of great players, a studio and the money. I was ready to start producing my debut disco album. In a blur of a few months, we cut twelve tracks in total. Larry and his fellow Ambition members Bobby Howard and Rodney Butler cut lead vocals on 'I Don't Need No Music', 'Small Circle of Friends', 'Put Yourself in My Place', 'Am I Dreaming', 'Storm Warning' and 'Thank You for Being My Girl'; Minnie Gardner on 'Good Good Lovin'' and 'Reaching Out for True Love'; and Tina and the girls from Venise on 'Perfect Harmony' and 'Happiness Is a Day with You'.

I can admit now that I was really winging it, but working with a crew of such talented, hungry young musicians like Andrei Carriere and Jim Anderson (guitars), Jeff Anderson (bass), Bob Stoloff (drums), Sa Davis, Russell Presto and C. L. Kelly (percussion), and Tony Carbone, Rollins Ross, Terry Gholson and Jonathan Klein (keyboards), I was able to create disco music that has proved to be timeless. I felt the record could compete with anything out there. We incorporated elements of the Philly and Motown vocal arrangements and were influenced by Eurodisco and the guitar grooves that Nile Rodgers of Chic was experimenting with. One session in particular stands out: we layered a live section of female Berklee College of Music string players over the bass break of 'I Don't Need No Music', and then Andre chugged a slick guitar through it. I knew the music was really working. The only problem was, I was running out of funds. I had cut too many tracks, without really finishing anything – a taste of things to come.

A few people were sniffing around our sessions, because in Boston nothing like these recordings had really been done before. Having so many musicians all wanting to hang out, it was a bit of a party too. Alan Schivek would pass through, and he loved what he was hearing. One night he brought in a friend of his named Jerry Moulton to check out what we were up to. Jerry's brother was Tom Moulton, *the* top remixer on the scene. Tom had arguably done the first 12-inch promo track, Bobby Moore's '(Call Me Your) Anything Man'. After listening to my music, Jerry said he might be interested in signing my project to the new label he was developing with his brother, Tom n' Jerry Records, distributed by Casablanca Records. Casablanca was *the* disco label, putting out hits by Donna Summer and the Village People. This sounded like an unbelievable opportunity. Then I heard the deal. Not so great.

The Moultons paid me $20,000 (with a promise of a bonus of $15,000 if anything from the record was certified 'gold' – yeah, very likely!). With that money I was able to pay Intermedia $6,500 and the musicians $3,000. I also paid myself back my $5,000. Jerry told me they'd use my songs and our arrangements, but not the actual recordings. They claimed that the masters weren't up to scratch, and they'd have to re-record everything in Philly, with Tom producing the new sessions. I would just get my songwriting credit and a third of the publishing. But they said they would still need to take all my tapes – not to use, but just to listen to them so they could copy my arrangements. This didn't sound right to me, but I had no other options.

Then they wanted to sign Tony and me to publishing deals, so we met with Jerry and the Moultons' lawyer, Toby Pieniack, in NYC that summer of 1978. We finalised the deal for the album, and Tony, who has an amazing memory, specifically remembers Jerry calling Intermedia's studio manager, Ross Cibella, getting our final bill for the recording and approving it on that call, while we there. But we both passed on the publishing deals because that offer was shit too, basically.

When the record was finally released in 1979, I first saw it at the Boston Record Pool. I quickly threw it on the turntable and realised straight away that I had been exploited. They hadn't re-recorded everything; the album, called *TJM*, was my production, performances and arrangements. Tom had replaced Bobby Howard's falsetto vocals with those of Ron Tyson, and there were some new embellishments on strings and horns. But that was it. Further proof was that all the musicians listed on the record were my guys. The worst thing was, Larry got no credit for his amazing leads; all the vocals were accredited to some bullshit act called The Brotherhood. To be sure, Tom had mixed the hell out of the material, and I was very proud of the results. At the very least, I should have gotten a co-production credit, but I was just named among the arrangers. At this point in my career a production credit would have made a huge difference to me, but at least the music was released, and I was able to experience hearing both 'I Don't

Need No Music' and 'Put Yourself in My Place' being pumped out by Larry Levan at Paradise Garage. The former was a top-ten *Billboard* disco hit and has proved to be a true classic, with Larry's 'And the music began to play' line being sampled in numerous hits over the last forty years. But I pledged to myself that I would never get burnt like that again, and that credit is everything.

7.

GOING UPTOWN

1978–81

'Bro, you gotta come uptown right now and see what these dudes are doing! They're hanging in the park, talking over tracks blasting out of big boomboxes! Someone's gonna make a million dollars on this shit!'

It was salsa legend Joe Bataan on the phone. We were working on a disco album, having been brought together by Howard Smiley, who had left TK to start his own company, Palm Productions. Howard had suggested Joe and I should bond, so we started to hang out a bit in NYC, before going into the studio. I remember Joe ringing me that morning, clearly excited, but the summer of 1978 was another really hot one and I was chilling in front of our noisy AC unit. My car had been stolen a week earlier, and the Bronx was a long way away from Kings Highway, especially in this heat.

'You really want me to come today?'

'Yup, you gotta!'

Joe convinced me, so I hopped onto the 2 train and made my way up to 125th Street. After lots of searching, I eventually found him sitting on top of a park bench in his Converse All Stars and shorts, looking ready for a b-ball run. He was always dressed like that, something I probably picked up from him that summer. He had a bottle of beer in his hand. It was hot, so I grabbed one too.

He nodded over to another bench. There it was – the boombox and a guy talking over Cheryl Lynn's hit 'Got to Be Real'. I'm not sure if I thought it sounded like a million-dollar-maker straight away, but Joe was convinced. He also made it clear to me that *he* was ready to rock the mic. What we had both witnessed were the early days of rap music before it was even called that. No reason Joe shouldn't be the one to make the million, I supposed. Ironically, it would be me who would eventually be one of the first to make a million dollars with rap, with the Soul Sonic Force. But I wouldn't even think about making a rap record until three years later.

When we started recording our album, a week or so later, Joe got off to a real quick start. He had his arranger, Marty Sheller, working away on his arrangements, one song being a track that sounded suspiciously like the 'Got to Be Real' we had heard in the park. *Why mess with the formula?* I thought. Joe was a real pro in the studio and got shit done quickly, knowing time was money. He was confident that 'Rap-O Clap-O' could be the first rap track to be a hit, and he wanted to finish it immediately.

Jocelyn Brown (Shaw) sang vocals – I met her for the first time during these sessions, and we've been friends and collaborators ever since – then Joe went in and did his rap over the track. I didn't really think much of it, being more into some of the disco-oriented songs we were working on, including 'Can't Put No Price on Love'. It was arranged by Ray Chew, Ashford & Simpson's arranger, and remains a personal favourite among my productions. Unfortunately, when the whole disco thing came crashing down, with the London US label going bust, 'Can't Put No Price on Love' ended up unreleased (until some forty-five years later, when Dave Lee released it on his ZR label). Joe took his songs and was later able to ink a deal with RCA, who released his *Mestizo* album, with 'Rap-O Clap-O' coming out in late 1979 as one of the first rap records and becoming a big hit in Europe.

Back in Brookline, Tony Carbone and I kept collaborating after *TJM*, bringing in another writer who I thought might fit into our disco vibe, a DJ/drummer named Russell Presto. Russell spun at a club in Revere called Jacob's Ladder, where he kept his drum kit set up so he could jam over records in a club setting, which was the first time I'd ever seen anyone do that. The three of us started messing around, recording beats and percussion. We wanted to make a DJ tools/disco-breaks record, with just percussion and bass lines. We wrote lots of bits that sounded pretty ahead of their time.

The three of us would jam in my apartment, where I now had my own old beat-up acoustic piano. One day Russell came up with an opening line: 'Let me tell you all a story, about the North End and its glory.' He and Tony were of Italian heritage, and the North End of Boston was its legendary Italian section, with all the best restaurants, etc. The words were a bit cheesy, but Italians in Boston did tend to love disco, and the sentiments my songwriting partners were creating were really pure, so we went with it – even to the extent of calling the group North End.

Tony and I had discovered a demo studio in Hopkinton that charged $15 an hour and had an engineer named Larry, who also played guitar. It was there, with Tina, that we demoed 'Kind of Life', along with another song, a duet between Tina and Tony called 'Drop It'. When 'Kind of Life' was completed, we all thought we had a hit on our hands. It felt like a classic pop disco song (I think we had the Bee Gees in mind). We were excited to get it over to our friend Danae Jacovidis, the DJ at Chaps. We all listened to it in the club. He loved the track, the lyrics and Tony's vocals, and suggested that we should let Mel Cheren at West End Records hear it. North End on West End sounded great to all of us.

We all travelled down to NYC to meet with Mel, whom I knew from Scepter Records. He was also from Boston, so that was another connection. He had a big office, which he shared with his business partner, Ed Kushins, and when I played him our demo, they were both blown away! He immediately offered us $5,000 to make the record. That seemed like a great budget to us, so we agreed. On returning home, we set up our new production company, Edge City Productions, and we were in business.

We went back into Intermedia, where by now I was very comfortable working. It was right on the extremely lively Newbury Street and was conveniently near one of Boston's top record shops, Newbury Comics, and also a great BBQ spot. Tony put a great rhythm section together and we got a great take of 'Kind of Life' on our second run-through. Since the mics were set up and we had a great drum sound, we decided to lay down a couple more rhythm tracks: 'We Can't Live Like This Anymore' and an instrumental cover of The Temptations' 'Cloud Nine'. On our dinner break, I happened upon a street musician playing harmonica for change. I thought he had skills, so I brought him into the studio and had him play on our tracks. His harmonica performance became one of the major musical hooks on 'Kind of Life'.

At this time I was going back and forth between Boston and NYC. During the recording process, I would pop into West End to keep Mel informed on how we were doing. He listened to the rhythm tracks but didn't seem to be impressed. I realised I should have played him the last rough mix, which featured the strings, horns and harmonica, first. When I finally threw it on, I got a big smile from him; he absolutely loved Tony's arrangement. I guess at that point he felt like he was getting his $5,000 worth.

We travelled down to NYC to finish the background vocals. Once they were completed, Tony knocked out his final lead, killing it in a few takes. The recording process was finished, and we were ready to hand over the track to Danae for the mix. But Tony, as the arranger, felt he should be around too, so I had to convince him that we should just let Danae get on with it. As DJs, Russell and I felt Danae would know what to do.

This time Tony was correct. Danae's mix had left out the horns! He just didn't like them and felt they were not important. Mel had a listen and figured that there was something else missing, and we all concluded that we should bring in that other Boston boy, John Luongo, for the remix. He went into Media Sound Studios in NYC and did his thing, adding a few bits of percussion, chimes and FX, and crafted (with additional input from Danae) what we had given him into a disco classic.

Mel and Ed loved the mix and got it over to Larry Levan, who was a sort of unofficial A&R man for West End. Larry loved 'Kind of Life' and helped break it by playing the shit out of it at Paradise Garage, before it was released in December 1979. The record eventually peaked on the *Billboard* disco chart at #18.

After the success of 'Kind of Life', Tony and Russell hooked up with some of the members of an active Boston gigging group, Breakaway, and took North End on the road. We also continued writing new songs, but Tony decided he wasn't meant to be a frontman.

While the guys were out on the road, I had an idea to cut a track that was meant to be the anthem for my beloved Boston Celtics. That year the team's marketing theme had been 'No More Games', and I directed Larry Woo and Terry Gholson to compose a song with that title, in the style of the McFadden & Whitehead anthem 'Ain't No Stopping Us Now', which was huge at the time. Larry and Terry came up with what I thought was a monster track, and I convinced local club owner and manager Roscoe Gorham to finance it. We started a label called Groove Hall Records, a take on the Grove Hall area of Boston, where his club, Roscoe's, was located. We recorded and mixed the track at Intermedia, and I drove to Philly to pick up the 45s at the Sound Makers pressing plant. Unfortunately, after we got the records to the Garden, the Celts lasted just two more games before they were knocked out. Strangely, the song became a northern soul classic in the UK, at one point garnering over £50 a copy.

Soul was in the air for me when we decided that the next North End record would feature a new singer (since Tony had stepped back), along with a new sound, a new studio and a new label. We wrote 'Happy Days' in an attempt to go further than we had with 'Kind of Life', sales-wise. We thought a more R&B approach might be easier to sell in the new 1980s disco environment. Inspired and influenced by Nile Rodgers and Bernard Edwards's work with Chic, we again wanted something uplifting. We had to find a singer who could do justice to what we thought was a great song.

Russell was DJing at Jacob's Ladder, and he would often meet bands passing through there. One of them, Sapphire, had a great singer, Michelle Wallace. Russell thought they wouldn't be doing any recording any time soon, so he approached her, and she seemed interested. We all met at Russell's apartment, and she blew us away, with a sound not far from Chaka Khan. Michelle was part of a great local singing family called the Wallace Sisters. She was anxious to get on with her career, and I think she thought 'Happy Days' could help her do just that.

We were now working in a shiny new studio in Boston, Century 3 on Boylston Street. Russell, as always, recorded his drums precisely (taping his wallet on the snare to deaden its ring), with a lot of time spent on getting the perfect sound and making sure the groove was slamming. He also overdubbed a cool vibraphone part. Tony played keyboards and wrote the arrangements. I brought in two new musicians to help, Maurice Starr and Michael Jonzun. They could both play any instrument, but in this session, Maurice thumped a great bass line, while Michael added rhythm guitar and synths; he also sang the backing vocals, along with Tina and Michelle. When Michelle took centre stage, she nailed it, and I thought we had everything we needed and were ready to mix.

Michelle Wallace.

I was still frequently travelling the 225 miles between Boston and New York and was starting to make further connections with the DJ/remixers there. While Paradise Garage was my main destination, I would also explore other underground clubs, and at a spot called Better Days I heard a DJ who I thought would be perfect to mix 'Happy Days', Tee Scott. Tee was from Queens, rocked disco funk and played legendary ten-hour sets that often featured a keyboardist named Andre Booth jamming over his mixing. It was the first place I'd ever seen that done. You could almost call Tee's style proto-house, and he ruled Better Days.

I played him our rough mix, which had gotten us a record deal with the fledgling label Emergency Records, which was owned by Italian record exec Sergio Cossa. Tee liked what he heard but said he had some ideas that would make it more of a Better Days track. He wanted to bring some of his guys in on it: Andre Booth on keys and a guitarist who played with him, Charlie Street. Tee convinced Sergio to let us work at Right Track Studios, with an engineer named Frank Filipetti. Right Track was a bit pricey, but a step up from where I'd worked before (I'd end up working there again years later with Bob Dylan, Carly Simon and Nona Hendryx). We went into Right Track's A room at night (as usual, the rates were cheaper for night sessions), and after spliffing up, Tee proceeded to have Andre do his thing, jamming over our track. He quickly came up with a hooky, synthy clav part that modernised the track immediately. Job done. Things had to be done swiftly: we were on a budget and so had to overdub and mix in one night.

Next, Charlie plugged in and started riffing, and when he hit on a George Benson octave thing, Tee and I both went, 'That's it!' We both knew straight away that it was so cool and right for the track. Frank was a great mixer (he later became known for his work with Foreigner) and got the sounds together in no time. We edited the mix as we went, meaning Tee decided on the bits and structure, and Frank did the actual cutting and assembling of the tape. We got the vocal version done quickly; blasting it back to check, it felt real good. We still had time to do an instrumental version (I don't think the idea of naming them dub mixes had even started yet). I thought of calling it 'Tee's Happy' because he seemed so happy with the results, but I had to convince Tee that it was OK to have his name on the mix.

'Happy Days'/'Tee's Happy' was released on Emergency Records in September 1981, peaking at #9 on the *Billboard* disco chart. The song had a long life after that: besides getting played heavily at Better Days, Paradise Garage and many other east coast clubs, Frankie Crocker played it tons on WBLS. So I finally had a hit record in the Big Apple. It was also a favourite with John 'Jellybean' Benitez at the Funhouse, and he used it as a reference when working on the song 'Holiday', even asking me if I thought he should keep it for himself or let his then-girlfriend Madonna have it for her record. I said he should let Madonna have it. When she did finally cut it, I was in the studio, and Tina was on backing vocals. Tina was the one link between both songs.

Tony, Russell and I continued to work together for a few more years, recording 'It's Right' for Michelle Wallace, which acted as the follow-up to 'Happy Days'. Our final record for her as a production team was 'Jazzy Rhythm'. Tragically, my North End collaborator and friend Russell Presto was gunned down at his home in Revere in 1984. The murder was never solved.

While we were going through the rather long process of recording and mixing 'Happy Days', I was also attempting to line up other projects. A producer needs to keep producing and have a studio to record in, because home studios didn't really cut it in the late 1970s and early '80s. Which meant cash was necessary to pay for one and make a record. By 1980 I was spending quite a bit of time in NYC, and it was there that I hooked up with my old friend Alan Schivek, who had started a production company with the help of a film producer named Bernard Spigner.

I ended up making four records with Schivek and Spigner (which they placed with the Posse label, a new disco imprint launched by the Rivkin brothers, who also owned Spring Records) between 1980 and 1981, and I used my Boston guys on all of them. We decided – or should I say *they* decided – on the group names Ritz and Glory. For the first Ritz release, Alan presented me with a track that had been started by Glenn Dorsey of the disco group The Joneses. It was called 'I Wanna Get with You', and Tina helped me finish writing it. Our edited horn intro from the track would be sampled numerous times, most famously by Stock, Aitken and Waterman on 'Roadblock' years later.

Both this and the first Glory track, 'Can You Guess What Groove This Is?', made some noise, enough for me to be asked to do follow-ups. Although those did not fare so well, the whole experience did mean that relocating to New York made sense. When we finally made the big move, in 1981, I told all my Boston boys that they always had a place to crash with Tina and me in the Big Apple. They'd take me up on my offer fairly soon.

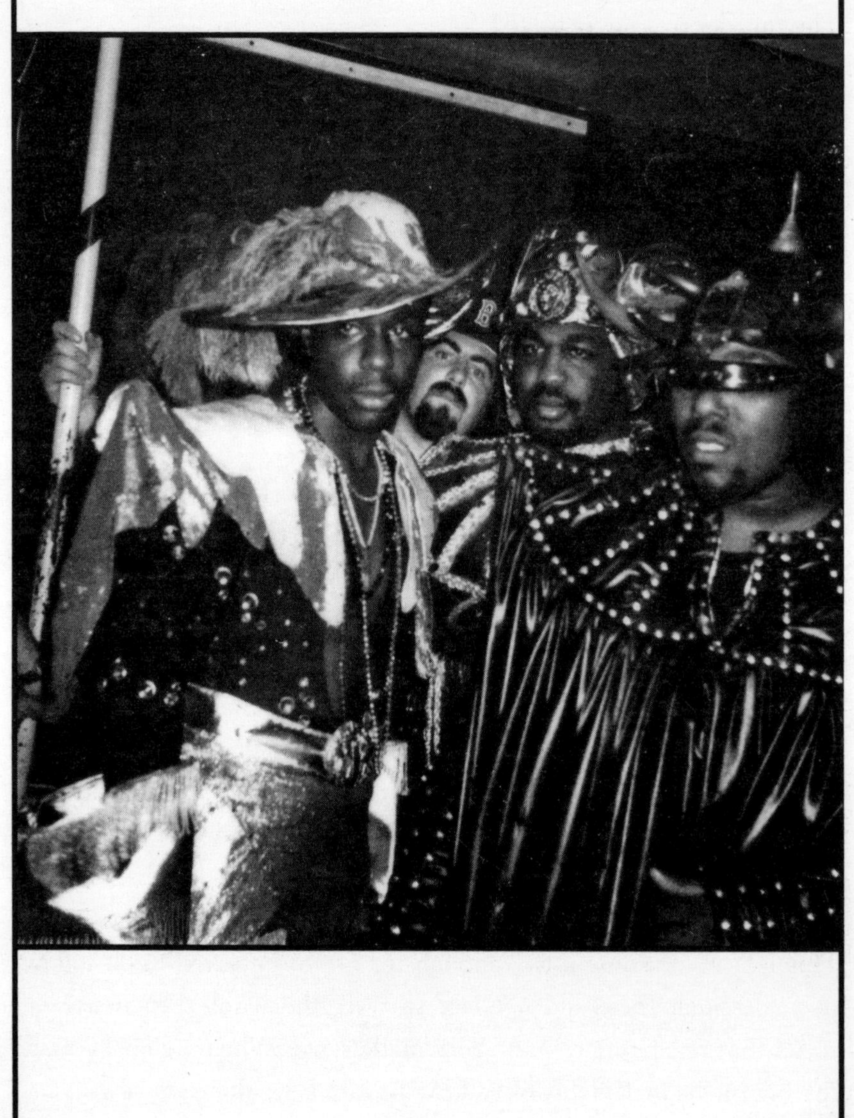

8.

JUST HIT ME

1982

I've probably told the story of the making of 'Planet Rock' more times than any other in my life. I guess that's rightfully so, considering I'm more known for making that record than any other.

It was only a couple of years after Joe Bataan had hipped me to guys speaking over records in the park that I finally got the opportunity to try my hand at it. Kurtis Blow and the Sugar Hill Gang had already had big hits by the time Tom Silverman approached me to help him out with his new Tommy Boy label. It was 1981, and I had just moved from Boston down to Brooklyn full-time. I was working in the warehouse of Cardinal One Record Distributors in Long Island City, first sweeping floors and building record shelves, and then as a record breaker (going through record orders and breaking them down by list price). Not very glamorous.

Tom and I met in his offices in Manhattan's Upper East Side, where he first broached the subject of me producing a record for his new label. I'd known him for a few years, having met him at the *Billboard* Disco Convention. Tom was publishing a trade journal called *Dance Music Report*, and I occasionally wrote reviews for him in return for free records.

He had decided he'd like to make records himself, so he launched Tommy Boy Records. I was one of the few producers Tom knew at that point, and I'd just had a hit with 'Happy Days', so he offered me the chance to make records for the label. He'd discovered a DJ named Afrika Bambaataa, who headed a group called the Zulu Nation. Bamb had three rap acts under the Zulu Nation banner: the Cosmic Crew, the Jazzy 5 and the Soul Sonic Force.

A few days later, I headed to the office to meet up with Bamb. He was wearing a puffer jacket with the hood up, which he typically did, no matter what the weather. I would later learn he was a man of few words, that it wasn't anything personal. Somehow it was decided that we'd commence our collaboration by recording with his group Jazzy 5. That was purely his decision.

We planned to meet up and record the next night at Intergalactic Studios, pretty much around the corner, which was owned by Rob

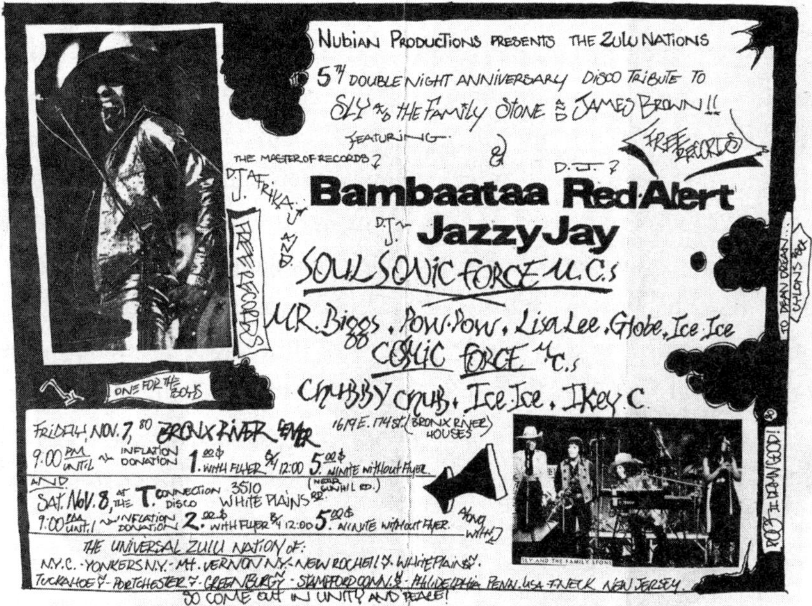

Party flyer for Afrika Bambaataa and the Soul Sonic Force, *c.*1981.

Manning and Chris Hanley, the guys from Everett Hafner's electronic-music class at Hampshire. I had to come up with a session band for the recording, and luckily, I had the perfect musicians for the job, having recently met some great young players from Queens through Tee Scott.

A big plus was that they were already into rap and production, particularly Andre and his buddy Marley, who hung out at that session and later ones. Yep, that Marley. Marley Marl. He stayed in the background, but I later found out that the sessions he sat in on were influential in his development as a producer. Throughout the years I've always had an open-door policy with my sessions and have discovered and helped develop a lot of young talent that way.

The musicians arrived early to set up their instruments and jam a bit. We then started on getting sounds, paying a lot of attention to the drums. Drums could make or break any disco, funk or rap record. I remember having an in-depth discussion with T Funk, the drummer Andre had brought along, about theories of drum miking and how he wanted his drums to sound. However we recorded his drums that night, it worked: they sound rocking to this day. I still have a cassette of the guys jamming, and listening back you can hear the progression of the final groove, and it all really rocks.

So we'd got the sound, and the band was ready. Only problem was, we hadn't picked what to cut for the rappers to rhyme over. Originally, all rap records were done over live cover versions of popular R&B or disco tracks (remember Joe Bataan had used 'Got to Be Real'). We had a big decision to make. Bamb and I brought along some records we thought might be suitable. At the time, Tom Tom Club's 'Genius of Love' was tearing up the charts. It would have been an obvious choice, only I was convinced that some other more well-known rap crew would use it. So I pushed for us to cut another record, a hot new club jam called 'Funky Sensation', which was originally by Gwen McCrae. It was slow and funky, but with a real disco vibe to it. Andre and the guys (who would soon be known as B. B. C. S. & A. and for their jam 'Rock Shock' on SAM Records) knew the original and were easily able to sit into a fresh groove and cut the fuck out of it. I thought we should call it 'Jazzy Sensation', considering the group was the Jazzy 5.

The rappers warmed to the rhythm track quickly and got to writing what would later be recognised as one of the classic first-generation party rockers. I decided the band should cut two distinctly different rhythm tracks. On the second, clubbier version I had my wife Tina try a 'Rapture'-style rap and called it the 'Manhattan' version (she was dubbed Tina B on the track). We later got Shep Pettibone to do remixes of both versions.

I remember Tom picking up the records from the Sound Makers pressing plant in Philly and going round to record stores, selling copies straight out of his boot. It was a very exciting time for us. 'Jazzy Sensation' quickly got radio play, with Mr Magic (of WHBI, one of the first radio DJs to play rap) jumping on it and giving it much love, which translated into good sales. This success enabled Tom to continue with the label and make another record. This was still very early in the rap game, and there really weren't enough good rap records being released.

Next group up was the Soul Sonic Force. This time Bambaataa and Silverman got more involved in the process. Unbeknownst to me, they had been working on a demo for 'Planet Rock', and when they played it for me, I don't really remember being blown away by it. It was mid-tempo and used the bass line from B. T. Express's 'Do You Like It' for its groove and some of Kraftwerk's 'Trans-Europe Express' for its melody.

Me and Shep Pettibone in Intergalactic Studios, NYC, 1981.

Both Tom and Bamb were set on using 'Trans-Europe Express'. I had often heard its handclap intro reverberating in the housing projects by the basketball court and park tables where I'd eat during my lunch breaks at Cardinal One. The Kraftwerk track had had a long life even at this point. It had come out in 1978 and had been getting club play ever since in New York.

Whenever I hit a new town, I'd always search out record stores. They were like our internet or social media platforms back in the day. You could always find out what was happening from the guys at the record store, and we quickly discovered a great one on Fulton Street, Music Factory, across from Junior's Deli. It was very close to the apartment on Warren Street where Tina and I lived, which we had rented from Mel Cheren, the owner of West End. We'd walk the mile to the shop every Saturday, and I quickly became friends with the managers, brothers Dwight Hawkes and Donnie Calvin. They'd DJ in the store and often play me new tracks and hip me to classics they thought I might not know and would appreciate. I could relax there and do my music research.

One day I walked in and was suddenly hit by a crazy electronic beat that struck me like a bomb. I ran over to Dwight, who was behind the decks, with a 'What the fuck is that?' look in my eyes. He noticed it and said, 'Yo, bro, this is "Numbers", the new Kraftwerk jam.' At that point I knew that I had to use this beat. I mentioned to Dwight that I was going to be cutting a new jam with Afrika Bambaataa and that this groove was the beat I was going to try out. I also invited him to come to the recording session at Intergalactic later that week.

After carefully listening to and dissecting 'Numbers', I realised that a live band wouldn't be the best way to get the sound and the mechanical feel. We needed a drum machine. I didn't own one and neither did the studio. We searched the *Village Voice*'s classified section, which was our Google at the time, and eventually found an ad proclaiming, 'Man with a drum machine – $25 a session.' I called the number and spoke to a guy called Joe, who told me he had a new drum machine called the Roland TR-808. I had never heard of it, and obviously hadn't used one, so I decided to go to Manny's Music, near Times Square, to check it out. I went over and heard some sounds and beats. It was very interesting, and I thought it would do the trick, so I called Joe back and hired him for the session.

Tom called me and said he and Bamb had found a guy who'd be perfect for keyboards, and that I should meet him at his office. On first meeting, John Robie seemed like an unassuming character, aside from the fact that he wore a yellow hat and pink T-shirt (I would later find out that he was colour blind). From his words and attitude, you could tell he was a rocker, but he had produced a down-tempo electronic synth track called 'Vena Cava' that Bamb had fallen in love with when he heard it on an early disco compilation released by the subscription label Disconet. Tom hired him for the session.

So we went into Intergalactic to cut a track for Soul Sonic Force with no real specific plans and using an unknown musician whom I had no prior connection with. I brought Donny and Dwight from the record store for support and retail feedback. Then there were Bamb, Tom and the members of Soul Sonic Force. The studio provided us with an engineer named Jay Burnett, who smoked like a chimney.

For a record that's known as a technological game-changer, we had very little equipment to work with. We had the rented TR-808, and Robie brought along his Micro Moog and a Prophet-5 (lugging them up the eight flights of stairs because the elevator was inconveniently turned off at night). But the studio did have a classic Neve mixing board, Studer tape machines, a few PCM delay units and a Sony reverb. And lastly, a *very* expensive computer, the Fairlight, which had a small library of samples. That was it.

First, Joe appeared with his Roland. We played him 'Numbers', and Bamb went through his records for beats, deciding on 'Super Sporm' by Captain Sky for the alternate break section. Jay, working those Neve EQs, got some great low end on the 808 going, while Joe programmed the two basic beats. I figured out how to rock the cowbell and threw down some other percussion patterns. The rappers had no patience for any of this programming and music-making, sneaking into the studio's live room and proceeding to bang on the drums, jump on the piano and sing 'Hound Dog', much to the bemusement of the record-shop managers.

When Joe was done, he quickly left, with his $25 in cash in hand. I remember him specifically not wanting a cheque, as he didn't trust them, and thus his full name was lost from the list of credits on this historical record. At least we had recorded a beat. It was approximately 129 bpm (Roland had failed to put a bpm screen on their new machine). But now I had some confused rappers on my hands. Understandably, they had expected a down-tempo groove like 'Jazzy Sensation', which was the normal rap template of the time. But we had tricked them with something new – this crazy uptempo electronic rock beat. They tried to find a pocket for the raps they had already rehearsed, but they got frustrated rapidly.

The main lyricist, MC G.L.O.B.E., was confident that he had made a good start on cracking the code for the pacing of the vocals on this futuristic-sounding track. But we all realised that the guys weren't ready to record the vocals and should work them out outside the studio first. So they left, with cassette in hand, leaving me and keyboardist Robie to get to work.

The B. T. Express bass-line idea from the demo wasn't going to work at this tempo, so I came up with a simple idea: we could put a bass synth down that would mirror and reinforce the kick-drum pattern, giving it a bass note. Robie got a fat sound on his Micro Moog and carefully played it all the way through the track. It achieved what I was looking for. Then we proceeded to add a few musical elements typically found in my favourite club tracks: some synth-clavinet rhythm parts à la D Train, a percolating arpeggiator line and explosive sound effects. Robie finally added strings that played the 'Trans-Europe Express' melody. It was sounding fucking otherworldly and extremely cool.

At some point we decided that there was a chance we might have an issue with Kraftwerk over using their melody, so I had Robie come up with an alternative melodic string line, which he improvised in a flash. He then sat down at the grand piano and played a big, minor-key, ornate chord progression. Lastly, I got my hands dirty, throwing down a high single-note piano part.

Jay got a mix together, and we sat back and listened. I think at that point I alone felt we had come up with something special, an epic track that seemed different to anything I had ever heard. It had this totally futuristic Afro–Euro electro-funk sound that I thought blew away the competition. That competition, in my mind, was Talking Heads and their experiments with an Afro sound. And this was still without a rap. I wasn't sure if Jay or Robie were convinced, but that really didn't matter to me.

I left that night, hopping on a subway out to Brooklyn with a rough-mix cassette in my pocket. I arrived home and played Tina the track, proudly claiming that we had just made musical history. I could see that she wasn't that sure. While Tom wasn't happy that we hadn't been able to complete the recording in one night, I remember he liked the direction the track had taken. Now the issue was going to be whether the rappers could live up to this new sound we had created. It would all be up to the G.L.O.B.E.

It seemed to me on our first meeting that John Miller (the G.L.O.B.E.) was the poet bard/nerd of the crew. So when we reconvened a few days later, he came in confidently, in the knowledge that he'd cracked the code. I listened and hoped for the best. He explained to me that he had created a new rap style, something he dubbed 'MC poppin''. It was rapping behind the beat, and it would pocket the up-tempo groove in a laid-back style.

But first Bamb had something he wanted to try. It was a party-starter shout that would become synonymous with 'Planet Rock': 'Party people, party people, can y'all get funky? Soul Sonic Force, can y'all get funky? Zulu Nation, can you all get funky? . . . Well, hit me!'

I had everyone go in to do the responses, giving it that live club-party vibe. It was the perfect intro for the track and would become a big hook. Then the G.L.O.B.E. got busy, laying his futuristic lyrical rhymes behind the beat, MC poppin' style. And damn if it didn't work. He coached the other members of the group, Mr Biggs and Pow Wow, patiently teaching them their new parts, and they laid them down smoothly. It was all going great, until Pow Wow missed one of his lines and instead scatted, 'Ze ze ze ze zah.' Tom immediately jumped out of his seat and said, 'Wow, that's amazing. We have to use that!' I agreed, and we kept the mistake and had Pow Wow expand on it for a featured scat solo. Another hook for the song.

Most of the music was complete, but we figured we should at least try to get something out of that expensive Fairlight computer. It had one of those little green TV screens and a small keyboard. As we messed around, scrolling through sounds, we found some explosions, which we threw into the break. Tom went over, stood over the keyboard and started hitting keys and scrolling, and – bam! – the orchestra hit. We all looked at one another, mouths wide open. That had to go in the intro.

Down the years there's been lots of questions about who did what on this record, as sometimes occurs when looking back at important cultural events. And with the ongoing controversy surrounding Afrika Bambaataa, we have unfortunately faced some erasure of the importance of the record in the history of hip-hop. What I can honestly say is that its creation was a collaborative effort. There were a lot of people involved, and Bambaataa's situation should not be to the detriment of all the other collaborators.

How the basic track was recorded was down to myself, Bamb and Tom, with great keyboard performances by Robie. After the written rap verses were recorded, I tried to get the rappers to incorporate what they did when they rocked a party, which meant using the calls and responses that they were known for, including their 'Rockin', don't stop it' party-routine bit at the end. I figured we needed all the hooks that we could comfortably fit in.

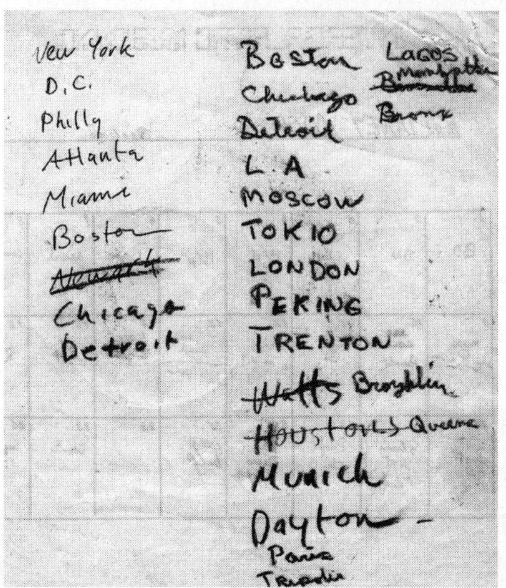

'Planet Rock' city shout-outs by me and Jay Burnett.

I had an idea for a chorus, which was the 'Rock, rock to the planet rock, don't stop' part. It was inspired by one of my favourite club tracks of that time, 'Body Music' by The Strikers. It provided a catchy hook. Then, since I had a feeling that 'Planet Rock' had the potential to reach beyond the States, I suggested that the city shout-outs we decided to do in tribute to James Brown should have a definite international flavour. Jay and I bounced random city ideas off one another, coming up with an eclectic, random list. I wanted to have an electronic vocal sound reciting the cities and the 'rock, rock' parts (à la Kraftwerk), but we hadn't rented a vocoder as we didn't have enough budget. Jay got creative and used a tight slap-back setting on a PCM 41 delay unit to get a metallic vocal effect. He then literally begged me to let him perform the electronic vocal parts. He'd got a cool sound, so why not? Another hook. A few months after the record's release, he wanted a royalty.

Next was the mix session, which, as I remember, went smoothly, with just Jay, assistant engineer Bob Rosa, Tom and I in the studio. Bamb and Soul Sonic weren't really interested in attending, which was fine by me, because having the artist attending a mix is never a great idea. They were all just interested in hearing it finished. Jay and Bob took charge of getting the sounds together with what little outboard gear we had, blasting the song through the big UREIs, while occasionally checking its sound softly in mono through the small Auratone speakers, which everyone called 'Awfultones'. We decided to mix down to half-inch tape on a Studer machine. I took charge of the record's structure, somewhat on the fly, attempting to arrange it like I'd mix an extended version of a club track, which was unique for a rap record.

The intro was mixed as it was recorded – with Bamb's 'party people' bit, along with the crowd and orchestra combining – to make a killer party-starter. We then followed the song structure as I recorded, editing in a few breaks and drops. One impromptu move I made in the mix – dropping the snare and leaving the claps to hit on the two and four beats – was very effective and has since become a standard technique in hip-hop production. After we had completed the vocal mix, Tom came up with the genius idea of having it segue straight into a separate beats track, which he aptly named 'bonus beats' – the first of its kind.

Next, we needed a B-side for the 12-inch. Typically, on a rap record this would be a straight instrumental of the A-side, only in this case there were so many elements to play with. I went for more of a dub approach, occasionally removing the beat and letting the bass line and claps carry the groove. This version felt more like the instrumental version that I had left the studio with that first night, while incorporating Jay's vocal stuff. I thought this version would get some play from DJs who weren't playing rap records, and I was right.

The rappers admitted years later, when interviewed for my movie *808*, that they thought 'Planet Rock' might be their first and last recording. It was true that it didn't fit in with anything that was out there back then. They felt that if it did hit, it would hit *big*, but they didn't think there was much chance of that.

We cut two acetates with Herb Powers Jr. at Frankford/Wayne mastering studio, one for me and one for Tom. I think the first place we tested 'Planet Rock' was at Rock & Soul record shop on Seventh Avenue. The owner, Shirley Bechor, had sold quite a bit of 'Jazzy Sensation', so she was anxious to hear our next project. She put on the heavy acetate, and after the 'party people' intro, which turned people's heads, and the kick hit – bam! – the massive low end killed one of her woofers. That's when we realised what the 808 could do if you're not careful. We went back to Herb, and he rolled the low end on the kick back a bit. But trust me, Shirley could pay for quite a few woofers with her sales of 'Planet Rock'.

Next I took the acetate back to the scene of the crime – my home lab, Music Factory. Dwight threw it on the decks. There, it didn't blow anything, but again you could feel the customers getting excited by this new sound. After the track was over, a bunch of people lined up to ask what that record was. One guy offered $100 for the acetate. Dwight smiled and pointed at me. That was when I knew we really had something.

So far all our retail tests were proving quite promising. Next, Tom and I tested it at Judy Weinstein's *For the Record* DJ pool's monthly listening session, just before Christmas. When the track dropped, people's heads jerked, really paying attention. It was one of the early 'What the fuck is that?' records of the 1980s. The DJs actually bopped to the record right there and then.

With 'Jazzy Sensation', Tom already had laid the groundwork with Mr Magic, Red Alert and the other radio DJs who were playing rap on the air, so those guys would be no problem, but getting 'Planet Rock' onto daytime radio would prove a bit more difficult. But we had the secret weapon: the non-rap B-side, which helped break the track on daytime.

'Planet Rock' pretty much exploded on release in NYC. Most club DJs introduced it to their audience via the instrumental B-side, but Jellybean Benitez at the Funhouse, one of the record's early supporters in the clubs, played both versions. He had attended one of the Intergalactic sessions when we were mixing the track, so he really felt a part of it. His club became my home base before long. He also had a reel-to-reel in his booth, so he would test my mixes in progress for me, slamming them out to a packed dancefloor. Baptism by fire, baby!

When we needed a radio edit of the rap version, Tom hired Jellybean to do it. I remember me, Jellybean and DJ Tony Smith sitting on the floor in the dim light of JB's apartment, trying to do the edit. While it started out as a quintessential NYC club record, pretty soon you could hear it everywhere, in every kind of club and all over the radio, with some people playing the rap and others the B-side, and some mixing both up, creating mad mega-mixes. This gave it an extra-long lifespan. It ruled the city and then moved across the States, and eventually the world, going gold quickly. And it created a new sound, which everyone else started biting.

'Planet Rock' most definitely changed my life. But what would I do next?

9.

P.L.A.Y.

1982

We now had a major international hit on our hands, which meant Afrika Bambaataa and the Soul Sonic Force were gone, constantly on the road, making all sorts of cash gigging. So we weren't really thinking about a follow-up yet, although in retrospect we should have had another Soul Sonic Force track ready to go.

I was turning my attention to starting my own label, Streetwise, but at some point, I got to thinking about all the music we had cut that magic night that hadn't made it onto 'Planet Rock'. Luckily, I found an instrumental version I had already rough-mixed using those additional parts and decided to bring the quarter-inch reel to the Funhouse. I told Jellybean Benitez what it was, and he let it roll. It started exactly like the 'Planet Rock' instrumental, but when those previously unheard dramatic piano chords dropped and the synth-clavinet parts and new melody hit, the crowd started barking like crazed dogs. That was their unique way of showing they loved a track. *Fuck!* When I heard the Funhouse crowd baying like that, I knew we had another smash on our hands. We could follow up 'Planet Rock' with another version that we had recorded at the same time with the same beats! To be honest, I liked this one more and thought we could take it further.

The additional music we had recorded was so ornately beautiful that it was just calling out for a soulful vocal. I didn't have to work too hard to convince Tom Silverman. Once he came to the Funhouse and saw the crowd's reaction, he was all in. But who could we get to sing it? I hadn't connected with many singers in NYC yet, but I did know a group in Boston called The Energetics. They were great singers and dancers, and they all looked very cool too. I convinced them to drive down from Beantown and come directly over to Intergalactic to work on the track, which was now called 'Play at Your Own Risk' (I named it after a sign that hung over a video game I often played at the Music Factory in Brooklyn).

I went into Intergalactic with the singers, Robie and a notepad in

Planet Patrol in Boston, 1983.

my hand. We were now collaborating a bit, and since he was already co-writer on the track, I figured he might be a help in finishing the song up. I was right on that front. We sat behind the console, with the five singers around a few mics out in the live room, and started offering up ideas, line by line. We'd start and stop, punching in lines as we wrote them, giving the individual singers their words and melodies. It was a strange way to write, but it worked.

The song ended up as I had envisioned it, with Herb Jackson, Joey Lites and Rodney Butler swapping lead duties (joined by Michael Jones and Melvin B. Franklin on backgrounds) and sounding like a futuristic Temptations, very much in a production tribute to Norman Whitfield, one of my main influences. Tom had come up with the name Planet Patrol for the back-up band's credit on 'Planet Rock', which came from a cartoon he liked, and he offered it to the singers. The guys were cool with it, so The Energetics were no more.

I asked Tom if we could bring in François K to help us with the mix. I loved the sound of the records François was mixing at the time,

Chris Lord-Alge, me, John Robie and Mike Jones at Unique Studios, 1983.

from Yazoo (who were known simply as Yaz in the States) to D Train. I thought he'd add to what we had on tape. He worked at Sigma Sound in NYC quite a bit, so we mixed there. We had some technical issues, and I remember François taking change out of his pockets and dropping quarters – his way of saying each minute of downtime was costing us money. We hired ace percussionist Bashiri Johnson to play bongos with sticks, which really took the track to a different place.

The record sounded amazing, and it was an immediate smash, exploding on impact. It meant that Tommy Boy had two huge records in 1982. I even got to perform on it, doing the 'Hey, buddy, buddy' and barking like the kids at the Funhouse. Years later, I agreed to license that barking for a new Miami bass track. That song became the first version of 'Who Let the Dogs Out'. Woof woof!

I'd have to say that 'Play at Your Own Risk' is right up there in my list of favourite records I've made. It's also the most painless follow-up I've *ever* made.

Unlike my next Tommy Boy production, the actual Soul Sonic Force follow-up to 'Planet Rock', which was one of the most difficult ones I've *ever* made. It took close to a year to complete.

BEST
Aretha

10.

TAKIN' IT TO THE STREETS

1982

The birth of Streetwise Records took place on the F train. For real. Late one afternoon I was travelling back to the Brooklyn neighbourhood of Cobble Hill, where Tina and I had finally settled. I had just spent a day hustling, running round a plethora of record labels in Manhattan, pitching my numerous 12-inch projects. I was deeply immersed in listening to my new closest companion, my Walkman, when I happened to look up and spot Paul McCraven, my old college friend. Paul was from New Haven, and we were flatmates in the legendary 'animal house' module at Hampshire College. We hadn't seen each other in five years or so, but we immediately fell into conversation, just like it was old times. I filled him in on my progress in the record business. Paul had gone down a way more conservative route, working for some serious investment bankers from Boston who were, he claimed, interested in getting into the music business. This seemed serendipitous to me. I told Paul how I really hated chasing labels for deals and royalty statements. I also thought I had pretty good taste when it came to discovering new talent.

We decided to meet up again, and I invited him to our apartment on Warren Street. He came by a few nights later. He and Tina had always been friendly at school, and we had a great night, discussing all our future successes. Paul was looking for a place in NYC, and we had an extra bedroom, so at some point it was decided that he should move in. It would be just like being back at college.

After Paul had moved in, Tina and I took him down to the Music Factory. I'll never forget that day and the buzz we felt on first hearing Denroy Morgan's 'I'll Do Anything for You' come booming out of the shop. It was a steaming-hot summer afternoon and downtown Brooklyn was rocking. You could always tell when a record was going to be a stone-cold hit just by the way the customers were smiling and moving. I remember that Paul and I said, 'Wouldn't it be nice if we had a hit like that, or even half as big?' Soon I would have a way bigger hit with 'Planet Rock'. That success gave us the credibility that would enable us to convert the idea of our own label into a real situation, when Paul and I convinced his friend, Boston banker Bob Alexander, to finance Streetwise Records.

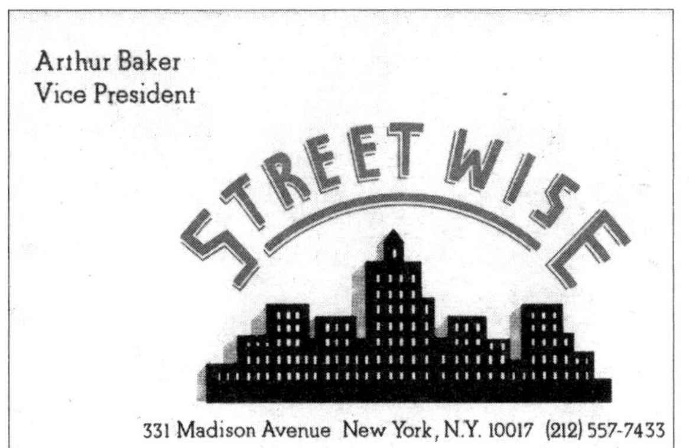

My Streetwise business card.

I had come up with the name Streetwise because I wanted the label to always stay close to the streets. However, the street our backers decided to stay close to was Madison Avenue, where our first one-room office was located – not the kind of street I had in mind. We had a top-heavy staff consisting of Bob, Jane Rifkin and Steve Memishkin, all of whom were bankers. Not very 'street' either! Paul was selected to be president, and I would be senior vice president, in charge of A&R. I still retained the freedom to produce for other labels, but having my own was like a dream come true. I began filling the place out with a 'street' promo team, with Paul and I hiring our college buddy Apache Ramos for radio promotion.

It was an exciting time, and I wanted Streetwise Records to make its mark quickly. My first signing was an import, 'Ease Your Mind' by the UK jazz/funk group Touchdown. I'd heard it played by Larry Levan at Paradise Garage and had fallen in love with it. I was very much taken by the new Brit-funk sound coming out of the UK, so I contacted the Record Shack label in London and licensed it. Since the original had been kicking around on import, I decided to do a few new remixes with my Boston friend Cosmo Wyatt. I decided to try one with a Latino slant, so I called my buddy Joe Bataan, who added his vocal flavour. We renamed this version 'Ritmo Suave', calling the B-side act

'Nuyorican' (interestingly, years later, Louie Vega would take the name Nuyorican Soul and redo the track). Both sides did well in the clubs, and it put Streetwise Records on the map in early 1982.

Next up was 'Be My Girl' by Pee Wee Ford, the bass player from the B. B. & Q. Band, who were hitting big with the track 'On the Beat'. I had originally mixed the Pee Wee track for Emergency Records, and when Sergio lost interest in the record, I asked him if I could license it for release on Streetwise. It was a down-tempo track, but it had a cool Luther Vandross/Change vibe, and I thought it could be a radio hit. I didn't know till years later that the vocals weren't actually by Pee Wee; they were by James 'Crab' Robinson, the featured singer in both B. B. & Q. and Change! But unfortunately, while being a pretty good record, it was not the most auspicious second release for the label. My partners weren't very happy. They were thinking, *You gave Tommy Boy 'Planet Rock', and all we got was Pee Wee?*

The pressure was now on to connect with something that would reward their faith in me. But I had no new artists and no ideas. So I went back to my laboratory, Music Factory. Lightning had struck once there, when I first heard 'Numbers' by Kraftwerk, and I was hoping that it could strike again. After some small talk, Dwight started DJing and dropped Eddy Grant's 'Walking on Sunshine', a song I'd heard numerous times in the three years since it had been released. Dwight claims he played it to me as a potential cover, after I came in sold on the idea of doing a version of Jimmy Cliff's 'The Harder They Come' (which I eventually did). But I remember things slightly differently. Nonetheless, I thought 'Sunshine' would be a great track to do, and I could incorporate elements of other popular club tracks to make it sound fresh. But who could sing it and do the song justice? Dwight pointed over to his unsuspecting brother Donnie and said, 'My brother can sing,' then pointed to Adrienne, the cashier, 'And the girl, she can sing,' and then finally, 'And I sing a bit.' Donnie remembers going 'gulp' like Scooby-Doo when he heard Dwight's claims, but I really didn't have many options, so I figured I'd give them a shot. We planned to meet up at my apartment, with Tina joining the rehearsal to balance out the background blend. After that first night, sitting on the floor in our apartment, it was evident that the four had a connection and could sing – or at least could sing 'Walking on Sunshine'. Sometime that night we decided on calling the group Rockers Revenge.

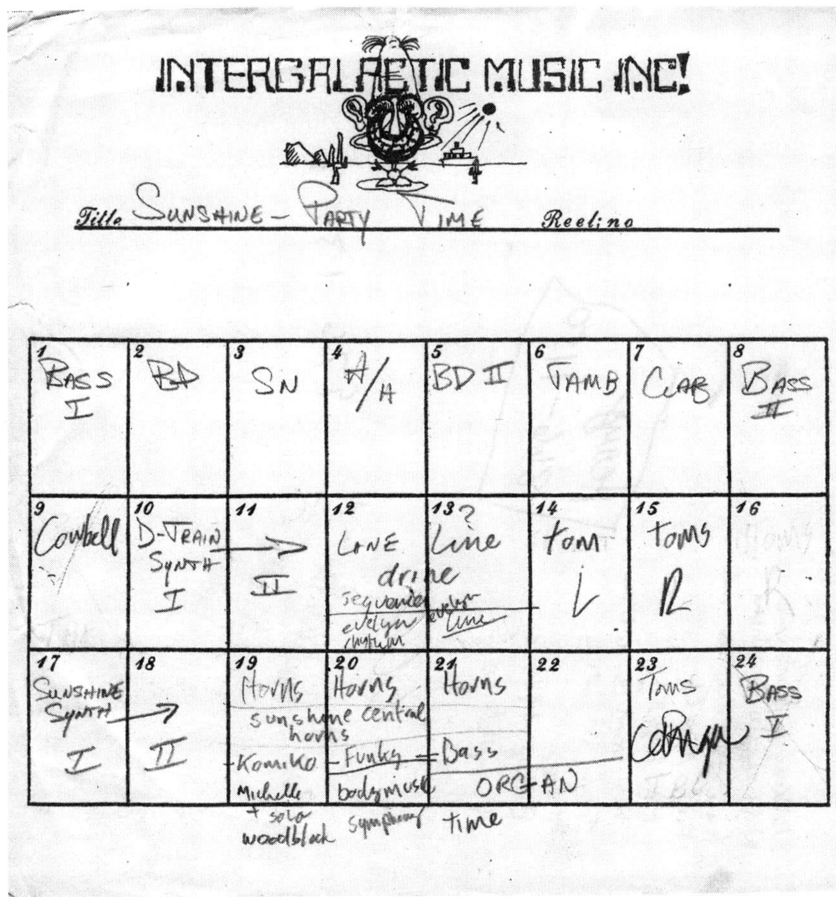

INTERGALACTIC MUSIC INC!

Title SUNSHINE – PARTY TIME Reel no

1	2	3	4	5	6	7	8
BASS I	BD	SN	H/H	BD II	TAMB	CLAP	BASS II
9	10	11	12	13 ?	14	15	16
Cowbell	D-TRAIN Synth I	→ II	LINE drive, sequencer, evelyn rhythm	Line, evelyn line	tom L	toms R	
17	18	19	20	21	22	23	24
SUNSHINE Synth I	→ II	Horns, sunshine horns, Komiko, Michelle	Horns, central horns, Funky body music	Horns, Bass, ORGAN		Toms, conga	BASS I

+ solo woodblock symphony time

Intergalactic Studios track sheet for 'Sunshine, Partytime', 1983.

I reached out to Fred Zarr, a keyboardist/programmer who had played on a few tracks I liked. We planned to programme the basic outline of 'Walking on Sunshine' at his parents' house. Not very glamorous, but we got the work done. Then we went in to cut the track at

Intergalactic. I had Bashiri Johnson play live percussion on the programmed track, and Pee Wee played the bass masterfully. Donnie, the shy brother, then killed the lead vocal, giving the song new relevance. I suggested some 'Hey, hey, ho, ho' ad-libs to him for the intro, which ended up becoming one of the hooks of the song. The girls blended perfectly, and their 'Do it, do it' became another hook. Fred played some of the clav riffs, syndrums and synth horn parts live, using the new Oberheim OB-8 synthesizer and the DMX drum machine. The sequencer had some issues with slippage, but since the percussion and bass were both played live, it gave the track more of a real feel.

All in all, I was confident that I finally had a winner for Streetwise. Donnie and Dwight didn't think much of what we had recorded and went back to their store gig. I had to get the track completed, so I brought Jellybean into Blank Tapes Studio with me and engineer Bob Blank. We mixed it specifically to work at the Funhouse, going back and forth between the studio and the club, checking levels and sounds until we had it ready.

Dwight, Tina B, me, Adrienne Johnson and Donnie Calvin at Music Factory record shop, Brooklyn, NY.

As I always would, I brought an acetate over to Paradise Garage, climbed those clunky metal stairs, handed it over to Larry Levan and waited. Then I waited some more. Finally, around 5 a.m., I left, thinking it wasn't going to happen that night.

The next morning I was woken by a call from my friend, Warner's promo guy Bobby Shaw, saying that Larry had played it five minutes after I had walked down the stairs! That was Larry. From that first play on, it was obvious that 'Sunshine' would be a NYC club smash.

A single play by Larry of a record could cause a tidal-wave effect. First, the clubbers would walk from the Garage to the Vinylmania record store, demanding the new songs they'd heard Larry play. Frankie Crocker, a DJ and the programme director at WBLS, would also be at the Garage to hear Larry play the latest records on Saturday nights. After Levan's initial play of 'Sunshine', we heard a rumour that Frankie would be playing it on his first show of the week. Paul, Tina and I sat glued to the radio, and when Crocker started to wax poetically about the track, I grabbed the phone and called our distributor, which coincidentally was called Sunshine Distribution. Its owner, Howard Rumack, who had also been listening, picked up the phone and put in an initial order for 10,000 copies!

The group started playing gigs all over the tri-state area, with an occasional late-night Saturday gig in Miami. The record made it in a flash to #1 on the *Billboard* disco chart. We had a real hit. Streetwise Records was on its way!

'Walking on Sunshine' quickly travelled to the UK, after London Records A&R man Tracy Bennett heard it during a Hudson River booze cruise while in NYC on vacation. He called me up a week later, when he was back home, and we did a UK distribution deal. The track exploded over there, selling 50,000 12-inch records in a few weeks and making it all the way to #4 on the national pop chart, which meant that Rockers were offered the chance to appear on the BBC's famous *Top of the Pops* TV show. A great performance would have taken the band and 'Walking on Sunshine' to #1 on the chart,

Billboard®

Survey For Week Ending 9/18/82

Dance/Disco Top 80™

© Copyright 1982, Billboard Publications, Inc. No part of this publication may be reproduced, stored in a retrieval system, or transmitted, in any form or by any means, electronic, mechanical, photocopying, recording, or otherwise, without the prior written permission of the publisher.

This Week	Last Week	Weeks on Chart	TITLE(S), Artist, Label
1	5	9	**WALKING ON SUNSHINE**—Rocker's Revenge—Streetwise (12 Inch) 2203 — WEEKS AT #1: 1
2	8	6	**LOVE COME DOWN**—Evelyn King—RCA (12 inch) PD-13274
3	3	11	**LOVE IS IN CONTROL**—Donna Summer—Geffen (12 inch) GEF 7-29982 (LP) GHS-2005
4	4	10	**JUMP TO IT**—Aretha Franklin—Arista (12 inch) CT-718
5	1	15	**SITUATION**—Yaz—Sire (12 inch) BSK 0-29950
6	6	9	**DO YOU WANNA FUNK**—Patrick Cowley Featuring Sylvester—(Megatone) (12 Inch) MT 102
7	9	7	**REDD HOTT**—Sharon Redd—Prelude (LP-all cuts) PRL 14106
8	2	14	**FACE TO FACE**—Gino Soccio—RFC/Atlantic (LP all cuts)
9	15	5	**DO IT TO THE MUSIC**—Raw Silk—West End (12 inch) WES 22148
10	10	17	**COMBAT ROCK**—The Clash—Epic (LP) FE 37689
11	12	10	**IT SHOULD HAVE BEEN YOU**—Gwen Guthrie—Island (12 inch) DMD 344
12	14	7	**THE MESSAGE**—Grand Master Flash—Sugar Hill (12 inch) 584
13	11	11	**MY HEART'S NOT IN IT**—Brenda Jones—Wave (12 inch) DL 1215
14	7	14	**BABE, WE'RE GONNA LOVE TONITE**—Lime—Prism (12 inch) PDS 435
15	16	8	**WHITE WEDDING**—Billy Idol—Chrysalis (12 inch) ETC 5002
16	19	9	**LOVE CASCADE/A WAY YOU'LL NEVER BE**—Leisure Process—Columbia (12 Inch) 44-02989
17	17	8	**VACATION**—The Go-Go's—I.R.S. (12 inch) SP-70031
18	22	7	**ABRACADABRA**—The Steve Miller Band—Capitol (LP) ST-12216
19	13	18	**GLORIA**—Laura Branigan—Atlantic (12 inch*) DMD 338
20	27	6	**YOU SHOULD HEAR HOW SHE TALKS ABOUT YOU**—Melissa Manchester—Arista (LP Cut) AL 9574
21	24	13	**DANCING IN HEAVEN (ORBITAL BEBOP)**—Q-Feel—Jive/Arista (12 inch) BJ 12004
22	34	4	**LOVE'S COMIN' AT YA**—Melba Moore—EMI-America (12 inch) (7803)
23	25	8	**SKI CLUB OF GREAT BRITAIN**—Haircut One Hundred—Arista (12 inch)
24	23	8	**IT'S PASSION**—The System—Mirage (12 inch) DM-4837
25	31	6	**I'M SO HOT FOR YOU**—Bobby O—O Records (12 inch) OR718
26	18	14	**SO FINE**—Howard Johnson—A&M (12 INCH) SP-12048
27	20	12	**DIRTY TALK**—Klein & MBO—25 West (12 inch)
28	21	13	**SOONER OR LATER/DON'T STOP WHEN YOU'RE HOT**—Larry Graham—Warner Bros. (LP) WBS-50065
29	39	5	**IN THE GROOVE**—Tomorrow's Edition—RFC/Atlantic (12 inch) DMD 309
30	50	2	**DON'T GO**—Yaz—Sire (LP cut) 1-23737
31	33	11	**TORCH/INSECURE ME**—Soft Cell—Sire (12 inch) 1-23694
32	32	8	**BACKTRACK**—Cerrone—Pavillion (12 inch) 429-02961
33	30	23	**I RAN**—A Flock Of Seagulls—Jive/Arista (12 inch) JIVE T14
34	26	19	**PLANET ROCK**—Soul Sonic Force—Tommy Boy (12 inch) TB-823
35	41	4	**LET ME TICKLE YOUR FANCY**—Jermaine Jackson—Motown (LP cut) 6017
36	36	7	**LET'S ROCK OVER AND OVER**—Feel—Sutra (12 inch) SUD 008
37	47	3	**DON'T GO WALKING OUT THAT DOOR**—Richard Jon Smith—Jive/Arista (12 inch) VJ 1200
38	40	5	**HUNGRY LIKE A WOLF**—Duran Duran—Capitol (LP cut) 12211
39	46	3	**UNDER THE BOARDWALK**—The Tom Tom Club—Sire

This Week	Last Week	Weeks on Chart	TITLE(S), Artist, Label
42	37	14	**I LOVE A MAN IN A UNIFORM**—Gang Of Four—Warner Bros. (LP) WB1-23683
43	56	2	**CAN'T BELIEVE**—Nancy Martin—RFC/Atlantic (12 inch) DMD 362
44	35	13	**INSIDE OUT**—Odyssey—RCA (12 inch) PD-13218
45	52	4	**YOU DROPPED A BOMB ON ME**—The Gap Band—Total Experience (LP cut) TE-1-3001
46	54	3	**RESPECT**—Zinga Washington—My Disc (12 inch) 4Z9-03139)
47	51	7	**CHECKING YOU OUT**—Aurra—Salsoul (12 inch) SG 369
48	38	19	**DO WHAT YOU WANNA DO**—The Cage with Nona Hendryx—Warner Bros. (12 inch*) 0-29969
49	57	3	**DANCE OR DIE**—Sweet Pea Atkinson—Island (12 inch) 0-99997
50	NEW ENTRY		**IF YOU COULD READ MY MIND**—Columbus Circle—Elektra 67893 (12 inch)
51	NEW ENTRY		**SECONDS**—Salsoul Orchestra Featuring Loleatta Holloway—Salsoul S9-376 (12 inch)
52	55	4	**RADIO**—Members—Arista (12 inch) CP-720
53	NEW ENTRY		**YOU CAN'T HAVE YOUR CAKE**—Brenda Taylor—West End 22149 (12 inch)
54	58	4	**LET ME FEEL YOUR HEARTBEAT**—Glass—West End (12 inch) 22145
55	NEW ENTRY		**KNOCK ME OUT**—Gary's Gang—Radar RDR 12000 (12 inch)
56	NEW ENTRY		**YOU TOLD ME YOU'D GIVE ME SOME MORE**—K.C. And The Sunshine Band—Epic [illegible] (12 inch)
57	59	2	**LOVE ACTION**—Human League—A&M (12 inch) SP 12049
58	60	3	**STEPPIN' OUT**—Joe Jackson—A&M (LP Cut) SP4906
59	NEW ENTRY		**REALLY SAYING SOMETHING**—Bananarama—London LLD 101 (12 inch)
60	61	4	**MOVE ON/STREET PLAYER/MECHANIC**—Fashion—Arista (12 inch) MINI CP-719
61	63	2	**WRAP IT UP**—Touche—Emergency (12 inch) EMDS 6529
62	65	2	**THE CRACK**—The Cosmetics—I.R.S. (12 inch) SP 7096
63	68	3	**DA DA DA YOU DON'T LOVE ME, I DON'T LOVE YOU AHA AHA AHA**—Trio—Mercury (12 inch) MDS 4019
64	62	7	**DANCE FLOOR**—Zapp—Warner Bros. (LP) WBL-23583
65	67	2	**SHE'S SO DEVINE**—The Limit—Arista (12 inch) CP 721
66	64	6	**EYE OF THE TIGER**—Nighthawk—RFC Quality (12 inch) QRFC 020
67	66	4	**SHY BOY**—Bananarama—London (12 inch)
68	70	2	**I MUST BE DREAMIN'**—Wanda—Elektra 69998
69	72	2	**CONNECTING FLIGHT**—Romanelli—21 Records T-1-0-301
70	71	2	**YOU GOTTA GET UP**—Majik—Gold Coast (12 inch)
71	28	16	**RIGHT ON TARGET**—Paul Parker—Megatone (12 inch) MT101
72	29	16	**I'M A WONDERFUL THING BABY/I'M CORRUPT/ANNIE I'M NOT YOUR DADDY**—Kid Creole and The Coconuts—Sire (LP) SRK 3681
73	44	14	**YOU AND ME JUST GOT STARTED**—Linda Taylor—Prelude (12 inch) PRLD 629
74	74	6	**TEMPTATION**—New Order—Factory (12 inch) Import
75	45	9	**SHE CAN'T LOVE YOU**—Chemise—Emergency (12 Inch) EMDS-6528
76	49	15	**KEEP IN TOUCH (BODY TO BODY)**—Shades Of Love—Venture (12 inch) VD-5021
77	73	7	**DON'T TURN YOUR BACK ON LOVE**—Freddie James—Arista (12 inch) CP 716
78	48	17	**DO I DO**—Stevie Wonder—Tamla

'Walking on Sunshine' makes it to number 1 on the *Billboard* Dance/Disco Top 80.

according to Bennett, but the band didn't go. In a decision of tragic proportions, they decided they couldn't leave their day jobs at Music Factory, even for just one weekend. They now claim they didn't know the importance of *Top of the Pops* and thought another chance would come around. They never got that chance.

11.

BEAT THIS

1983

How do you follow up an iconic, game-changing record like 'Planet Rock', a track that got unanimous accolades from such diverse publications as the *New York Times*, the *Village Voice* and *Rolling Stone*, a song that just wouldn't go away, spawning many sound-alikes and our own great 'Play at Your Own Risk', while also trying to run your own hot new record label? You either buckle down, focus and just do it, or you consume lots of cocaine. I tried my best to do all of these.

I had arrived in NYC from Boston in 1980 as a clean-living guy, having given up using any drugs in 1979, after a year-long bender fuelled by my mother's death. And throughout the making of 'Planet Rock', 'Walking on Sunshine' and 'Play at Your Own Risk', I had remained drug-free. But the pressure and the late nights finally got to me, and I started to partake. I'm not gonna lie, it was fun at the start.

The doors to my three favourite clubs – the Funhouse, the Garage and Danceteria – were always open to me, and with Danceteria being a spot that pretty much never closed, constant distractions were available nightly. And, of course, I was doing my research, listening to what Jellybean, Mark Kamins, Freddy Bastone and Larry Levan were playing. Robie and I, usually with Tina in tow, would leave the Funhouse at closing time and hit after-hours clubs like Save the Robots, usually after checking in on our friend John King at Chung King Studios. All fuelled by cocaine. And I'm not gonna lie, it was fun at the start, and it fuelled the party and the work.

'Planet Rock' had peaked on both the R&B (#4) and the pop charts (#48) in July 1982. When you have a hit record, it really pays to have a follow-up ready to roll. Unfortunately, we hadn't even recorded one yet. This time Tom Silverman and Afrika Bambaataa hadn't given me any ideas to work with, so it was left to me and Robie to create some more magic for our rappers. First, we needed to decide on a beat.

It wasn't easy coming up with another definitive groove after 'Planet Rock''s had taken over the universe. We felt the pressure. I vividly remember sitting on the floor at Robie's apartment, alternating between the DMX and an 808 drum machine plugged into my boombox, trying to jam my way to a magic beat. After banging away for what seemed like years but was actually about six months, it eventually dawned on me: I was looking for another perfect beat.

At least now we had a theme. The guys were finally back home from their tour, and I called the G.L.O.B.E. with my concept for our new record, 'Looking for the Perfect Beat'. He seemed to like it and got to work on the lyrics. But we still needed that killer beat. Robie and I consciously decided to make 'Looking for the Perfect Beat' entirely original, with no samples or replaying of other people's ideas; something more like a hip-hop symphony than a typically sparse, raw rap record. In programming the drums, I rocked from beat to beat, randomly changing up as a conscious challenge to other producers. We ended up laying the original drums down at Unique Studios, switching back to the TR-808 after flirting with using a DMX; the 808 was definitely part of the sound of Soul Sonic Force. From there we travelled to numerous

Engineer Mark Berry and me at Vanguard Studios, 1983.

studios in our quest for that perfect sound, that perfect follow-up, that perfect beat. Robie was composing the music on the fly, playing two light, marimba-sounding chord-progression parts by hand. They interacted with each other, creating a unique call-and-response sound (a template that would later be very successfully sampled by the creators of Miami bass, in songs such as 'Whoot There It Is').

Record sleeve for 'Looking for the Perfect Beat' by Soulsonic Force.

The song became a continuous work-in-progress. We kept adding to it until our last mix session, which was due to either an inability to make final decisions or just too much cocaine. Or both. Tom Silverman booked the large room at Vanguard Studios for us to lay the vocals down. We reverted to the basic-formula party-starter chant, this time actually using a real vocoder. The G.L.O.B.E. had totally rocked the rhymes, coming up with amazing lyrics. Again, he ran through the parts with Mr Biggs and Pow Wow. They had brought a large posse of young ladies with them, giving the guys a captive audience to perform to. The vocals went down smoothly. The women also provided the call-and-response choir, which came in very handy. The 'beat this' vocal break came together sonically when I accidentally sent the kick drum to a reverb chamber that created the explosive beats of that section – another one of those 'oh shit' moments. I also thought we should create some soulless electro vocal parts (à la Thomas Dolby's 'She Blinded

Me with Science'), so I decided to perform the mad-professor voice, saying 'looking for the perfect beat' myself.

As we left Vanguard, everyone was happy with what we had. There were vocal hooks galore, and the beats were rocking and definitely club-friendly. And I thought we had a totally new sound that everyone – the group, the label and friends – was responding to. We booked time at Sigma Sound to finally finish the song. Whenever Robie and I went into a studio on our own, there was a good chance we'd have some cocaine, which really wasn't great when you're mixing. It dulls the hearing of the high end, so typically you get a very bright mix, with not much low end. Robie was known for sparkling-bright records with *no* low end.

Blow can also make your decision-making functions somewhat suspect. But sometimes not. My instinct (or drug paranoia) this time was that there was still something missing, that the track needed one more hook to bring it home, but I wasn't sure what. I mentioned this to Robie, who started playing over the track. At one point he played something that immediately stood out, and I said, 'That's it!' It was a catchy, hooky synth line, a call to the dancefloor, and it gave us the final piece of the puzzle. We were now finally ready to mix a follow-up that we could be happy with. We got the mix finished and the song released right at the end of 1982 (but, alas, we still didn't get enough low end on it).

'Perfect Beat' didn't do the sales that 'Planet Rock' had, but it was extremely creative and added another new element to the hip-hop landscape. We had done something different and not copied ourselves. In any case, Tom was so happy with the outcome that he decided to offer me $33^1/_3$ per cent of the Tommy Boy label to come in house as his partner, but on an exclusive deal. I turned him down hard, mentioning I already had my own label. That might have been a long-term mistake.

New York Times critic Robert Palmer named 'Looking for the Perfect Beat' as his top single of 1983, calling it 'an ingenious small symphony in rap rhythms, and a dancefloor favourite', noting that it was 'the year's most widely imitated new sound'. It was ranked at #13 in *NME*'s 'Tracks of the Year' for 1983.

12.

POP FRENZY

1983

While I was trying to get 'Perfect Beat' in the can, I also had my own label to run. Streetwise had its hit and was on its way, but I needed more music to release, quick. So first I used a page out of my 'Planet'/'Play' handbook and released a rap version of 'Walking on Sunshine' with a new dub, featuring an alternative bass line. We called it 'Sunshine, Partytime', and it did the job. It was a great companion piece to the 'Sunshine' 12-inch and also had a cappella and dub versions, giving DJs the tools to make their own master mixes with.

Then a few gifts landed in my lap, as I started to get tapes being sent to me from the UK. Both 'Sunshine' and 'Planet Rock' were rocking the British charts, and I was getting a lot of UK press, but since I wasn't travelling over there (or anywhere really, as I refused to fly, part of the paranoia of taking too much cocaine) I was a bit mysterious, something of an enigma, and that attracted artists. One group in particular flooded me with tapes of their demos. They were called Freeez (I never did understand the spelling), who had recently hit the UK charts with a song called 'Southern Freeez'. They were really keen on me producing their album, but I listened to a few of their demos, and they didn't knock me out. In any case, I wanted to be involved in the actual writing of songs with the bands I was going to produce. That way, I thought, I wouldn't get bored by the material I was producing.

Freeez were signed to a new label in the UK, Beggars Banquet. But since I was quite busy, I sort of forgot about them. That was until they showed up unannounced at the door of my office. These guys had flown over from London to New York to bum-rush me in my own office. They were persistent, I had to hand that to them. I felt sorry for them, given they had flown over from London with no guarantee from me, and I guess I was an old softy back then, because I agreed to produce their album despite everything else I had on the go. I did negotiate with Beggars that Streetwise would have the rights to release the album in the US, which turned out to be a very good move.

We were scheduled to enter Unique Studios in mid-October to record an album. There was only one issue we had to deal with first: they had no tunes I wanted to record. There was also no way we could compose an album at Unique. We needed somewhere to write. Luckily, Fred Zarr had just the place. We had used his small home studio to work out the programming for 'Sunshine', but since then he had acquired a lot more equipment and taken over his entire childhood house. He had a programming room in the basement, with a bunch of gear – synths, drum machines and sequencers. It was the perfect writing room. Or it would have been if it weren't out by Kings Highway in Brooklyn, which was a long subway ride away from Manhattan. But that's where Freeez were going to have to write.

In the midst of this, I got a call from one of my friends from Boston, Maurice Starr. Could he crash at my place in Brooklyn for a couple of nights? 'Sure,' I said, 'no problem.' A few days afterwards he appeared at my door, a lot later than Tina, Paul and I had expected him to arrive. He looked a bit down, which was unlike Maurice, who was usually up and optimistic. He explained he had spent all day visiting record labels, pitching a new act he was working with. Everyone had turned him down. I was curious. I said, 'Maurice, I have a label, remember? Let me hear your act.' He handed me a cassette, and I popped it in. A funky drum-machine fill with electronic claps hit me, followed by a rap and then this chorus that grabbed me and had my housemate Paul coming in from the other room: 'Candy girl, you are my world . . . you look so sweet, you're my special treat.'

As soon as I heard those words and melody, I knew straight away that this shit was a hit, and I was so sure that I wasn't going to let Maurice leave my apartment. He explained that the group were some kids from Boston called New Edition, and the song was called 'Candy Girl'. It sounded exactly like a Jackson 5 song, but not one you'd heard before. Paul and I played it for our partner Bob Alexander, and even he could see the potential. Paul went up to Boston a few days later to meet the kids (who were only twelve and thirteen years old!) and their parents to sign them up.

Now I had both a Freeez album to co-write and produce and a New Edition album to help Maurice finish up and mix. I started the Freeez process in October and New Edition in November, both at Unique Studios, all while also working on a couple of 12-inches for Streetwise that we wanted to get out by the end of the year, along with 'Perfect Beat'.

First, and most importantly, we needed to make a proper follow-up to 'Walking on Sunshine', after the stopgap of 'Sunshine, Partytime'. I decided to finally do that cover of my Jimmy Cliff favourite 'The Harder They Come'. I had both Fred and Robie working on it, and we finished it up at the end of November with a John Potoker mix at Sigma Sound for a late-December promo and early-1983 release. It became a huge record for Jellybean at the Funhouse and was a staple on New York radio. We even cut a video for it.

Local groups were also starting to approach the label, and when some rappers called the Awesome Foursome appeared one day and auditioned for me right there on the street, I signed them and cut a track. I decided that doing a rap over one of my favourite Afro disco tracks, 'Soul Makossa', would work. I went into the studio with Robie to cut 'Funky Soul Makossa' at the beginning of December, right after we had completed 'Perfect Beat'. It was a painless record to make, which we also released at the beginning of 1983, and it became another Funhouse smash.

Next up was New Edition's 'Candy Girl'. *This could be the big one,* I thought. Maurice came to NYC, and we worked together at Unique, quickly taking the track from demo to final record. I had Bashiri Johnson in to play congas and tambourine, and I worked on the drum programming and arrangement. Maurice and his brother Michael had already done most of the heavy lifting, getting the group to sing in tune (almost) and rap their bits. Frank Heller, my new engineer, worked on the mix with Maurice and me. We put 'Candy Girl' to bed quickly, with the mix going down in one day, which was a record for me. After we got a pumping Herb Powers mastering job, I had a few test pressings cut and was anxious to test it out in a club.

It was a cold winter's night in January 1983 when Tom Silverman and I ventured up to see Afrika Bambaataa and Jazzy Jay DJing at the Bronx River Center. We were clearly the oldest and whitest guys in the place, with pretty much everyone decked out in snorkel coats, it was that fucking cold. There was a group Tom wanted to check out, and I wanted 'Candy Girl' to get its baptism by Bronx fire. I handed the test pressing to Jazzy, and he gave it a quick listen and then cut it right into the beat. The funky drum-machine beat slammed in, and by the time the first chorus had ended, there was total mayhem. It seemed like the entire centre was jumping and singing along. Tom looked at me with an approving smile. He knew.

New Edition's debut album, *Candy Girl*.

We decided to rush-release the track at the end of February and planned a party for it and the new Rockers Revenge track at the legendary Copacabana Club, with both acts performing live. By the time the event happened, 'Candy Girl' was already getting radio play. New Edition's performance was pretty choppy, but the crowd loved them. We had planned an in-store event at the Rockers' Music Factory the next day, and the kids there went crazy when the boys lip-synced to their track. We definitely had a big one on our hands.

With Rockers and the Awesome Foursome ready to roll, and 'Candy Girl' scheduled for February, Streetwise finally had an actual release schedule and a bit of breathing room. Me, not so much. I still had that Freeez 12-inch and album to get ready. I had been working with the Brits to sculpt an album that would somehow connect their earlier jazz-funk style with the NYC club sound and the electro vibe I was becoming known for, and hopefully we'd have a couple of smashes in the process. Not easy.

Andy Stennett, me, John Rocca and Peter Mass at a Freeez recording session in Unique Studios, 1983.

The band started to disintegrate in front of my eyes when the drummer, Everton, left NYC. I mean, we were experimenting with drum machines, but realising this was cutting him out, I had tried to involve him more, letting him do raps on the funky 'We Got the Juice' and 'Can U?' And we even tried some live drums on 'Juice', but that didn't work, and he bolted back to London.

We had decided to finish the album before releasing a single, and that ended up being a great decision. The last tracks we recorded, 'No Need for Greed' and 'Pop Goes My Love', were more electronic-based, but neither felt like a first single.

I was really taken with the work Vince Clarke was doing with Alison Moyet as Yazoo. I loved the keyboard sounds he created and how Moyet was a soulful woman who sounded like a man. I thought having John Rocca, Freeez's vocalist, sing in his higher range would reverse that process. I went in with Andy Stennett, the keyboardist, and put down a piano over a straight Roland TR-808 drum pattern, leaving the herky-jerky syncopations I had recently used on 'Perfect Beat' behind. Robie then put down a synth bass line. I took the instrumental rough track home to live with.

We were running out of time. I had lunch at Shun Lee West with my lawyer, Joe Zynczak, and discussed this. I was pretty down and feeling a lot of pressure. Afterwards I hopped into a cab to get crosstown to Unique for the session. While I was in the cab, I was listening to the track on my Walkman, and out of nowhere the chorus of 'A E, A E I O U' popped into my head. By the time I arrived at Unique I had the chorus written, singing it into my Walkman. I got Robie, Tina and John Rocca to sing the backgrounds. I remember Robie giving it a bit of Bowie in the way he exaggerated the letters, while I was going for the classic Chic backing-vocals sound. But in any case, it sounded like a hit.

We realised that we still needed an additional part to drive the track, since at this point it was somewhat mellow. We needed one of Robie's master synth hooks. He laid a cutting Morse code-type synth part down, playing it live. That was definitely what was missing. Next, Jellybean, who I had invited to help on the mix, asked if we could sample the vowels on the studio's new Emulator sampling synth and then have Robie play them as a syllabic solo. This turned out to be a real game-changer. Soon everyone would be sampling vocals in this way, and along with the Roland beats and orchestra hits, we had refined the signature sound of Latin freestyle and electro records.

At this point we ran out of time at Unique; also, John Rocca was meant to be leaving the next day. I called Vanguard Studios to see if they had any available time, and luckily they did. The next day we went in with a few lyric ideas, and we punched in a vocal line by line, similar to how we had recorded the 'Play at Your Own Risk' vocal. I had John do the spoken-word bit, which he wasn't wild about but did nonetheless. We also had to slow the tape down so John could reach the high notes. This ended up making his voice sound even more feminine. He finished his vocal as a cab waited to take him to the airport.

Then, just as I completed work with one British band, another one arrived, making their first appearance in my life.

A dour bunch of Mancs who went by the name of New Order.

13.

OUT OF ORDER

1983

When, at the start of 1983, I received a call from my friend Michael Shamberg about an English band that would potentially like to work with me, I was hot, in demand and out of control. I don't remember being very excited about the idea as I already had a lot on my plate. When the band sent me some demos, I put them in a stack and probably didn't even listen to them. What I did pick up was that New Order were the remnants of Joy Division, whose lead singer, Ian Curtis, had committed suicide just days before their big US tour, and that they were dour. That didn't seem too appetising to me, so I probably let it sit for a while more. Eventually, Shamberg pushed me on it and somehow convinced me to add this band to the growing stack of records I had to produce.

Whatever demos I'd heard on tape probably didn't increase my enthusiasm, although in retrospect I wish I'd kept those tapes. When Freeez had showed up with no songs I was happy with, I'd sent them out to write at Zarr's place. It would become my conveyor-belt halfway house for wayward British artists whom I thought needed a hit.

I had almost finished the Freeez album when New Order arrived in NYC for a three-week stay. I'm pretty sure, looking back, that they weren't too happy with being in a queue behind some southern jazz-funkers. My first impressions of New Order – Bernard Sumner (aka Barney), Peter 'Hooky' Hook, Stephen Morris, Gillian Morris and manager Rob Gretton (who went everywhere with them) – were that they seemed like a shy bunch. They had a rep from that pinnacle of journalistic excellence, the UK press, of being moody and forbidding. Indie friends would ask me, 'What are New Order really like?' Truth is, I didn't know yet, because I was still working on Freeez's 'I.O.U.' By the time I finally got round to starting work with them, they'd been in NYC for two weeks of the three they had scheduled. Now I just wanted the band to come up with a couple of ideas we could record and which I could help produce and mix into dance hits. My credo at the time was that I had to become a member of any group I produced. Which meant co-writing with them. Which meant at the very least coming up with the title and the beat. So I dragged them out to Fred's place in Brooklyn, sat them in front of some synthesizers and waited for something to happen.

Rob Gretton, Peter Hook, Bernard Sumner and Stephen Morris writing the lyrics for 'Confusion' at the Iroquois Hotel, 1983.

They never told me back then, but years later, I found out that they usually spent lots of time hanging around talking and eventually they'd come up with something. Well, this was like that, but in Brooklyn and sped the fuck up. I also discovered later that they found me intimidating, despite the fact that there were five of them and only one of me. A rather large and gruff me, I admit, but still. At some point I think I came up with some beats. Or should I say, I took my 808 with the grooves I had programmed and made a few subtle cowbell and rimshot revisions to them. New Order added some bass and arpeggiator ideas from their Pro-One synth, and then it was finally time to make the trek from Kings Highway to my home base of Unique Studios, right smack in the centre of the jungle of Times Square.

The band were staying in the same convenient Times Square hotel, the Iroquois, that Freeez had crashed in. I don't think they were impressed when they found out they were sharing their rooms with some cockroaches. Adding pressure to the situation, we didn't have much time in which to record, which was my fault because I kept setting things back. Eventually, we made it over to Unique, where we quickly laid down some 808 beats, Juno string chords and a Pro-One bass part. But we didn't have any lyrics. Ah well . . . We repaired back to the hotel and sat around in a roach-infested room, looking at each other.

The whole situation was a bit confusing, so I remember deciding that we should call the track 'Confusion'. Made sense to me at the time. *Job done. I've done my part,* I remember thinking. Somehow the lyrics were written by committee, including Rob. I don't think I had heard Gillian's voice yet. She had been added to the band after Ian's demise and was still feeling her way, it seemed. I have a few pictures of the writing session, which really help freeze the moment. The band are smiling. Were drugs part of the picture? At some point they were spoken about, I seem to remember.

So we had some lyrics and two days left at Unique. Bernard attempted a lead vocal, but it seemed like he had somehow caught the flu. For some reason, I brought John Robie in (to Hooky's eternal consternation) to play a very strange show-off metal guitar solo. Then Simon Topping from A Certain Ratio threw down a timbale solo. I added my rat-a-tat-tats and shouts and convinced the group that it was quite alright to have the title sung as a refrain, which I don't think they had done before, although it was shouted rather than sung – 'CONFUSION!'

New Order's 'Confusion', on Streetwise Records.

Tina B jumped in with Gillian and added her attempted posh British accent (we hadn't figured out that Mancs have a totally different accent and aren't posh) to the 'why can't you see?' bit. They were the first female backing vocals to appear on a New Order record, and they started a trend (one Robie continued with on 'Shellshock').

I brought the band and the rough mix over to Jellybean at the Funhouse, just to get some feedback – positive, hopefully. The crowd went off, barking and breaking to it. I could relax. The band seemed happy. But there was still the mix to do, which I had Jellybean and Robie jump in on with me. At the same time, we thought it would make sense to start on a follow-up before the band left. So, going for a different sound, I brought my DMX drum machine into the B room at Unique, and we all started to jam.

This track had a darker, more traditional New Order vibe to it, with Hooky playing more of a part in its development. After a lot of discussion, we decided to call it 'Thieves Like Us'. The band remember Jellybean having something to do with the title, but I'm pretty sure it was from some graffiti I saw on a wall somewhere. Whatever the case, we didn't get too far on it, but Hooky did lay down a few great bass riffs. No vocals were attempted, and the band took the tape with them back to Manchester so they could work on it.

I'm not sure what New Order thought about the crazy success that 'Candy Girl' was having as they headed back to the UK. After we released the record in early February, things went haywire. Within a week our friends at London Records had made us an offer we couldn't refuse. Roger Ames and Tracy Bennett both thought it was potentially a #1 record in the UK. They were right. 'Candy Girl' had an extremely long chart life on release, both in the UK and the US. It hit #1 in the UK on 28 May and spent thirteen weeks in the charts. It hit top spot in the *Billboard* R&B chart on 14 May, nearly three months after its release.

By the time New Order returned to town to attend the New Music Seminar, we had just released Freeez's 'I.O.U.', and it was everywhere, the anthem of the summer in NYC. It was a pop dance record that I figured would be a hit with all demographics. It made it to #1 on the *Billboard* dance chart within a month of release and stayed there for two weeks. It went to #2 on the UK pop chart, kept off #1 by my future friend Paul Young's 'Wherever I Lay My Hat (That's My Home)', and remained in the top ten for eight weeks and top five for six.

Meanwhile, New Edition were in the US top ten with 'Is This the End', with Streetwise dropping their debut album, *Candy Girl*, on 19 July 1983. It would stay on *Billboard*'s black chart for forty-four weeks straight. I was on a big high, and Streetwise was the top indie dance label in the UK and US for sure.

While all this madness was going on, New Order were meant to play a gig at Paradise Garage and shoot a music video. At some point someone in the Factory camp – probably Anthony H. Wilson – came up with the genius idea of featuring me and the Funhouse in the video for 'Confusion'. Tony was the ideas guy, the huckster, the salesman, the dreamer, the schemer, the intellectual TV presenter – think David Frost meets Donald Trump, in the nicest possible way. He ran Factory Records and paid the bills. Occasionally. I really didn't like the idea of being in the video – I was shy. But somehow Tony convinced me. It was to be helmed by a respected director named Charles Sturridge, who had made *Brideshead Revisited*. I was told I didn't have to act. 'Just be yourself,' they said. They would film me riding in a cab (not a limo) to the Funhouse, handing a tape to Jellybean and watching the crowd dance.

It was a steamy, hot summer's night when we shot the video. Hooky remembers Tina and I having a fight outside the club (not an uncommon occurrence at the time), which led to her smashing not just our car, but two innocent bystanders' vehicles. A synthesizer might have been thrown at some point – I'm not clear on that one. In retrospect, the making of that video was very important – not for me, especially, but in capturing that moment in the history of NYC. Nothing captures the club energy that was everywhere in New York in the 1980s like the 'Confusion' video. Watching it now in its new remastered version takes you right back to those times, much like how *Taxi Driver* shows New York as it existed then.

When 'Confusion' (both the video and record) was rush-released a month later, it did extremely well and brought the band more exposure in NYC clubland, and even a bit in the world of hip-hop. And it added to the strength of Streetwise. Still, it was overshadowed by the ever-lasting, muscular thumping of the blue monster, 'Blue Monday', which had preceded it. Some people thought I'd produced that track too, but I hadn't and have never once claimed to have done so. I think that rumour might have come from one Anthony H. Wilson, as I was a hot name in the UK, and Tony never missed an opportunity to hype something up. The truth is, someone had sent me New Order's album *Power, Corruption & Lies*, and I had mentioned '5 8 6' as a groove I would like to work on if they ever did another track in that vein. That. Was. It. Nothing else. I don't even remember the band playing 'Blue Monday' to me when we were working on our stuff. I did eventually get tired of talking about it, though.

One late winter's night in 1984 I had been doing a club crawl and was standing outside Kamikaze waiting to get in. I heard a beat that sounded vaguely familiar. At the time, my beats were getting bitten fairly frequently, so no biggie there. But this sounded *really* familiar, so upon entering I made my way to the metal ladder leading to the crow's-nest DJ booth, quickly climbed up and looked down at the black label on the spinning record. To put it in the Manc vernacular, 'Those bastards!' It was 'Thieves Like Us'. The DJ handed me the record when he was finished. No production credit! But at least I had my writer's and publisher's share. I guess they had recut it; never really knew, actually. I recently found my rough mixes of the track, and they still sound pretty good forty years later.

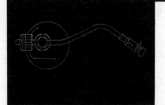

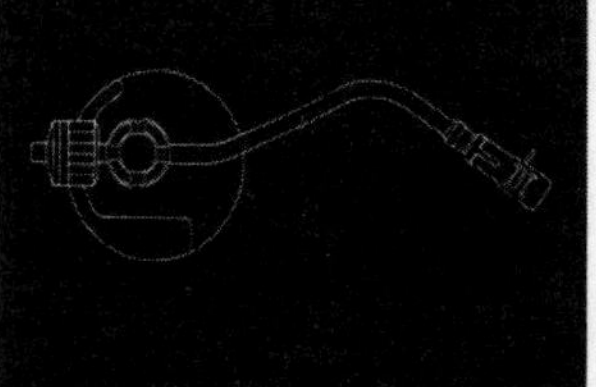

T LA ROCK
JAZZY JAY

RICK RUBIN
INVITES YOU AND A GUEST
TO CELEBRATE THE
STREETWISE RELEASE OF
T LA ROCK AND JAZZY JAY
PERFORMING THEIR HIT SINGLE
"ITS YOURS"
PERFORMANCES BY
SPECIAL K AND COOL MOE DEE
(OF THE TREACHEROUS 3)
THE BEASTIE BOYS
D.J. AFRIKA BAMBAATAA

WEDNESDAY JULY 4th, 11AM

2ND FLOOR OF
DANCETERIA
30W 21 ST

14.

IT'S PARTY TIME

1984

The Streetwise team would end 1983 with a celebratory dinner party and state-of-the-label meeting at Windows of the World restaurant, in the penthouse of the Twin Towers. How the hell did we end up there? Good question.

First of all, there was that record called 'Candy Girl'. New Edition were the hottest new act in the US and UK. Freeez's 'I.O.U.' was also huge. We were selling records but were out of our depth management-wise, giving retailers lots of credit. But everything looked so positive! We thought sales would never end and that people would pay their bills. It looked like Streetwise was on top of the world. But we were about to get in over our heads, and there were some signs that I should have noticed.

Rockers' 'The Harder They Come' had been released at the end of 1982, but it hadn't sold much, despite being an instant classic at the Funhouse and getting tons of play on WKTU. It hadn't really translated to the UK, or even the rest of the US. Since I was so busy with my other projects, I let Rockers take charge of their own writing and producing, which turned out not to be the right move.

We released New Order's 'Confusion', and although it did well in the clubs and in the UK, it had disappointing sales in the States. Then the Freeez follow-up, 'Pop Goes My Love', didn't come close to 'I.O.U.' in terms of sales. And in the midst of all of this I decided to start a sister label for Streetwise to enable us to release more records. I called it Partytime Records, and I wanted to make it our rap label.

My old intern Marley Marl and Andre Booth had an interesting rap record called 'Sucker DJ', by a girl known as Dimples D. It was a novelty answer record to the Run-DMC track 'Sucker MCs', and on 15 March 1983 it became our first Partytime release. Unfortunately, the good luck we had with 'Candy Girl' didn't pass over to Dimples D. Another Partytime act, Cuba Gooding Sr., pulled a gun on his producer, Gavin Christopher, during a recording session, so we weren't upset when his lawyer wrote, asking us to release him from his contract.

But I did make a few good moves. I hired Yvonne Turner, formerly of Downstairs Records, to come in and do A&R for us. She helped connect us with quite a few acts, and 1984 would prove to be a strong year for our records in clubs, with singles such as Colonel Abrams's 'Music Is the Answer' (with Yvonne's remix), John Rocca's 'I Want It to Be Real' (with my remix), Dominatrix's 'The Dominatrix Sleeps Tonight' and my Loleatta Holloway track 'Crash Goes Love' killing it in the clubs. Unfortunately, none of these did much sales-wise. We had been spoiled by New Edition and Freeez.

Oh, and I then had the idea to try and sign the Godfather, James Brown!

Somehow, I got a meeting with him, probably through my lawyer, Joe Zynczak. It was arranged that I'd go see him at his hotel. The desk called his room, and I was told to go up. I entered the room to some strange electrical sound. JB's wife, Adrienne, met me and apologised for the fact that James was getting prepared for a gig. Out of the corner of my eye I saw JB sitting under an old-school pink hairdryer, the kind they used to use in a beauty parlour. He was wearing a dark-cranberry velvet smoking jacket.

It was a dimly lit, old-school hotel suite. Adrienne ushered me in, and I sat down. She sat next to him and started to do his nails. I gave him my best sales spiel, telling him what a fan I was, how I had met him in Boston some years earlier as a young journalist (forgot to bring the picture, unfortunately), about Streetwise, New Edition, what I was up to, and how I'd love to make a record with him.

He asked me where I worked. I said I had my own studio, which was available any time for us to go in and work on our music. He looked at me very seriously and had just one question.

'What floor is your studio on?'

Interesting, I thought. *I wonder why he's asking that?* I told him it was on the second floor. He looked a bit disturbed.

'A studio should be in the basement, that's where you get the best bass on your records. That's why they call it a *bass-ment*!'

I didn't know if he was joking and really wasn't sure how to respond.

CABLE ADDRESS: UNICTRACT NEW YORK
TELEX NO. 62705

AGENCY
INC
218 WEST 57TH STREET SUITE A
NEW YORK, N. Y. 10019
582-7575

June 7, 1984

Mr. Bob Alexander
STREETWISE RECORDS
25 West 43rd Street
New York, N.Y. 10036

Dear Bob,

James Brown requested this day that I write to you and advise you that the agreement between James Brown and StreetWise is now null and void due to StreetWise's failure to make payment on June 1, 1984 as per the agreement.

Bob, I am sorry that this situation did not work out but I tried to buy you some additional time with a minimal payout. However, I guess this also was not in your best interest.

Sincerely,

Jack Bart

JACK BART
PRESIDENT

JB/ds

"The Universal Name in Theatrical Entertainment"

ANY OFFER CONTAINED IN THIS LETTER DOES NOT CONSTITUTE A CONTRACT.

Cancellation of James Brown's record deal with Streetwise Records.

I tried to sway him by saying we had great Neve EQs and got very deep bass on our records, but I don't think it convinced him. He mentioned the clay in Georgia having something to do with his bass too. We chatted a bit more, then said our goodbyes. When I walked out of there, I really hadn't gotten a feel for whether I'd succeeded in getting the Godfather to cut a track with me for Streetwise or not.

In the end it didn't happen, and I always assumed that we just hadn't clicked. But recently I found evidence that my partner Bob Alexander actually *had* closed the deal, signing a contract with the Godfather, but had not sent the advance to him in a timely fashion. So because of that we lost out, and JB ended up making a record at Tommy Boy with Bambaataa called 'Unity'. No idea what floor they recorded that one on.

One legendary artist did end up making it over to Streetwise: Mac 'Dr. John' Rebennack, the legendary Night Tripper. I had been a huge fan of his through 'I Walk on Guilded Splinters' and 'Right Place, Wrong Time'. It came about through Ed 'Duke Bootee' Fletcher, whom I met after Grandmaster Flash and the Furious Five's legendary track 'The Message' had blown up. Fletcher had written and rapped the majority of 'The Message', despite not actually being in the Furious Five. He was a bit pissed off that he hadn't got enough credit and had a new track that he was shopping called 'New York, New York'. I didn't feel it was right for us, but then he played me a demo of a track called 'Jet Set' and told me that he could get Dr. John to make the record.

This sounded like a great idea. I knew Fletcher played percussion in Dr. John's band and so could probably make it happen. Dr. John was also represented by Bob Schwaid, an old-school manager whom I'd first met when I was behind the counter at Discount Records in Boston. We met with Bob and the good Dr., who actually looked pretty rough, as if he could use a good doctor himself. Later, Bob explained that Mac was in need of a bit of rehab, and our sizeable advance would help pay for it. Sounded OK to my partners and me as we were pretty flush with cash (and credit) at the time, with New Edition selling tons. The record came out, was critically acclaimed and helped get Mac well and back on form. Multiple Grammys followed – just not with us.

So Streetwise was now a very eclectic label with a wide range of artists. We even signed Eartha Kitt, who made a record called 'Where Is My Man'. Apache and I saw her perform at the Rainbow Room, and she came and sat on my lap during her show.

At that year-end dinner, we found out that we had been named the best independent label of 1983 by *Cashbox*. But I was starting to lose my focus. Too much cocaine, working on too many well-paid gigs.

Partytime? Well, there was a rap record that Jazzy Jay brought in that piqued my interest. It was very raw and sounded like a live rap show. It used the crowd-response vibe that I had championed with the Soul Sonic records, but it included real scratching, which we had never done. Jazzy's partner on the record was this college kid called Rick, a long-haired white boy. He looked a bit like a younger version of me. I loved the record and wanted to sign it to Partytime. The only thing was, the kid had very clear ideas on how he wanted it to be released. It had to have a unique sleeve, not a generic Partytime cover. He had his own logo and layout. In the end I agreed to it, because the record was strong, and the sleeve was cool. We had a large number of sleeves printed: I think 10,000, thinking it couldn't possibly sell

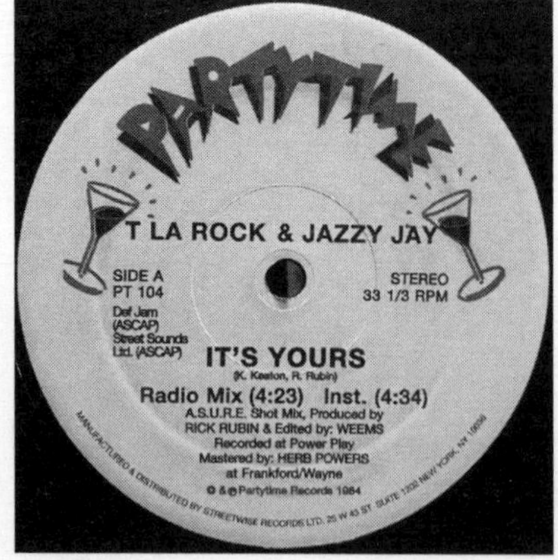

T La Rock and Jazzy Jay's 'It's Yours', released on Partytime records.

more than that. When we sold out, we wanted to keep selling the record in our Partytime sleeves, and this caused something of a problem between me and Rick, the kid. Rick Rubin was his full name. The track was T La Rock and Jazzy Jay's 'It's Yours', and it was the first-ever Def Jam record.

That issue wasn't my fault, but others were. With hindsight, I just took my eye off the ball and went for the cash of the big-name remix. Which left my partners to make some dodgy A&R decisions I didn't agree with. The label was run into the ground, and a lawsuit with New Edition and MCA Records didn't help.

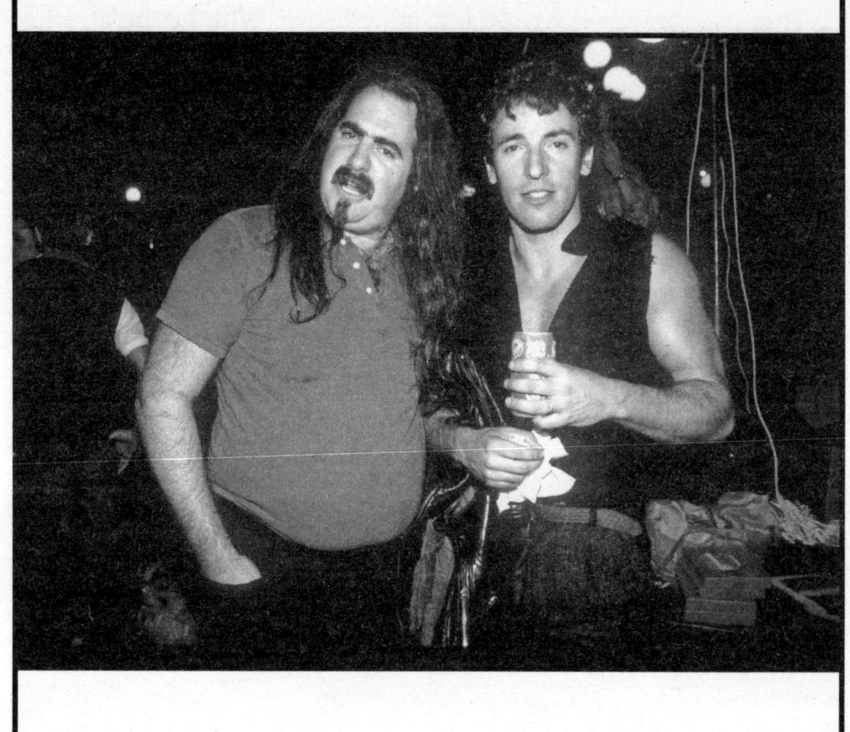

15.

JUST WANNA HAVE FUN

1984

I never realised how important my remix of 'Girls Just Want to Have Fun' was to my career until I started looking back for this book. It's not one I ever really think or talk about, but it was actually the first remix I was hired to do after hitting with my five big productions of 'Planet Rock', 'Play at Your Own Risk', 'Walking on Sunshine', 'I.O.U.' and 'Confusion'.

I was on a roll and actually a bit too busy producing to do remixes. Wasn't even looking for them. I remember Joe Zynczak mentioning a new artist he was working with, Cyndi Lauper, whose boyfriend/manager Dave Wolff shared an office with Joe. Epic Records had hired Jellybean to remix her debut single 'Girls Just Want to Have Fun', but the mix hadn't been accepted. There were even false rumours at the label that he had sabotaged it, as he was going out with Madonna at the time and maybe didn't want any competition for her.

Joe said they were looking to get another remix done and asked if I would be interested. The song already had a buzz around it, and the mix was needed immediately. It would give me a shot at being a hero at Epic, if I could succeed where my boy Jellybean had failed. I called my poker-playing buddy Rick Chertoff, who had produced the original, and he was happy for me to do it. So I said, 'Why not?' and 'What would it pay?'

I went in to do the mix. I didn't change the track drastically (these were the days before that kind of remix), but I sampled Cyndi's vocal into my Emulator and messed around, playing it myself. Then I stretched out sections, adding drum breaks and drops to the arrangement, and did some wilder dub passes. I had fun with it, making the track a bit more joyous and danceable than the original. It was approved and rushed out quickly, hitting #1 on the *Billboard* dance chart on 24 March 1984 and gaining lots more radio play in the process.

Someone who was listening was an artist who was just finishing up his own album. Bruce Springsteen heard my mix of 'Girls' on the radio and liked it, 'thought it was fun', and decided that it might be a good idea for me to get my hands on the upcoming first single from his new album. That was what set the ball in motion for me to remix 'Dancing in the Dark'.

Bruce's team made a call to my friend Joe McEwen, an ex-WBCN DJ and journalist who did A&R at CBS. I was a little surprised when Joe got in touch, because I hadn't heard from him in a while. He said he had been speaking with Jon Landau, an ex-journalist friend and Springsteen's manager, and he thought that it might be a good idea for me to get my hands on Bruce's new single and remix it. This was hugely exciting to me, as I had been a Bruce fan since day one. I had

042784(1)2

MIXING SERVICES AGREEMENT

AGREEMENT made as of the 23rd day of April, 1984, by and between BRUCE SPRINGSTEEN c/o Jon Landau Management, Inc., 136 East 57th Street, New York, New York 10022 (herein called "Artist") - and - ~~SHAKIN' BAKER MUSIC~~, INC. c/o JOSEPH ZYNCZAK, Esq., 65 West 55th Street, New York, New York 10019 (herein called "you"). Arthur Baker

WITNESSETH:

In consideration of the mutual covenants and conditions contained herein, the parties hereby agree as follows:

1. ENGAGEMENT

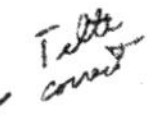

Artist hereby engages you, upon the terms and conditions of this Agreement, to furnish the personal services of ARTHUR BAKER ("Baker") to remix the Master Recording embodying the performances of Artist entitled "Dancing in the Dark" (the "Master"), for the purpose of creating a new version of the Master that is suitable for use on a twelve-inch Single, and you and Baker hereby accept such engagement. You shall cause Baker to render his services diligently, conscientiously and to the best of his ability and in accordance with first-class standards of performance in the phonograph record industry.

2. MIXING PROCEDURE

(a) The mixing services to be performed hereunder by Baker shall include editing, sweetening and such other work as may be necessary to obtain the new version of the Master that is described in paragraph 1 hereof. All mixing sessions hereunder shall be held at the Power Station in New York City or such other studio that Artist shall designate. Artist shall have the right and opportunity to have his representative(s) attend each session. The Master to be mixed hereunder shall be mixed in accordance with the rules and regulations of all unions having jurisdiction. The parties hereby acknowledge that the services to be rendered hereunder by Baker are "technical" and "creative" services. Accordingly, the Master shall be subject to Artist's approval as technically and creatively satisfactory, which approval shall not be unreasonably withheld. Upon Artist's request, you shall cause Baker to re-mix the Master until, in Artist's judgment, a technically and creatively satisfactory Master is obtained.

(b) You shall deliver to Artist a fully mixed and equalized two-track 15 i.p.s. stereo tape for the Master. Furthermore, you shall deliver the Master in both a vocal version and an instrumental version. The Master shall be delivered to Artist in New York City at a place designated by Artist. Each and every original session tape and part thereof, and each and every mother, master, acetate copy or other derivative, shall also be delivered to Artist or kept available for Artist and subject to Artist's control at the recording studio where recorded.

Cover page of my contract with Bruce Springsteen for my remix of 'Dancing in the Dark', 1984.

actually won his debut album in a radio competition, after I stopped at a phone booth and called in. Don't remember the question, but I won the album. So of course I was interested. I asked for a listen; in fact, he may have played it to me over the phone.

After my lawyers got the business sorted, we scheduled a night session at the Power Station, which was Bruce's studio of choice, in order to do some listening and overdubs. I brought Robie with me to play some keys, and Chris Lord-Alge to engineer. Both guys were pretty outrageous characters, and I pleaded with them to be on their best behaviour. Chris was from Jersey, so I figured he might show Bruce the proper respect. But Robie? I wasn't too sure. Joe planned to be there to make the intros between me, my guys and the Boss, but by the time he arrived I was in full 'Spector' mode, and Bruce was there watching me and Robie work with 'his eyes wide open' (according to Joe). Bob Clearmountain, the legendary mix engineer, was also there to help show Chris around the place. They had an SSL mixing board that Chris was already familiar with.

Bruce just chilled, watching us mess around and experiment. I felt that 'Dancing' sounded a bit unfinished and wanted to add the type of arrangement embellishments that Phil Spector himself might have used (minus the gunshots). Robie couldn't help himself and got into some kind of argumentative discussion with Bruce pretty quickly, but when he expertly played a few glockenspiel samples, along with dulcimer, which were more like parts Bruce himself might have recorded, things fell into place. We didn't really add anything outside of the E Street realm. Things were going swimmingly, until the power cut out, which left us without air conditioning. Luckily, the board and all the equipment stayed powered up, so we continued working. Bruce volunteered to go out and get a case of cold beer himself. He got back in a flash, and we all slammed down some cold Buds. Bruce left a bit later, thanking us, and you could tell he was happy with the direction we were going in.

Bruce later had some nice words to say about the experience of working with me, and said that when he'd first heard my dance mix of 'Girls Just Want to Have Fun', he thought it was 'incredible'. He explained to *Rolling Stone*: 'So I hooked up with Arthur. He's a character, a great guy. He had another fellow with him, and they were really pretty wild. They'd get on the mixing board and just crank them knobs, you know. The meters were going wild. I didn't have much input. The entire thing is Arthur Baker. He's really an artist. It was fun to just give him a song and see what his interpretation of it would be.'

Bruce also said that before we worked together, 'I was always so protective of my music that I was hesitant to do much with it at all. Now [after me and him had worked together] I feel my stuff isn't as fragile as I thought.'

That evening, once Bruce and Clearmountain were safely gone, one of us, I'm not sure who, pulled out a wrap, and we did a few lines and worked through the night. That was the only time Bruce attended one of my mix sessions. I did later mix 'Cover Me' and 'Born in the USA' for him, but he didn't turn up for the sessions, so we had to fetch our own beers!

The next day we went over to my new studio, Shakedown (which gets its own chapter shortly), to add some background vocals with my crew – Cindy, Will, Craig, Lisa – both answering Bruce's lead and also doubling up the chorus. I returned to the Power Station with Chris for the final mixdown, which meant EQing, doing the arrangement and taking a couple of passes of the song. A few edit sessions at Shakedown later, we completed the remix.

I waited anxiously to get final feedback on the mix. Bruce had never let anyone touch his music in this way, and although he seemed to like what he had heard in the studio, that was pre-backing vocals and final mix. I was incredibly relieved to get word back from Joe that the Boss loved it.

The 'Dancing in the Dark' single dropped on 9 May, and my 12-inch 'Blaster' remix hit the shelves and clubs on 2 July. I wasn't prepared for it to be quite so controversial with some of Bruce's fanbase. I was in bed in Brooklyn early one morning, when I was awoken by my radio going off. As I started getting ready for the day, I was stirred by the WNEW DJ stating, 'And that was the controversial Arthur Baker remix of the Boss's new single. What do you all think?' He was actually taking listeners' calls on my mix!

'Someone should kill that guy!' yelled the first caller.

'Bruce couldn't have approved that shit!' shouted the next.

Very angry fans.

So, yes, there was a lot of media buzz about this remix, and a bunch of controversy. But a lot of actual club play too, with my mix making it all the way to #7 on the *Billboard* Hot Dance Music/Club Play chart. Amazingly, it also had the most sales of any 12-inch single in the US in 1984. Job done.

At least, that was my experience of the record. But it took me forty years to get the entire story. In 2023, I went to my first Springsteen gig in over twenty years, on my Sun City partner (more on this later) Little Steven's invite. I took my wife Annette (we had married in 2010 – more on her later too) with me to experience the power of the Boss's inspiring show at the Hard Rock Casino in Fort Lauderdale. Steven threw an after-gig dinner. No Bruce or band showed, other than the background vocalists, the horns and the percussionist, as Bruce didn't want to risk getting Covid (which he would a month later).

Steven's managers were there, and my wife was speaking to them and their wives. They introduced her to a gentleman who happened to be Jon Landau, Bruce's manager. He came up to me, and after a few niceties asked if I had ever heard the behind-the-scenes story of 'Dancing in the Dark'. 'No,' I said, 'but better late than never.' Landau went on to explain that Bruce hadn't really been convinced about releasing 'Dancing' as a single. He didn't feel like it was really him, and he was worried that his fans would respond the same way (we were talking about his original version of the song, not the remix). After I had done my mix, Bruce had taken the acetate to a dance club in Asbury Park, New Jersey. When the DJ popped it on and the crowd went off, an excited Bruce had called Jon on the phone. He was ecstatic and at that point decided that he'd be happy to release it as the first single from *Born in the USA*. Jon said that without the crowd's reaction to my remix in the club that night, 'Dancing' might never have been a single, and the entire path of the album might have been completely different. When the original version of 'Dancing' stalled in the UK, they re-released it with my remix, and it became a hit in Europe. I have to say, that was nice to hear, even if it was forty years after the fact!

After the success of 'Dancing in the Dark', I soon heard back from my friend at Epic Records, Lennie Petze. He was Cyndi's guy. He had two things on his mind. Firstly, he wanted me to meet a friend of his, a manager who was interested in working with me called Tommy Mottola. Yes, I knew who Tommy was, both through the Savannah Band song (he is mentioned in the lyrics of their hit 'Cherchez La Femme') and through Hall & Oates, whom he managed. 'I'd be happy to meet him,' I said.

Secondly, there was a new Cyndi single coming up called 'She Bop'. He was going with Cyndi to a gig in Boston and wanted to know if I'd like to join them for dinner and work on a remix while we were there. He'd booked Synchro Sound (which was on the site of the old Intermedia studio). 'Sure,' I told him, 'I'll do it.' It sounded like fun.

We went into Synchro, and I was surprised how bare-bones it was compared to what I was now used to in NYC. But thankfully they had an AMS delay unit, which we used for sampling some glass, some laughs and some of Cyndi's vocals. Then it was down to making a few breaks out of the cool rock beat that her drummer had laid down on Rick Chertoff's original production.

When we took a dinner break at an Italian restaurant close by on Newbury Street, I witnessed the power of Cyndi's new-found fame. 'Girls' had been one of the top records of the past year, and her video was everywhere. Not surprisingly, there were fans lined up all the way through the restaurant to our table, patiently waiting to say hello and get her autograph. Afterwards we went back to the studio and worked through the night, pretty much finishing the remix. I took my passes back to Shakedown, and the Latin Rascals (Tony Moran and Albert Cabrera, the young editing team I had discovered through their medleys for WKTU) edited a 12-inch vocal and dub. My vocal version was then also edited down for the single – although uncredited, unfortunately – and 'She Bop' was released at the beginning of July. The 12-inch made it into the top ten on the *Billboard* dance chart, peaking in September 1984.

By the end of July, the Springsteen juggernaut was in full swing. The tour was taking off and would hit Giants Stadium in East Rutherford, New Jersey, on 19 August. A new single, 'Cover Me', had just been released, when I got a somewhat panicked call from Joe McEwen, which was unlike him, as he was usually a very mellow guy. 'Have you heard "Cover Me"?' he asked. 'Sure,' I told him. I had a copy of the album and had listened to it (it wasn't one of my favourite tracks, to be honest). 'Well, it's the new single, and Bruce doesn't want to play it live. He just doesn't feel it. He thinks it needs something, but he can't figure it out. He'd like you to give it a look, remix it, and hopefully it'll inspire him to come up with some arrangement idea for his live set.'

I thought, *Wow, that's pretty cool, potentially helping to arrange a track he'd play live in front of fuck knows how many Broooce fans.* I just hoped I'd find something that would do the job. I went into the studio with Bruce's recording engineer, Toby Scott, for a listen. First thing I thought was that the current bass line would have to be replaced. My theory has always been that people dance to the bass; if the bass grooves, people will groove. I had just signed Mojo Naya, a reggae group, to Streetwise, and the bass player, a chilled Rasta named Brian Rock, grooved massively. He'd give 'Cover Me' an entirely new vibe. Looking at the track sheet, I saw 'BV' (background vocals), quickly pulled up the corresponding fader, and suddenly this amazing, soulful female vocal magically appeared, riffing on the words 'cover me'.

Wait . . . is that . . .? I thought. I realised almost instantly it was my old friend Jocelyn Brown! I called her. 'Jocelyn, is that you on this Springsteen thing?' There was silence for a second. She said, 'Oh, yeah, baby, I did that session a few years ago as a demo.' She had forgotten about it. I promised her that 'I'm gonna get you out there with those killer ad-libs'. She was pretty happy; I could feel her smile through the phone.

So I had my direction: Brian back on bass, my new guy from Sugar Hill, Gary Henry, on keys and Bashiri Johnson on percussion. Their playing instantly melded together with Jocelyn's ad-libs and Bruce's vocals and guitars, and I was inspired to go into full dub-fest mode. I used Toby as my mix engineer, sure that he'd know how to get Springsteen's basic sound, but decided I'd go extreme and then roll the craziness back, if necessary. I drenched Bruce's and Jocelyn's vocals in Lee Perry-like space echo delays, constructing breaks and drops and melding a new intro out of this new dub symphony. When the overdubs were complete, the track felt totally natural and organic, like it was meant to be this way from the jump, which would possibly give Bruce something he could use for his live arrangement. But the real test was yet to come – the Boss.

Joe again sent the mix over to Jon Landau. Word got back to me that Bruce had loved it and thanked me. Now he could play his new single live in Jersey, and I should be there to hear it.

The show was on 19 August 1984. It was a Sunday, and I was way out in the Hamptons at my friend, lawyer Owen Epstein's house, so I had some serious driving to do to make it to Jersey for the gig. We got there just in time for me to hear Bruce and Patti Scialfa, his bandmate and future wife, singing the intro of 'Cover Me', with their voices dubbed out just like my remix.

I would later go on to do one more remix for Bruce, 'Born in the USA', again using Toby as engineer, but mixing at my own Shakedown studio. This time I pretty much used what was on tape, adding some bells and hand percussion and lots of delays and FX. I went bombastic and brought out the rage and explosiveness of the song. When I met him in 2023, forty years later, Jon Landau admitted to me that my version of 'Born in the USA' was his favourite of the three mixes I had done.

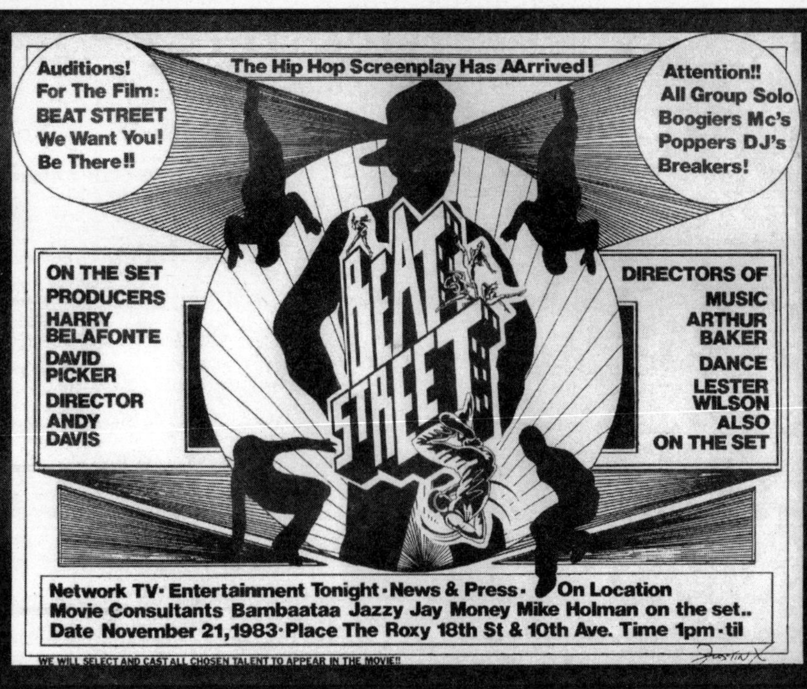

Auditions!
For The Film:
BEAT STREET
We Want You!
Be There!!
The Hip Hop Screenplay Has AArrived!
Attention!!
All Group Solo
Boogiers Mc's
Poppers DJ's
Breakers!
BEAT STREET
ON THE SET
PRODUCERS
HARRY BELAFONTE
DAVID PICKER
DIRECTOR
ANDY DAVIS
DIRECTORS OF
MUSIC
ARTHUR BAKER
DANCE
LESTER WILSON
ALSO ON THE SET
Network TV· Entertainment Tonight· News & Press· On Location
Movie Consultants Bambaataa Jazzy Jay Money Mike Holman on the set..
Date November 21,1983· Place The Roxy 18th St & 10th Ave. Time 1pm· til
WE WILL SELECT AND CAST ALL CHOSEN TALENT TO APPEAR IN THE MOVIE!!

16.

ME AND MR B.

1984

I was working in the studio one night when I got a call from a journalist friend of mine, Steven Hager. Steven had interviewed me for an article he had written for the *Village Voice* about the Funhouse scene, 'Beatin' It with the Juice Crew'. Steven really had shone a light on the whole electro scene; me, Robie, Jellybean and Tom Silverman were all interviewed.

Steven wanted to meet but didn't say why. We met up the next day, and he filled me in on something he had been working on. He had written a film script about the nascent hip-hop scene, and he wanted to call it *The Perfect Beat*. I was flattered that he had chosen that name, so I definitely wanted to know everything. He had originally met with Jane Fonda, who liked the project enough to offer him $500 for the script. $500? Thanks, but no thanks, Jane. He then met with David Picker, who was a top producer with a lot of clout. He had served as president of United Artists, Paramount, Lorimar and Columbia Pictures, before becoming an independent producer. While at Paramount he had helped develop *Saturday Night Fever*, *Grease* and the 1981 Academy Award winner *Ordinary People* – some big-ass films. Picker had brought in Harry Belafonte as his film production partner, and they had a deal with Orion Pictures. Steven wanted me to be part of the creative team and produce the music for the film.

I thought about it. I was already under deep pressure work-wise. I had Soul Sonic, Planet Patrol and Rockers Revenge to think about, along with Streetwise and opening my own studio. I was also doing way too many drugs in the process. But I felt that I was in the zone, so I told Steven, 'Yeah, of course I'm in.'

Steven organised a meeting at Harry's office. Harry was a larger-than-life character, a movie star, and he took over a room. He was seated behind a big desk. After shaking hands with us, he randomly asked us if we were Jewish. Steven said no, and I answered in the affirmative. Harry jumped out of his chair, opened the closet door and said, 'OK, come out, Hymie,' and Picker pops out of a closet. They both had a big laugh. An interesting start to a business meeting. They

My first solo record, 'Breaker's Revenge' from *Beat Street*, on Atlantic Records.

made a dynamic team. Harry was charismatic and had that gruff voice and stature that immediately commanded attention. But David was no shrinking violet either. He was smooth; you don't get to run studios without being slick. They both started to pitch me the project, which wasn't actually necessary, but they were in full sales mode and had already convinced the suits at Orion. Harry famously said that if he had been white, he would have been president, which after spending time with him I would have to agree with.

One of their early decisions was to change the name of the film. No longer *The Perfect Beat*, it would now just be a succinct *Beat Street*. Sounded a bit corny to me, but I'm sure I didn't push back. Even if I had, it wouldn't have mattered. I was happy just to be in the room. Steven had given me the brief on the film, but then I read his script. Put it this way, it was a lot grittier and far more realistic than the corny one that eventually ended up getting shot. And he was still only paid the same $500 that Jane Fonda had offered him for it!

At the time, I was confident that with great music, we could produce a film that would be the *Saturday Night Fever* of hip-hop. Obviously, Picker, who had also been involved in that film, thought so too, and Harry was definitely a believer, as he had put his name behind it. That may have been why he began making decisions that started to homogenise *Beat Street* from day one.

There was still my business deal to be negotiated. Steven recently told me that Picker and Belafonte thought I was asking for too much (when I heard what he got paid for the script, I could understand why they thought that). There was mention of Quincy Jones as another possible option, and Picker had said they had a good relationship. But I'm sure Q would have asked for much more, so at the end of the day I got the gig.

My job description was threefold: (1) I'd help find the artists to perform in the film and on the record; (2) I'd write and produce the material they'd perform; and (3) I'd work with the record labels in helping to negotiate deals. I thought finding the acts would be easy. This was going to be the first Hollywood film to showcase our scene, so who wouldn't want the chance to be included on the big screen? I didn't really think about the budget and the business side of things initially.

Harry and I started brainstorming what the film's musical concept should be, agreeing on my initial idea that the soundtrack should be at least a double album: one of new material, and the other an album of b-boy classics from the likes of James Brown and Jimmy Castor. We wanted to stay true to the musical roots of the culture, and using some of the tracks that had helped give birth to breaking was essential.

They still needed to select a director and wanted Steven's and my input, so we went to a screening of *Stony Island,* the debut film of a new director they were interested in, Andrew Davis. It also featured a young actress, Rae Dawn Chong (the daughter of Tommy Chong, of famed stoner comedy duo Cheech & Chong), whom Harry and David were thinking of for the lead. It was an early-morning screening, and I had probably been in the studio working all night, because I fell asleep halfway through. Steven said I hadn't missed anything; he wasn't impressed either. Despite this, Harry and David had hired both the film's director and its lead actress.

Rae Dawn Chong, Franc Reyes and Tonya Pinkins at Shakedown Sound's Valentine's Day opening party.

Andy Davis seemed a strange choice for director, seemingly having no connection to the world of hip-hop, but they had seen something in *Stony Island*. They then slotted Guy Davis (the son of legendary acting couple Ossie Davis and Ruby Dee) for the male lead. Harry eventually slipped in his daughter Gina into the film, and his son David was hired to produce some of the music. Once both Davises were in, it was decided to do some 'street' castings at the Roxy, the famous hip-hop/roller rink downtown on the West Side. Our entire team was out in full effect: Belafonte, Picker and Andy Davis, along with me and Lester Wilson, the director of dance, and 'Money' Mike Holman, a hip-hop impresario who was deep into the breaking scene. I brought Afrika Bambaataa and Jazzy Jay in to provide the jams, and they blasted out current tracks like 'White Lines', alongside breakin' classics like 'Just Begun'. We were looking for groups, solo performers, boogiers, MCs, poppers, DJs and breakers. Everything and everyone

B-boy audition for *Beat Street* at the Roxy.

turned out, and it was a bit of a madhouse. I hung out with Harry behind the big glass window in the VIP lounge overlooking the mayhem. I eventually made it down to the dancefloor and watched all the great breaker crews trying to out-rock each other to Bamb's and Jazzy's DJing squads, such as the Rock Steady Crew, the Dynamic Breakers and the all-female Dynamic Dolls Crew. I slipped out as things were ending, not having noticed any acts I was specifically interested in.

However, the next day I got a call from Picker. He told me to be on the lookout for this very young Puerto Rican girl he and Harry had met at the casting named Brenda K. Starr. She was in the Dynamic Dolls breaker crew but had sung a bit and was very outgoing and determined. Harry thought she had something and that I should check her out for the soundtrack. A few hours later, I got a call from Brenda, and I told her to come to Shakedown. Being around just fourteen, she showed up that afternoon with her mother Beverly in tow. But then again, New Edition were that age too, so I gave Brenda a serious listen.

She sang an interesting choice for her audition, 'Love on a Two-Way Street', which had been a big hit for The Moments in 1970 and, more recently, Stacy Latissaw. Brenda was a bit out of tune, but she was confident and had a nice voice with a cool vibe. A Puerto Rican Jew, her mother was a PR, while her dad, Harvey Kaplan, was keyboardist in the classic group Spiral Starecase, of 'More Today Than Yesterday' fame, so she had heritage. I figured I'd give her a shot. She already had an idea for a song called 'Vicious Beat', so I started messing around, searching for a 'vicious' beat to go with it. The pressure would be heavy in terms of writing and accumulating material that the director dug and the producers approved. I thought that would be where the real hard work and disagreements would occur, and I was correct.

Harry made me and the world aware, through a *New York Post* interview, that we were under an extremely tight deadline. The film was scheduled to premiere at the Cannes Film Festival in May. No ifs or buts. There were rumours that a few other movies on hip-hop culture were being planned by other production teams – one of them headed by Harry's friend Sidney Poitier – and obviously Harry wanted to make sure *Beat Street* was the first. Before too long it became apparent to him and David that Andy Davis was out of his comfort zone, and that a new director with more of a feel for the subject matter and black culture should be brought on board. They picked Stan Lathan, who had directed Redd Foxx's *Sanford and Son* TV show, among others. This seemed to be a step in the right direction.

Although my new studio, Shakedown, was just about fully up and running, I was still doing most of my work over at Unique's new MIDI room with Chris Lord-Alge. It was fully stocked with all the newest gear, and owner Bobby Nathan had everything MIDIed up, which gave me lots of options synth- and sound-wise. I was getting bored with the 808 sound and had started moving on to the more organic sound of the Oberheim DMX drum machine, along with the Oberheim DSX sequencer. Chris was on top of both, programming-wise, so we started knocking out tracks in early December.

Me, MC G.L.O.B.E., Mr Biggs, Pow Wow, Ahmed and Afrika Bambaataa at Shakedown Sound, recording 'Frantic Situation' for *Beat Street*, 1984.

Those initial sessions produced the beat that would become '(Only Love) Shadows', eventually sung by Lisa Fisher. We made a bunch of rough demos specifically for the breakin' scenes, since the director wanted stuff to shoot to asap. Other assignments included providing tracks with scratching that the lead actor could perform to. I brought Jazzy Jay into Shakedown to experiment on beats and scratches for that. Lip-sync scratching, anyone?

Towards the end of December it became apparent that I needed a keyboardist to help me finish up some important tracks, so I called in Fred Zarr. I trusted Fred's talent and demeanour; we had already successfully worked together, and he had become Madonna's chief keyboardist after his work on her song 'Everybody'. I got Brenda in with her 'Vicious Beat' idea and had Fred pull up those pop-dance sounds he was known for. He got into the groove quickly, and we arranged a great track under her vocal. Brenda still had some issues with pitch, which is typical with young singers, but that helped give 'Vicious Beat' the sassy New York PR attitude that would become the trademark for all the Latino freestyle singers who would follow Brenda.

Fred also added keyboards on a track that Tina and I had just started, 'Nothing's Gonna Come Easy', which was composed for the scene where Guy Davis's character is fighting with his mother over being a DJ. It eventually was used in the Roxy audition scene, giving Tina the opportunity to take part in the film. Harry, watching her performance, expressed his opinion that it was a great song, and if Donna Summer had sung it, it would have won a Grammy. Tina also remembers having to provide her own costume and choreography for the scene.

When I got back to work after a short new year's break, one of my first assignments was to compose a song for the important montage scene, which featured the girls getting primed for their night out at the Roxy. I had initially given the assignment to the group The System, and they had composed a song called 'This Is My Night' for Chaka Khan. The track was great, but the business deal to bring Chaka in came to a screeching halt, and although The System were in the film's audition scene playing their 'Baptize the Beat' track, Chaka's song was not in the film. It did, however, end up on her *I Feel for You* album.

I had to get on to a replacement for the Chaka track asap, so in early January I went into Unique's studio B with Chris and two friends of his, Carl Sturken and Evan Rogers, a new young writing/production duo he thought I should meet. Before we started, I referenced Michael Jackson's 'Don't Stop 'Til You Get Enough' as the vibe we were after, and we began jamming a groove together. I put down a DMX beat and came up with the bass line, Chris played some keys, and Carl played a funky rhythm-guitar line. Then Evan started riffing on a 'this could be the night' lyric idea. The song came together really quickly. Tina came by and helped us finish up the lyrics from a girl's perspective.

Next we needed a female singer to deliver this important song. Carl mentioned a young vocalist called Cindy Mizelle, whom he had worked with in the West Street Mob and was now gigging at a place called the Cellar Club. I decided to go by and check her out. She had a great voice and was very cute too, real artist material. After the set, Carl and I went backstage, and I spoke with her. She came to Shakedown a few nights later with Carl and Evan and knocked the vocal out like a real pro.

During the shooting, Bamb and Soul Sonic approached me about what they thought was the lameness of the film and the mood on set. In their eyes, it wasn't a true reflection of the scene, it wasn't keeping it 'real'. I remember Mr Biggs saying, 'Yo, Artie, this shit ain't right! We can't smoke, we can't drink, we can't swear. This ain't *real*. Talk to Harry, man.' Which I did. A few times. Unfortunately, to no avail.

Ad for *Beat Street*.

Harry started to take more control over the music, handing quite a bit over to his son, David. I had a lot on my plate, and looking back, I can admit that I was under a lot of pressure, while my cocaine use wasn't helping things. Some of the decisions Harry made creatively were, in retrospect, correct, but having his son produce quite a few tracks didn't work. The film also suffered from horrible fake graffiti and a production designer who was known for films like *Barry Lyndon*, who just wasn't right.

On 5 June 1984, Tina and I went to the *Beat Street* premiere at the Alice Tully Hall, a very large theatre. I thought the film was pretty bad and was almost tempted to get up and walk out a few times. Jellybean was there with Madonna, and we avoided them afterwards because I was embarrassed by how the film had turned out. There was an after-show 'hip-hop party' at the Roxy.

Billed as the 'music and breakdance explosion of the summer', *Beat Street* opened on 8 June to mixed reviews and business. But after its time in the movie theatres, it became one of the top film rentals of that year and is now considered one of the first films to expose breaking and hip-hop to the world. It has since been name-checked by artists such as Nas and Lin-Manuel Miranda and by many of the Olympic breakers for its importance.

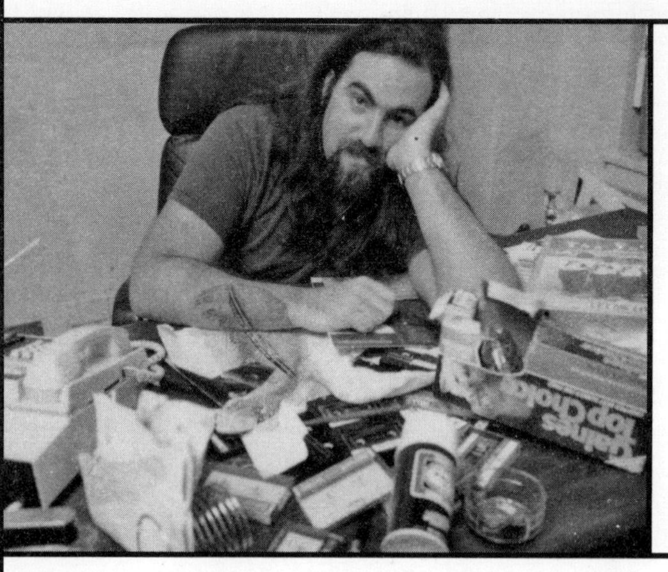
Gaines

17.

SHAKEDOWN SOUND

1984

Around the time the *Beat Street* project started, I decided to open my own studio. After having spent a lot of time and money at OPP (Other People's Places) studios, in late 1983 I decided it might be time to finally take the plunge and open my own. Why the hell not? My career was exploding. I had my own record label, with lots of records to make for it, and I had all the *Beat Street* work coming. There was more than enough in the pipeline to keep me and a studio busy full-time. Although my days of big-name remixes hadn't yet come to pass, it looked like they might be a real possibility soon, so the idea of collecting studio costs along with my mix fee definitely appealed to me. On top of that, both Intergalactic and Blank Tapes, where I did a lot of my studio work in New York, were closing, so I needed somewhere new.

With my burgeoning career, I really needed my own recording complex, a place with multiple studios where I could work on various projects at the same time. It would need a live-recording room with a state-of-the-art console where I could work on mixes, a separate smaller control room for overdubs and writing, and an editing/listening room. The other major bonus of having my own studio would be I could leave my mixes up on the board if my drug use didn't allow me to focus on finishing them before crashing out, which was starting to be a problem.

So I pulled the trigger and signed a lease for the fourth floor of 222 West 37th Street, right in the centre of the fashion district, which my father had roamed through during his NYC work trips in the 1960s and '70s. I needed to have the studio up and running asap, but the realistic ETA was early 1984, so I needed somewhere else to work in the meantime. When Jay Burnett mentioned a new Times Square studio called Unique that he was working at, it luckily turned out to be the perfect transitional home base for me. The owners, Bobby and Joanne, were a very cool musician couple, and they had all the newest and most cutting-edge gear, for no extra cost: things like a wall of MIDIed-up keyboards, the AMS sampler and the Emulator. Bobby would work through the night making samples for his Emulator and creating mega synth sounds with his bespoke MIDIed-up grand piano. As a bonus, Unique had a crew of interesting clientele rolling through, so bumping into acts like the two Billys – Idol and Ocean – and creative producers and musicians such as Keith Diamond and Bobby O was a plus. The Christmas parties were also a hoot, you could say. Spending a few hours with Mr Idol and his bag of white Christmas cheer was pretty memorable.

Unique also had a team of inventive in-house engineers. Jay was there, but he was extremely busy on the back of the success of 'Planet Rock', so he wasn't always available for recording. So I started off with a new engineer, Frank Heller. We worked together on the New Edition and Freeez albums in Unique's A room, and then on the New Order sessions in their newly opened B room. He was a very good engineer, just a little too anal at times. He'd spend hours labelling our half-inch mix boxes, although I admit they did look nice when he'd finally finished.

But when I was introduced to this somewhat crazed engineer from 'Joisey', who had made his bones at Sugar Hill Studios and could play, program, mix and experiment, I was sold. Chris Lord-Alge immediately became my main man, working with me on remixes such as 'Dancing in the Dark', the Rolling Stones' 'Too Much Blood' and Diana Ross's 'Swept Away'. His mix theory was just to give them the wood – the hard snare sound that was his trademark. Add a bit of reverb to it and – boom! – it rocked. His programming graced a lot of the tracks on the *Beat Street* soundtrack. He loved to sample; nothing was safe when he was working the AMS, creating massive drum sounds with this technique. We loved to use Unique's B room as our programming and overdub spot, with clients such as Ric Ocasek and his girlfriend Paulina crunched behind us, making out on the small couch, as we worked on The Cars' 'Hello Again'. Diana Ross passed out on the same sofa after drinking red wine, snoring through our 'Swept Away' mix session. We recorded Billy Crystal's 'You Look Marvelous' in that room, along with the Soul Sonic Force's 'Renegades of Funk', as seen in the BBC's *Arena* hip-hop documentary 'Beat This'.

When Unique started to get booked up, we'd occasionally have to move around to do mixes at other studios, such as the Power Station, Electric Lady and Right Track. With the ongoing pressure of the *Beat Street* film project, the opening of Shakedown Sound was coming just when it was most needed. I started work for the film at Unique, writing and recording track after track there, but when my studio opened with a rockin' Valentine's Day party, it was right on time. Shakedown Sound immediately became my clubhouse, workspace and party spot. I made sure it would be comfortable for working there non-stop, 24/7, so it had a shower, a kitchen, a massage chair (which Diana Ross adored) and a ping-pong table (which Daryl Hall and John Oates loved).

You are cordially invited to attend the opening of

ARTHUR BAKER'S
New Recording Studio

'SHAKE DOWN SOUND'

Valentine's Day
Tuesday, February 14, 1984
Six P.M. 'til Midnight

222 West 37th Street
2nd Floor
New York, N. Y. 10018

R.S.V.P. (212) 947-9170

Invitation to the Shakedown Sound opening party.

As head engineer, I brought in a guy I had met at EARS Studio in Jersey, when I worked there mixing 'I.O.U.' with John Robie. Andy Wallace was a bit older, had built studios before and was a great engineer. He helped me with purchases and setting up the place, and later became known as Butch Vig's engineer on Nirvana's *Nevermind* album, along with producing the Jeff Buckley album and engineering Slayer for Rick Rubin. He was Shakedown's first in-house engineer, but as you'll discover in the next chapter, his tenure was short-lived.

Our first board was the Trident 80B; most of the *Beat Street* productions were mixed on it. We had plenty of outboard equipment, including a rack of Neve EQs and a plate reverb. We also had our secret weapon: a large white photo/dance space that we dubbed 'the room of doom'. The rounded cement walls created mega drum sounds. We also had access to an eight-floor stairwell in the evening. Keith LeBlanc would set up his drums there and rock all night, making John Bonham-type sounds.

My dad, who was in the process of setting up his own fashion brand called Mr Coats, decided it was a great spot for his showroom, so he borrowed my office a few days a month and became part of the Shakedown family. He'd bring me Boston Chinese food in lieu of rent! Billy Crystal loved the place and would always ask about Irving. My dad got on well with many of the artists and producers who used the studio. He and Randy Muller, producer and arranger of such acts as Brass Construction, B. T. Express and Skyy, had many discussions about the clothing industry, as Randy's wife was a designer.

My friend Shep Pettibone began to use Shakedown as his mix room, and for a few years he was my main client. We had great fun hanging out together, doing loads of drugs and occasionally assisting each other

Me and Tina B at Shakedown Sound, 1984.

with difficult mixes. I remember helping Shep when he had totally lost the plot on a Pet Shop Boys mix, and he helped me on quite a few, one Jeffrey Osborne track in particular. Either he or I would come into the studio in the morning, ready to start a new remix, only to find the other one, wasted by the board, still in mid-mix after having worked all night. It felt like Shep was mixing everything at one point, even before his work with Madonna. No matter how great his mixes were, I would find it really annoying to have the same thing being played over and over from the edit room. Songs like Phyllis Nelson's 'I Like You' or a B-52's track on repeat could really do your head in.

John Doumanian, Woody Allen's best mate, once sent over a nineteen-year-old female singer called Sophie for me to check out. I let her throw down four songs, with keys and vocals. I thought she had a nice voice, but not much more than that. I probably didn't pay her enough attention. A few years later, that same singer, Sophie B. Hawkins, was Grammy-nominated as Best New Artist and went on to have a great career.

Lynn Shaffrin, a lawyer I knew at Grubman, Indursky & Schindler, the top music-industry law firm in NYC, sent her friend, who was a keyboardist and singer, over to see me. I didn't happen to be there that day, so he left a card for me to get in touch, but I never did get round to calling him. His name? Harry Connick Jr. Another one that got away!

Mr Magic, the hip-hop radio DJ, came in late one night with this big guy who made beats with his mouth. Keith LeBlanc happened to be in the studio that night and put down a few rough beats for the guy to beatbox to. His name? Biz Markie. I thought he had talent, but he seemed a little strange.

Jay brought a young, pre-record-deal Adam Yauch, later known as MCA from the Beastie Boys, in as an assistant engineer intern. He'd occasionally run errands on his skateboard, and he, Jay and I wrote and produced one pre-Def Jam track, 'Drum Machine', together.

But it was when we started the Sun City project that Shakedown really made its bones. We were there 24/7, with legends such as Miles Davis, Lou Reed and Peter Gabriel coming in at all hours.

Running a studio wasn't easy, and I had to make sure that I had enough business to keep it going when things slowed down, so I'd have to court clients and engineers, which really wasn't my thing. I remember when Dave Ogrin, whom I was trying out as an engineer, asked if I was interested in getting Larry Blackmon of Cameo to use the studio. Larry had heard about Shakedown and the vibe, and now that I had a fifty-six-channel SSL board (the company Solid State Logic was a new manufacturer who made fully computerised mixing desks), he wanted to check out the studio.

'Of course,' I said.

The only issue was, Larry used a Sony thirty-two-track digital tape machine, and we didn't have one. Larry owned one, so he had it carted over. It made it into the elevator no problem, but when it was wheeled down the hallway to the SSL control room, the external doorway was just an inch too small. *Shit,* I thought, *there goes a potentially huge client leaving.*

Why I had a sledgehammer in the studio, I do not remember, but I started swinging and knocked enough out that the machine could make it through into the SSL. Unfortunately, after a few hours Larry decided he really wasn't feeling the Shakedown vibe and left. With my doorway in pieces. Yes, I was still doing cocaine at the time.

The saga of the first Shakedown sadly ended when the building was sold and I was forced out. I probably hadn't read the lease properly, but once the building was sold, my lease was up. I remember the last day, when we had a studio wake and all tagged the walls with our autographs. I ended up having to move my SSL into an existing studio owned by a dude named Todd, whom I didn't have any vibe with at all. I parked my board there and tried to get on with work, but it wasn't happening. That was another partnership that ended up in court.

Both of my boards ended up in my Jersey City loft when I moved my operations out there in the early 1990s.

18.

TWELVE BARS OF BECK

1984

In 1984 I got a call from Lennie Petze to see if I wanted to work on a Jeff Beck album. As was often the case, the A&R folks were surprised that I had knowledge about and love for the acts they offered me to work with, thinking I was just the electro remix guy. But I had been a fan of Jeff's, from his time in The Yardbirds to the Jeff Beck Group album featuring Rod Stewart, through the Cozy Powell 'Orange' LP to the *Blow by Blow* album. Most of his records were in my collection.

I was given the mission to finish up his latest album, *Flash*. They wanted me to do additional production on a track called 'Ecstasy', which had been started by Nile Rodgers, and to come up with a few new songs. Jeff was one of those guys who never seemed to age. Everything about him – his playing, his look and his attitude – seemed forever young. I'll never forget handing him a Roland synth guitar and watching him really trying to make it sing, and the way he figured it out, playing a magical flute sound with it. Lots of memories from a few weeks of work.

Our first guitar session was at Electric Lady Studios in NYC. We had already done some initial recording at Shakedown. I brought my main engineer, Andy Wallace, over to continue engineering the project. As he was a bit older than most of my guys, he knew his way around artists and rock'n'roll. We were getting settled in at studio A, and Andy was setting stuff up so that Jeff could play from the control room.

I had written a track with Tina called 'Gets Us All in the End', which I guess could be considered an electro-rock anthem. I thought it was an interesting song and was really excited that Jeff and the A&R team liked it enough to agree that we could cut it. Looking back, it seems sort of an odd choice for a Jeff Beck album, but back then I thought of self-written productions as collaborations with the act – i.e. not the typical producer–artist scenario. We had the instrumental with backing vocals on it, and Jeff was all hooked up and ready to go. When the tape rolled, he played an amazing solo, a real rock'n'roll blinder. We were all going nuts in the control room as it was going down. It was an

UNIQUE RECORDING
STATE OF THE ART 24 TRACK STUDIO

701 SEVENTH AVENUE
NEW YORK, NEW YORK 10036
921-1711

DATE	CLIENT
DEC 22, 1984	EPIC
ARTIST	PRODUCER
JEFF BECK	ARTHUR BAKER

ENGINEER	ASSISTANT	WORKSHEET	REEL #
TLA	AK	1 of	of

*TK17 HAS BEST "S" ON VERSE & B RDG

TITLE GOING FOR THE KILL MASTER SLAVE

1	2	3	4	5	6	7	8
Track	Cymbals		bell gtr Amp	bell gtr room	So of doom Amp	Room	heavy gtr Amp
9 heavy gtr room	10 gtr Hi Part chorus B V	11 harmonizer ATTOP Hi Parts B	12 DX7	13 gtr Midi	14 James Brown	15 Choruses Girls Mel	16 [illegible]
17 Chorus Boys	18	19 Chorus Screech	20 Chorus Boys II	21 B.S. Riffs GP Harm	22 Will Riffs	23 Craig Riffs GP Harm	24 SMPTE

Take	No.	Time	Comments	Take	No.	Time	Comments
			LD VOC WILL V1				

TITLE

1	2	3	4	5	6	7	8
9	10	11 BJ HIGH PART	12	13	14	15 Mel Voc V	16 Verse Bero 2
17 3 "S PASS"	18 4	19 5	20 6	21 HARM 1	22	23 HARM 2	24

Take	No.	Time	Comments	Take	No.	Time	Comments

☐ 15 ips ☐ Dolby ☐ No Noise Red. ☐ 1 k Tone ☐ 100hz Tone
☐ 30 ips ☐ Dbx ☐ 10k Tone ☐ Dolby Tone

*NEW GROUP CHORUS @ 42D ON 15, 16, 17, 18, 19, 20

Crumpled track sheet from the Jeff Beck recording sessions, 1984.

extended track and it went on and on, while Jeff's solo kept building and building. I felt as if I had witnessed real genius. Supercharged, I turned to Andy and said, 'Let's hear that!'

He looked at me and said, 'What? I was still setting up.'

I then realised he hadn't recorded it.

I freaked out. Looking back, maybe I should have been calmer, but . . . I fired him from the gig on the spot. I went to the other room and called Chris Lord-Alge. Now, Chris was a bit out of control, but the one word he lived by was 'AIR', as in 'Always In Record!' In a very stressed state, I told Chris, 'Jeff Beck, Electric Lady. Get over here *now*!'

Chris hopped in one of the ex-police cars he drives and set off from Jersey. I got a call from him an hour later, saying he'd been stopped by the cops for speeding. 'But not to worry,' he said, 'it's cool. Tommy's on the way.' Tommy was Tom Lord-Alge, Chris's younger brother. Chris said Tommy had amazing ears and would be better than him in a few years. I was doubtful of that but had no problem with him working as Chris's assistant. But this was Jeff Beck!

Still, I really had no choice, and fortunately, it all worked out. Tommy came in and brought a fresh vibe to the sessions. He was more experienced as a live-gig engineer and knew his way around guitars. Jeff ended up playing a bunch of mind-blowing solos, and Jimmy Hall from Wet Willie killed the vocals on my song. 'Gets Us All in the End' was chosen as the second single from the album and got tons of radio play.

While we were working on the record, Jeff had taken a side job, playing on Tina Turner's new album. He was so proud of playing with her and talked about how she had carved her name on his guitar. Sometimes during recording Jeff would start on a blinding solo, and after a while he would sort of peter out, claiming he'd got bored with whatever he was playing after twelve bars. Considering he came from the twelve-bar-blues discipline, it made some sense. I attempted to get around that by challenging him that if he didn't play it, I'd end up chopping and pasting his solos.

Master tape for the Jeff Beck project.

When we finished the album, Jeff left something behind: a small Seymour Duncan amp, which had various switchable tube plug-ins. This technology enabled Jeff to get his huge sounds without stacks of amps and speakers. The amp remained in Shakedown for years.

A decade or so later, Jeff and I would bump into each other quite a bit, after I moved to London and opened up my restaurant, Harlem. We spent a few late nights at Martin Miller's hotel, drinking Miller's gin and just shooting the shit. The last time I saw him was in around 2014 at SARM West Studios, by Portobello Market. We discussed the possibility of him cutting tracks to score my friend Chris Hanley's new film, *London Fields.* Chris and I went by SARM to hear the tracks Jeff was working on. He was really excited about his new music and going on tour to Japan.

Unfortunately, the film was set back, and Jeff never got to work on it.

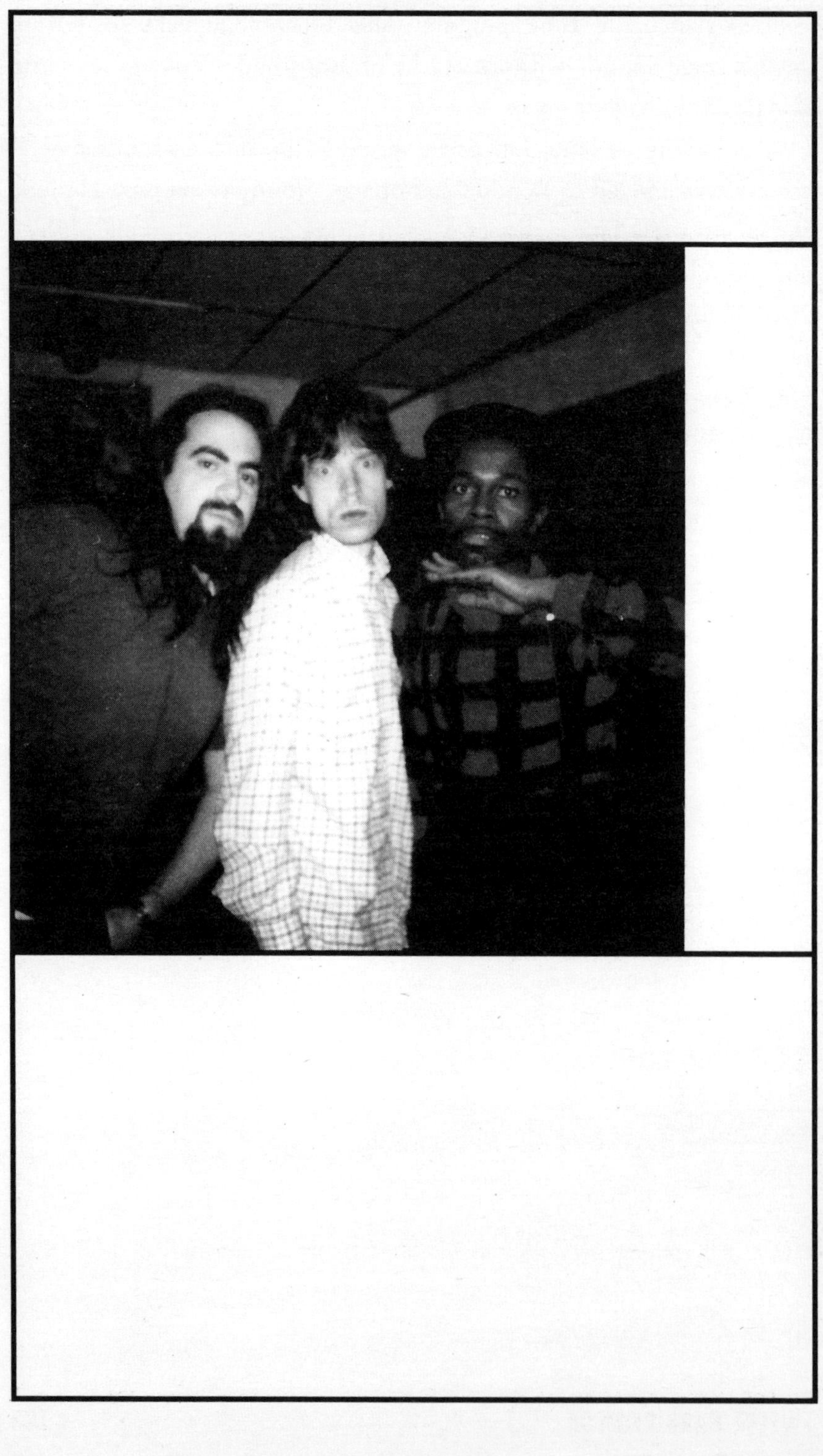

19.

TOO MUCH DRUGS

1984

In 1972 I was in the crowd for the infamous Boston gig by the World's Greatest Rock'n'Roll Band, the Rolling Stones, which saw the band come on stage five hours late, having been arrested for drugs in Providence, Rhode Island, earlier that day. Boston's mayor, Kevin White, got the Stones released, letting the crowd know by showing up at the Garden and giving the legendary 'My city's in flames' speech. He announced that the Stones were coming and he'd keep the Boston T subway open all night, if the concert crowd could keep their cool. Then Stevie Wonder, the opening act, came out to play a second set.

When Jagger and company finally showed up and played 'Gimme Shelter', all hell broke loose! I stayed till the very end with my four stoned high-school friends, hopped the T to Newton, then walked the six miles to Needham High and crashed on the grass, until we were woken by other kids arriving for school. We were pretty legendary after that.

Having said all that, imagine how I felt a little more than ten years later, when I was offered a chance to do a remix of the Stones track 'Too Much Blood'. Mick Jagger, in my opinion, is one of the greatest frontmen and singer-songwriters in the history of rock'n'roll. And he knows this, and upon meeting you he lets you know it pretty immediately. But then he *is* Mick fucking Jagger.

I'm pretty sure I was first approached to do the mix for the Stones by Tony King, whom I had known as a young DJ, when he was head of disco promotion at RCA. Tony started working with the Stones in around 1983. The band were releasing their records through Atlantic, who had just released the *Beat Street* soundtrack that summer, with my 12-inch of 'Breaker's Revenge' doing well. Also, the Springsteen mixes had been just released and had made lots of noise, so that probably brought me to their attention.

The original song had a lot of appealing elements. It had a very African, Fela Kuti vibe, with jazzy Rhodes piano, choppy guitar parts and particularly mental, hooky Jagger vocals, with lyrics that went on about some cannibal chap. He also had some wild stream-of-consciousness, spoken-word stuff, which seemed to be directed towards one Michael Jackson. Cool. I immediately knew what to do with it.

First, we attempted to sync the Stones' performance to a sequencer, so that we could program 808 beats to it. Unique Studios' owner Bobby Nathan and Chris Lord-Alge, my engineer, tried everything to make it work. Chris, who was also a drummer, ended up tapping a kick click to Charlie Watts's funky, yet totally out-of-any-semblance-of-time, drum track. We eventually had to give up on syncing and went for live overdubs. I replaced Bill Wyman's somewhat leaden bass part, again using my guy, Brian Rock, who had also played the bass on my 'Cover Me' remix for Springsteen. Bashiri Johnson came in to add percussion, and Robbie Kilgore, keyboardist on such tracks as Shannon's 'Let the Music Play', threw down some keyboard funk. It all sounded pretty tasty. First job done.

We next reconvened at Electric Lady Studios, in the Village, on 5 November 1983. There we'd start mixing, getting levels and EQs. This was Chris's domain. I vaguely remember Mick coming in, fairly sober, listening intently and being seemingly happy. He went out for some Italian and came back hours later, pretty drunk, and almost fell asleep while trying to get involved in adjusting the fader levels. But somehow we got the sound and the levels correct.

Next came my favourite part: doing passes, mutes and drops on the fly. I'd let the two-inch master tapes roll and start doing my thing live, recording down to half-inch tape. I might do a predominantly percussion pass, then an instrumental with dub vocals, a keyboard-heavy pass, a bass dub one . . . Just throw them down almost like live performances. Very high while doing them, but hopefully someone was taking notes (usually the assistant engineers). I ended up making eighteen reels of passes! We'd sort it out later. I left the studio around midnight, wasted, and crashed at the Gramercy Park Hotel for a day and a half.

Then I had to get back to the edit. We ended up with three great versions. I was very happy with the results, which brought a new energy and groove to the original while keeping the spirit of the Stones. And they were definitely different from anything else out there at the time. And Mick and Atlantic loved them – Mick, enough to hire me to help him finish his debut solo single, 'Just Another Night'. That track was pretty much complete when Mick came over to Shakedown. He showed up with Tony King and Fonzi Thornton; the plan was for him to work on his lead vocals. The staff were obviously very excited to see Mick. My studio manager, Rhonda, remembers having to convince him to let her make him a cuppa (tea, that is). My friend and bass player Doug Wimbish, who knew Mick, fired up a joint, which Mick took a couple of hits on, getting pretty toasted.

Me at Shakedown Sound, 1984.

I had worked with Fonzi before. He was one of the top background singers in NYC and also a vocal coach, so he was there to help Mick with his vocals. A stoned Mick did a few passes, but he was having some pitching issues, which could have been caused by Doug's spliff. My engineer, Andy Wallace, went out to the piano to hit some notes to help Mick, and then my dog, Sheba, who happened to live in the studio at the time, wandered into the vocal booth. Mick leaned over to shoo her away or pat her (I don't really remember), and she squatted and peed a bit. She was a very shy dog. I don't think Mick was happy. Anyway, after some work we ended up finishing the vocals, and Mick left town to travel to Colombia, to work on a Stones film with Julien Temple. He gave me no specific instructions, just basically told me to do my thing. Which I did.

The track was already grooving, with Sly Dunbar and Robbie Shakespeare playing great drums and bass. I added some Bashiri on percussion, background vocals from my crack crew, including Lisa Fisher, Cindy Mizelle and Will Downing, and sax by Jeffrey Smith of the Family Stand. I was pretty convinced Mick would love it when he got back.

He hated it.

He went through what I had added and said that the Stones had done all of it – the background, percussion and horns – before. I tried to explain that I was trying to go for the vibe of 'Caribbean Queen', the Billy Ocean track that was hitting worldwide. 'Just Another Night' had a similar pulsing groove, topped off with sax and female vocalists. Jeff Beck had actually played on it. But this was Mick's first solo release, and he couldn't be convinced.

Looking back, I understand him being somewhat nervous and trying to stay away from anything that related to the Stones (in his mind). François K ended up doing the final mix, using Jagger's vocals from our Shakedown sessions, and it was released in February 1985 (I was credited as co-producer for additional production). All good. No problem.

A few years later, imagine my surprise when the second Jagger solo album, *Primitive Cool*, comes out, and who is included in the list of producers? My friend Keith Diamond, Billy Ocean's producer, a beautiful dude who passed away way too soon. Background vocals were by Lisa, and Jeffrey Smith's sax was all over the album – and Lisa has been singing backing vocals with the Stones ever since then!

Well, it does prove I would have made a great A&R man for Mick. He just took a little while to come round to my way of thinking.

20.

WE ARE THE CHAMPIONS

1984

I was surfing a tidal wave of work, and while my lawyer, Joe Zynczak, had done a good job as adviser, I thought I needed someone more high profile to help me navigate my career. Enter Tommy Mottola and Champion Entertainment. In 1984 you couldn't get more high profile than that. Like many people, I had first heard of Tommy in the lyrics of 'Cherchez La Femme', a 1976 song by Dr. Buzzard's Original Savannah Band, which included the opening line 'Tommy Mottola lives on the road . . .'

Tommy managed August Darnell, the brains behind Dr. Buzzard and Kid Creole and the Coconuts, but his biggest clients were Daryl Hall and John Oates. Tommy was a larger-than-life character, who often pushed his Italian-American roots, subliminally suggesting links with the underworld. He was brought to my attention as a potential manager by Lennie Petze, who was the head of A&R at Epic Records, and he set up a meeting with Mottola for me.

I went into the austere surroundings of the Champion Entertainment offices on 57th Street and was shepherded into Tommy's office. He had an imposing desk and was surrounded by numerous awards and platinum records, plus hunting paraphernalia and duck decoys. Tommy was a serious hunter and famously ate what he killed. He made me an offer I couldn't refuse: he wanted me to become part of the Champion family. Which sounded very cool to me, for a couple of reasons.

First, I have to admit that I was a huge Hall & Oates fan. I thought they had been making the best pop music of recent times, and they had roots similar to mine: Philly soul and Motown. Their track 'I Can't Go for That (No Can Do)' had blown up around me when I first moved to Brooklyn in 1981 and had been an inspiration to me in my work over the last few years. So when Tommy offered me a chance to work with Daryl and John, I was all in.

Second, although success was all around me, I was a bit out of control back then. Tina and I weren't getting on. My drug use and her career focus had us living different lives, so we separated around this time, with me moving out of our 57th Street condo. I thought I needed a team that would keep me in check, while also forwarding my career and getting me onto the A-list.

Tommy and Champion seemed to tick all the boxes. Also, I'd have to change my legal team to Grubman, Indursky & Schindler. They represented everyone – record labels, artists and managers, often all on the same deals. I had first noticed their letterhead when signing the contracts for my Springsteen mixes; they repped the Boss, and they repped the label too. Well, that was the biz.

The first project Tommy offered me was the chance to co-produce Diana Ross with Daryl Hall. Not a bad entry into the world of Champion. I listened to a demo for the song 'Swept Away', and it sounded like a hit for Hall & Oates, rather than Diana Ross, but I figured I could add a cool dance element to what was a pretty pedestrian demo. Tommy arranged for us all to meet at Shakedown to listen to some music and hang out a bit.

My crew were pretty excited the night Daryl and Diana got out of the elevator at Shakedown. Tommy had dropped them off in his limo, which he kept on call 24/7. I had already met Daryl and hung out with him, but this was my first meeting with Ms Ross, which is apparently what she liked to be called. We put up the demo, and Diana sang along to it and decided she loved it. I think the idea of it being a duet (with Daryl) may have been kicked around. We then left and had one of those legendary New York nights out. Diana, Daryl and I borrowed Tommy's limo and drove around the city, getting smashed on red wine.

Daryl and I returned to Shakedown from 8–10 May 1984 to record the backing track for 'Swept Away'. I had my engineer, Jay Burnett, on the session and brought in Robbie Kilgore. Daryl had two members of his band, G. E. Smith and Tom 'T-Bone' Wolk, to handle guitars and bass. I programmed the DMX beats, while Robbie came up with a magical, sparkling arpeggiator line, a marimba line and some synth horn stabs that, along with my hard-rocking beat, gave the song a different personality from the original demo. Daryl really got into what was being laid down. We were clearly creating a new vibe for the song.

I could tell he liked the set-up at Shakedown, with the ping-pong table, the clubhouse feel and the fact that lots of young creative people were hanging around. He definitely felt comfortable there.

Once we started cutting the vocals, we needed forty-eight-track capacity, so we moved proceedings over to the Hit Factory. The studio was in the same building as the legendary Studio 54 club – something Diana pointed out when she first arrived. She actually made quite the entrance, regally exiting her Bentley, resplendent in a floor-length mink coat. Entering the control room, looking incredibly glamorous, she said her hellos to Daryl and me, then quickly ducked into the ladies' room, only to reappear moments later, ready for work . . . in a tracksuit!

Looking into the vocal booth and seeing Daryl and Diana waiting for my instructions could have been intimidating, but once I began blasting out the track, Diana started hopping up and down energetically like a rabbit in her tracksuit. This broke the ice and put a smile on my face. The sound of their voices blended really well, but there were some obvious issues with pitching. Imagine having to tell Daryl Hall and Diana Ross that they were out of tune! But it had to be done, and they dealt with it like the pros they were. We got the vocals done in a few sessions.

When she was almost out of the door after the second session, back in her full-length-mink-coat glamour, Diana received a delivery. She was seeing Gene Simmons from Kiss at the time, and this huge box arrived that he had sent over. She had no idea what it was. When she opened it up and pulled out a huge two-foot chocolate cock, we all had a good laugh.

After a false start mixing 'Swept Away' at Right Track Studios, we ended up at my old home base, Unique, with Chris Lord-Alge behind the board. We were pretty well into the mix when Diana showed up, anxious to hear where we were at, as it was the last track to be completed for the album. I ordered a bottle of her favourite red wine, and after a few glasses she fell sound asleep in the control room. There we were, trying to mix her record, and all we could hear was her snoring.

To be fair, it was a real late session. When she woke, she took the mix home, and the next afternoon called me to say how much she liked it and that she wanted to cut another track with me for the album. I was really jazzed, only to get a call the next morning from the label to confirm that the record had already been mastered. But when Diana heard the final 'Swept Away' dub mix, she asked me if I 'was on Pluto' when I did it. That was probably one of the best artist reactions I ever got.

Gold album for Diana Ross's *Swept Away*.

The experiment of me working with Daryl was deemed a great success, so much so that I was asked to work on the next Hall & Oates album. A few days before the sessions were scheduled to commence, I got a call from Tommy Mottola. He thought I should have a bonding/listening session with John Oates, since we had yet to meet. Also, Tommy wanted me to check out some songs John had written for the album.

I already had something scheduled for that day, which happened to be my very first meeting with Bob Dylan! I figured it wouldn't take more than an hour, but it kept going on, and I couldn't just tell Dylan that I had to leave to meet John Oates. So I arrived late at Shakedown. John was already there, hanging with my staff. I apologised, we chatted a bit, and he handed me a cassette. I popped it in, and we listened to a few songs. They weren't very memorable on first listen, but of course I gave positive feedback.

He then handed me something he said he had just written, which he thought might be good for The Stylistics, my new Streetwise signing. Both he and Daryl were obviously huge fans of the Philly group. I had already signed Maurice Starr and Michael Jonzun to produce them, but we were still on the lookout for tunes. I put John's new song on, and an amazing glockenspiel-topped chorus immediately hit me like a ton of bricks. To me it was the sound of a #1 record. But not for The Stylistics. For Hall & Oates.

I looked at John. 'Man, this is a fucking number-one record for Hall & Oates!' He wasn't sure. He still thought it could be a hit for The Stylistics. Which it would have been, but Tommy would have killed me if I had recorded it with the soulsters. Just then, he conveniently called up to see how things were going. 'Tommy, John's written a number-one song, but he thinks it's good for The Stylistics!'

Tommy said, 'I'll be right there,' and hung up the phone. He got to Shakedown in what seemed like seconds and ecstatically seconded my opinion. Now the main objective would be to not fuck up the song, 'Out of Touch'.

We were encamped at Electric Lady Studios, in the Village, to record the *Big Bam Boom* album. When I say 'encamped', I mean it: we were in for the long haul to cut a hit album. Tons of gear were delivered: Mickey Curry's drum kit, amps of all types, numerous guitars, the band's very expensive Synclavier (an early digital synthesizer and polyphonic sampler that cost over $100,000 back then) and a new Fairlight CMI (which stood for Computer Musical Instrument). Both synths were carefully unpacked and set up. Daryl had requested a ping-pong table, after enjoying the one I had at Shakedown. All meals would be catered by Balducci's Italian deli, which was right around the corner. No expenses were spared; this was definitely high-level record-making.

There were plenty of chiefs on this project. Daryl and John were producing, and Tommy had already promised engineer Bob Clearmountain that he would be credited as a producer on the project. And T-Bone Wolk was credited as arranger, alongside Daryl and John, leaving me the odd man out. I wasn't very happy. My $50,000 fee softened the blow, but still, I was a producer. My title would only be 'mix consultant and additional arrangement', and I would get no points. But John knew that I'd be important to the making of the album. 'Instead of making the record and then giving it to Arthur, we decided to integrate him in the process, have Arthur involved in the process from the beginning. We came in with germs of ideas that we'd develop with Arthur and Bob Clearmountain,' he said. 'That way the songs would evolve, and we would not have to remix the record.'

However, I had a plan: getting a co-write on the album might help ease the pain.

After setting all the gear up we quickly began playing around with it, specifically checking out the potential of the Fairlight. The novelty of using our voices to create samples of instruments kept us occupied for the first few sessions. It was sort of an expensive, computerised, robot version of a human beatbox. As we started using the samples to create drumbeats, I remember feeling that Mickey Curry was getting increasingly pissed off. Considering that Hall & Oates had brought in ace drum programmer Jimmy Bralower to work on the record, I figured Mickey was starting to feel a little redundant. Tommy made us aware that we had to keep Mickey engaged and feeling part of the process. Reason? He needed the drummer to be happy and ready to tour after we finished the album. (The fact that Mickey was also Bryan Adams's drummer and received points on his albums was also a touchy subject.) So Clearmountain (who also mixed/produced Adams's albums), embracing the new technology of sampling, began working with Mickey in getting his big bam booming drum sounds sampled. When I later met John Taylor from Duran Duran/Power Station, he mentioned how Power Station had used *Big Bam Boom* as a reference for their own album.

So we were becoming a team, all pulling together and working hard and late. The forthcoming tour meant there was definitely a tight schedule. The very straight Clearmountain, who was clearly the best mix engineer in the biz, would call it a day fairly early. Daryl and John kept somewhat reasonable hours at the beginning of recording, but I'd always stay late, experimenting on nocturnal ideas with Jay B, T-Bone, G. E. and Robbie Kilgore, often having a bit of 'fun'. I'd slip in occasional late-night-line sessions with the band members after the 'parents' had left. Then I'd drag myself back to the Mayflower Hotel, where I ended up living after Tina and I separated. Both Daryl and Tommy also kept rooms there. It was like a college dorm.

One night I was going up to Daryl's room to hang with him and Tommy. In the elevator was a girl in a raincoat who got off on his floor. I let her out first and followed her down the hallway. She knocked on Daryl's door, and he let us both in. She took off her coat, and she was pretty much butt naked. Daryl had a song he was working on called 'All American Girl', and he had decided to call one up and interview her. We ended up putting her on the track. I doubt they discussed royalties or clearances.

When we started cutting, we worked using a combination of programming and live performing. One track that used that combo was my pick as a future hit, 'Out of Touch'. We got the beat programmed, with help from Jimmy, and T-Bone hit a steady bass groove. John then replayed the keys that he had laid down on the demo, and he and Daryl put down the background flawlessly. The track, which was obviously very important, was coming together quickly, but it was getting late, so we decided to prepare ourselves for the weekend break. John readied to leave for the Hamptons. He packed his stuff, said his goodbyes and left. Daryl sat in the control room with me, Clearmountain and Jay. He then asked us to get him that trusty old standby, the Shure SM58 microphone.

Although John had clearly written the bones of the song, Daryl stayed behind, attempting to write the verses and perform it. I didn't know if this was how they typically collaborated, but sitting in the control room watching Daryl going full stream-of-consciousness and coming up with a genius melody and dummy lyrics pulled out of thin air was pretty inspiring. While the words were still a work in progress, the melody and phrasing felt complete. I don't remember how the fact was broken to John, but the song was now Daryl's to sing lead on, although they worked on the lyrics together.

We were well into the album when Tommy started counting possible singles. 'Out of Touch' would definitely be the first, and it was decided that 'Method of Modern Love', one that I was particularly involved with producing, with its hip-hop beats and modern arrangement, would be number two. Then there was another track, more of a sleeper, with its Oates-penned, old-school chorus: 'Possession Obsession'. John had obviously planned to sing lead. Tommy called me: 'Listen, you've got to talk to John and tell him to let Daryl sing "Possession". It'll be a hit with Daryl singing.' I agreed with him. 'But . . . how can we do that to John?' I said. 'You're the manager. You should do it, Tommy.'

He didn't. John sang lead, and 'Possession' would peak at #30 on the *Billboard* chart.

I really wasn't getting to do as much as I would have liked on the record, so late at night, with time on my hands, I'd mess around in an empty studio, just making beats. One night I got a kicking beat going on the DMX and programmed a bass line with Jay. The next morning Daryl heard it and hopped in with some guitar. We then had G. E. double my bass line on guitar. This thing was rocking. I sampled up some vocals Daryl had on another track, triggering them off a conga pattern – '*Chica, baila!*' – then another line that worked particularly well, 'Dance on your knees.' Everyone loved the result. It was a rocking dance track and a statement tune. But how could it be used on the album? It was decided that it would be a great intro for *Big Bam Boom*, mixing right into the first single, 'Out of Touch'. It was also included in the video version, which was inspired by a drawing I had on the wall at Shakedown showing an oversized kick drum. And I had 50 per cent writing on the track! I knew that would earn me quite a bit in the future.

As we were finishing the recording of the album, I felt we were one hit short. 'Some Things Are Better Left Unsaid' was looking like the third single, but it didn't feel like a top-ten song to me. One day Daryl and John were sitting by a piano, messing around, singing some old classic. At that point it became totally clear to me that we should cut something stripped-down for the true fans, a piano ballad that would feature Daryl and John's voices and soul. I brought it up with Tommy. He said there wasn't time, that the album was great as it was. So that was that.

When all was said and done, there would be only eight full tracks and my 'Dance on Your Knees' bit (at one minute twenty-seven seconds long) on *Big Bam Boom*. Left off the album were two other songs we had recorded: 'Foolish Pride' (which Daryl would use for his solo album) and 'Rockability' (which would be included on the next Hall & Oates album, *Oh Yeah*). 'Out of Touch' was released on 4 October 1984 and went to #1 on 1 December, staying there for two weeks. *Big Bam Boom* was released on 12 October and went on to sell 2.5 million copies.

Once the album was done, I had time to work on new projects, with Tommy acting as my adviser. My friend Dick Wingate at Epic Records (whom I had just worked with on Boston band Face to Face's record, producing their top-forty hit '10–9–8') had signed another Boston band I was already familiar with, 'Til Tuesday, and they wanted me to produce them. The band's manager, Randall Barbera, was a friend from Boston, and he had been trying to get me to work with the band for a couple of years. I spoke to Tommy, telling him about the offer, but he said, 'Nah, they're not happening. They're not a priority at Epic. You should work with Carly . . .' He had recently signed Carly Simon, who was also on Epic, and he wanted me to produce and mix a couple of her tracks. The album, *Spoiled Girl*, produced by Don Was, was pretty much completed. I went with Tommy's suggestion.

I had a good time working with Carly. She was an entertaining and extremely classy woman. We had some great chats about New England and music. After we completed the project, along with an ad-lib track for one of the songs I was working on for my solo album, Carly gifted me a pill box from Tiffany's, which I still have today. Much as I enjoyed working with her, though, the project didn't further my career at all. The record peaked at #88 on the album chart. Epic had me go back in and remix her second single, 'My New Boyfriend', after the album was released, but nothing really happened with it.

'Til Tuesday? Well, when they hit big with 'Voices Carry', a song I'd really liked as a demo, I was pretty upset I had missed out. The video for the record, featuring Aimee Mann, their striking blonde lead singer, was on MTV non-stop, and 'Til Tuesday went on to win the 1985 MTV Video Music Award for Best New Artist. Daryl Hall saw the video and decided he wanted 'Til Tuesday to open part of the *Big Bam Boom* tour, which started on 26 October 1984 in Bangor, Maine. Proved I had good ears, I guess.

Still, Tommy did help me hook up a sweet artist deal with Lenny Petze and Epic, but personally I was a bit of a mess at the time. I started working on my solo record, but I was spending a lot of late nights getting high and going out, sometimes with my boys, but occasionally on my own. I often hung out downtown at Danceteria, visiting my friend, DJ Mark Kamins, and had brought him 'Out of Touch' for its first club play. One frigid January night I went there on my own to check out one of my favourite singers ever. Amazingly, the 'thin man', Eddie Kendricks, was performing there. I had never seen him perform solo live, but I went with no expectations; I just thought it might be a fun gig. Besides all his hits with The Temptations, he had more disco classics under his belt than just about anyone – 'Boogie Down', 'Date with the Rain', 'Keep on Truckin''. I also wondered if he was signed. I hadn't heard of any new records recently, so I thought that it would be amazing to get in the studio with him for my solo album. The show was great, and he played all his hits.

Left: Tommy Mottola, David Ruffin and Eddie Kendricks at Live Aid.
Above: Live Aid VIP guest pass.

Afterwards I went to the empty backstage area and started a conversation with him. I introduced myself (it was obvious that he had no clue who I was), but when I bigged up my Hall & Oates credentials, he became interested. He relayed that he wasn't signed at the moment and mentioned that neither was David Ruffin – and they were back working together!

First thing the next morning I called Tommy Mottola and told him about my chat with Eddie. He was extremely excited, especially considering that The Temptations were Hall & Oates's main inspiration. He called Daryl and John, and they were all in. The summer of 1985 would be a big one for them. Tommy had quickly organised a Hall & Oates featuring Eddie and David gig at the famed Apollo Theatre in Harlem. It was recorded for a Hall & Oates album, but I received no credit for the hook-up whatsoever. The next two shows were on an even grander scale. Their 4 July gig at the Statue of Liberty was filmed for MTV and led off with my version of 'Dance on Your Knees', going into 'Out of Touch' as Daryl and John jumped out of their helicopter onto the stage. I watched proudly from the wings, already wasted in the blazing sun. A week later, they'd appear at the Live Aid gig in Philadelphia, a homecoming of sorts for them.

One time Tommy, Daryl and I were riding around in the limo when we decided to get some food. We head down to the Village, to a spot called Joe's. It was an unassuming little Italian, very quiet. I noticed Morris Levy was sitting all the way back at a corner cable facing the door. Tommy went over and said hello, and then we all sat down and ordered. I spied Daryl holding something and glancing at it under the table. It looked like a bag of weed. Tommy noticed it too and quickly – and I do mean quickly – grabbed Daryl and pulled him out of the door and threw him into the limo, shouting, 'Are you fucking crazy?! Do you know you could have got the entire place busted if the cops came in?' I really can't remember if we went back in for our food.

Knowing Tommy had a connection with Morris, when I started negotiating with Levy about him taking on the Streetwise debt and us becoming partners, I asked him for his thoughts. Tommy paused and told me, 'Nah, do not do it. Do not get in business with Morris. He'll end up with everything.' That was the one time Tommy was 100 per cent correct. My business dealings with Morris were a disaster.

I eventually stopped working with Tommy, but then, in 1988, he was hired to run US operations for CBS (now Sony Records). He launched a CBS-associated label with Walter Yetnikoff and Jerry Greenberg called WTG Records. I was invited to a festive Christmas record-release party at the end of 1988 at Media Sound Studios on 57th Street for their new signing, Eighth Wonder. The band featured the British actress/singer Patsy Kensit, who at the time was married to Dan Donovan from Big Audio Dynamite but would later marry Jim Kerr from Simple Minds, then Liam Gallagher from Oasis. Eighth Wonder's single 'I'm Not Scared' was written and produced by Neil Tennant of the Pet Shop Boys.

I saw Tommy at the party and went over to say a quick hello to him, Walter and Jerry. It was their bash, so they were pretty busy with people, and I left them to it and started roaming the place. In the crowd I noticed my old protégée, Brenda K. Starr, whom I hadn't seen in quite a while. Before I could get to her, she ran over to me and gave

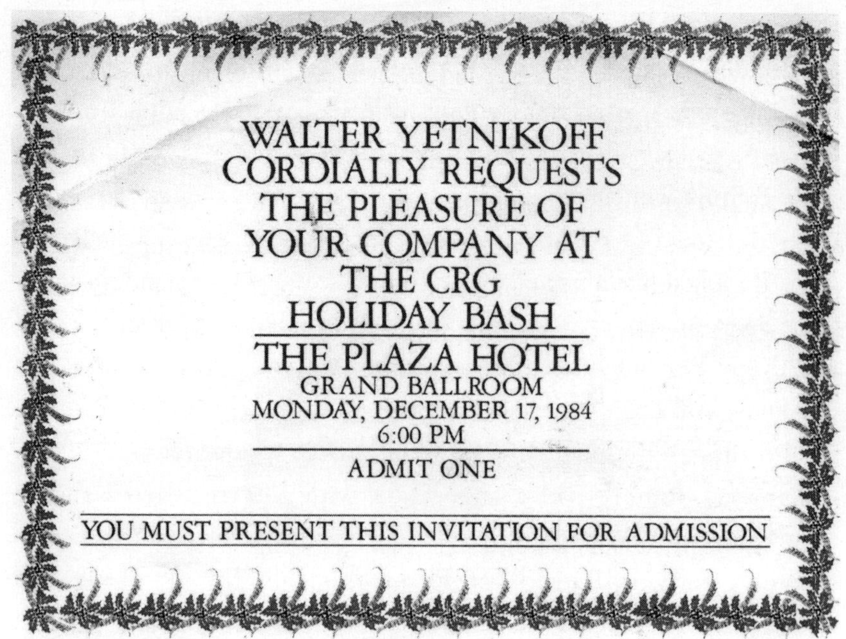

WALTER YETNIKOFF
CORDIALLY REQUESTS
THE PLEASURE OF
YOUR COMPANY AT
THE CRG
HOLIDAY BASH

THE PLAZA HOTEL
GRAND BALLROOM
MONDAY, DECEMBER 17, 1984
6:00 PM

ADMIT ONE

YOU MUST PRESENT THIS INVITATION FOR ADMISSION

Invitation to CBS Records' Holiday Bash, 1984.

me a hug. She started raving about her new backing singer and introduced me to this quiet girl standing beside her. Brenda kept talking about how amazing the girl and her demo of self-written songs were. She convinced me, and we agreed to go over to my studio after the party to listen to it. As they walked off, I looked up and saw Tommy motioning to me to come over to him.

'Who's the broad with the body?' he asked.

'Brenda?' I answered.

'Nah, I know Brenda. The other girl . . .'

'She's Brenda's backing singer.'

'Any good?' he asked.

'I don't know. Haven't heard anything.'

'Go bring her over,' were his last words.

I brought Brenda and her background vocalist over. Brenda did the intros, starting with Jerry, but when the girl went to hand Jerry her demo, Tommy grabbed it. We all said our goodbyes, and Brenda, her background singer and I got a cab back to Shakedown. We went into my edit room, and the girl handed me her cassette. I put it on and was immediately blown away by the voice and the song. It was the amazing voice of Mariah Carey, and the song was 'Visions of Love'. It sounded like a final recording! I couldn't believe it; the voice was levitating out of the speakers. All I could think was, *I've found the next superstar*. She was a combination of Madonna and Whitney Houston. Then I remember Tommy got the tape, and he obviously wanted to fuck her, so sure he'd listen to it.

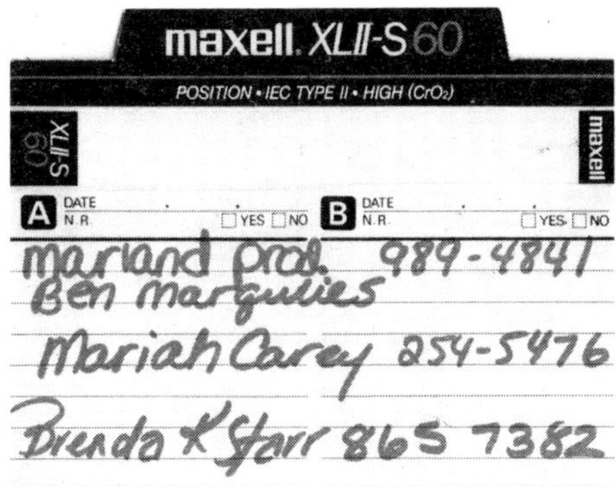

Mariah Carey's demo cassette.

After the girls left I called my new manager, Bennett Freed, a Brit based in LA. I emphatically told him about the girl, the songs and the situation with Mottola, and pleaded with him to get on the next flight. I even offered to pay for a first-class seat with my credit card. But he wanted me to FedEx him the tape first. We both ended up losing out. I tried my best to get in there. I called Mariah's writing partner/producer, Ben Margolis, warning him that Tommy would cut him out, bringing in other producers, and that I could bring her to MCA or Warners, but it was all to no avail.

Tommy got Mariah.

21.

MARRIED TO THE MOB

1985

The one time I didn't listen to Tommy Mottola would be the one time I really should have done.

It was when he told me to stay away from Morris Levy. Tommy knew.

Morris was infamous in the world of pop music. He had owned the Birdland jazz club and dealt with all the jazz legends way back in the day. He had signed such early rock artists as Frankie Lymon and the Teenagers, and he was even on the copyright as a writer on 'Why Do Fools Fall in Love?' People would joke about the thought of Morris sitting by a piano with Frankie, working out the first lines of that song . . . but not to his face. He was also behind Roulette Records and had recently been involved with Sugar Hill Records, partnering up with the label's owners, Joe and Sylvia Robinson, for their 'Rapper's Delight' smash. And he was connected in a way that would eventually see him convicted and put him behind bars, before dying of cancer (although wild rumours also had him in a witness protection programme, living out his life in Australia).

You did not mess with Morris. Even Tommy knew this. So why did I? You could say I was desperate. Which I was. I just didn't want to lose my label.

My partners had mismanaged Streetwise, and our staff had let distributors rinse us on the credit we had given them. By then we had actually lost New Edition. It seemed that Maurice Starr had signed an underage group under Massachusetts instead of New York law. That case was in court, and the lawyer bills were out of control. Jheryl Busby of New Edition's new label, MCA, offered me a chance to produce tracks with the group, despite the legal dispute, but I turned him down out of loyalty to my partners – the same partners who quickly walked away, leaving me holding the ball.

So in order to stay afloat, I was going to give Morris half of the pie. Naively, I thought that maybe our Jewish connection might protect me. Nah, I was probably just very high at the time. He sold me on our partnership by saying that by sharing all the expenses with him

331 Madison Avenue New York, N.Y. 10017 (212) 557-7433

AGREEMENT made as of the 8th day of October, 1982, by and between STREETWISE RECORDS, LTD., whose address is 331 Madison Avenue, Suite 903, New York, New York (hereinafter referred to as "Company") and the company known as "Boston International Records, Inc.," whose address is 20 Linwood Square, Boston, Mass., 02119 ,(hereinafter referred to as the "Producer") with respect to the group known as "The New Edition" (hereinafter referred to as the "Artist").

1. Employment. Company hereby contracts with Boston International Records and Maurice Starr for the purpose of making master recordings, from wich phonograph records will be produced which embody the recorded performances of The New Edition and for those purposes that are normally related thereto. The Artist shall not perform as a featured artist for any other company during the term of this contract.

2. Services. Company hereby enters into a production contract with the Producer for the musical selection "Candy Girl" to be performed by the group known as The New Edition (the Artist). Company also obtains the right of first refusal on each of the next three records by the Artist produced by the Producer, individually and separately, and a right of first refusal on an album produced by the Producer and recorded by the Artist.

3. Producer Compensation. Company agrees to pay Producer a royalty of 10 points based on the average applicable or recommended retail prices ($4.98) for the musical selection "Candy Girl" less a standard percentage of the retail price which is an allowance for packaging and which currently is established at 10 percent, for 90 percent of all such records and tapes sold within the United States under authority of the company, on both sides of which are only performances recorded according to the terms of this contract. Company also agrees to pay an advance of $5,000.00 for recording costs of "Candy Girl". This payment shall be considered a non-returnable advance to Producer which will be recouped from any royalties or payments due the Producer from the Company.

4. Subsequent Services and Compensation. If Company exercises its option on any of the three singles (individually) or on the album, Company will pay an advance of $5,500 for the first single optioned, $6,000 for the second, $6,500 for the third. The advance with respect to the album, if the Company exercises its option, will be negotiated at the time and neither will unreasonably withhold its agreement. Producer will receive a 10 point royalty on each of the options executed and the advances will be considered non returnable advances against royalities.

New Edition's contract with Streetwise Records.

and the other distributed labels, which would make it a lean operation, all the income would stick to our ribs. He had made a similar deal with the great TK Records man Henry Stone, whom I'd occasionally sit with, commiserating on our situations. But have I mentioned yet that

Morris was the model for the character of Herman 'Hesh' Rabkin in *The Sopranos*? The horse-breeding record-industry character? Check. Yep, that was my new partner.

The scariest shit was the guys who'd be just hanging out in his office at all hours of the day, sort of like the Soprano crew: tracksuits, diamonds and gold. They'd typically show up just when I'd be called in to report on the label. This was over ten years before *The Sopranos* and my friend Steve Van Zandt's star turn in the series. When the show came out, it was like déjà vu all over again.

In the beginning things were somewhat chilled. I was invited up to the family farm with Tina, and we hung with Morris and his son, Adam, who was getting involved in the business. The record business, that is. It was a great place: good food and lots of horses and countryside. Tommy actually had a home close by, I think. He convinced me that I could sign whatever I wanted, that the label was mine. At first nothing really changed. I was still doing my drugs and being irresponsible, messing around, which wasn't the best look when dealing with Morris. There was literally no way he didn't know what I was up to.

I was doing plenty of remixes, working on big acts like Bob Dylan and the high-profile Sun City project at my studio, while making no income for Morris. He definitely wouldn't have liked that. I specifically remember one day in the office, when Moishe (his Yiddish nickname) was holding court with his crew. He was telling a story about star 1960s singer Tommy James ('Crimson and Clover', 'I Think We're Alone Now'), who had been signed to Roulette. Tommy was a legendary junkie, according to Morris, and when it was obvious it was affecting his productivity, Levy figured he'd have his guys take him to the farm and clean him up cold turkey. Which they did. We all hung on his words, as Morris joked that 'We got him clean, and he nevah had another fookin' hit! Ha-ha . . .' We all laughed, as it was pretty funny. But was he trying to tell me something?

We had put out John Rocca's 'Once Upon a Time' and a few novelty records. Then we released a few Stylistics records, but none were an 'Out of Touch'. There was the lawsuit and negotiations with MCA, which I was kept out of. Who knows how much Morris was getting kicked back? I was kept in the dark and was too out of it to care. This definitely wasn't going to end well for me.

Finally, when Morris pushed for us to do a blind bid against one another for the label, I figured that at least it was going to be over. With my lack of focus and concentration, I just threw out a number, without doing any due diligence. And unfortunately, I lost. Levy never really cared about the label or the catalogue. It would turn out that Starr had owned the name New Edition, and Morris would broker a deal that had MCA paying a couple of million dollars for the name, which he and Starr ended up splitting.

I called my next label Criminal Records. A few years later, when I started working on the Quincy Jones documentary project, producer Courtney Ross mentioned that she thought she'd like to do her next movie on Morris Levy. I kept quiet on that idea.

22.

RUM AND COKE

1985

At the start of 1985 I got a call from my old Boston buddy Joe McEwen at CBS. Joe was the one who had hooked me up with the Bruce Springsteen remixes.

'Hey, man, are you interested in meeting with Dylan?'

'Are you fucking kidding me?'

Joe told me that Don DeVito, Bob Dylan's A&R guy, had reached out to him about setting up a meeting. Whoa! I was instantly thrown back in time, remembering the first occasion I heard that iconic voice. It had been on 'Like a Rolling Stone', coming out of our family's car radio during some road trip. The second I heard it I found myself consumed by the song, the words and the harmonica. Man, that refrain – the 'How does it feeeeeeel? . . . to be on your own . . . like a complete unknown, like a rolling stone . . .' – was like a magic trigger that awakened something new in me.

'Like a Rolling Stone' was released in July 1965. I was only ten at the time, but somehow it resonated and stuck with me. That started a long history between me and Bob. I got his *Greatest Hits* album around my birthday in 1967. That was part of the big score from my little scam with the Columbia record club. You could buy ten albums for the introductory price of $4.99, but then you were meant to be locked in forever at exorbitant prices. I joined but used my neighbour Mrs Merowitz's address, unbeknownst to her. When she brought the package over, I greedily opened it and had the start of my record collection. I'd chosen lots of funk and soul, and lots of greatest hits albums: The Temptations, Sam & Dave, Otis Redding, Sly and the Family Stone, and Bob Dylan's *Greatest Hits*, which came with a free poster that I proudly hung up in my room, next to my ironic 'Nixon/Agnew for President' poster. A few years later, I was even able to use my love of Bob to do my eleventh-grade final English project on his poetry. My English teacher was a young hippie named Phil Wallis, who totally 'dug' Dylan, so he was very engaged in my work. I remember writing a poem about how cool it would be to be Dylan's kid. It would have blown my mind if you had told the teenage me that years later I'd be playing basketball with Dylan's actual son, Jesse, in the recording studio.

I finally got to see Dylan live on 14 January 1974 at Boston Garden, during his unforgettable reunion tour with The Band, when they had furniture on stage and all the musicians were wearing make-up. It was Dylan's first proper tour since 1966.

So, did I want to meet Dylan?

Of *course* I fucking wanted to meet Dylan! But the idea of working with him was both mind-blowing and intimidating.

I was to go over and meet Dylan at the hotel he was staying at, the Essex, on 59th Street, near the southern border of Central Park. It was winter, so I hopped in a cab, and I must admit it was a nerve-racking ride. I wouldn't usually get that nervous about meeting a big artist for the first time, but come on, this was Bob fucking Dylan.

After getting reception to call his suite and let him know I was on my way up, I took the elevator to his floor and found an open door into his suite, but no Bob. He suddenly appeared out of nowhere and gave me a limp-fish handshake. Mmmm. Looking around, the first thing I noticed was that there were trays of food on catering racks scattered all around the room. Dylan obviously ordered room service and ate in his room a lot; I guess he didn't want to go out and get hassled in the restaurants. But the thing was, room service hadn't picked up the trays for, like, *days*, so there were all these discarded trays of food everywhere.

Dylan had a pile of cassettes and started playing me different songs. He probably played me about fifteen or twenty, and he kept asking me, 'Well, what would you do with this one?'

I said, 'Let me hear one a few times and focus.'

So we hung out in the hotel room for a bit, listening and talking stuff over, but it was somewhat stunted. Dylan was quite focused on the track that at the time he was calling 'Brownsville Girl', although during recording the title would change to 'New Danville Girl'. It was over ten minutes long, and he told me how he had written it with playwright Sam Shepard.

At the time, I presumed Dylan didn't have a clue about what I did or how I worked. Looking back, I guess what happened was, DeVito had seen the success my Springsteen mixes had had and wanted someone to help bring Dylan into the 1980s and finish the album that Bob was self-producing. For his part, Dylan might have thought I might not get where he was coming from, if he even thought much about it at all. I mean, I was best known for making hip-hop or electro records (apart from the Springsteen and Cindy Lauper remixes), so Dylan might think I didn't know much about him. But I was totally aware of his back catalogue and everything he had done. I was a fan, and I let him know that. I mean, it wasn't like I was going to go in and try to get Dylan to go electro, right?

Anyway, Dylan must have thought the meeting went well, because I got a call the next day saying I'd got the gig, and we went from there. The sessions were at the Power Station, because Dylan had worked there on his previous record, *Infidels*, and it was the top line-recording facility in NYC. It was this old power station, with a lot of wood panelling, which made it feel a bit like a ski lodge in the middle of New York. It was on the West Side, in Hell's Kitchen, not far from where Studio 54 had been. It's been gentrified now, but in the mid-1980s it was still a pretty rough neighbourhood. The building had cathedral ceilings and a regulation-height basketball hoop. I remember one day Bill Graham, the infamous concert promoter, paid a surprise visit with one of his sons and Bob's kid, Jesse. It immediately brought me back to that high-school poem I had written. Next thing I know, we were all hoisting jump shots. Not sure if Bob joined in, but he was definitely there with us.

I was living in the Mayflower Hotel at the time, so I was close enough to walk to the studio. At the first Dylan session I attended, he was cutting a track called 'When the Night Comes Falling from the Sky' with members of the E Street Band – Steve Van Zandt on guitar (more on him later) and Roy Bittan on keyboards. After a few takes were in the can and the guys had left, Bob expressed concern to me that it 'sounded a bit too much like Springsteen', and I was like, 'Well, yeah, you're using *his* band. Wasn't that the idea?!' But Bob decided he didn't like it, so he canned that version.

The next night I arrived in the studio to the sight of the legendary drum and bass riddim-makers Sly and Robbie in the big room, ready to rock steady! I scoped Sly sitting in the drum booth, relaxing behind his syndrums, with the *Daily News* sprawled across the tom-toms. He would actually read the paper while he played!

I got involved, and we cut a rollicking new take, which I eventually ended up overdubbing with percussion ace Bashiri Johnson and Face to Face guitarist Stu Kimball. This version was very different to the previous night's take, more like the Hendrix version of 'All Along the Watchtower', and it ended up on the album.

I soon realised that Bob didn't really like the studio all that much, and after all those years spent making records, I guess it was understandable. He was known to be a road dog; he loved travelling and playing live. He didn't want to hang around. He'd order takeout soul food from Sylvia's pretty much every night, although that seemed to be more for the female background singers than him. Sylvia Woods had opened her restaurant in Harlem in 1962, and she was known as the 'Queen of Soul Food'. I don't really remember Dylan chomping on a rib during downtime; in fact, I don't remember him eating anything much.

There was a lot of rum and coke during those sessions. Dylan was drinking the rum (Mount Gay), and I was snorting the coke (but not in front of Bob). One night I happened to pick up a cup that I thought was my coffee, but it was Dylan's, and it was a very strong rum hot toddy!

Bob would like to start his sessions at 5 p.m., work for about three hours and then leave. I'd then stay up all night, working on the record and doing drugs. I had lots to do on the tracks. I was basically trying to take the songs I had heard on those cassettes, which he had started with various different producers, and make them sound like a cohesive album.

When Bob did show up at the studio, the one thing he spent a lot of time on was the lyrics. He loved to work and rework them more than anything else. Which I understood because, you know, he's Bob Dylan, man, and people are going to be examining and deciphering those lyrics forever. I remember him struggling over a line about a Jersey cow, and me and the musicians trying to save the cow. In the end I think we lost that battle.

Dylan would often make out like he understood little or nothing about the recording process, but most of the time he'd just be messing with you. He loved to test me and mess with me, joking around and asking me things like what a bee of sound was, as opposed to a dB?

A rather more trying situation occurred when I came to record Bob's vocals. He'd want the background singers to record their vocals with him on the same mic, which would cause huge problems for me if I later wanted to punch in any new lines or take out dodgy backing vocals. We ended up putting two mics across from each other to separate the tracks, and somehow it worked.

Another issue was Dylan's inability to tune his guitar. He really didn't have much patience for the process, and as this was pre-digital tuners, it could take some time. Bob came upon the unique solution of taping down the lower strings, which weren't needed for his chicken-scratching parts. It worked!

A different tuning issue led to a bigger waste of time. One night I arrived at the Power Station a few minutes late, to find Mark Knopfler holding court in the studio with Bob. I was a big Dire Straits fan and was happy to meet Mark, who had produced Bob's last record. Mark was also cutting his album at Power Station, so it made sense that he'd drop by. He took a listen to one of the tracks and exclaimed, after some seemingly intense focus, that he'd heard a part he'd like to play. I thought, *OK, cool*, and we all agreed. First, he tried to tune to the track, which he failed at. He suggested that the chords played throughout the track by his keyboardist, Alan Clark, would lock the tuning in for him and give him something to play to. So Alan came in, dragging his synth behind him, and after thirty minutes tuned to the track. Then he took another thirty minutes to lay a pad down. Finally, Knopfler re-entered the studio to play his potentially song-saving part. He listened intently once. A quiet hush over the room. By now, it had been a few hours since he had listened to the song for the first time. After a pause, he looked over at me and Dylan, shrugged and said, 'Mmm, actually I don't think this needs a guitar part,' then walked out. Bob and I looked at one another in utter disbelief, and Bob exclaimed, 'Imagine doing an entire album with him!'

Another superstar intrusion to our sessions occurred at Right Track Studios, where we moved for the mixdown after we'd finished recording at Power Station. I came in early one day, coffee in hand, walked into the control room and was surprised to find Bob already there, sitting by the board with somebody who had their back to me, the two of them locked in conversation. The visitor turned to look at me, and it was fucking Mick Jagger, whom I'd worked with recently. Jagger drawled out, 'Why, hello, Arrrthurrr, just talking to Bob about you . . .' with an annoying grin.

At first Bob would hang around Right Track during the initial mixing process, sort of waiting for something to happen. He would chill on the couch that was in front of the huge SSL console. In mixing, you play the song over and over, stopping and starting – not very relaxing. So we were listening back to the music, when I heard some dissonant sound that didn't belong. I stopped the tape and looked around, to see it was Bob playing guitar and singing his version of Madonna's 'Like a Virgin'! He looked at me and asked, 'Can we make a record like Madonna? Or Prince?'

I think I said, 'We can do whatever you want, Bob, as soon as we finish with this mix.' Which led to a lengthy discussion about the amount of time it took him to mix down his absolute classic album, *Blonde on Blonde*. He claimed it had taken them only four days to mix all fourteen songs. I tried to explain that *Blonde on Blonde* had been recorded on only eight tracks, while our recorded music was now contained across forty-eight. I don't think he was convinced.

I suggested that he go see a movie, while I carried on mixing. He came back a few hours later, fully animated and excited. He had gone to see *Mask*, starring Cher, and it had blown him away. 'I didn't know they still made movies like that! Actually, I didn't think they ever made movies like that!' He thought Cher had been great. It was the most animated and impressed I think I ever saw him.

Towards the end of the recording, I thought we needed one last song to end the album, so I suggested to Bob, 'Why don't you pick one song, and we'll just do a live recording? Just you and the acoustic and harmonica, like you used to do, no bells or whistles. I'll just add a little reverb on it.'

He agreed and came in the next day to record it. We set everything up old-school in a small vocal booth: just Bob with guitar, harp and a mic for his vocal and a stand for his lyrics, with the lights set down low. He launched into this delicate, spiritual-sounding song that I'd never heard before, with a smoky refrain of 'and all I see are dark eyes'. I was enthralled. The first take was magic, but we laid down a second just to make sure we had it. As his guitar and harmonica rang out at the end of the second take, I gave a thumbs-up and turned to run out the door to catch a train to Boston, as Stu Kimball and I had planned to see the Celtics play the Bulls (with their rookie, this kid named Michael Jordan). Looking back, I think I should have stayed a few minutes more to appreciate that magical moment.

Twenty years later, I would find out the secret of the song we had recorded that night, 'Dark Eyes', when I bought a copy of Dylan's memoir, *Chronicles*. I read the book as a fan, not expecting to be mentioned at all, as *Empire Burlesque* was really just a short footnote in his long career. I was surprised, somewhat shocked when I got to a section where Bob reminisced in detail about my request for him to do a live song to conclude the album. What he never told me at the time was that he had gone away and written the song that night, after I'd suggested that to him . . . and that was the only time he'd done that for a producer in his career. It was a unique moment, and I had no idea at the time. I guess I just presumed it was a song that he'd had kicking around for a while. Of all the things that had happened in his long career that he could have talked about, most of which didn't even get mentioned in *Chronicles*, Bob chose that incident in the studio.

The album was released on 10 June 1985, to mixed reviews, more positive than negative. Afterwards I didn't hear from Bob for a few weeks, so I was surprised when he called me up one day. He wanted to know if he could use my studio to rehearse with Keith Richards and Ronnie Wood. They were going to do a surprise set for Live Aid. I said, 'Sure, anything I can do.' But I never heard back from him after that. When I was later in the Live Aid audience and watched their set, it was fairly obvious that they hadn't rehearsed.

I also asked Bob to be on the Sun City record and video I was working on, and he came through for me on that, recording his vocals in Los Angeles as the last lead cut for the record. I used his line as an echo to Jackson Browne, which worked well.

Having worked with Bob gave me entry to a few of those amazing Dylan events. In November he had an album-release party for his *Biograph* compilation in the basement of the Whitney Museum. It was *the* most star-studded party I've ever been at, to this day: Lou Reed rubbing shoulders with Martin Scorsese; Billy Joel and Judy Collins; Robert De Niro and Harvey Keitel; Debra Winger and Rick Danko; Pete Townshend and David Bowie. It was a crazy evening. I was probably the only person in a suit that night; Dylan had even fixed my tie! There was a great photo in the press of me standing next to Bob, with Judy Collins on his other side, as well as Scorsese, Lou Reed and Billy Joel.

Bob kept in touch, and he sent me an invite to go see him perform at Madison Square Garden on 16 July 1986. He also wanted to discuss me doing his next album, so I guessed he was happy with the results on *Empire Burlesque*. But, believe it or not, a traffic violation would end my chances of doing so.

Around lunchtime on the day of the gig, I was transporting some records to Shakedown in my old Merc, accompanied by my friend Joey Carvello, my studio assistant Cathy Williams and Stu Kimball. Loaded up, we headed down Seventh Avenue. It was a hot summer lunchtime in New York, and the streets were rammed with pedestrians and cars. I noticed a sign on the corner of West 37th Street saying only commercial plates were allowed to turn into it during daytime hours, but I ignored it, thinking the boxes and my studio gave me the right to make that right.

Bob Dylan and Carolyn Dennis at Power Station Studio, 1985.

Out of nowhere, a brownie appeared (in NYC we used to call traffic wardens 'brownies', as they all wore brown uniforms). She started yelling at me to back out into Seventh Avenue, as I had already turned down 37th. Attempting that would have been nuts and dangerous, as a wave of pedestrians were crossing behind me in a constant line. But the brownie was insistent. She was having none of it and got in front of my car and tried to force me to back up. I'd had a late night and was very hungover, I have to admit. Joey, who was sitting in the front passenger seat, reached his long legs over onto the gas pedal, and the car lunged forwards. The brownie faked that she had been hit. I decided to stand my ground and pulled the car over to the kerb. I got out and told her to call the cops; I wasn't moving the car. I had Joey, Stu and Cathy get out – no need for them to get involved – and handed Stu my large wrap of coke.

Next thing I know, two cop cars pulled up, out of nowhere, and I was thrown against the wall and cuffed. A number of people had gathered and were watching this develop. A businessman stepped out of the crowd and handed me his card. He said he had seen the entire thing and that his father happened to be a state Supreme Court judge; he'd try to help me out. While I was being led into the cop car, I told Stu to go down to Dylan's gig and tell him that I was sorry, but I had been detained.

Me with Joey Carvello and Stu Kimball.

I ended up being taken down to what were called the Tombs, the central NYC holding pen where they take you when you've been arrested. With the one call I was allowed, I dialled my lawyer friend, Owen Epstein. He got there quickly and took my Rolex for safe keeping. I was held overnight, and after going in front of the judge for arraignment (in my dirty white sweatpants and shirt) and pleading not guilty, I was released.

I was out, but boy, was I pissed off. I managed to get hold of Stu to find out what had happened with Dylan the night before, and when he told me, I was even more pissed off. Stu had gone backstage at Madison Square Garden after the gig and told Bob I couldn't be there because I'd been arrested and thrown into the Tombs overnight. Bob just looked at Stu and said, 'Couldn't he have come up with a better excuse than that?' I probably couldn't, it was such a crazy story, but that ended my working relationship with Bob.

Stu also claimed he had flushed the wrap of coke I gave him down the toilet, which I was *really* pissed at, but in my burnt state I actually believed him. Years later, he finally admitted to me that he and Cathy had done all my drugs after the Dylan gig!

I decided I wasn't gonna take this shit lying down. The brownie claimed I had hit her with my car, so this was serious, a felony. She had also immediately stopped working, having put in a disability claim. I knew I hadn't touched her with my car. She was pulling a scam. I called a friend who was a criminal lawyer and told him to hire a private investigator and follow the bitch (sorry, but this was 1980s NYC). The PI finally tracked her down, hanging out in the Bronx, smoking crack!

We counter-sued the city of NYC for $5 million, claiming I had lost the possibility of doing Bob Dylan's next album. I had my day in court, and the judge tossed out the state's case against me after listening to the brownie's story. I was sitting in court with Cathy, and as the brownie walked down the aisle after testifying, she leaned over and said something threatening to me. Cathy jumped out of her seat and tried to smack her. Mayhem.

We ended up settling for $75,000. My lawyer got $25,000 and I got $50,000, which was the same amount as my fee for *Empire Burlesque.*

LIVE
AID

23.

'(AIN'T GONNA PLAY) SUN CITY'

1985

If you ask me which song I'm most proud of being involved with in my long career, I can answer in a second. No contest. It's the song I spent four stressful, intense months of my life working on for free. Its journey as a song and a project was not a predictable one, and it didn't sell as many or chart as highly as some of my big hits. But it's a song that made a real difference.

The song is '(Ain't Gonna Play) Sun City'.

In mid-June 1985 I was hired by Cyndi Lauper and Lennie Petze to help mix Cyndi's 'Good Enough', the lead single for Steven Spielberg's new film, *The Goonies*. I was also asked to come up with a track for the movie's big octopus scene, so I cut a song called 'Eight Arms to Hold You' with my sessionaire buddies Jimmy Bralower and Robbie Kilgore, which became an electro anthem. We called our act the Goon Squad. Unfortunately, our scene was cut from the film, but there's an embarrassing video for the song that can be found online.

Cyndi and I went into the studio together to mix 'Good Enough'. It was another one of those late-night weekend sessions since the mix needed to be submitted on the Monday morning. We were comfortable with each other and chatted while working. She told me she thought her song had some African musical vibes in it, and then we randomly started discussing South Africa and the evils of apartheid. I'd witnessed first-hand racism by South Africans when I was kid, and it had stuck with me. It seemed that my mother's family tree had a distant branch that had crossed from Poland down to South Africa. I don't remember them being mentioned often, but one day a few of our South African relatives made a surprise visit. Our meeting with them didn't last too long: just one visit and one meal – or should I say, appetisers. That's because they spewed out some racist stuff at the dinner table. I was only around six years old at the time, but I remember my dad showing them the door. That event has always stayed with me.

I'm a bit hazy on that session with Cyndi, although I do vividly remember slapping her hand kiddingly when she tried to interfere and move a fader! And we definitely worked all night. A day or so later, I called up my new friend and collaborator Steve Van Zandt – or Little Steven, as he was known in those days – to tell him about my discussion with Cyndi about apartheid. Steve and I had already written a few songs together at the Power Station during Dylan downtime: 'You Don't Have to Cry' for Jimmy Cliff and 'Addiction', which we cut with Eddie Kendricks and David Ruffin.

'Steven, we should do an anti-apartheid song,' I remember suggesting.

'I've already got one,' he answered immediately. 'I wrote and demoed it the other night!'

Synchronicity strikes again. Steven came over to Shakedown and played me his demo. 'Sun City' used the resort of the same name as a symbol of the evil of apartheid, urging artists never to play there again, or in South Africa in general. Many major stars had been tricked into thinking that Bophuthatswana, where Sun City was located, was a separate free country and it was fine to perform there. This was a lie. While bands like The Beatles and Hall & Oates had refused, acts like Queen and Tina Turner had played in the resort. And Nelson Mandela, the spiritual leader of black South Africans, was imprisoned on trumped-up charges. Steven and I felt we could really change things through a song. And Steven had that song.

In its first demo form, '(Ain't Gonna Play) Sun City' threw down in a primitive Motown-goes-punk-anthem style. It was extremely catchy and rocked real hard. It also led with the line 'We're rockers and rappers, united and strong,' which really piqued my interest. After a few listens, I offered to bring in my crew to start on a more elaborate demo.

The next night, 15 June, we reconvened at Shakedown. I had my keyboardist Richard Scher come by to help out. He intuitively threw down a clavinet part and composed a Yamaha DX7 log-drum track that ended up being the one consistent track stabiliser and a big groovalising hook of the song. I then grabbed my singer of choice at the time, Will Downing (who happened to be passing through Shakedown that night), to provide an alternative lead, making it a duet with Steven.

We thought we needed to beef up the chorus with background vocals, so the next night I got Tina B, Lotti G and B. J. Nelson (whom we had dubbed BLT) to come in and add their background flavour to the mix. Although Tina and I were on again/off again personally, we still had a good working relationship.

In those first two sessions we put a great demo together, with 90 per cent of what we recorded making it to the final record. I was excited because I thought we had something that could potentially make a difference. The Sun City project was extremely important to me, and I was all in on it – with my time, my studio and whatever energy I had left in my body. After completing our demo, Steven and I stayed up the rest of the night brainstorming and started making a wish list of people we wanted to approach for the record. Between us we knew a lot of the top artists of the time, from cool underground acts to the world's biggest pop icons. I thought we had something really hot musically, and the cause was beyond reproach. I was confident we could pull in anyone. But Steven, being more the insecure artist, had doubts and needed more confirmation. It was *his* song and vision, and I was there to help make it a reality. He had someone specific in mind to run it by whose opinion he really respected, and it just so happened to be someone who'd been a big influence on me growing up, but whom I had never met.

Enter Danny Schechter, who was known as the 'news dissector' back in the 1960s/'70s, when he was the news director on Boston's WBCN, my number-one radio station as a teen. He was our punk political commentator, and a mentor to me without knowing it. During the Vietnam War, it was Danny who helped school WBCN's young listeners. He was now an Emmy-winning producer on ABC's *20/20* news show.

Unbeknownst to me, Steven and Danny had already been speaking about doing an anti-apartheid project, before there was even a 'Sun City' song, so he was excited to hear about what we had been up to. He listened intently to our new demo and loved it. He thought the lyrics were spot-on, as I did, even when Steven wanted to continue crafting them. Danny was also all for naming the artists who had already played the Sun City resort and been put on a UN blacklist. Steven and the girls had rapped some of the offenders' names in the breakdown of the demo, but I disagreed with shaming acts, because unless we named everyone who had played there, we'd be making a judgement call on who we were outing. We ended up not naming names, but not before the original demo with the name-checks had been mistakenly sent out. My friend Nelson George made mention of it in his *Billboard* column, but nothing really came from it. Danny was convinced that we had something special, and he wanted to help. There was plenty he could do, but he'd have to do it undercover since it might conflict with his role as a *20/20* producer, so he was unable to put himself out front.

Our planning sessions started. Steven and I lived close to one another, on opposite sides of West 57th Street, between Eighth and Ninth Avenues. We would have breakfast meetings at the Sunrise diner, fine-tuning our artist lists over bacon and eggs, writing them down on greasy placemats, which Steven would then take away with him and invariably lose. So we'd have to start the lists over and over, eventually reaching fifty names. Steven thought it was a bit of a fantasy, considering we had no record label and no money. I, being more at home in the actual record industry, was always more confident that we'd find a label and get any artist we wanted. But then again, I was on drugs at the time (a fact I didn't share with Steven) and sometimes a bit out of touch with reality.

But in the end I was right.

When making those original lists, we'd assumed the record would feature more alternative, less mainstream acts, since we were looking for more of a street sound. I had access to most of the rappers, guys with strong opinions who hadn't had the chance to participate in Live Aid or 'We Are the World'. Steven and I both wanted to feature their voices heavily. But I figured that with Steven being a fucking rock star and having played with the biggest rock star in the world, we could get anyone. Which we sort of eventually did.

Steven came up with the name Artists United Against Apartheid, which made sense, particularly with that rapped first line of the song, 'We're rockers and rappers, united and strong', signalling who we were (although we could have added jazzers, Rastas and salseros to that line too – in the end we had them all).

We started approaching the names on our wish list. In his memoir, Steven mentioned me as the chief schmoozer of the team, but we both had our own artist connections and called them in. I had recently been working with Hall & Oates, Bob Dylan, Nona Hendryx, Jimmy Cliff, Cyndi Lauper, David Ruffin and Eddie Kendricks, and knew or worked with a lot of the top rappers – Run-DMC, Afrika Bambaataa, Kurtis Blow, Melle Mel, Scorpio and Duke Bootee of the Furious Five. The inclusion of the rappers – including the godfather of rap, Gil Scott-Heron, and the godfather of dub rap, Big Youth – made a very important statement. This was an all-inclusive project, and it acknowledged the importance of hip-hop as a major art form and vehicle of social change.

All the artists we approached agreed to come on board, except for Cyndi Lauper, who was planning a statement record of her own. My friend Rick Newman managed Pat Benatar, so we were able to get her. Steven and I both knew Bono and Peter Wolf, so they were also in. Steven had his wish list of top-tier artists who had influenced him: Peter Gabriel, Gil Scott-Heron, Miles Davis and Melle Mel, plus newly discovered political artists Rubén Blades and Peter Garrett. Then there were his friends and rock-star connections: Darlene Love, Clarence Clemons, Bonnie Raitt, Jackson Browne, Joey Ramone and Lou Reed. And finally, there was the elephant (not) in the room: the Boss. We never actually discussed Bruce; I just figured Steven would deal with that one in his own way and according to his own schedule.

Slowly but surely, we kept adding to the list and started recording artists. Danny brought in Hart Perry to be in charge of making sure things were being documented on film, and he and his crew were on call 24/7. David N. Seelig shot still photos throughout the process. I brought in two lawyer friends of mine to help us navigate the numerous label clearances and get a record deal: Owen Epstein, U2's lawyer, and Rick Dutka, the head of business affairs at Tommy Boy. Both of them gave us great direct access to potential record labels. I thought Tom Silverman and his label Tommy Boy might be a good landing spot for the project. Tom also ran the New Music Seminar, which would be a great launch pad for 'Sun City'. Another early option was Chris Blackwell and Island Records.

While we were putting out feelers, the recording of 'Sun City' commenced at Shakedown on 31 July 1985. A crew of rappers, including my guys Afrika Bambaataa, Melle Mel and Duke Bootee, were first up. I had worked with all three before, so this was a great session to get the project rolling. Doug Wimbish introduced me to George Clinton, who came in too.

My open-door policy meant artists would be coming in and out at all hours of the day and night. The policy extended to my friends as well, and it was often organised chaos at my studio. Late one afternoon, for example, Bonnie Raitt and Kashif had been scheduled to cut their vocals. Bonnie was first in the vocal booth, having cancelled the soundcheck for her gig at the Ritz that evening to record her part. Kashif was listening and waiting to do his thing. I was behind the desk producing but had taken a quick second to get a coffee, when the outside buzzer rang. There was no security downstairs, so guests would have to be buzzed in. I picked up the phone, and a gruff voice went, 'Hey, it's Miles. Let me in!' Shit! Miles Davis had actually shown up!

There had been a rumour that Miles wanted to get on the record, and Danny Schechter had been enlisted to see if we could actually get him in, and here he was. Steven, Danny and I all looked at each other pretty nervously. Miles had a rep. But we all went to greet him, and there are some pictures of that day, and Miles is smiling in them, so someone must have said something funny, because I really don't recall seeing any other pictures of Miles smiling anywhere.

Recording session for 'Silver and Gold' at Right Track Studios, NYC, 1985: (from left) Steve Lillywhite, Kirsty MacColl, unknown, Bono, Steve Jordan, Ronnie Wood, Keith Richards, me, Steve Van Zandt, Tina B and Chris Lord-Alge.

Bonnie, who had come out of the booth so that Miles could record, approached him, saying, 'Mr Davis, I love what you do with your horn.'

Miles responded, 'Yaah, that's just my thing.'

When he went into Shakedown's small booth, a camera had already been set up and had been shooting all day. We were nervous about Miles being OK with the filming, but Danny was the most nonplussed of the three of us, so he strolled into the booth and asked him if he minded being filmed while he played. Miles answered, 'Bring it on, bring it on . . .'

I put a mix up in his headphones that was basically drums and Richard Scher's omnipresent log drum, with no vocals. I just wanted him to play freely, without being distracted. Steve wanted him to do a couple of takes, one with a mute and one without. His playing was amazing. He spoke through that horn. But at the end of the first take he started speaking, almost in a whisper: 'You can't go in there, you're the wrong colour.' As on edge as we were, we thought he might be talking about the cameraman. We sort of freaked. But then we realised he was speaking as the voice of South African apartheid. I kept the tape rolling to capture this impromptu performance. When he was done, we all just looked at each other in silence. He had been amazing. Then Danny, being Danny, went and asked Miles if he could do it again, just to make sure we got it. I wanted to kill him. But Miles happily performed another vocal. When he was later asked about his contribution to the record, he replied: 'South Africa makes me sick. South Africa makes me ill. I jumped at the chance to help out with this record.'

Peter Gabriel was another artist Steven really wanted on the record. His track 'Biko' had educated Steven and transfixed him with its beauty and meaning. We had been trying to get in touch with Peter, when I heard he was recording at the Power Station. I got him on the phone, explained where we were at with the recording and asked if he could come to Shakedown. He agreed and showed up at the studio on his own, when the place was fairly empty. As with Miles, I just gave him the log-drum track with some beats and told him to do whatever he felt like doing. He started chant-singing and constructed an amazing, incandescent hymn before my eyes. He doubled and then tripled the line 'No more apartheid'. He did take after take, until declaring he was finished. It was incredible, but Steven and I soon realised there was no place we could use it on the main version.

One of our engineers, Tom Lord-Alge, was a Gabriel fanatic and ended up volunteering to work on the track, so the next night I took the tape over to Unique Studios' B room, where I had spent many nights recording the *Beat Street* album and various Tommy Boy records. Keith LeBlanc had set up his drums and was ready to rock. And with just the log drum as a guide, Keith laid down eight minutes of a beat. He wanted a second go at it, so I muted his first drum track, and he again recorded to the log drum. When we played back what he had done, I accidentally put both takes on. They were so close that they phased! It was an unreal feat of dexterity.

Steven later threw down some guitar against the beats and Peter Gabriel's voice, and Doug played a thumpin' bass and Zoe Yanakis keys.

It became its own very special thing. Steven was a little nervous that Gabriel might not like what had been done with his 'thing'. We sent it to him in the UK, and he absolutely loved it. 'No More Apartheid' was complete.

While we were recording all this great music with amazing artists, we still had no one confirmed to actually release the record. Both Tom Silverman and Chris Blackwell had pulled out of the running for different reasons. Luckily, there was a new label that seemed like a possibility: Manhattan Records, run by Bruce Lundvall, formerly of CBS and a friend of Steven's. The label was distributed by EMI, so it had the reach and cash that we needed. Negotiations were begun, and we came to a deal in early September. Bruce was a real jazz aficionado, and when he was presented with the idea of incorporating Miles's and Hancock's already-recorded parts with a new performance by jazz legends bassist Ron Carter, drummer Tony Williams and guitarist Stanley Jordan, he really perked up. So we had the other maestros come in, and another track, 'The Struggle Continues', was birthed.

It became evident that the project was quickly shaping up to be an entire album. Some of the other sessions are memorable for somewhat non-musical reasons. One night, unbelievably, I had Eddie Kendricks, David Ruffin, George Clinton and Bobby Womack all in Shakedown at the same time, hanging and singing. These guys had made half of my favourite soul records. But it was 1985, and none of us were choir-boys. When I nipped into the bathroom to take a few private lines, I quickly heard a knock on the door. It was the entire crew. I guess I hadn't fooled these pros. They were looking for a few hits, and I'm not talking about the musical type. 'Open up, man!' they shouted in harmony. The bathroom was only the size of a phone booth, but I had to open the door and sort them out.

The drugs would often come out as soon as Steven left. Cocaine was standard studio fare at that time, and quite often it was required to motivate some of the engineers and musicians, who were working for free. We were pretty much in the studio non-stop. Steven might

Clockwise from top left: John Davenport, Keith LeBlanc, me, Tom and Chris Lord-Alge and Little Steven at Electric Lady Studios, NYC, mixing '(Ain't Gonna Play) Sun City', 1984.

go home at 9 p.m., but work would continue. I'd be hanging with the Lord-Alge boys and Doug and Keith, working and having fun.

I specifically remember one night towards the end of mixing at Electric Lady. Chris Lord-Alge and I had been working on the mix all night and were happy with what we had. Steven came in bright and early the next day, and after having a quick listen, basically pulled down the faders, ready to start on the levels all over again. Chris and I just looked at one another.

Getting the music mix right was sort of the easy part. Actually, no, that's a lie. Nothing was easy about mixing the main version of 'Sun City'. After originally thinking we'd have the artists sing specific lines, we'd get enthralled with the performances and let these amazing vocalists sing the entire song, which was great at the time but now gave us so many decisions to make. We had to choose who sounded best singing each specific line, matching sounds and levels, getting the proper ad-libs and making sure everyone shined. That was the most difficult part of making the record. Think about who was singing. I mean, some of the greatest singers ever. *Ever*. It wasn't easy. The technology then was far from where it is now, and everything was on tape. We had recorded three hundred tracks of vocals and music over thirteen master tapes. We'd have to bounce all that down to three tapes, and then sync up three machines to do the mix. We did have basic computerised mixing, but it was nothing like today. So many fader moves had to be made that we'd all be on the board at once, working the faders to make the changes from singer to singer sound as smooth as possible. But when we were done, it really worked. We got nominated for a Grammy for Best Rock Vocal. Which was only right. But we lost out to the Eurythmics. Who have one singer. A great singer, but c'mon . . .

As we were closing in on the final 'Sun City' mix, along with all the additional tracks that were born out of the sessions, we started thinking about the video. Steven and I had earlier made contact with MTV, who would be a very important ally in making the record a success. The channel was having its own racial issues, as it was being criticised for not playing many black acts. We had a meeting with Les Garland, who was MTV's senior vice president and head of programming. Les was a real character, an ex-record-label promo guy who actually had a putting green set up in his office. He liked the project and immediately offered MTV's help with shooting the recording sessions. I then remember laughingly telling him that we had already been using some of his camera team. He thought it was funny too. So MTV became our partner in *The Making of 'Sun City'* long-form video.

We contacted Kevin Godley and Lol Creme, hoping they would direct the music video, as they were *the* hotshot video directors at the time and had a great feel for the new technology that we thought would make the video something special. Unfortunately, after we had decided to shoot on 10–11 October, to coincide with a major

Broadcast Music, Inc. 320 West 57th Street · New York, New York 10019
212 586-2000 Telex 127823

FRANCES W. PRESTON
PRESIDENT
CHIEF EXECUTIVE OFFICER

February 20, 1987

Mr. Arthur Baker
c/o Howard Comart, CPA
1775 Broadway
New York, NY 10019

Dear Arthur,

Congratulations on your Grammy nomination for *Best Rock Performance by a Duo or Group with Vocal,* and *Best Music Video, Long Form.*

This is indeed a great honor, and one that is *richly* deserved.

You are a winner, regardless of the outcome, but you certainly have my best wishes toward taking home the coveted awards.

We at BMI are very proud to be associated with you and hope that the future holds many more honors for you.

Sincerely,

Frances

Frances W. Preston

FWP:sg

SERVING MUSIC SINCE 1940

A letter from BMI president Frances Preston, congratulating me on 'Sun City' receiving a Grammy nomination.

anti-apartheid rally, Godley and Creme realised they had a prior commitment they couldn't get out of, but they would be available to edit the video. Steven and I were both friendly with Jonathan Demme, so we reached out to him, and he was able to do the shoot. Hart Perry, who had been involved in filming the studio sessions from just about day one of the project, would go out to LA and shoot the scenes there.

So many of the artists came to NYC from all over the world for the video shoot and final celebration in Washington Square Park, and they came on their own dime. The first day, Jonathan hit the streets of NYC, shooting at various locations, with Bruce Springsteen, Eddie Kendricks and David Ruffin walking down the streets of Hell's Kitchen, singing; the rappers in East Harlem; and Bono, Jimmy Cliff, Joey Ramone and Darlene Love in the East Village. Having star combinations working the streets of downtown NYC was the basic artistic theme of the video. There were some great performances captured that day. Afterwards we met up at the hotel, had a group meal and prepared to take the bus down to Washington Square Park for the group celebratory shoot. I think it was only at that meal that a lot of the artists first realised the scope of what they were involved with and who else was on the record.

The bus ride was another bonding moment, and I remember Charlie Wilson of the Gap Band (who hadn't featured on the record but flew in for the video) leading the bus in singing his hit 'Party Train'. When we all finally made it to the park, our high spirits went up another notch. This was gonna be a real park jam. There was some security provided by the NYC police, but I don't think they realised the degree of celebrity that would be on show in the park. Very soon a big crowd gathered. Once they realised that stars like Bruce, Bono and Run-DMC were in the house, the hoots and hollers started. Jonathan Demme took charge and started shooting the assembled group of stars. He had Duke Bootee address the crowd and explain what was going on in his own inimitable style.

After a take of everyone standing and singing the song's chorus, Peter Wolf came to me with an inspired suggestion: everyone should dance to the track, like in a conga/soul-train line. Once that was put into effect the real mayhem that you see in the video started. It was a true celebration of what we had accomplished, and everyone was getting down, me included. But through the haze of partying, I suddenly realised we should probably get some of the participants to record vocals in sync with the filming. I suggested this to Jonathan, and after a few tries we got Bruce, Eddie and David, who were now best friends, to nail some of the ad-libs I had chosen on the record.

Everyone went back to their hotel rooms or homes to prepare for the next afternoon's big anti-apartheid rally uptown. Everyone except Steven and I, that is, as we had to go back to Electric Lady to work on the mixes, which were meant to be mastered on Monday, and also Bono and Peter Wolf, who went to meet up with the Stones at Right Track Studios for a late-night session. Which could have been a dangerous evening.

What actually happened was, Bono got a crash course in the blues from three masters, Peter Wolf, Keith Richards and Ronnie Wood. He had never really paid much attention to the blues until then; you could tell by listening to the sound of early U2 – not a tinge of the blues. But that night they played him some of the classics, like the old country blues of Son House and Robert Johnson, and he was hooked. U2 would go on to record their next two huge albums in the US, recording at Sun Studios in Memphis with B. B. King.

Next afternoon I got a call from Bono. He asked me if I could get my hands on an acoustic guitar, like *now*. He had a few songs he wanted to write. OK, cool. I made a call, got a guitar and had it dropped off at Bono's hotel. He stayed up late working on his ideas, but I really had no clue about what he was up to at that point.

Next night there was the anti-apartheid rally at the Citicorp building. To be honest, at this point my main concern was finishing up the record. I was fully in mix mode, with the Monday deadline looming, working full-on through Saturday night, when Bono showed up, ready to record a new track he had just written called 'Silver and Gold', inspired by the mining economy of South Africa, the exploitation of black workers and the slave wages they were paid. We quickly miked his voice, his guitar and his foot stomp and recorded the song. It was a transcendental performance, with his foot stomp keeping the beat.

Keith LeBlanc, who was hanging with me at the studio, volunteered to overdub a cardboard freight box as an additional drum. It added more drive and urgency to the track. But there wasn't really much time to spend on experimenting on a new track, considering our Monday deadline, and the mixing had come to a standstill while we were recording. Bono really wanted to add Keith Richards onto the track, so we let him take the tape over to Right Track with him. Peter Wolf tried to track Keith down, but the Stones' recording hours were fully nocturnal.

We finally got a call at 5 a.m., and Bono, Steven and I, along with Zoe Yanakis, Tina B and Tom Lord-Alge, made our way from Electric Lady to Right Track to meet with Keith and Ronnie. When we arrived, it was a classic Stones session, with a big focus on a fully stocked bar in the centre of the live room, along with a plate full of illegal substances; it would have been impolite not to take part in the social amenities. Then we listened to their new album, *Dirty Work*.

After a few hours Bono eventually got round to playing 'Silver and Gold' to the Stones duo, and Keith and Ronnie became the final members of Artists United Against Apartheid by playing guitars on it, with Ronnie famously using a switchblade to play his slide-guitar part. We kept Bono's original vocal after further attempts did not better it.

It was now Sunday 12 October. We had a day until mastering, and we still had this last track to mix. Steven went home to get some rest, but Bono, Tom and I headed over to the Power Station, the third recording studio in less than a day, to see the 'Silver and Gold' tapes in action. I was really shattered, and when we arrived and I realised that we'd have to wait to align the tape heads to our tape, I gave up and went home to try to get some sleep. I expected to come in the next morning and help finish the mix. Tom and Bono had other plans, however, deciding to stay and work through the night. In the morning Steven came in to find the pair pretty much out of their heads, not really knowing what they were hearing any more. But Steven checked the mix, made a few small changes and thought they had nailed it. By the time I made it in, the track had been deemed finished.

That afternoon, Monday 13 October, Steven and I took the mixes of the album over to Bob Ludwig at Masterdisk. We had finally completed the recording and mixing of the Sun City project. The single was released towards the end of the week, on 16 October.

We still had the video to finish and were very excited when Godley and Creme confirmed that they were able to fly in to do the edit. They were on an amazing streak of great videos that had all got strong MTV play, including Herbie Hancock's 'Rockit', Duran Duran's 'Girls on Film', Frankie Goes to Hollywood's 'Two Tribes' and their own 'Cry'. We had strict a deadline from MTV, who were already promoting the video's world premiere, so we booked Godley and Creme in at the International Production Center, which donated a Friday-to-Monday-morning chunk of time to edit the thirty hours of footage down to a seven-and-a-half-minute music video. I went over to meet them. Hart Perry was already there, taking the lead on coordinating the edit. First things first, Kevin needed some spliff asap. I quickly sorted him out, and the edit room soon became a smoky edit shebeen. We pretty much left them to it, occasionally dropping in to see how much they had accomplished.

Everything was going smoothly with the edit when I met Hart in the editing suite. The video was looking cutting-edge. They had used the footage Demme had shot – and it really looked great – putting their stamp on it with special effects and animation. A large part of it was finished; all that was left was the vamp-out. But as we watched, Godley and Creme started packing up. I queried what was up. They replied that they had a flight booked and were off to the airport!

Hart and I looked at one another. We were completely shocked. We had to deliver the video to MTV by twelve noon the next day! So we had no choice: we had to finish the edit on our own and stay up all night doing it. Hart was a director in his own right, and I was very opinionated, so we figured we could handle it. I called up a friend, who came by with enough ammunition to keep both of us up all night.

We decided to make those last two minutes of the video big, spirited fun. I wanted to make sure that everyone got their moment, especially my friends, who had worked so hard throughout the production of the record. We chose a few somewhat incongruous moments, like Bono kissing a member of the Fat Boys, Lou Reed doing a spin, Peter Wolf performing a shimmy and Herbie Hancock doing his version of the moonwalk. I even threw in a bit of myself dancing.

When Steven showed up the next morning, he was surprised that Godley and Creme had left and that Hart and I had actually finished it. I'm pretty sure he liked it, which was good, as we had no more time in which to mess with it. We walked it over to MTV that morning, just in time, as it premiered that evening. The album was released on 25 October.

On 30 October Steven, myself (I was late, having had another pre-event fight with Tina) and the other Sun City organisers – Rick Dutka, Owen Epstein and Danny Schechter – along with many of the artists who had performed on the record, went to the UN to present the first

United Nations

The United Nations Special Committee against *Apartheid*

expresses its great appreciation to

Arthur Baker
Artists United Against Apartheid

for his valuable contribution to the
international campaign for the elimination of *apartheid*
and the establishment of a non-racial and democratic society in South Africa

Chairman
SPECIAL COMMITTEE AGAINST APARTHEID

Declaration from the United Nations for our work on 'Sun City'.

pressing of 'Sun City' to the secretary general and the chairman of the Special Committee Against Apartheid. We were each presented with a framed declaration from the Committee for our work against apartheid, and the 'Sun City' video was premiered to the artists and UN representatives.

Once the record was released it wasn't always smooth sailing. Manhattan Records had a promo guy whom Steven and I were sure was a good-ole-boy racist, and even Bruce Lundvall had problems getting the guy to do his job. MTV gave us loads of play, and our *Sun City* long-form video, about the making of the track, got nominated for a Grammy, but we barely touched the top forty.

Still, we spread the word, educated, and raised over half a million dollars, and no artist ever played the Sun City resort again. 'Sun City' was selected as record of the year by some of the most influential music critics around, and it topped the prestigious *Village Voice* international jazz and pop critics' poll for Best Single of the Year. We were also nominated for two Grammys in 1986: Best Long-Form Video and Best Rock Performance by a Duo or Group.

Some four years later, when Nelson Mandela was released from prison, I did feel some pride for helping make that happen. A celebration was planned in NYC: a reception and dinner hosted by Robert De Niro at his Tribeca Film Center and Grill, attended by some of Hollywood's biggest stars, to honour the Mandelas and raise money for the African National Congress. Steve and I were there, but I had sort of hopped off the Sun City train years earlier, so I was in the cheap seats, and while I caught a glimpse of the great man, unfortunately I didn't get a chance to meet him and shake his hand.

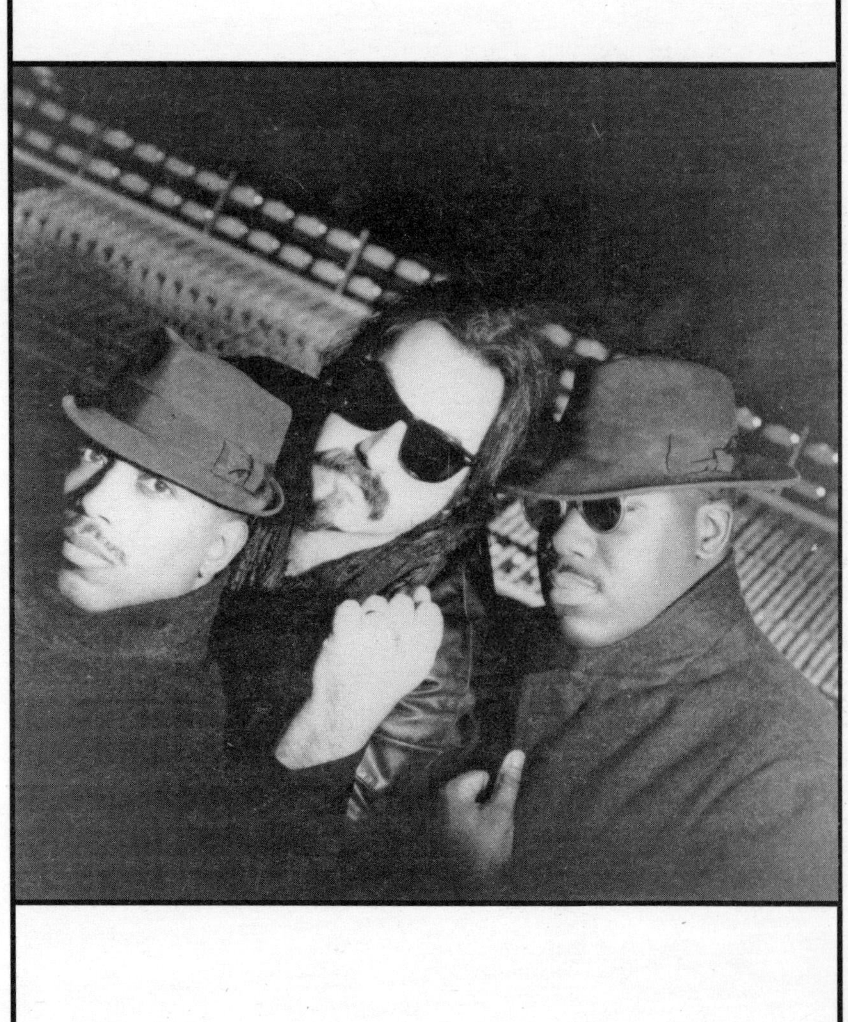

24.

'TURN ME LOOSE'

1986

After close to three years of non-stop work and the pressure of major projects such as *Beat Street*, Hall & Oates, Beck, Dylan, Diana, Springsteen, 'Sun City' and attempting to complete my own album for Epic, I decided I needed to reboot, refocus, concentrate on getting back to the streets and produce some dance music. And I didn't even consider taking a rest.

Working with so many major rock acts, I had become consumed by the world of rock'n'roll, and it (and cocaine) had taken over my expensive solo project. While my album featured many of the amazing artists whose records I was already working on – Nona Hendryx, Carly Simon, Jeff Beck, Face to Face, Eddie Kendricks and David Ruffin – it lacked what I was known for: risk-taking and street excitement. I was now working in expensive studios, and it sounded like it, in the wrong way. There were some good songs, but unfortunately, the record lacked soul and sounded way too 1980s polished. To be honest, I can't even say what actually happened to the project, other than that the album was never released.

Also, Streetwise had gone down the drain, so I was almost back to square one. I started Criminal Records (as a tongue-in-cheek poke at Morris Levy) and decided its focus should be on pure dance music – the new sound of house. I felt house was a logical way back to my roots. It had a soulful, disco-on-a-budget sound and a real do-it-yourself ethos, which in reality was what we NYC guys had been following for the past four years (from 1982 to 1986) anyway, but house was more focused on sampling the disco that I loved and had grown up with.

My first two releases on Criminal tried to capture that house vibe, starting with a remake of Dhar Braxton's 'Jump Back' (which had just come out on Sleeping Bag Records), sung by Will Downing under the alias Wally Jump Jr. and the Criminal Element, which was mixed in June. Our second release was '(I Want to Go to) Chicago' by R. T. & The Rockmen Unlimited, and it was my tribute to Chicago and house music.

It seemed as if I really had my ear to the ground, because it was ready for release just as the New Music Seminar of summer 1986 began. That NMS will be forever known as the seminar where Chicago house invaded New York. I had my new Criminal promo team, led by my old Boston buddy Joey Carvello, ready to promote our 'Chicago' track at the seminar.

Towards the end of the year, Tony Wilson, the owner of Factory Records, had tried his damnedest to finally get me on a plane to Europe, this time to work with a new group he had signed, Happy Mondays. I listened to their tape and thought the songs were weak. Tony said it was all about their live show and he'd get me over to the UK to see them perform. That I couldn't do, because I still had a bad fear of flying. I had even missed the opportunity to meet Pete Townshend and Ringo Starr, who had both played on the Sun City record but had done their recording in London. Nightlife and drugs had finally consumed me. A faint memory of leaving the New York Music Awards with Seymour Stein in tow, in a search for stimulants, thus missing out on a major moment – receiving the Producer of the Year Award 1986 – stands out. And when I found myself prone on the bathroom floor of a club in search of droppings, only to see Nile Rodgers on the same mission, it was the last straw! I was passing up some great opportunities, plus throwing lots of my hard-earned cash at scum dealers. And my health was horrible – my weight was up to twenty stone! So I finally decided to quit drugs.

Tina and I checked out a few rehab places in NYC, but I thought they were all too expensive. *I'll do this on my own*, I thought. Then I would fly over to Europe and go to MIDEM, the annual music-industry trade show in France, with all the great new music I was working on at Criminal.

First two weeks in, I'd done no drugs, and my clean-up seemed to be going really well.

Then New Order showed up.

I got a visit from Michael Shamberg. He told me about an indie film being directed by a woman named Beth B, who was well known on

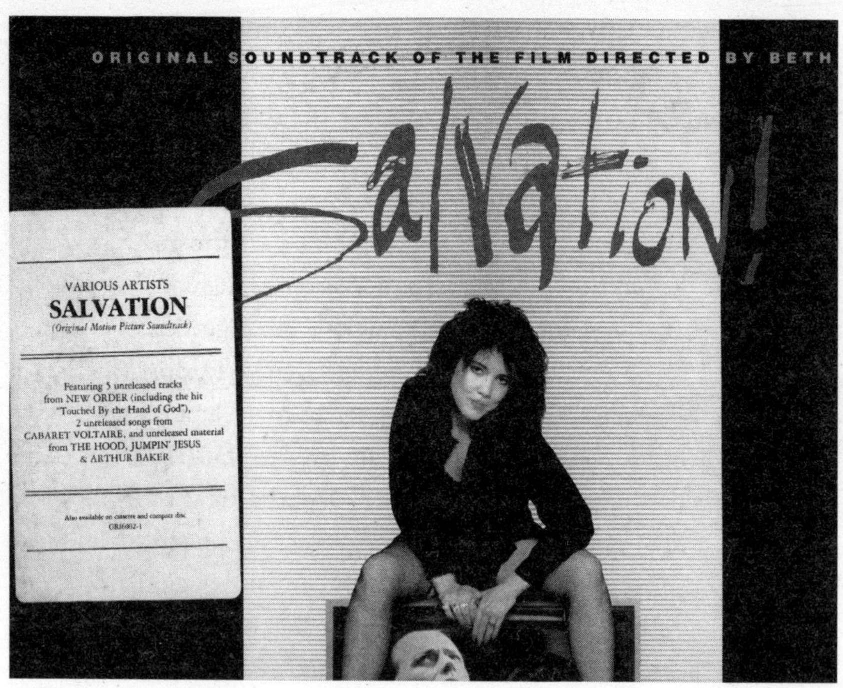

The *Salvation! Have You Said Your Prayers Today?* movie soundtrack album.

the NYC downtown scene. The film was called *Salvation! Have You Said Your Prayers Today?* It was an ironic swipe at the culture of TV evangelism. *Timely and cool,* I thought. He had convinced New Order to start on the soundtrack and wanted me to finish it up. They had cut five tracks at Pluto Studios in Manchester with producer Michael Johnson. I looked at the footage and listened to the music. The film was raw but pretty good. New Order's music was rockin' but needed finishing. One track in particular, 'Touched by the Hand of God', had real potential and excited me. *Would love to get my mitts on that one.* I also thought that the instrumental piece called 'Let's Go' could really use vocals, that there was a great song hiding there. Being an indie film I knew there was *no* money at all. And free studio time would also be needed. Shamberg knew I had my own studio and that getting more involved with film soundtracks was something I was very interested in doing. It would be cool to get to work with New Order again. I was in.

My cleansing was going well, until New Order came to town to check out how things were going with the soundtrack. I went into Shakedown one night with Barney to write lyrics and cut some vocals on the 'Let's Go' instrumental. I proudly told him that I was through with cocaine. It was obvious he wasn't convinced when he laid about twenty of those mini-lines he was known for across the mixing console. I looked at him and then at his scrawny lines, and it took me no more prodding. I took a credit card out, ran them all together and snorted the entire long line. After an inconsequential, messy, drink-and-drug-fuelled session, I somehow made it back to my apartment on the Upper West Side, convinced I was having a heart attack. I promised the divine spirit there and then that I'd quit the evil drug if I were allowed to see the morning sun. The next day I tossed what I had left down the sink and happily quit drugs once more for the next seven years.

I wouldn't see New Order again until we caught up in California a couple of years later, in June 1989. I happened to be in LA, working in the studio with Debbie Harry on a few tracks for her *Def, Dumb & Blonde* album. Gary Kurfirst, who managed Debbie, Talking Heads and The Ramones, lived in the Hollywood Hills and was having a party to celebrate the Ramones' gig in LA. Debbie and I went to the party on our way to the show, pulling up in my rented red convertible Mustang (I must admit, it felt pretty good riding around LA in a convertible Mustang with Debbie fucking Harry in the passenger seat!). We rang the bell, and the door slowly opened. Debbie and I both did a double take. It was Timothy Leary!

Or, on this occasion, Timothy leering.

Then Tina Weymouth from Talking Heads appeared. Timothy tried to talk Tina, Debbie and me into dropping some acid and exploring the Hollywood Hills. Debbie and I refused politely and rode off into the night to see The Ramones.

That same rented convertible Mustang enabled me to hit the road to San Diego, where I would catch up with New Order on their *Technique* tour and finally see them play 'Touched' live. After the gig, I

Chris Frantz and Tina Weymouth (Talking Heads/Tom Tom Club) with me at Sigma Sound, NYC, working on the Tom Tom Club record.

offered to drive a few of the guys back to the hotel for the after-party in the Mustang, which for Brits was not a common ride. Shamberg, Hooky and Mike Pickering (who was the tour DJ) all piled in. I was showing off a bit, driving too fast, when the flashing lights of a state trooper broke up our conversation. He made me walk a straight line, touch my nose with my eyes closed and count to ten backwards. After passing all the tests, I somehow talked my way out of a ticket, telling the officer that we were on the way back to the hotel from the gig, that Hooky was in New Order and I was their producer, and 'Yes, sir, I won't be driving any more tonight.' As he pulled away, I sighed with relief. Then I turned to see Pickering holding a bag full of a white substance. Fucking close call.

I wouldn't get to work with the band again until seven years later, when I was hired to remix '1963', finally getting that vocal on 'Let's Go' in 1994 for a 1995 release.

After that one-day, New Order-induced relapse, I really got back on the wagon. This time I decided to do a drug-cleansing fast, my theory being that I'd get so high from the fasting that I wouldn't miss the coke buzz. I did this successfully, and after a few weeks of fasting, consuming only a daily protein drink, I was in a state of near hallucination. This had the added bonus of getting me into a very creative place. One night a song idea came pouring out while I was in this state. I really loved the act of songwriting. I was self-trained and couldn't really play the keyboards. But when the spirit moved me, an idea might just fly into my consciousness. I was in such a heightened condition I was seriously convinced this song might bring about world peace. I literally ran over to my keyboard player and co-writer Richard Scher's apartment, a few blocks away, and we wrote and recorded the skeleton of my new song idea, 'The Message Is Love'.

We went into Shakedown on 18 December and cut a demo. As Steve and I had done with 'Sun City', I got Will Downing to sing on it, and he killed it. It wasn't a dance song at all; in my head it was more like 'Hey Jude' and spoke of world peace and unity. Richard and I felt that we really had something special.

The MIDEM music conference in Cannes was coming up at the end of January, and it was a great place to do business. I had already prepared lots of new music for my Criminal label that would be available for licensing there. I still wasn't flying, but I figured a trip to Cannes would be a great way for me to get over that fear, since I'd be travelling with a gang of my lawyers. There would be no way I could wimp out of the flight at the gate with the entire firm of Grubman, Indursky & Schindler accompanying me.

So we all set off, and I sat with my attorney, Bob Flax. The firm took over the upstairs of a 747, with bespoke catering provided by Alan Grubman and the Carnegie Deli, with huge deli sandwiches for everyone. The flight was great, the drinks were flowing, and I landed in a jovial mood.

I had finally made it to Europe.

Above left
Sorcerer Sound session, 1983 – Fred Zarr, Robbie Shakespeare, Sly Dunbar, John Robie and me (*courtesy of AB collection*).

Above right
Afrika Bambaataa, Pow Wow, MC G.L.O.B.E., me and Mr Biggs at Unique Studio, 1982 (*courtesy of Jacques Chenet* / Newsweek).

Left
Bond International Casino 'A Valentine Affair' flyer, 1983. The infamous snowstorm extravaganza gig (*courtesy of AB collection*).

Bruce Springsteen, Zoe Yanakis, Steve Van Zandt, Danny Schechter, me and Richard Scher on the bus going to Washington Square Park for Sun City video shoot, 1985 (*courtesy of David N. Seelig*).

Yes, Miles does smile! Don't know what I said. Miles Davis, Steve Van Zandt and me at Shakedown Sound Studio, Sun City Session, NYC, 1985 (*courtesy of David N. Seelig*).

Guardian Angel Lisa Sliwa, film director Matty Rich, me, BMG VP Trish Heimers, RCA VP Miller London, former Reagan press secretary James Brady and the Rev. Al Green at the Ebenezer Baptist Church in Harlem at an event to promote handgun violence awareness and 'Leave the Guns at Home', 1991 (*courtesy of Ebet Roberts*).

Martin Scorsese, Lou Reed, Ian Hunter, Judy Collins, Bob Dylan and me attend a party to celebrate the release of *Biograph*, Dylan's career retrospective box set, held at the Whitney Museum of American Art, in NYC, 13 November 1985 (*Vinnie Zuffante / Stringer / Getty Images*).

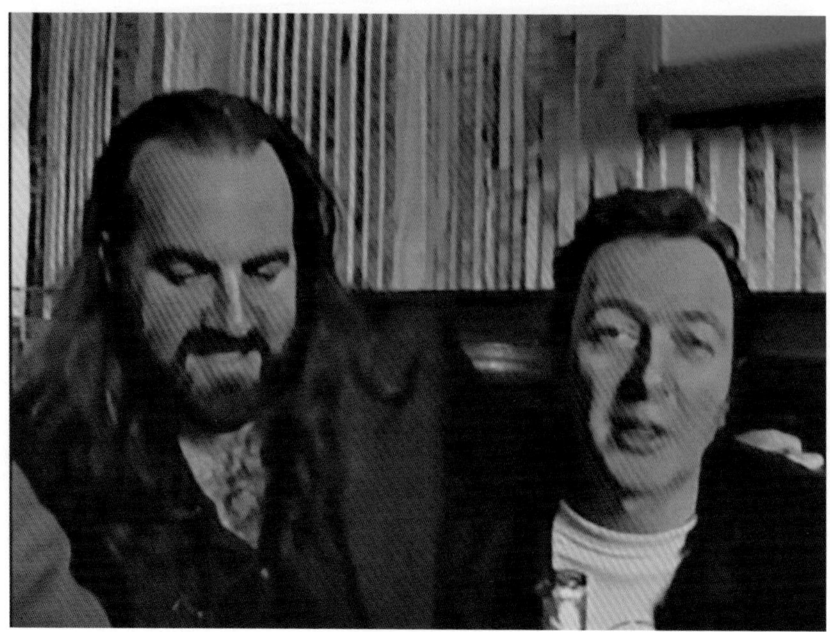

Me and Joe Strummer at the Elbow Room Chapel Market opening party, 2002 (*courtesy of AB collection*).

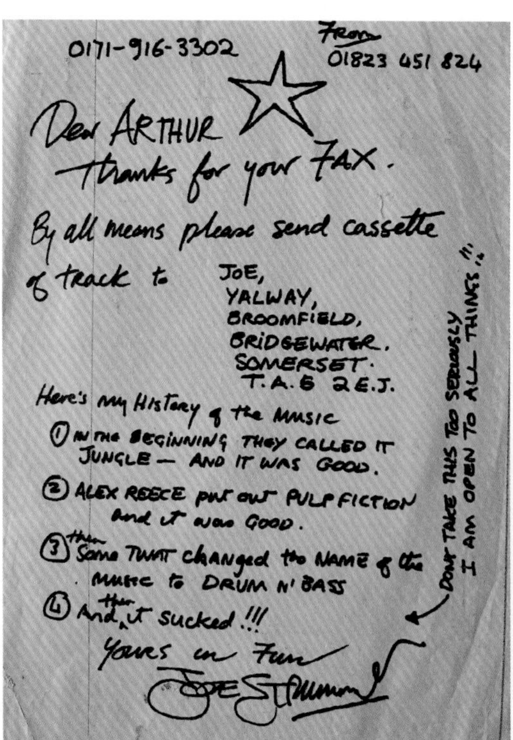

0171-916-3302

From 01823 451 824

Dear ARTHUR
thanks for your FAX.

By all means please send cassette of track to JOE,
YALWAY,
BROOMFIELD,
BRIDGEWATER.
SOMERSET.
T.A.5 2E.J.

Here's my History of the Music

1. IN THE BEGINNING THEY CALLED IT JUNGLE — AND IT WAS GOOD.
2. ALEX REECE put out PULP FICTION And it was GOOD.
3. then Some TWAT changed the NAME of the MUSIC to DRUM N' BASS
4. And then it sucked!!!

DON'T TAKE THIS TOO SERIOUSLY I AM OPEN TO ALL THINGS !!

Yours in Fun
JOE STRUMMER

Left

Rejection letter to me from Joe Strummer, 2001 (*courtesy of AB collection*).

Below

Me and Gabby Mejia at Submercer, NYC, 2010 (*courtesy of AB collection*).

Lumar LeBlanc, Bootsy Collins, Novena Carmel, me, George Clinton and Bernie Worrell attending Finding the Funk Film Panel at SXSW Music and Film Festival, 2013 (*Mindy Best / Contributor / Getty Images*).

Me and Annette in Barcelona, 2004 (*courtesy of AB collection*).

Above left: Me and my dad in Boca Raton (*courtesy of AB collection*).

Above right: Annette, me and the Rabbi at our wedding in Ibiza, 5 July 2010 (*courtesy of AB collection*).

Right: Annette, Amarone and me in London, 2014 (*courtesy of AB collection*).

Below left: Me, my dad and Amarone in Boca Raton, 2015 (*courtesy of AB collection*).

Below right: Amarone and the matriarch of our family, my aunt Dodie in Beverly, Massachussets, 2024 (*courtesy of AB collection*).

Above left: Me, Annette and Amarone at home in Miami, Florida, 2022 (*courtesy of David Dines*).

Above right: Amarone and me watching the Boston Celtics beat the Miami Heat. Miami, 2024 (*courtesy of AB collection*).

Above left: Amarone and Annette by the kitchen table. Miami shores, July 2020 (*courtesy of AB collection*).

Above right: Me, Annette and Amarone at Tribeca Film Festival, 2024 (*John Lamparski / Stringer / Getty Images*).

In session at the Bridge Recording Studio, Miami, December 2022, with José Parlá (*courtesy of Lisa Leone*).

Amarone instructing me on my opening set for New Order / Rockers Revenge gig at the Fillmore Miami Beach, 17 January 2020 (*courtesy of AB collection*).

25.

MY EUROPEAN ADVENTURE

1987

On my first day in Cannes I walked around town, armed with a Criminal compilation cassette and rough mixes from Will Downing's album. Bob Flax was repping me, and he introduced me to many international record executives. But my most successful meeting I organised myself. Chris Blackwell, the owner of Island Records, was in town. Chris was a buddy of mine, and we had already set aside some time to meet in the penthouse of the Martinez, an art deco hotel on the promenade, where Chris usually stayed.

When I got to Chris's suite, we immediately spliffed up and reminisced for a few minutes. I then slapped Will's demo tape on. Chris was blown away by the songs and Will's amazing voice, a godly combination of Luther Vandross and Teddy Pendergrass. He offered me a deal on the spot, mentioning that I could work with Joel Webber, who was his top A&R guy in the NYC Island office and an acquaintance of mine from the New Music Seminar.

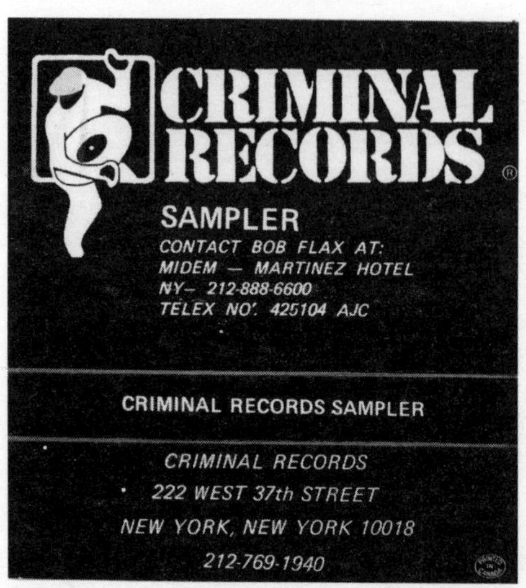

Criminal Records sampler cassette for Midem, 1987.

On that trip I would meet three people who would become lifelong friends. Not really knowing the scene at MIDEM, the next day I went to the convention centre and started schmoozing. Forgetting about my success in Europe, I was surprised when lots of the attendees started approaching me, having recognised me from New Order's 'Confusion' video. I first met a young French-Canadian DJ named Robert Levy, who had a radio show in Paris. He told me that he played all my records and asked if I'd be a guest on his show. He spoke English very well, which was obviously a big plus, because my high-school French wasn't cutting it at all. He also introduced me to an interesting young French-Algerian girl at the Martinez pool named Sophie Bramly. I soon realised she was the legendary Sophie that Afrika Bambaataa often mentioned, a well-known hip-hop photographer and journalist. She asked if she could interview me for an article for *The Face*, the UK music and style magazine. I agreed, so we sat by the pool for the interview. Sophie also was developing an idea for MTV, which ended up morphing into the show *Yo! MTV*, which she presented and on which I'd be a guest. (It would later be appropriated by Fab 5 Freddy as *Yo! MTV Raps*.) Like Robert, Sophie spoke great English.

Me with Sophie Bramly on her show *Yo! MTV*.

So right there and then, after meeting these two very cool people, I decided to change my plans and, after Cannes, make my way to Paris first, instead of London. Which turned out to be a great idea.

The last person I met at MIDEM was a young guy named Paul, who was representing a dance label from the UK called, interestingly enough, Champion Records (my manager Tommy Mottola's company was Champion Entertainment). Paul mentioned he DJed a bit and also did some promotion for my friends at Def Jam Records. Champion would love to put out my records in the UK, he said. I sort of paid that no mind because I was already hooked up in England with A&M, CBS, Chrysalis . . . a whole bunch of labels. We exchanged details, and I told him I'd be in touch.

After all my UK success, I had lots of connections there and a list of people I'd meet when I finally made it to London. I had unintentionally created a bit of a mystique around myself thanks to my fear of flying and not showing up in London while I was really hot (not to mention all the opportunities I might have missed by not going over there at the height of my success). But now I was headed to Paris to meet my two fantastic, cool, hooked-in tour guides. Robert had the underground club scene covered for me. He played at the biggest, hottest dance club in Paris and also had *the* dance radio show in France. Sophie also took me to Bandouche, a very chic, but edgy, spot. Through her I met all the hippest, hot, breaking French acts and artistes – people like Philippe Starck, Les Rita Mitsouko, Étienne Daho and Caroline Loeb (I'd eventually collaborate with Étienne and Caroline on a track called 'Paris Sens Interdits'). Loeb had this amazing record called 'C'est la ouate' that had been played non-stop at Cannes and was everywhere in Paris. When I met her, I was already a fan, obsessed with her record. I immediately tried to license it for the States, only to be beaten to it by Seymour Stein and Sire.

I loved everything about Paris – the food, the people and the music. It was a very special place for me from the start. I could easily get lost in my head and come up with new ideas there. I noticed on that first visit that the sounds of African music were everywhere, thumping out of bars, being played by live bands and on records. All the Manu Dibango/Fela Kuti vibe that I had loved in early disco music was all around you in Paris. I was inspired by it, and many musical concepts started percolating in my head.

Then, when Sophie and I walked by the opera house on our way to see the Moulin Rouge, a real idea was hatched. I'd just have to wait till I got to London to do anything about it.

When I finally made it to London, all I wanted to talk about was the French music scene. Everyone looked at me like I had drunk some bad French rosé. It was 1987, and the UK record industry and the country's DJs thought they were at the top, followed by the States. The French? C'mon!

But I had come to London with a cool Paris-inspired idea already concocted in my mind, which I wanted to get down asap. For some reason I decided to call Paul, from Champion, to ask him if he knew a studio in town that I could book quickly. He said he didn't, but he'd find me somewhere. I then called the only keyboardist I knew in London, Andy Stennett from Freeez. Paul called back and said he had organised a studio for me. When we all met up there and I told them my Paris-induced concept, I'm not sure what they thought. They may have figured I was nuts, I guess.

The idea was to create a sound clash between African *makossa*, house music and opera. I wanted to call the act Jack E Makossa and the record 'Jackin' the Opera House'. I called a singer friend from NYC, Catherine Buchanan, who happened to be in town and said she could sing a bit of opera.

When Paul arrived, he sheepishly admitted that it was his first time ever in a studio. A couple of years later, Paul Oakenfold (or Oakie, as he was known) would feel very comfortable in a studio, and also in DJ booths and stadiums across the world. But for that session he didn't have much to offer. Andy covered the keys, Catherine hit the opera's high notes, and I rocked the bass line and drums. I was pretty satisfied by the results.

We played Paul's boss, Mel Medalie, the track, and he loved it. The fact that it had novelty value helped seal the deal. He also was able to get Stock, Aitken & Waterman engineer Phil Harding to provide a remix. I'd keep American rights, he'd release it in the UK, and we'd split the rest of the world. I'd get all of the publishing, since I wrote the sucker.

On release it did well in both the UK and the US, but predictably (to me), it did amazingly well in France, eventually becoming the theme song for the top radio station in Paris, NRG. Sophie also created a fun animated video for it, which got MTV play (you can still find it online).

While at MIDEM, I had decided to take on a rep for the UK, Stephen Budd. Stephen managed Tony Visconti, the famed David Bowie and Marc Bolan producer, and his studio, Good Earth. He helped sort out some remixes for me in London, one being a cover of Sly and the Family Stone's 'Running Away' by The Colourfield, Terry Hall's (from The Specials and Fun Boy Three) new group, which I mixed at Visconti's studio.

Then I got a few interesting tracks to remix. First was a cover of the Buzzcocks' 'Ever Fallen in Love' by the Fine Young Cannibals, from my friend Jonathan Demme's film *Something Wild*. I already had a couple of my own songs in the flick: a Jimmy Cliff track, 'You Don't Have to Cry', which Little Steven and I had written and recorded at the Power Station with Sly and Robbie on drums and bass; and my remix of Sister Carol's cover of 'Wild Thing'. For my Cannibals remix I brought their singer, Roland Gift, back in and had him ad-lib over my new percussion-and-Rhodes-piano-led groove. He sounded a bit like Mick Jagger scatting over a Norman Whitfield psychedelic soul thing. My extended club version made a lot of noise throughout the UK.

Then I was hired by a softly spoken young A&R man named Pete Edge to remix a track by his new signing, a three-piece act called Living in a Box. Their debut song, also titled 'Living in a Box', was coincidentally co-produced by my old engineer, Tom Lord-Alge. It was a real pop song in a polished electro mode. I dubified it, pedalling a new deep bass line throughout it and adding live percussion. I basically gave it a bit of an organic 'Walking on Sunshine' vibe.

The lead singer had a real soulful voice, although he had blond hair, and his delivery was obviously Bobby Womack-inspired (Womack later would cover the track). I pulled out all my mix tricks: big drops, occasionally taking the drums out completely. Pete was a bit spooked by these drops, fearing that the crowd would lose the groove and leave the dancefloor, so I acquiesced, taking a few of the big drops out of the vocal version but keeping them in the dub. I felt it was right up there with my 'Too Much Blood' and 'Cover Me' remixes, although unlike them, this one was totally drug-free!

My 'Turn Me Loose' track was also about to drop, so London Records had Wally Jump Jr. – Will Downing, Craig Derry and myself – do some press. The main event was to perform the song live on the TV music show *The Tube*. I got to climb into bed with the host, Paula Yates, on 13 February 1987 for her interview treatment. I talked about our new record, but she also wanted info on Rockers Revenge, New Order, Freeez, New Edition and Afrika Bambaataa, since I hadn't been to London when they had hits, so no one in the UK had heard me talk about them. When Paula asked me what new and exciting records I had coming up, I really enthused about the 'Living in a Box' remix I'd just done. I promised that the band and my mix would hit the top five. A month later, they did.

On that first trip to London, I was only in town for about three weeks, but I remixed a ridiculous amount of records in that time: seven in total, by The Colourfield, Funkrew, Le Baron, Big Trouble, Nick Kamen, Living in a Box and Fine Young Cannibals. I even had to fly my new editor, Junior Vasquez, over to keep up with the cutting, which was unheard of. My first trip to London was a big success, both creatively and financially.

NOMINEE

Arthur Baker

THE 29TH ANNUAL
GRAMMY AWARDS

26.

LOOKING OUT FOR LOVE

1987

When I flew out to LA to attend the Grammys on 24 February 1987, I was on a bit of a natural high: all the work coming in, I had made it to Europe, I was off drugs *and* 'Sun City' had been nominated for two Grammy awards. My old friend Billy Crystal was the host, and I thought it would be amazing if we won something. I crashed down to Earth a bit when we lost to the Eurythmics and fucking Sting! I mean, *seriously*?

While I was in LA, I got a call from Michael Ostin, head of A&R at Warners (and son of the president, Mo Ostin). He wanted me to come and see him at Warners' offices in Burbank. I thought, *Mmm, interesting*. He didn't give me a clue as to why he wanted to meet up.

As I waited to be ushered into his office, I ran into Craig Kostich, head of dance promotion at the label. We exchanged hellos, and he asked me why I was there. When I said, 'To see Michael,' he was curious, as he knew nothing about the meeting. I entered Ostin's office, which was decked out with endless gold and platinum records, and he told me he had been in London a few weeks earlier and had seen my interview on *The Tube* and then watched as my mix of 'Living in a Box' went up the charts and lived up to my prediction. When he said, 'Let me play you something,' I could tell he must have something special for me. Then he blasted out this tribal tom-tom groove, topped with an Emulator-sampled vocal riff.

I was sold.

It immediately reminded me of the vibe of Kate Bush's 'Running Up That Hill'. The first time I had heard 'Running' was on a late-night solo ride out to the Hamptons. I had pulled my car over so that I wouldn't lose the radio signal before I could find out what it was, and this track had a lot of that. But it was only when the chorus came in with a catchy, poppy refrain – 'Looking out for love, big, big love' – that I realised it was Fleetwood Mac. It was 'Big Love', which was scheduled to be their new single.

After the track ended, Michael said, 'Can you do something with that?'

I answered, 'Oh yeah, I can make that a number-one club record.' I was that confident, and in my mind I already knew what I would do with it. He seemed happy.

When I left the office, Craig approached me immediately. 'So what did Michael play you?' he queried. '"Big Love",' I answered. He was very surprised. 'That's not a dance record!' he said, in a somewhat smug, challenging way. I said that I thought it was, and that after I was done with it, it would be a number-one dance record – with his help, I added, as he was one of the top promo men in the dance world, and I wanted him on my side.

Michael had arranged for me to go over to Lindsey Buckingham's house in Beverly Hills to meet him and pick up the multitrack. I was starting to feel a bit ill and was scheduled to fly back to NYC the next morning. I was still a nervous flier, but at least I was going to fly back with Tina. I went over to Lindsey's home studio, and he talked me through what was on the tape. He was cool and inquisitive, but I didn't reveal what I was planning. He said I could use whatever I wanted on the tape. Cool.

That night my stomach was really upset, and I felt like I was getting the flu. My friend and doctor, Mike 'Dr Hollywood' Wiechowski, happened to be in town, so he came by the Bel Age in Beverly Hills, where we were staying, and gave me some Compazine for the nausea. I took them, no problem. The next morning Tina and I got picked up by a Music Express car. I was feeling a little off, but I figured it was the flu. As I said, I was still a very nervous flier, so I thought it was that. But as the 747 started its ascent, I started feeling very twitchy. I suddenly lost control of my arms and couldn't breathe. I realised I was having an allergic reaction to the medicine. I had had a similar reaction when I was in college, working at my dad's friend's coat factory. They had given me Benadryl, but we were on a fucking plane. I communicated all this to Tina, gasping. It was not good. She told the stewardess the situation, and they asked if there was a doctor on board. There wasn't, but a nurse came up, and she convinced the pilot that he should land the plane. Quick.

Tina recently told me that the crew had an EpiPen but could not administer it without a doctor present! We landed in Denver, with four-hundred-plus angry passengers giving me the evil eye as I slowly departed the plane. There was an ambulance there, and after a few tries, the young nurse was finally able to find a vein and hit me with the Benadryl. Immediate relief. I felt how a junkie must feel that first time – I was gone. They took me to the hospital to check me out, and Tina asked if I wanted to go back via train or on the next flight. 'I'm so high I wouldn't feel anything if the plane crashed,' I said, so we got on the next plane to New York.

Once back in NYC, I got to work immediately on the 'Big Love' remix. The single was due to drop at the end of March, so it was a tight schedule. I started pulling up faders and looking at the track sheet. There was a track that was simply labelled 'Stevie'. I pushed up the fader, and there was this soulful, gritty voice, singing the 'big, big love' chorus. But then she took it further with her shouts of 'house on a hill'.

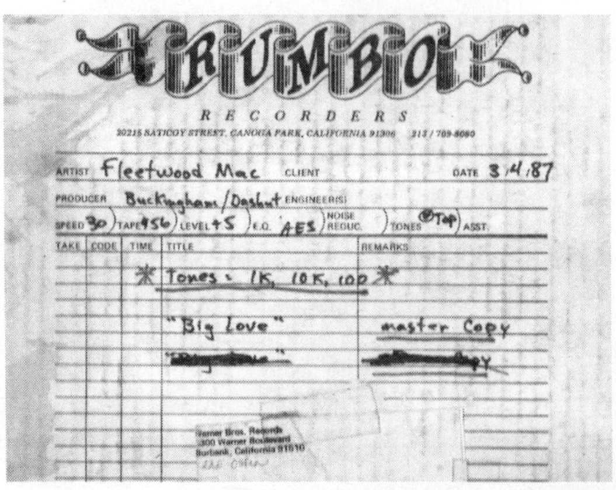
RUMBO
RECORDERS
20215 SATICOY STREET, CANOGA PARK, CALIFORNIA 91306 213/709-8080
ARTIST Fleetwood Mac CLIENT DATE 3/4/87
PRODUCER Buckingham/Dashut ENGINEER(S)
SPEED 30 TAPE 456 LEVEL +5 E.Q. AES NOISE REDUC. TONES (Top) ASST.

TAKE	CODE	TIME	TITLE	REMARKS
			* Tones - 1K, 10K, 100 *	
			"Big Love"	master Copy

Warner Bros. Records
3300 Warner Boulevard
Burbank, California 91510

Two-inch tape box of 'Big Love' from Lindsey Buckingham's recording studio, 1987.

House! I had the vocal riff I needed. I decided to do a house remix. I called Bob Rosa in to engineer and tried a new keyboardist, Gary Rottger, who would put a rhythmic piano part down. But when push came to shove, I reached out to keyboardist supreme Mr David Cole (who would later become one of the Cs of C+C Music Factory; RIP,

David). He rocked the vocal samples and laid down a smokin' piano solo.

Once the mix was complete, I thought I had come up with something extremely special. So I was very confident when I sent Ostin the remix. He loved it, but . . . only one issue: Lindsey had a problem with me using Stevie's vocals. He had failed to make it clear that this was *his* song. Fuck. He had told me I could use anything that was on the tape! It must have taken some convincing from Michael, but Lindsey eventually agreed to let Stevie's vocals be used on my two dub mixes. It peaked at #7 on the dance charts.

I've always thought of this track as one of my most important remixes, seeing that it was the first house remix of a rock song. And it was totally legit; it worked on the dancefloors and kept a great song intact. Michael and the band were happy enough with the outcome, so much so that they quickly ask me to remix the next Mac single, 'Family Man'.

With 'Big Love' blowing up, I was pretty hot once 1987's New Music Seminar came around and I had lots of visitors dropping by. Dave Dorrell, an underground London DJ who played at Raw, on Tottenham Court Road, rolled in. He played me a new song of his, which I thought was really cool. I then dropped a test pressing of my new track, 'Put the Needle to the Record'. I had put it together with my new protégée, Gail 'Sky' King, whom I had met recently while on a late-night research trip to the Red Parrot. The Parrot had an upscale, club-head crowd, with music that echoed the Paradise Garage sound, while also playing funk and hip-hop. On arrival, I was hit by a track that sounded vaguely familiar but was rocking in a new way. I had to know what it was, so I eased my way through the crowd to the booth. Surprisingly, I found a bespectacled, smiling young woman rocking the decks (back then there were very few female DJs). I introduced myself and asked Gail what she was playing. It was the bootleg 'Rock the House' by Mr. K. I invited her to Shakedown the next night (with the record, of course) so she could help me produce a new track featuring the bass line.

Gail came in, showing no nervousness, and immediately got to work. She was all biz. This was pre-looping, so she had to ride the record in against a percussion beat I had made. It took a while, but eventually she got it. I quickly decided this should be my sample record. Sampling was controversial at the time, and if there was going to be a legal test case, I wanted this track to be *the* one. So we sampled lots of the hottest tracks of the day. I again called David Cole in, and he rocked a couple of passes of mischievous solos using the vocal samples. Keith LeBlanc then laid down some funky drums over the top. Lastly, we grabbed a vocal off 'Drum Machine', a song that Shakedown intern and future Beastie Boy Adam Yauch and Jay Burnett had done years earlier, and 'Put the Needle to the Record' was born. I planned to release it under the Criminal Element Orchestra moniker.

Photo shoot for the Criminal Element Orchestra project, 1988.

I played the track for Pete Edge, who had hired me to do the 'Living in a Box' remix, and he was so blown away he immediately made me an offer.

But back to Mr Dorrell. I remember handing him a test pressing of 'Needle' and helpfully suggesting that he should try a vocal sample on his instrumental too. Thing is, I didn't mean *my* vocal sample.

Just a few months later, I got a call from Pete. He said the track was going well, but there was another record out that had the exact same vocal sample. And it had been released on the *same* fucking day – 5 September 1987. He told me it was a record by a London DJ, Dave Dorrell, and his group M|A|R|R|S called 'Pump Up the Volume'. He had sampled the hook from my fucking record!

Let's just say I wasn't pleased.

27.

SOMETHING GOIN' ROUND INSIDE MY HEAD

1988

When I played Chris Blackwell Will Downing's demo tape in Cannes, I withheld one song as I thought I had enough ammo without it to score Will a record deal. The secret weapon I kept in my bag was 'The Message Is Love', which had been composed and demoed a few weeks earlier in New York. I planned to use that song in my quest for my own solo album deal in the UK. I was aiming to sign to A&M, as I already had a great working relationship with Mike Sefton and Jeff Young, who had signed the Wally Jump Jr. album to their label Breakout/A&M. It felt natural for me to bring my solo album over to them, and Mike set up a meeting for me with the head of A&R, Chris Briggs. Chris was already a legend in the UK music industry for signing Def Leppard, ABC and Gang of Four, and for being hard-drinking and fond of partaking in the fruits of the job.

At our first meeting, not really knowing much about Chris, I proudly declared that I'd just made it to my first half-year of being drug-free, thinking he'd be happy to have an artist who might actually be reliable. He looked at me somewhat in disbelief and sadly murmured a disappointed 'Oh . . .', and after a pause, 'Ah well, I'll sign you anyway.' He did let me know that he thought most people who didn't partake were 'boring'. I promised him that I was far from boring and still loved my red wine. Years later, when he was the one who had quit drugs and drinking, I often thought of his comment as we had lunch.

I hadn't demoed many songs for my album, and the first few I played for Chris were merely politely responded to. He didn't really light up, until he heard the sound of Will singing, 'Love is the message, and the message is love.' Immediately, his demeanour changed. He already loved that voice from my Wally Jump records. But this was a proper song, and he said he thought I had a hit. 'Message' without question scored me my solo deal at A&M. But, naturally, he also wanted to sign Will. Bit of a problem there, Briggsy, as I'd already made a deal for him with that other Chris – Blackwell. Briggs was not happy, but he figured we'd be able to get a 'featured artist' for Will on my record. So then I had to go back to Blackwell, play him 'Message' and try to convince him to let me use Will's vocals on my record. Blackwell wanted the song for Will's album, and if he couldn't have it, then Will's vocal couldn't be used for my album. Impasse.

I had a similar issue with Blackwell a few years later, with the Stereo MC's track 'Human Being (Bedrock Steady)', which I worked on for the *Flintstones* soundtrack. MCA wanted it as the first single from the soundtrack, which was released in 1994, which was great as it was going to be a huge movie. But Chris refused, saying it would conflict with the band's new studio album. The annoying thing was, that record was delayed and delayed, and was finally released only in 2001, seven years later.

So it looked like we couldn't use Will's amazing vocals. This was a huge issue for me, and everyone at A&M loved his performance. But Briggs believed we'd find a way to work things out, and my deal was agreed. We began discussing the UK artists I could collaborate with on my other tracks. While continuing the writing process for my LP in both NYC and London, I was also working with Will on his album, which we were meant to deliver by the end of 1987. We hit the deadline, and the album was mastered right before Christmas. Around that time Will and I again hit pay dirt, with our Wally Jump medley of the Archie Bell & the Drells tracks 'Tighten Up' and 'I Can't Stop Dancing', which made it to #24 on the UK pop chart, keeping my friends at A&M happy.

I loved having the opportunity to spend more time in London, staying in first-class hotels all over the city. I had some major regrets for not having made it over earlier in my career to enjoy my first wave of success. That said, if I had been in London while I was still doing cocaine, it might have ended very badly. Now I was clean and able to appreciate the magical time I was having.

An exciting new music scene and sound was taking over, and cutting-edge venues were popping up everywhere. One evening I journeyed to a new club called Shoom with Sophie, where DJ Danny Rampling and his wife Jenny held court. It was down in a cavernous dark basement, and I'll never forget opening the front door and being hit by a gust of hot steam. We carefully navigated our way down the stairs into the smoky darkness and were hit by house music and screams, with only the occasional strobe to break the blackness. Shoom couldn't have been more different to the clubs in NYC I had spent the 1980s going to.

When Will's debut record, 'A Love Supreme', was finally released in March 1988, it was an instant smash, peaking at #14 on the national UK chart. This helped me secure another collection of remixes in London, meaning I could spend even more time there. I was also making new connections, hanging and working with great up-and-coming British acts. When I was offered the opportunity to remix the piping hot, hip-hoppy 'Buffalo Stance', from new artist Neneh Cherry, I jumped at it.

She was an uber-cool young woman with great fashion sense and was part of the new Buffalo-style wave of fashion and music hitting the UK. We got to chat in the studio before I remixed the track, and this gave me additional insight into her musical ethos. I also met Cameron McVey, her producer/boyfriend, who worked with a collective from Bristol called the Wild Bunch, some of whom would soon become Massive Attack. An entirely new sound was about to explode, and I was fortunate to be there to witness it and be involved in a small way.

By early 1989 'Buffalo Stance' was a smash, and my 'Half Way to House' remix made it playable in more traditional house-playing clubs. Through Cameron and Neneh, I discovered the Wag Club, where Tim Simenon, who had co-produced 'Buffalo Stance', DJed. I remember walking up the steep stairs and discovering a spot that was reminiscent of Danceteria, a place where anything went, music-wise. Tim played an eclectic mix of NYC hip-hop, disco, world music and much more.

Around this time I also met a larger-than-life DJ who navigated the streets of Soho in a Rolls-Royce! Steve Walsh was a true London character with a passion for music and food, both of which I loved too. He turned me on to a great, very late-night Chinese in Soho called Lido, and we'd go there before or after hitting the Wag or the Limelight, where my old friend Paul Oakenfold played at his Raid club night.

When Paul launched his new more house-focused night, Spectrum, at Richard Branson's Heaven club, below Charing Cross station, things really went to the next level. It was a huge venue, and Paul would go off, playing the Balearic sounds that he and Danny Rampling had discovered in Ibiza that summer.

Then I started hitting the raves around Heathrow Airport, going with my new mates Martin Fry and Mark White from the group ABC. I met them when I was hired to mix their production of Paul Rutherford's version of Chic's 'I Want Your Love', which helped soundtrack the new 'Summer of Love'. The ABC boys were deep into it. The calls of ecstasy were heard everywhere when I attended my first warehouse rave with Martin and Mark, somewhere out in the wilds of deep west London. It was my first time in a bouncy castle and first time taking an E. I remember the evening ending with cold pizza and then finally finding a black cab after walking what felt like halfway back to Soho. After that night out bonding, Martin and I went in and cut a track called 'Mythical Girl', which my old friend Jocelyn Brown provided ad-libs for, much in the style of the ones she had sung on Springsteen's 'Cover Me'. I thought we had a single.

By the autumn of 1988, I was frequently popping back and forth between London and NYC, bringing that UK rave knowledge and spirit with me back to New York, while also trying to run my Criminal and Minimal labels. I had experienced the deep spiritual sound of Fingers Inc. at rave gatherings in London and reached out to the voice of those great tracks, Robert Owens, through my friends at 4th & Broadway. He agreed to come in and created a song, 'Silly Games', over a rough track I had cut a few days earlier.

Then I somehow snagged Jimmy Somerville from Bronski Beat for a collaboration. He composed a beautiful song, 'I Believe in Love', over an atmospheric guitar-led track I'd cut at Shakedown with my old friend Angelo Petraglia from the band Face to Face. I was really excited by how both the song and album were shaping up – it felt like a classic soundtrack LP in search of a movie.

Me and Angelo Petraglia at Shakedown Sound.

Andy McClusky from Orchestral Manoeuvres in the Dark, who had just hit with the song 'If You Leave' from the movie *Pretty in Pink*, was introduced to me by A&M, and we went into the studio together in November 1988. I sculpted a track that wasn't that far away from OMD's hit, but also incorporated a bit of a reggae groove. Andy wrote a great song over it called 'Walk Away'. I got Shirley Lewis, one of the backing singers from Wham!, to come in and do ad-libs. She was part of British vocal royalty, her sister being Linda Lewis. I was super-happy with it, as was A&M.

During the recording, Andy and I had become friendly, so I met up with him in Liverpool, while on my way to Manchester. I was with my friend Mary Calderwood, the editor of the pop magazine *Smash Hits*. When I told Andy we were going to spend the night raving at the Haçienda, he was keen to come along. I called Bernard Sumner, whom I had planned to have dinner with before going on to the Haç. I told him that I was with Andy and that he wanted to join us that night.

'What are you doing with that Scouse bastard?' said Bernard, possibly jokingly.

I explained I had made a track with him. Bernard said, 'OK,' and we were on our way.

The competition between Manchester and Liverpool reminded me of the one between Boston and New York, to put it in American sports-rivalry terms. OMD had also been an early signing to Factory, with the song 'Electricity', so there was some history there. Bernard was not a fan of *Smash Hits*, after the magazine had reported on his late-night escapades with some groupies while on tour in LA, so I told Mary to keep her place of employment to herself.

Frankie Knuckles, me, Christina Visca, unknown, unknown, Junior Vasquez, Leotis Clyburn, Rosie Lopez and Bobby Shaw at Baseline, NYC, 1988.

When we got there, everything was civil. We had dinner at a posh restaurant and then some drinks, and things were loosening up. I noticed Bernard dropped some sort of pill. At one point a waiter came up to Andy, excusing himself and telling him what a fan he was of OMD, and could he have his autograph? Andy happily obliged and looked at Bernard smugly, in a 'Well, he didn't even notice you' way.

Bernard immediately shot back, 'Andy, we don't have fans that old!' Ouch.

I had written a track that I thought would be perfect for Neil Tennant. Unfortunately, he wasn't available, and I had no other ideas. I was on the phone to Sophie and mentioned where I was at with the album, and she suggested I give Étienne Daho a shot at the track, whom she had introduced me to on my first trip to Paris. So Étienne and Caroline Loeb, singer of my favourite French track 'C'est la ouate', wrote the lyrics, and Étienne did the vocals and added some production elements. It was a love letter to Paris, which I totally related to.

Then I cut a track at Shakedown called 'It's Your Time', which was written with the husband-and-wife team of Lotti Golden and Tommy

John Warren, Mac Quayle and me, from the sleeve of *Merge*, my album with the Backbeat Disciples.

Faragher. I had co-written quite a few songs with Lotti, including many of the ones on the Brenda K. Starr album, and she had sung backgrounds on 'Sun City' and numerous others. I used a cavalcade of my NYC musicians, including Skip McDonald of the Sugar Hill studio band on guitar and Jeffrey Smith of the Family Stand on sax. Shirley Lewis sang lead on it.

The label gravitated towards this track, which had a very Chicago, Inner Life/Ten City-like feel, as the album's first single. We added a female cockney rap, by UK rapper Rhythum Asyllum, in a somewhat corny attempt to catch the Neneh Cherry vibe. We filmed the video in Times Square, during the winter, driving around in an open-topped white limo. Shirley and the rapper travelled over from London, along with stylists Stephanie Lange and Sara Blunstein, two women whom I met for the first time that day and I'm still friends with today.

I decided to name the project Arthur Baker and the Backbeat Disciples, with lots of my musician buddies as the band. Looking back, it would have been more appropriate to have called them the Breakbeat Disciples, but I guess I was already shedding some of my streetwise awareness.

As for the 'Message Is Love' situation, things were now getting

Phillip Damien, Bobby Khozouri, Tiny Valentine and Cevin Fisher – the Backbeat Disciples.

somewhat desperate. My album was near to completion, and I still hadn't found a singer for the song. Although I was a UK signing, the 'Message' demo found its way to A&M's LA office and Gil Friesen, who was president of the label in the US. He also loved the song and said he would try to help. We now had the entire label, even its US president, searching for a lead singer. Who at A&M could do the song justice and hopefully make us forget about Will's lead vocal on the demo? Jeffrey Osborne was on the label, but he had just released something.

'Wait, what about Al Green?'

I'm not sure who suggested Al first; probably Gil. An opportunity to work with the Reverend would be up there with working with Dylan for me. He had just come out of pop retirement, duetting with Annie Lennox and the Eurythmics on 'Put a Little Love in Your Heart'. Was it possible?

When the M of A&M, Jerry Moss, decided to get involved, he made it happen, and I finally had my singer. Two years after laying down the demo, we had my favourite soul singer – and the perfect voice for 'The Message Is Love' – ready to rock it. Now to record with the Reverend Al Green.

AL GREEN AND ARTHUR BAKER RCA

28.

REV IT UP – ME AND AL GREEN

1989

When I received word from A&M that Al Green had agreed to sing 'The Message Is Love', I was ecstatic. I had been a massive fan of his ever since I first heard 'Let's Stay Together' in 1971. But the initial euphoria wore off when I was faced the actual reality of working with an iconic artist with a reputation for being somewhat difficult. But then he is Al fucking Green!

Although the label had agreed to front Al a chunk of money from my album's budget as an advance, I still had to get our contract signed before we could do any recording. So when I made my first trip down to Memphis to meet the great man, I had my attorney, Bob Flax, in tow. This was both for moral support and to help get the deal closed. We flew in on the first early-morning flight out of Newark and made it to Al's office right on time. It was a one-storey brick dwelling set on a grassy patch close by the Reverend's Full Gospel Tabernacle Church. We were let in by his assistant. She greeted us with Southern hospitality, apologising on behalf of Rev. Green, telling us he was running late. We sat for what seemed like an hour.

It looked like Al wouldn't be showing any time soon. I asked the assistant if I might be able to speak to him on the phone. She rang him up and handed me the phone. After some niceties, I mentioned we hadn't eaten yet, which we could do while he made his way to meet us. I asked him for a suggestion for a good spot where we could get a down-home Southern breakfast. I loved soul food (I would later open up my own soul restaurant, Harlem, in London). When he immediately answered, 'Shoney's,' in his high-pitched southern drawl, I thought he was either kidding or assumed I didn't want the real soul thang. But I absolutely wanted the real deal. Shoney's? That was a chain through the South that I had stopped at during family road trips to Florida. But he promised me that their breakfast buffet was amazing. We took his word for it, went down there, and fair play to Al, the breakfast was amazing. We ate and waited and waited. Still no Al.

We dropped back into his office, and his assistant got him on the phone again. He apologised in a husky, low voice and said he wasn't feeling well. We agreed we would leave it for now, and that I'd come back down to Memphis once he'd signed the contract that I left with his assistant. Then I asked if he knew a great BBQ place for dinner. He laughed and suggested a local spot called RJs. We stopped there on the way to the airport, and I picked up a big bag of ribs to take on the flight back to New Jersey.

When the contract was finally signed, I went back down to Memphis, and we hit the famed Ardent Studios on 2 March to record Al's vocals. He loved Ardent because they had this legendary Elvis Presley microphone, the Shure 556, which the Rev. always used. He was a passionate Elvis fan and often spoke about him in hushed tones. Al listened to the track in the studio, relaying that he knew it from the cassette I had sent him. I wasn't totally convinced, but I had him give it a go. He let loose with an emotionally charged, classic Al Green vocal on the very first take. It was great, the only problem being, it wasn't really *my* song. Yeah, he had got most of the lyrics correct, but the melody was entirely different to mine. I said to Al, 'Beautiful man, loved what you did, but could you listen to Will's vocals again, just to get the melody?'

We listened to the cassette a few times more, and he seemed to be figuring out the tune. Then he went back in. This time the melody was spot-on, but there was absolutely none of the fiery emotion of the first pass. At all. After we listened back to that second take, Al looked me in the eyes and said, 'He ain't gonna sing it no better than that!' I was a bit confused. 'He'? Did he mean Will? Then I realised he was talking about himself in the third person. Ah, OK. This was a new one for me. I instantly tried to live in Al's reality and just went for it.

'Do you think the second guy could teach the first guy the melody?'

Al seemed to like that. He went back in and killed it. Goosebumps. We took one more pass after that, and he ad-libbed his ass off. Will who? I flew back to Shakedown with four takes of Al fucking Green singing my song!

After a bunch of careful listening, I realised Al's vocal still needed a bit of work, as he had missed a few important lines here and there, and some special phrases Will had sung were missing. As luck would have it, Al was going to be in Boston in early April. I met him there, and we did an hour-long session in Century III Studio, punching in those few lines I needed and singing the chorus melody straight to reinforce the background parts. We finally had a fantastic vocal in the can!

So, after my A&R men Mike Sefton and Chris Briggs listened and offered feedback, and a few mix updates were completed, my debut solo album was finally finished and approved. A&M then got on to shooting a video for 'The Message Is Love'. It was decided that we'd send out director Martha Fiennes, sister of Hollywood actors Joseph and Ralph, and her director of photography to film people around the world waving flags adorned with the word 'Love'. *Sounds like a fun gig for them,* I remember thinking. Then me, Al and a white dove would appear in the concluding scene together. If you look at my bit with Al, I'm spinning a plastic globe on my finger like a basketball, and Al's attempting to lip-sync, but at least we look like we're having fun and the video was in keeping with the message of the song, while not being too cheesy. It did the job.

When the song was released as a pre-Christmas 1989 single, the fact that Al Green was singing lead got us some insane prime-time US TV appearances. I mean, *The Tonight Show*? Johnny Carson? Waiting in the green room in the Burbank studio before the show with Al, preparing to hit the bandstand to play tambourine with the Doc Severinsen Orchestra as Al Green sang a song I composed, is truly one of the more surreal moments of my life. Al, of course, showed no nerves. He's a true pro. He was fairly animated and chatty, joking around with not a care in the world. I, on the other hand, was sweating bullets, despite the fact that all I had to do was play tambourine. In a crowning moment in my family's life, Johnny Carson held up my album and spoke my name while introducing us. It's hard to describe how special that moment was for me, unless you also grew up watching Johnny. Some of my most memorable exposures to the world of entertainment came through him, and now here he was, introducing me. Al just

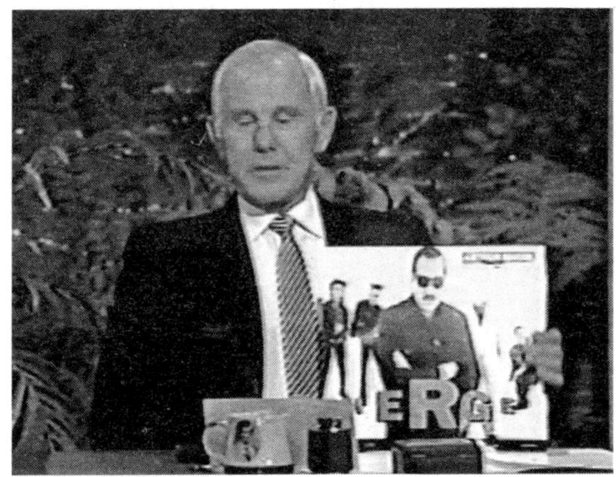

Johnny Carson holding my album on *The Tonight Show.*

nailed it, while there was a fleeting view of me rocking the tambourine. (Unbelievably, while writing this book I found the VHS my dad recorded of the show in my archive, and it's still pretty nuts to see it.) Afterwards, we departed in a limo and headed for the Mondrian hotel, and it was like someone had pulled the plug on an electric toy. Al totally collapsed and went into a dream state. I hadn't experienced that side of him at the time, but I would after future gigs.

So we had got some great exposure, but unfortunately, the song just didn't hit the way it was expected to. The new beast, MTV, was in its prime, and it didn't give us the plays we needed to make it a hit. In retrospect, if it had been marketed as an Al Green single, maybe it would have been easier to promote, because no one knew who I was, and Al was Al.

In Europe, it was a different story. The song was much more successful there, especially in Germany, where, as chance would have it, the fall of the Berlin Wall had just taken place, on 9 November. We couldn't have timed the release better, as the lyrics resonated perfectly with the times, and the sing-songy chorus hook was easily sung along to, even without knowledge of the English language. It's success meant the Al and Arthur show had to hit the road in Germany. In a surreal moment, here I was, travelling all over the newly united country, which was in a state of euphoria, with Al Green. First, we spent a few nights in Berlin, in the same hotel as David Hasselhoff. It was surrounded by hundreds of his fans, all hoping for a glance of the Hoff. We passed by the Berlin Wall quite a few times; seeing people gathered around it throughout the night, illuminated by lit garbage cans, chanting and pulling pieces of the Wall down, was something I will never forget.

The next few singles from the album didn't fare as well, so I was dropped by A&M. The fact that we had spent a lot on the album, with three videos, all the remixes and the tour support, made this understandable. But fortunately for me, I was picked up almost immediately by RCA. Their remit was to make more of a US-style dance album. Nonetheless, they had been attracted by my Al collaboration and were hoping for a repeat.

I started work on my next album, *Give in to the Rhythm*, collaborating with RCA's US team. I was writing housier stuff and decided on using singers such as Táta Vega, Darryl Pandy, who had sung on Chicago house classic 'Love Can't Turn Around', and Leee John from London group Imagination. But providing a follow-up to 'The Message Is Love' was going to be difficult. The first issue was whether I could actually get Al to do another vocal for me. But after some business wrangling (and also helping him secure a new solo record deal with RCA), he agreed to team up with me one more time. Now I just had to come up with the right song. Al was very particular about what he'd sing, as he should have been. Lyrically, it could be about love in a spiritual way, but no relationship stuff that would put his Reverend-ness in question. An uplifting political statement might work.

I had first met Greg Phillinganes at a party at Quincy Jones's house. I was already a fan of his, aware of the amazing keyboard and arrangement work he had done on some of the greatest songs ever recorded, by artists such as Michael Jackson, Stevie Wonder and Eric Clapton. His playing immediately brought funk, soul and class to anything he touched. Also, it was clear from our first meeting by Quincy's pool, when Greg shared some hilarious stories of playing with the greats, that he had a great sense of humour. We decided to keep in touch. I knew that I'd love to collaborate with him in the future, but I wanted to wait for something really special. And writing a song for Al Green was definitely something special. When I called Greg about it, he was over the moon, declaring that Al was one of his favourite singers. We scheduled a writing session for a few days later.

On the day of the session, I picked up a copy of *Rolling Stone* and came across an article on rap. KRS-One was talking about his social consciousness and crime, relating that he always told the crowd at his concerts, 'When you come to see me, leave your guns at home.' I immediately thought, *What a great song title and message*. I had really wanted to write something with a positive message, and when I saw those words, I decided that an anti-gun-violence anthem would be perfect. I thought someone needed to speak out about the mass shootings that were already an epidemic in the US. I started messing with a chorus melody and some lyrics, which were somewhat ready by the time I arrived at Greg's apartment in Burbank.

When I got there, I found he had a very basic studio, much like many of my other collaborators. But he had this one special ingredient: his amazing talent! When I sang him my chorus idea and he started to jam on it, it was pure magic. The synth-bass fills he casually played took me back to Michael Jackson and Stevie Wonder; you could hear how big a part he had had in the sound of their records. And then, when he started singing my chorus, it was delivered with so much pure soul. *Wow*, I thought, *this song already sounds like a classic*. We worked on some lyrics together, and 'Leave the Guns at Home' was pretty much written.

I continued with the recording back at Shakedown, having planned that Greg and I would meet in Memphis for a session with Al. I flew in from New Jersey and Greg came in from London (where he was working with Eric Clapton) to record his keyboards and Al's vocals at the former Hi Studios, which had been renamed Weylo Studios. Upon entering the darkened room, it was revealed to us that it had been an old theatre, with carpeted walls that deadened the sound; this was a huge part of what had made the legendary Booker T. & the M.G.s drummer Al Jackson's drum sound on his Hi recordings so unique and recognisable. We were also shown the legendary wooden box that had been used on the stomp intro on 'Love and Happiness'. This was where all the Reverend's early classics had been moulded and produced by Willie Mitchell, and as we entered the control room, there was Willie himself, sitting on a couch speaking with Al. Having Mitchell in the studio was almost more nerve-racking than working with Al, since I'd already worked with the Reverend.

Greg had flown in on his dime. He said he had to be there, being such a big Al Green fan. He had worked with all the legends, but having a song he co-wrote being recorded by the Reverend was something particularly special. When I introduced them, I could see what a big moment it was for Greg; he was like a little kid.

First, we needed to get Greg's piano and organ laid down for Al to sing to, so Greg sat respectfully at the piano and laid down a beautiful first take. Then he was brought over to the organ that had been all over all the Hi classics. He sat down to play a rocking organ part. After a few more passes, he said he had to make his way to the airport. He was worried about getting caught in an oncoming blizzard and had to get out that night, since he was on a two-day break from being Clapton's musical director during his residency at the Royal Albert Hall. But before Greg left, I wanted him to witness Al throwing down.

But when we rolled the tape to start recording (with Al on his favourite microphone, which we had borrowed from Ardent), something worrying happened: the twenty-four-track machine started to jam. The engineer, Willie Brown, looked worried. We weren't sure if it was the tape or the machine, but then Mr Mitchell jumped in and lent a hand, as most studio owners would. But this was Willie Mitchell! He actually had his hand on the tape reel, gently pushing it, making sure that the twenty-four-track reel kept turning. This time Al really knew the song, and when he sang it, both Greg and I smiled big smiles. I think he got two takes down before the machine stopped turning, and then the Reverend was gone.

I stayed over that night and ended up going to dinner with Willie. He entertained me with many old Memphis war stories. And there was one that was not so old, about the Scottish band Wet Wet Wet, who had moved to Memphis to cut an album with him. He was not greatly amused by having to entertain the Scottish lads: 'What the fuck am I gonna do with these white motherfuckers?' he asked me.

I guess he didn't consider me a 'white motherfucker', because he definitely entertained me.

I decided to hire Willie to arrange the horn parts for the track, and he got the Memphis Horns to play them. It was an amazing day in Memphis. Next stop Detroit, where I recorded the Ron Winans Family & Friends Choir at their own Selah Studios, which was total magic. The icing on the cake for the track was bringing the great Táta Vega in on ad-libs.

When the track was finally finished and mixed, we needed to shoot a video. At the time, I really liked REM's video for 'Losing My Religion', and I referenced it in our search for a 'Leave' director. I wanted something with similarly strong images. Shots of Al performing to camera were cut in. Greg came over to be in the video, in which we both appear as fleeting images: his hands are shown playing piano, and I'm standing, the two of us in silhouette.

RCA started the PR machine and got Al into New York to do a few things. We went into the studio on 10 October to record some additional city shout-outs, so that we could do personalised versions of the song for places that hadn't been mentioned on the record. A few days after that, I got a call from RCA, saying that they had been able to collaborate with Sarah and James Brady's gun-control organisation, the Center to Prevent Handgun Violence, and had organised a press conference to promote awareness of handgun violence. Al and I would go up to Harlem and meet with James Brady, the press secretary who had been paralysed during the attempted assassination of President Reagan in 1981. That the song had reached Brady was a very big thing for me. The meeting was scheduled for 11 a.m. on 17 October, so RCA made sure we got there particularly early, taking Al and me to Sylvia's soul food restaurant, just around the corner from the church. We tried to get something to eat, but before we could order, a line of women gathered, right up to our table, trying to get autographs and a word with the Rev. Many of them pulled out photos of their children and told Al respectfully that these children existed because of him. He smiled and was very kind to them, while I was trying to get my chicken and waffles. I finally got some food, and then we made our way to the Abyssinian Baptist Church. We met with Brady, who had some kind words for us and presented us with a plaque thanking us for the work we were doing in support of gun control. Al then had a few words with legendary Harlem civil rights leader Reverend Calvin Butts, before jumping into the pulpit and performing our song to an audience of schoolkids.

Then RCA scored us something perfect: *The Arsenio Hall Show*. It was planned that Al and I would fly out together from Newark Airport to LA on 19 November 1991, accompanied by one of the label's A&R men. We met up at the airport and went to check in. I had a first-class ticket that had been supplied by either the show or RCA. But Al, who was travelling with his niece, had apparently cashed in his first-class ticket for two economy seats and forgotten that fact. Or his assistant had done it and not passed on the information. The label guy tried to explain that RCA hadn't changed the ticket. Al looked at me.

'I didn't have anything to do with this, or even know about it,' I explained to the Rev. Which Al didn't believe at all. Things didn't go well from here. All he saw was that I was in first class, and he wasn't. I offered him my first-class seat and also spoke to the stewardess to try and get an upgrade for him and his niece. She said she could move them after we were in the air.

But he went off on an 'Al Green, thirty million records sold, and they put him at the back of the bus' rant, wouldn't accept the upgrade and stayed in economy throughout the flight. When we landed, he wouldn't get in the limo that was there to pick us up. There was a really bad vibe. We checked in, and the next morning, as I was getting ready to go to the sound check, I got a call from the A&R guy, who told me that Al wouldn't do the show if I was at the rehearsal. I was really pissed off and didn't go. That night I watched the show from my room, steaming. The next morning, I got a call from Al. He goes, 'Where were you last night, Artie? Why'd you miss the show?'

Me and Al in the studio in Boston.

That was Al One. The guy who didn't want me at the show was Al Two. That was how it was with Al – predictable in his unpredictability. He was also predictably unpredictable during his live performances. Sometimes he was great; sometimes he was more take-the-money-and-run. One night he was playing a gig in LA, and the audience was full of stars, from Pete Townshend to Quincy Jones. Al killed it that night. After the last song, the crowd were on their feet, yelling for more and assuming he'd come out and play another of his classics. Quincy came over to ask me where Al was, and wasn't he going to come out for an encore? I answered that 'encore' was not in Al's vocabulary, and that he was probably already halfway to his hotel. Which he was.

I had managed to get Al a great overseas deal with BMG International through a German executive named Heinz Henn, whom I had met during the success of 'Message Is Love'. He was a huge Al fan and was very excited about making a full album with him. I was brought on board to produce part of the album and executive-produce the rest. I had the idea to also bring in David Steele and Andy Cox from the Fine Young Cannibals as producers. Their work with their singer, Roland Gift (whose voice was somewhat reminiscent of Al's), on the track 'She Drives Me Crazy' had resulted in a huge hit, and I thought they had an understanding of the old Hi sound and could modernise it in that cool British way.

Al came to New York to record at Shakedown, which had relocated to Pyramid Sound's former studios, but when he showed up for the first session and saw a cat, he was immediately out of there. Al didn't do cats. Once I had the animals removed, we managed to do a few sessions there, recording some of Al's vocals for 'Love Is a Beautiful Thing', which ended up being the first single. Al was still reluctant about singing anything even close to having a sexual connotation; he'd just say, 'Al can't sing that.' Thus, 'baby' would become 'maybe', no matter how strange it would sound. He was fine with spiritual love, but definitely not the sexual kind. It was his album, and he's fucking Al Green, so it was what it was.

We also worked at Tommy Faragher and Lotti Golden's Upper West Side home studio, where we recorded the vocals for the track we co-wrote, 'Keep on Pushing Love'. The day of the session, we were all sitting around the piano, working out the song, when Al went, 'This really sounds like Al. I don't know if his publisher could agree to this, 'cause it sounds so much like Al,' adding that he should have a writer's credit and publishing. He wanted 25 per cent of the song, and we were fine giving it to him. I guess he thought it was a pastiche of his style, which, of course, it was. He started the song with an ad-lib – 'Oh, I love this . . . somebody, somebody say bless him' – in response to our negotiating. Luckily, I had hit 'record' and caught the throwaway comment. I had to keep it on the record.

The last track I cut for the album was a cover of The Temptations' 'Don't Look Back', which would become the title track. Al performed it as a duet with Curtis Stigers, an up-and-coming artist on Arista Records and a favourite of Clive Davis, the legendary head of the label. This song would give me nightmares for years.

BMG was a German company that owned RCA and Arista Records at the time. Heinz Henn was from the head office, which gave him some sort of overlord power over BMG/RCA/Arista. Or at least, that's what he thought. And since Heinz had been very involved with the making of Al's record, I think he took it very personally when there were issues with us getting the album placed on one of the BMG labels for the US. Arista had passed on the album, and it finally ended up being released in the US a few years later, after I had helped get it signed to MCA.

What was the nightmare?

Whitney Houston was trying her hand at acting, and Clive Davis at Arista was putting together the soundtrack for the movie she was starring in, *The Bodyguard*. I sent my friend, Arista A&R man Richard Sweret, Al's album. Clive got back to us, saying he loved the track 'Don't Look Back', and requested it for the *Bodyguard* soundtrack. But Heinz turned him down cold. He told me – get this – that instead of being on the *Bodyguard* soundtrack, he thought it should be the fourth single from Al's album. That one stupid decision cost Al and me millions and a share of the Grammy for album of the year, which went to the *Bodyguard* soundtrack.

I never told Al about that. Had he known, he might have killed Heinz.

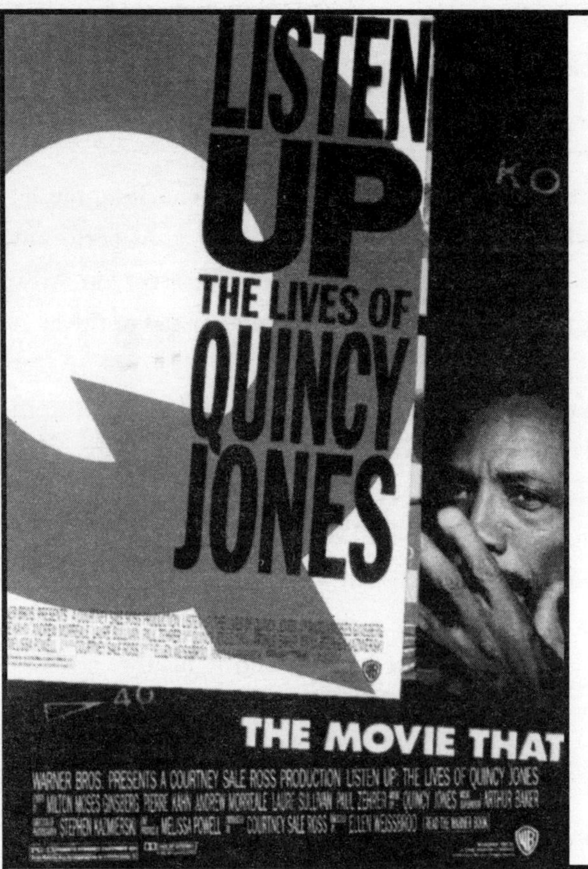
LISTEN
UP
THE LIVES OF
QUINCY
JONES
KO
40
THE MOVIE THAT
WARNER BROS. PRESENTS A COURTNEY SALE ROSS PRODUCTION LISTEN UP: THE LIVES OF QUINCY JONES
MILTON MOSES GINSBERG PIERRE KAHN ANDREW MORREALE LAURE SULLIVAN PAUL ZEHRER QUINCY JONES ARTHUR BAKER
STEPHEN KAZMIERSKI MELISSA POWELL COURTNEY SALE ROSS ELLEN WEISSBROD

29.

LIVING THE LIFE OF QUINCY JONES

1989–90

It was late July 1989, and I was back at Shakedown in New York, after being pretty much out of touch in the UK for a while. I was straightening up my office, going through my messages, when my friend Michael Ostin, vice president of A&R at Warner Records, rang me. In an aggressive, annoyed voice, he said, 'Arthur, have you been getting any calls from Courtney Ross?'

'Yeah, I got some messages here about some Quincy Jones documentary. I figured it was some guy doing a school project.'

'You *idiot*! That's Steve Ross's wife! Steven Ross, the head of Warner? You need to call her back right *NOW*. She's been chasing you for weeks to be the music supervisor on her Quincy Jones doc.'

'Fuck!'

Not a good look. I took Courtney's number from him and quickly hung up. I immediately dialled the number, and the woman who answered said, 'Ross residence.' I told her who I was, and she handed me over to Courtney. 'Courtney Ross, hello.' She made some joke along the lines of, '*Finally* . . . you actually exist!' and said something about guessing I must be pretty busy. I apologised profusely. She then asked if I could come over and see her at her apartment.

'Sure, when?'

She laughed and said, 'How 'bout now?'

After a bit of navigating, I arrived at the Rosses' apartment, a sprawling triplex mansion decked out tastefully with art and flowers. Courtney ushered me in. She was a thin, blonde beauty, a Southern cowgirl in jeans – not what I expected the wife of a New York City media tycoon to look like. She enthusiastically started describing the Quincy project to me, how important it was to her and Steve and to the world, and how Q had thought that I'd be the perfect person to organise the music for it. She made it clear how impressed he had been with my Sun City project. It had followed right on the heels of Q's 'We Are the World' record (I thought maybe it had made him wish he had been more creative and outside-the-box with his project). I was immediately seduced and sold.

'So, are you free to go to LA with us?' said Courtney.

'Sure. When?'

'How 'bout tonight?'

What? It was clear time was of the essence. I called my new girlfriend, Joanie, and quickly explained what was going on. Joanie and I had been going out for a year or so (after Tina and I had gotten divorced) and were living together. I had met her in 1988, while working on an album for MCA, where she was a vice president. It was by a British/French duo called Jet Vegas. I thought the record was pretty good, but unfortunately it died a death when it came out. Joanie was really excited by the prospect of me working with Quincy and told me I had to go. Being in the industry, she knew how important getting a gig like this was. Also, her dad, Richie Kamuca, had been a jazz musician and had worked with Quincy, so she had an extra layer of respect for the man.

Courtney got me a car, and I went home, packed my bags and headed straight back to the Rosses' place, pronto. We jumped into their limo, drove over to the heliport and got into the Warners helicopter, heading for East Hampton Airport, where the Warners private jet would be waiting for us. It was my first-ever helicopter ride. It was 25 July 1989, and my year-long journey on *Listen Up* was just starting.

When we landed at East Hampton, I noticed a woman and two guys standing by the jet. Steve had joked that a few friends were going to hitch a ride with us. I looked closer . . . it was Barbra fuckin' Streisand! Steve, gracious as always, introduced us all. One of the guys was Robert Zemeckis, director of *Back to the Future*, and the other was Barbra's son, the actor Jason Gould. We hopped on board the spacious Boeing 727, which was full of couches and had a large dining table. The seats were better than those in first class. The stewardess told us the plane had every Warners film ever made on board. Champagne was served, and there was a huge mountain of shrimp cocktail and other food set out. But once airborne there was more serious business to be dealt with: it was time for gin rummy. The teams were me and Courtney vs

Steve and Barbra. I wasn't an experienced player, but I figured it out as we went. Barbra would decide on the stakes: when she won, it was a quarter a point; when she lost, it was 10 cents a point. Who was going to argue with Barbra Streisand?

This was around the time of the Time/Warner merger, which was very big news. It had to be confirmed by the Senate, and Steve went to plead his case in front of Congress. But Barbra had a very serious question for Steve about it: 'What are you going to do about all that Warners *stationery*?'

We all laughed. Months later, Steve told me he had a truck full of old Warners stationery delivered to Barbra's storage facility in Brooklyn.

The flight was over too quickly, and we said our goodbyes to Babs and crew. I got in a car with Steve and Courtney, destined for Quincy's house in Beverly Hills. There was some traffic, so Courtney had time to tell me what I should expect while I was in LA. She wanted me to meet with Q to discuss his thoughts on the music for the doc and hang in the studio with him for a bit. I remember thinking what a cool gig this was going to be.

We arrived at Quincy's, a big ranch house with lots of long hallways. Q gave me a warm hello and complimented me on my work, especially the Sun City record. He and the Rosses had some personal business to get to, so they ducked into a Grammy- and platinum-disc-laden room and closed the door, while I headed out to the pool to chill a bit.

There was a lot of activity, people rushing everywhere. It looked like they were setting up for a big party. After about half an hour, Q and the Rosses reappeared, looking like they were preparing to leave. Quincy shook my hand and said, 'Hey, I'll see you later. You got to come back tonight. It's my girlfriend Verna's birthday, and I'm throwing her a little party.'

I said, 'Really, are you sure?'

'*Definitely*. You'll have a good time.'

We got into a BMW, and Steve kindly had me sit next to Courtney. He took the jump seat, and we headed over to the Beverly Hills Hotel.

The Rosses got out and headed to their room, saying we should meet at the bar in an hour. I was then led by the bellhop to my room. I figured they'd got me a small suite. But it was at this point that it became clear to me that nothing was going to be small and no expense would be spared when it came to the production of *Listen Up: The Lives of Quincy Jones*. The bellhop led me through a beautiful winding garden to a three-room bungalow with a fully stocked kitchen. It hit me right then that I'd scored a great gig.

We met at the bar, had more champagne, then got into the BMW and headed back to Quincy's. Verna Harrah, the birthday girl, was a film producer and the widow of William F. Harrah, the hotel and casino magnate. When we arrived, the scene was reasonably calm. I got another quick hello from Q and was then left to mingle with the early guests. I went out to the pool area and saw a guy setting up at the keyboards. We started chatting, joking about the scene that was about to happen. That was my very first meeting with Greg Phillinganes.

Guests started pouring in. At one point I was navigating through the kitchen when I saw, at the end of the hall, two very tall, older gentlemen engaged in an intense discussion. I looked closer and suddenly realised they were Gregory Peck and Jimmy Stewart! Amazed, I said to the person standing next to me, 'Did you see who that is?'

'Yeah, I know. Crazy!' he said. I turned to see that that someone was Lionel Richie!

That's how Q rolls, but for a first introduction to his world, it was pretty intense. He had a ridiculously diverse crew for Verna's birthday bash, everyone from the LA mayor Willie Brown to Tommy Lasorda, manager of the Dodgers, while the entertainment included Don Rickles doing his classic shtick of taking the piss out of Frank Sinatra! You couldn't make this shit up.

A few days later, I was at Ocean Way Studio in Hollywood, at a Quincy session for his *Back on the Block* album, which was being recorded at the same time as the doc was being shot. He was working on a cover version of the Brothers Johnson track 'I'll Be Good to You', which he originally produced in 1976. This time it would be a duet between Chaka Khan and Ray Charles.

The first thing you noticed when you entered a Quincy session was the abundance of amazing food, all laid out to make the dopest buffet you'd ever experience, like on a high-end cruise ship, complete with beautiful flower arrangements everywhere. As I entered the control room I heard loud laughing, and there were Quincy and Ray Charles, kickin' it hard. These guys had known each other since Q was fifteen and Ray not much older. I immediately felt privileged to be able to sit back and observe their history – and history in the making. They got into a heavy chat about divorce, a subject they (and I) knew something about. They were speaking specifically about Johnny Carson's recent history-making divorce. Ray started riffing on how a woman would turn your pockets inside out, and everyone cracked up. Q ended up using it as an ad-lib on 'I'll Be Good to You'.

Ray went into the booth and knocked his part out in a few great takes. It was really cool to be there for the vocals session, considering I would be doing the 12-inch dance mixes for the song. But I had no fucking idea at the time that my remix of the track would go to #1 on the *Billboard* dance chart and that I'd be working on the Quincy project for over a year!

Benny Medina was another part of the equation. I met him soon after I started on the project. He was a young A&R man at Warners and a songwriter with obvious aspirations for bigger things. He told me about a TV pilot he was developing with Quincy, which they were both very excited about. One day I was with him and Q, riding around LA on an errand. I was told we were off to pick up the rapper Fresh Prince, aka Will Smith, at an MTV outdoor event. Will was riding big at the time off his track 'Parents Just Don't Understand'. Quincy, Benny and I walked through the crowd, grabbed Will and led him back to the car. They started talking about their next destination, which was Brandon Tartikoff's house. Quincy apologised to me, explaining they were going inside to sign a contract with Tartikoff, who was the president of NBC at the time, and would be out in a few minutes. That contract was the agreement for NBC to produce the *Fresh Prince of Bel-Air* TV show, which was actually based on Benny's life story.

I stayed in the car, listening to the radio, chilling and relaxing. The few minutes turned into an hour, understandably. When they finally came out, they had a contract in their hands, and the deal was done. Quincy and Benny then asked Will where he wanted to go to eat to celebrate, and he chose . . . Fatburger! So we went over to a Fatburger drive-thru in the limo, ordered tons of stuff and rode around LA, celebrating the deal for *The Fresh Prince of Bel-Air*!

As soon as I started working on *Listen Up*, I realised the director was an odd pick to direct a movie on Quincy Jones. Ellen Weissbrod was the polar opposite of Courtney Ross: she dressed in black, with dark hair and a total downtown vibe, while Courtney was a blonde who dressed in bright colours. I still have no idea how their collaboration happened, but I can't say it was smooth. Often I ended up being put in the middle of things. From early on I was known to be Courtney's guy. She did hire me, and Ellen probably thought of me as Courtney's spy. Steve thanked me for being there to help his wife on many occasions.

The number of amazing interviews they managed to get, through the access that Courtney and Quincy had, was incredible. From his old friend Barbra Streisand to my buddy Miles Davis to Frank Sinatra to Michael Jackson, *all* the greats were interviewed and sang Quincy's praises. Not in a corny way either; it was totally sincere. They respected Q 1,000 per cent. The timescale was crazy: they had most of these interviews done before I came on board, but it was still over a year until the film was finished and released. They had four editors working on the cut full-time.

My job was to familiarise myself with Quincy's vast catalogue of film scores, along with all of his records, and to use his music to score the documentary. Initially, I thought it would be fun and easy, and doing it with today's technology *would* have been easy. But the technology of 1989 meant it wasn't so fun or easy. *Listen Up* was being edited on the old-school flatbeds, which meant the music selections would have to be transferred to tape that would also be placed on the flatbed. It was a very clumsy technique and not easy to experiment with.

I ended up spending a lot of time playing around at home with videos of scenes and cassettes of the music. Which was not fun. Then I started sampling sounds from Q's records in the studio and looping stuff up. Some of the best outcomes of my experimentation would eventually be used in the movie and my remixes. While I was working on the score, Quincy was finishing up his album at Ocean Way with the great Bruce Swedien. He was incorporating a lot of the current rappers into the title track, 'Back on the Block'. I was hanging around the studio and would show Quincy some of the loop ideas I was working on. Hearing them, he asked if I'd like to try to do some club remixes of 'I'll Be Good to You'. I happily agreed. This would be outside the scope of my work on the film and additional pressure, but I already had a few ideas in terms of where I'd take the mixes. I came up with three very different vibes: one that used the original music Quincy had produced; one a more Soul II Soul-style version; and then a house vocal and dub. The package ended up topping the *Billboard* dance chart in February 1990, which scored me loads of brownie points with Warners, Quincy and Courtney.

As the editing team closed in on a final cut of *Listen Up*, which would be screened at the Edinburgh Film Festival in August 1990, I was deep into finalising all the music cues, along with the additional task of composing a new song for the film's grand finale. I must admit, the task of composing something that would stand out among the classic Q productions and put a smile on the audience's faces was a scary proposition. It needed to be a hit. It wasn't as if we had any time either; we had to nail it quickly and in one attempt.

A diverse range of collaborators would eventually come together from both Quincy's world and my younger, 'streetier' connections. I began working on the track at Shakedown with two new discoveries of mine: a pair of unsigned, unpublished young female singers called Judy

A signed photo from Quincy Jones.

Titus and Charisma. Things got serious when Courtney's clout brought in the legendary Arif Mardin to help with writing and arranging things. Arif had cut such classics – and favourites of mine – as Aretha Franklin, the Average White Band and Hall & Oates. Quincy also introduced the great Siedah Garrett into the stew. She had been part of Michael Jackson's team and was a genius writer. Finally, Benny Medina, a man of many talents, threw down some input, nailing the bridge section. Once finished, it was a great, uplifting song that combined pop, soul, rap and gospel. Song-wise, we had it. But who was going to sing it?

It was decided that artists on Warners and a few others who had already featured on *Back on the Block* would make the most sense. I cut Big Daddy Kane during a memorable session at Shakedown. Kane rocked his rhymes and had his hype man in the booth to provide the grunts and ad-libs you hear on the record. Ice-T and Melle Mel were both recorded at Encore Studios in LA, along with Al B. Sure!, Tevin Campbell, James Ingram, El DeBarge, Siedah Garrett and Karyn White. Karyn's session was particularly memorable because she had her boyfriend in tow, Terry Lewis (of Jam and Lewis). Terry sat quietly while Karyn sang, but he was obviously a presence. Recording James Ingram was a particular high point for me. He absolutely slayed the bridge in just a few takes.

Now it was my job to travel the world to get the final few elusive vocals recorded. First up was a trip to Detroit in the July heat to record the incredible voices of The Winans in their beauty parlour/recording venue, Selah Studios. I had to hang out in my hotel, waiting for word of their availability. I didn't see much of Detroit as it had seemed pretty desolate on my ride from the airport. Also, it was so hot and humid that I just stayed in the hotel. When I finally hit the studio with the Winan family, some real magic happened. Their gospel harmonising brought the tune up another notch, and it was well worth the trip.

Then there was the holy grail, the one voice that Courtney would not take no for an answer on – Mr Ray Charles! First, I had to get the lyrics printed in Braille. Not a big deal. I then had the lyrics and a cassette shipped to a few different locations, since Ray was always on the move. After a few weeks of waiting, we heard that he was in the south of France. Courtney was on a mission and organised for the Warners jet to go to Cannes to pick him up. Meanwhile, Ellen, the director, and I flew over to Paris and booked the best recording studio in France, Studio Plus 30. We waited for Ray. And waited. Two days went by, and nothing. Then, on the third day, Ray turned up at the airport in Cannes, boarded the Warners jet and promptly disappeared. He pretty much hijacked the plane and went missing for a day! Nobody had any idea where he had gone. Finally, another day later, he arrived in Paris with an entourage of fur-coat-wearing, champagne-swigging characters right out of a Truffaut film.

I introduced myself to Ray and told him I had been at the Quincy session for 'I'll Be Good to You' in LA, had done the remix and was a huge fan. Then I handed him the lyrics (in Braille) and played him the track. But . . . Ray didn't want to sing his part.

'Naah, man, this shit's too high. Give it to some girl . . . Give it to Michael Jackson!'

Panic. I didn't even want to think about all the money Courtney had spent on getting him, Ellen and myself to the studio. She definitely wouldn't be happy if that classic Ray Charles vocal wasn't on her film's title track. I decide to plead with him.

'Ray, do you know how much cash Buck [the nickname Ray and Quincy used for Courtney] has spent getting us all here first class, with you on the Warners jet, plus the studio and five-star hotels for days? If I don't get you on the track, she'll go crazy. You know what she'll be like if I come back empty-handed . . . Really, man, just give it a shot – you'll kill it.'

Luckily, Ray knew exactly what Buck was like. He paused and thought. It looked like my approach had won him over.

'Yeah, OK, man,' he said, and his assistant led him into the booth. I ran the tape, and Ray nailed the vocal as only Ray Charles could, laying down four takes. He absolutely killed it. As he was leaving, I remembered that the woman who had done the lyrics in Braille had asked me to get Ray to sign them. So I asked. Big mistake.

'Hey, baby, signing for sighted people . . . I can't sign *nothing*!'

I immediately got it. People could put anything down for him to sign, and he wouldn't know what it was. But I had got the killer vocal.

With our title track now mixed in various versions and the final cut of the film completed, we prepared to depart for the Edinburgh Film Festival. Warners had a big profile at the festival, with *Listen Up* and the new Clint Eastwood film *White Hunter Black Heart* both premiering there. On 24 August the company threw a big dinner, and Joanie and I got seats at the head table, sharing it with Steve and Courtney, plus Quincy, Clint Eastwood and their dates. I introduced Joanie to Quincy by her full name, Joanie Kamuca, and Q responded with 'Are you Richie's kid?' When she responded shyly in the affirmative, Quincy said, 'Your dad was a beautiful dude.' After she thanked him, he added, with a smile on his face, 'Not a nice guy, a beautiful guy. When we went out together, no girls paid any attention to me!' Not sure what Joanie thought about that, but I thought it was funny.

Thanks to the pressures of the film and various other personal situations I had gotten myself into, Joanie and I weren't really getting along in Scotland. When we had another fight before the dinner, me being me I sort of panicked and proposed to her on the spot, thinking maybe she'd accept, maybe not. But she did, and we made our way to the dinner. We were sitting there happily with Quincy and Clint, when Steve got up to give a toast. It was a packed house at a Warners-sponsored affair, and everyone was listening to the big man. He started talking about someone who had stood by Courtney throughout the making of the film, and how talented he is. I was thinking that he was talking about Quincy, when he dropped the line '. . . and he's just proposed to his girlfriend tonight!' Everyone got up and toasted me and Joanie, who had obviously told Courtney straight away. Boom. I left Scotland engaged. We decided to get married that December.

I thought the film was done and my job finished after Edinburgh. Not so fast. There was another premiere scheduled for 4 October at the Apollo Theatre in New York, followed by a big gala dinner and party. The event would salute NYC's first lady, Mrs Joyce Dinkins (the wife of the city's first black mayor, David Dinkins), and Mr Quincy Jones . . . with a live show that someone would have to produce. Yep, me. With Arif Mardin.

So SIR Studios were booked, and we rehearsed a band featuring musicians such as George Duke and Wayne Shorter, and singers like James Ingram and Patti Austin. Courtney also somehow convinced Miles Davis to perform. Arif and I set up the running order. Our plan was that the show would open up with a choir that included Caiphus Semenya and Andraé Crouch. After their song, they'd part to reveal Miles and band. At least, that was the plan: he'd do his one song, and then Patti Austin and James Ingram would do theirs. We thought this was a great idea.

The night of the premiere should have been a celebration for me. Seeing and hearing my music at the Apollo should have been an amazing event, leaving me with golden memories. But I had a show to produce. While the film was screening, I was over at the tent, trying to organise things. Miles showed up and was chilling in his trailer when I approached him with our plan. He wasn't having any of it. He wanted to

Dinner Ticket

An evening of dining, dancing

and entertainment

to salute

Mrs. Joyce Dinkins

and

Quincy Jones

Thursday, October 4th

under the tent adjacent to

the Apollo Theatre

ADMIT ONE

Not transferable

Ticket must be presented at tent entrance.

(over)

Ticket for dinner after the *Listen Up* film premiere at the Apollo Theatre in NYC.

go on first, do his one song, then get the fuck out and head off into the night. I couldn't see any way of convincing him, so I just agreed to it.

I went out into the audience and spotted Arif at the front table, sipping champagne with his wife. I asked him when he was coming backstage to help out. He looked me straight in the face and said, 'Arthur, I don't do windows.' It's one of my favourite lines ever. Unfortunately, that night I did all the windows, and swept up afterwards.

Miles went on stage to great applause and started playing, pretty much with his back to the audience. He played a long song that sounded great. Then he launched into another, then another. At that point Flavor Flav from Public Enemy hopped out of the crowd to try to give Miles a hug. WTF, Flavor? Davis turned his back on him, while two huge security guards lifted Flavor by his arms up into the air, with his legs still moving as if he were trying to run away, like in a cartoon. The funniest shit ever. Miles finished his last song and left.

James Ingram and Patti Austin also sang, and there was an amazing performance of 'Back on the Block' by an all-star group of rappers and singers. But the craziest thing about this gig is that it does not exist anywhere online. The crew filmed everything during the making of the documentary, but there's literally no record of that night and the performances of 'Back on the Block' and 'Listen Up'. Very strange.

After all the work I'd put into the film, record and show, Courtney and Steve graciously paid for my honeymoon with Joanie in St Barts, after we had married at the apartment of our friends Herbie and Donna Schinderman, witnessed by a few of our close friends. The plane into the island was notoriously hardcore, and as I was still a paranoid flyer, I asked the Rosses if we could boat it in from a nearby island with a bigger airport. They agreed. They truly were a nice couple.

The film was released in October 1990 to mixed reviews. It has to be one of the most expensive documentaries ever made, but it captured interviews with some of the greatest artists ever, most of whom are no longer with us. They all spoke of a one-of-a-kind musician and person: the hugely talented, funny and generous Quincy Jones.

Another one-of-a-kind man, Steven Ross, died a little over two years after the release of the film. He was sixty-five. I attended the tribute to him at Carnegie Hall on 12 February 1993. Quincy was the musical director of the event. Sadly, while I was completing this book, the great Quincy Delight Jones passed away. I hadn't seen him in many years. I had planned to reconnect and bring him a copy of the book in person once it was published.

A Classic Hit For The Young At Heart

PAUL YOUNG

"What Becomes Of The Brokenhearted"

THE FIRST SINGLE FROM THE ORIGINAL MOTION PICTURE SOUNDTRACK

Fried Green Tomatoes

PRODUCED BY ARTHUR BAKER • CO-PRODUCED BY TOMMY FARAGHER

WRITTEN BY JAMES DEAN, PAUL RISER AND WILLIAM WEATHERSPOON

MIXED BY MICHAEL BRAUER

AS FEATURED IN THE UNIVERSAL FILM, NOW IN THEATRES

MCA.

30.

‘BUELLER? BUELLER?’

1991

A few months after my work on *Beat Street*, I received a clearance request to use 'Looking for the Perfect Beat' in a trailer for a new film starring Eddie Murphy, with an option for its use in the film itself. *Beverly Hills Cop* went on to be a massive hit worldwide, but 'Perfect Beat' didn't appear on the soundtrack. A new song called 'Axel F' by Harold Faltermeyer replaced it in the film and was a huge hit off the back of this mega-movie.

After *Beverly Hills Cop* came out, I always had my suspicions that 'Axel F' had been influenced by our track but never had any solid proof. Until five years later, when my friend Kathy Nelson invited me to Daytona Beach for a music-producer screening of a rough cut of the new Tom Cruise film *Days of Thunder* and to meet its producers, Simpson and Bruckheimer – the same team that was behind *Beverly Hills Cop*. Don Simpson, the legendary party animal of the pair, started up a conversion with me. 'Hey, Arthur, good to meet you. You produced "Perfect Beat", right? The one we used in the trailer for *Beverly Hills Cop*? Love that track. What did you think about the way we ripped it off for "Axel F"?'

I wish I could say I had something clever to say in response, other than 'Yeah, nice record,' but I figured I might still get a song in *Thunder*, so I didn't want to rock the boat.

I started a short involvement with the films of John Hughes when I was approached to complete 'Left of Centre' by Suzanne Vega, featuring Joe Jackson, for inclusion in his movie *Pretty in Pink*. Hughes had also chosen two New Order songs, 'Thieves Like Us' and 'Shellshock', for the soundtrack. The album, which was released on A&M, ended up going gold during its initial release.

After that success, John Robie and I were approached by David Anderle, head of A&R at A&M. He and Hughes wanted us to produce the soundtrack for *Ferris Bueller's Day Off*. It sounded like an amazing opportunity. The label got us tickets to fly out to LA to meet up with Hughes and start working with him. The only problem was, I *still* didn't fly. My cocaine paranoia was still raging in full effect back then, but with work offers starting to slack off a little, this was too big an opportunity to pass on. So I got some Valium from our friend Dr Hollywood, and Robie and I boarded the 747. We started drinking and playing poker. I grabbed his arm more than once as the plane bounced along. He convinced me that the turbulence was nothing. I remember winning quite a bit during our flight-long poker game. Upon landing Robie admitted to me that we had just experienced some of the worst turbulence he had ever flown through. But we made it.

We started working in a small room over at the Universal lot, discussing music ideas with Hughes. He liked the Yello track 'Oh Yeah', so we planned to do a remix of it. I spoke to Martin Fry from ABC about doing a track for the album, and a few other ideas were rolling in. Hughes spoke to us about his plans for an A&M-associated label for his soundtrack albums; the *Ferris* soundtrack would be its first release. He had a meeting scheduled with Anderle and wanted Robie and I to come with him.

We entered Anderle's large office, which was on the old A&M film lot. It was full of memorabilia and photos from his illustrious time in the business, which in his early days had seen him work with the Beach Boys, Elektra Records and The Doors. He went on to join A&M in 1970, working with such acts as Kris Kristofferson, Rita Coolidge and Delaney & Bonnie. He always seemed like a mellow, cool old hippie. He was also a painter and truly understood the artist mentality. He had very successfully taken charge of A&M's film-music department, supervising the music for *The Breakfast Club* and *Pretty in Pink*.

After some small talk, Hughes launched into the reason for this meeting: Hughes Records. He felt that his success with such films as *Sixteen Candles, Weird Science, The Breakfast Club* and *Pretty in Pink* had proved his A&R chops and that A&M Records should be grateful to do business with him. For some reason, and I never really figured it out (it may have been ego), Anderle, Mr Mellow, was totally against the idea. No discussion. This made no sense to me, but that was that. There would be no official soundtrack album released and no Baker/ Robie producing the music for *Ferris Bueller's Day Off*.

I had met Jonathan Demme through Michael Shamberg and New Order, and we had then collaborated on the 'Sun City' video. So when he started on his new film, *Something Wild*, I got a call to see if I had anything suitable for the soundtrack. Steve Van Zandt and I had cut a track with Sly & Robbie (on Dylan downtime) for Jimmy Cliff called 'You Don't Have to Cry', which slotted in nicely. Then I played Jonathan a track I had cut with Tina called 'Testimonial', which he loved and put in the film, though it didn't make the soundtrack album. He also had me mix the end-title track, 'Wild Thing' by Sister Carol.

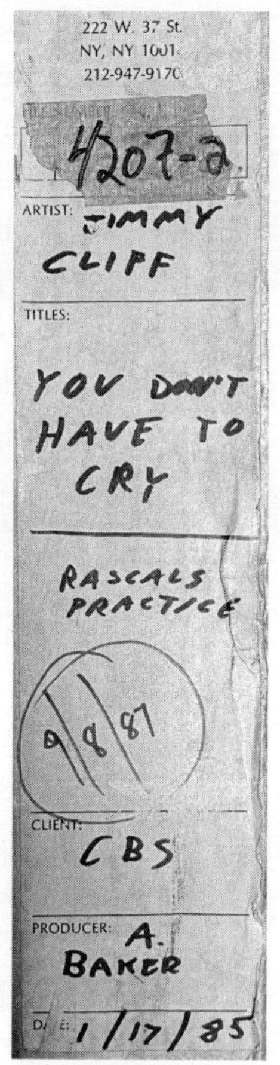

Jimmy Cliff's multitrack tape.

A screening and dinner in midtown New York was organised for the people involved with *Something Wild*. I sat and watched the movie for the first time and thought it was amazing. Both Jeff Daniels and Melanie Griffith were riveting, and the pace of the film was perfect . . . until the high-school reunion scene, which featured two full songs by The Feelies and connected the two halves of the film. I felt it just went on and on and on. It was probably ten minutes long. Then Ray Liotta entered the picture and blew us all away.

Afterwards, I approached Ed Saxon, the film's producer, with my thoughts on the section. I think he agreed, but he said, 'Why don't you mention it to Jonathan?' I didn't think it was my place, so I didn't. We then went out for dinner with the film and record-label people, and Tina and I got into one of our infamous arguments. I remember this only because Kathy Nelson, who was MCA Records' vice president for films, caught the action and mentioned it to her best friend, my wife-to-be Joanie, when we first started going out a couple of years later. Must have been a biggie for her to remember it.

Kathy ended up being very important in my career as music supervisor, hiring me to work on both *The Flintstones* and *Fried Green Tomatoes at the Whistle Stop Cafe*, my most creatively satisfying film project. To an outsider, *Fried Green Tomatoes* wouldn't have seemed like the most obvious project for me to take on – the story screamed middle-of-the-road – but Kathy convinced me that it was going to be a big film, and it had a stellar line-up of amazing actresses: Kathy Bates, Jessica Tandy, Mary Stuart Masterson, Mary-Louise Parker and Cicely Tyson.

ACT III PRODUCTIONS
1327 Ocean Boulevard
Suite D
Santa Monica, CA 90401

As of October 29, 1991

Mighty Love, Inc.
f/s/o Arthur Baker
12 E. 32nd Street
3rd Floor
New York, New York 10016

RE: "FRIED GREEN TOMATOES AT THE WHISTLE STOP CAFE"

Gentlemen:

The following shall constitute the essential terms of the agreement ("Agreement") between MIGHTY LOVE, INC. ("Lender") f/s/o ARTHUR BAKER (hereinafter sometimes referred to as "Baker") and ACT III PRODUCTIONS concerning our engagement of your services as music supervisor for our motion picture entitled "FRIED GREEN TOMATOES AT THE WHISTLE STOP CAFE" (said motion picture, together with any trailers, lead-ins, promotional announcements, commercials and previews thereof, shall be collectively referred to herein as the "Picture"), and your services in connection with the production of sound recordings (the "Masters") for possible inclusion in the Picture, and phonorecords, if any, derived therefrom ("Album"):

1. **SERVICES.**

(a) Lender hereby lends to us and we hereby engage Baker to perform for us all services customarily performed by music supervisors in the motion picture industry, including, without limitation:

(i) The supervision and coordination of all musical material to be used in the Picture and in audio-only phonorecords, if any, derived from the Picture (collectively, the "Album"), including, without limitation the background musical score, bridging, incidental music and themes (the "Score"), any original songs written for the Picture and/or the Album, any existing songs or other musical compositions licensed for use in the Picture and/or the Album, and any and all recordings of any of the foregoing (all of the foregoing songs, recordings and other musical material to be supervised by Baker hereunder shall sometimes be referred to as the "Music").

(ii) The selection and recommendation to us, for our approval, of (A) composers, songwriters, lyricists, recording artists, musical performers, music producers and other personnel for the creation, performance, production and recording of the Music; (B) existing compositions and phonorecord masters to be recorded and/or licensed for use in the soundtrack of the Picture and

My contract for *Fried Green Tomatoes at the Whistle Stop Cafe.*

She organised a trip to Atlanta so I could meet the producer, Jordan Kerner, and the director, Jon Avnet. It was during a major heatwave in the summer of 1991, and it was over a hundred degrees when I got there. Everyone seemed stressed by the heat. First, I met Jon, who was a New Yorker, Jewish and a big basketball fan. We hit it off immediately. He was a long-time production partner of Jordan's, but this was the first film he'd directed, and he had also co-written the script. He exuded that New York confidence. Still, it was a big deal for him. It was sort of a chick flick, but with a soulful Southern edge.

Jon wanted to use recognisable songs that people could lock in to and immediately connect with – maybe some classic Motown, but also gospel and rootsy blues stuff. In my mind I started to scan for artists I could reach out to who would fit the bill. Kathy could also supply some acts from MCA. The song list came together quickly, as did the artists, and I ended up making my way over to LA to cut some of the tracks, close to where the film was being edited. As always with movies, the pressure was on to get the music finished so that the editors could cut the scenes to the final tracks. I got some of my LA friends to play on the sessions: David Palmer (ex-ABC and The The, along with Rod Stewart) on drums, Gregg Sutton (Dylan, Lone Justice) on bass, Tommy Faragher (keyboardist/my long-time co-writer) on keys and arrangements, and Paul Pesco (Madonna and The System) on guitar. I also had great background vocalists, including Sly's sister, Rose Banks.

As for singers, I think I first reached out to Bono. He had written 'Silver and Gold', a great blues track, for the Sun City project, and I thought he might be up for trying his hand at a country-blues cover. He sent me a great note thanking me, but U2 were in the midst of rehearsing for their tour, so no go. I then thought of Peter Wolf from the J. Geils Band, who had schooled Bono on the blues the night before he had penned 'Silver and Gold'. He said he was in and had an idea he really wanted to try: a song called 'Rooster Blues'.

Next up was my friend Taylor Dayne. The director wanted a Motown song for a specific lip-sync scene in the film, and I asked Taylor if she'd be up for recording The Marvelettes' classic 'Danger Heartbreak Dead Ahead'. It had been a hit, but it wasn't one that had been covered to death. Taylor was better known for ballads and dance tunes, but she loved the song's vibe and nailed it, dancing in the studio as she did so.

There was a spot for a big tear-jerker, so I decided to give Paul Young a call. I loved his voice, and on top of that his cover of 'Wherever I Lay My Hat' had kept me from having a UK #1 with 'I.O.U.', so I figured he owed me! Being an old soul boy, I assumed that he knew and loved Jimmy Ruffin's 'What Becomes of the Broken Hearted', another Motown classic that hadn't been covered to death. I was right. Tommy and I laid down an 808 beat and built the song around it, giving it a much more modern vibe. Although it took us a while to nail Paul's final vocal, in the end we got there. I felt like we had our hit single.

And this time I was right. It was the first single release from the soundtrack, quickly shooting all the way up to #1 on the adult contemporary chart, while peaking at #22 on the *Billboard* pop chart. As the song climbed both charts, I pleaded with MCA president Larry Palmacci to make a video using footage from the movie, along with coverage of Paul singing. It would have been cheap, easy and a no-brainer. Unfortunately, it was never done, and 'What Becomes' was at that point the last pop top-twenty-five record without a music video!

Kathy was able to score two great new young R&B acts, Jodeci and Aaron Hall (from the group Guy), for the project. I had always wanted to recut The Association's 'Cherish' and thought that with Jodeci, we could cut both a new jack/hip-hop take and also one closer to the original MOR track. The two versions could each get their own play in the film.

I went into a small studio in New Jersey to record the two brothers from Jodeci, JoJo and K-Ci. They were among the most rockin' of the new jack vocalists, almost like a modern Sam & Dave, and they brought a youthful, soulful energy to a song that had been written way before they were born. I added some scratches and samples, and the track worked both in the film and on the dancefloor.

For me, the most enlightening and surprising experience on a record full of them was working with Aaron Hall on the gospel song 'If I Can Help Somebody'. Aaron, who was considered one of the most soulful singers of his generation, reminiscent of Stevie Wonder, sat down at the piano, played and got the song down in one take. We added some backing vocals and a few vocal corrections, and what we had was pure church ecstasy. For a full-on dose of the soulful shivers, it was up there with working with The Winans and Al Green. He also entertained us with stories of his pit bulls, as his side hustle was raising dogs.

The rest of the album consisted of some Marion Williams gospel classics and a track by Patti LaBelle, who sang 'Barbeque Bess', which was produced by Hal Willner, who was helping me out at the last minute, while I was in LA finishing the album.

We had everything done, except the end-titles track. Which was, of course, the most important track of the entire movie. I screened the final scene a couple of times, and it finally dawned on me that I had already worked on a song that would work perfectly: Bob Dylan's 'I'll Remember You', a track from *Empire Burlesque*. I found a copy and played it for Jon and Jordan, and they loved it. Now to find a singer who could do it justice.

My old friends and collaborators Michael Baker and Axel Kroell had been working with a gritty, soulful blues singer, a young white kid who had played piano in a gospel church in Hartford, Connecticut, named Grayson Hugh. I thought he had the chops to do it. I spoke to Kathy, and we got Grayson approved and rushed out to LA to cut the track. For this song I called in my friend Greg Phillinganes and drummer Steve Ferrone (who were both playing in Eric Clapton's band), with Gregg Sutton on bass and Paul Pesco on guitar. Grayson played a Hammond B3. I had two of my NYC crew, Fonzi Thornton and Tawatha Agee, on background vocals, joined by Rose Banks and Alex Brown, who provided the churchy vocal ad-libs. Grayson and I worked on the vocal arrangement, adding a catchy new background-chorus answer part, which, in my opinion, made a great Bob Dylan song even better. It was perfect for the film's end titles, and all those involved with *Fried Green Tomatoes* were very happy. I'm still very proud of the work I did on it.

A year or so later, I got a call from Bob Dylan's manager, Jeff Kramer, who told me Bob wanted to meet up. This came as a big surprise, because I hadn't heard from him in years. I was really curious. I was given an address, which I drove to in the flashy red Mazda convertible I always rented when I was in LA. When I arrived, I figured it had to be the wrong place. It was a run-down, old-school motel; old ladies in hairnets were sitting in lounge chairs by the small pool. *Strange place to be staying,* I thought.

I walked around and finally spotted an open door, and there was Bob, arranging stuff on his bed. I thought, *Why would Bob be staying here?* So I asked him. He told me it was because his house was under reconstruction. I guess that made sense; he had to stay somewhere.

After some small talk about his boxing gym (he told me that he was keeping it as a private club and wouldn't allow anyone in for fear of someone getting hurt and suing him), and Bob showing me some chords he had learnt in Brazil, he started talking about *Fried Green Tomatoes,* how much he had dug the film and what a great job I had done with his song. He loved the gospel background vocal parts we had added. Which meant so much to me. Then he asked me if I wanted to go and see Dion and the Belmonts that night. Unbelievably, looking back, I said sorry, but I already had something on. I can't even remember what the fuck that something was . . . But what could be so important that I turned down an invitation from Bob Dylan to go and watch Dion and the Belmonts?

Presented to
Arthur Baker
to recognise sales in the United Kingdom
of more than 300,000 copies of the
Parlophone
album
"Wildest Dreams"
1997

31.

'WHATEVER YOU WANT'

1993–6

On 23 February 1993 I drove out to Brooklyn from my Upper West Side apartment to meet my friends Fred Zarr and Taylor Dayne for a songwriting session. I had run into Taylor a few nights earlier, and we decided to try our hand at writing together with Fred. Fred's studio was in the basement of his family home, where I had stashed Freeez and New Order for their own songwriting sessions years earlier.

When the three of us got together that morning over coffee, I had a few basic song ideas in mind and had brought some examples to listen to. I was really taken by Seal's 1991 release 'Crazy'. It's not uncommon for writers to use existing songs as templates. A good writer can come up with something great without showing where their inspiration came from, though sometimes listeners might be able to hear it. You have to make sure not to be so close that you could get sued.

We got right into one song idea. I programmed some beats and a bass line. Fred took it from there and added some beautiful chords, but I specifically wanted the bass to just pedal through the chord changes. Then Taylor, who has a very soulful voice and can really sing, started riffing. The song started to take a U-turn from its inspiration, and everything fell magically into place, giving that one thing you look for as a songwriter: goosebumps.

We then tried a dancier thing. It had a great groove, but we were more excited by our first attempt. Taylor took the two instrumentals home and promised to get some lyrics written within a couple of days. We planned to reconvene a few days later.

The morning of our second session, I got in my car and took the same route I'd taken many times, going down the West Side, cutting under the World Trade Center and then on to Brooklyn. I would usually listen to the radio, but this time I threw on the cassette with our new tracks. It was winter and the roads were a bit icy, so it took me longer than usual. When I arrived, Fred and Taylor were outside, looking a bit shaken. I asked them what had happened.

'Didn't you hear?'

'No. What are you talking about?'

'There was a bombing of the parking garage under the World Trade Center!' Taylor responded.

'What? I just drove through there thirty minutes ago, on my way here!'

Realising I had come close to having been right in the midst of it, I sat down, a bit shaken. We went inside and watched the news reports. Six people had been killed and more than a thousand injured, and the bomb had carved out a 100-foot-wide, several-storeys-deep crater. Fuck, I was lucky.

We decided that we were all safe, so let's get to work. Taylor got on the mic and immediately blew Fred and me away as she channelled Tina Turner. Her vocals and the lyrics were stunning. The song would be perfect for Tina. After some more work on the lyrics, Taylor finished up, and then Fred and I started to mould the track further, adding arrangement embellishments and sampled guitar hits. We'd finish a rough mix at Shakedown over the following week or so. Next up was getting it to Tina Turner herself.

I had met Roger Davies, Tina's manager, through my friend Harriet Brand, who was vice president at MTV Europe. Harriet was a close friend of Tina's and had introduced her to her future husband, Erwin. She had also brought me as her plus-one to Tina's birthday party in LA the year before. I got Roger's details and sent him the tape.

We didn't hear anything for a while but were super-confident that she'd love it. But when we got the call, it was a pass. We were really surprised. The situation was, Tina had recently done a greatest hits album with a few new tracks, but we had just missed that opportunity. There were no new recordings planned. We were gutted.

I'd heard that Naomi Campbell was in the process of recording an album for CBS. I got a call from her A&R person, David Massey, asking me to come in. I brought 'Whatever You Want' with me, along with a few other tracks. When he heard it, he lit up – he thought it was a hit. 'But do you think she can sing it?' we asked. I offered to go into Unique Studios with Naomi to give it a try, to see if she could find her way around the difficult range and melody. Obviously, there was a lot of excitement among the mostly male staff, and I have to admit I was a bit nervous that I'd be put off by her beauty. I mean, c'mon . . .

When Naomi arrived, she seemed pretty chilled, though she was probably a bit anxious at having to do the vocal. We entered Unique's B room, sitting on the floor in the live room, and listened to the demo vocals. She gave it a good old college try, but it was obvious she didn't have the vocal dexterity to pull it off. We tried more of a sexy spoken technique, but I thought it really wasn't happening. But she was cool and took a quick rough mix back home with her. I called David and said I didn't think it would work with Naomi.

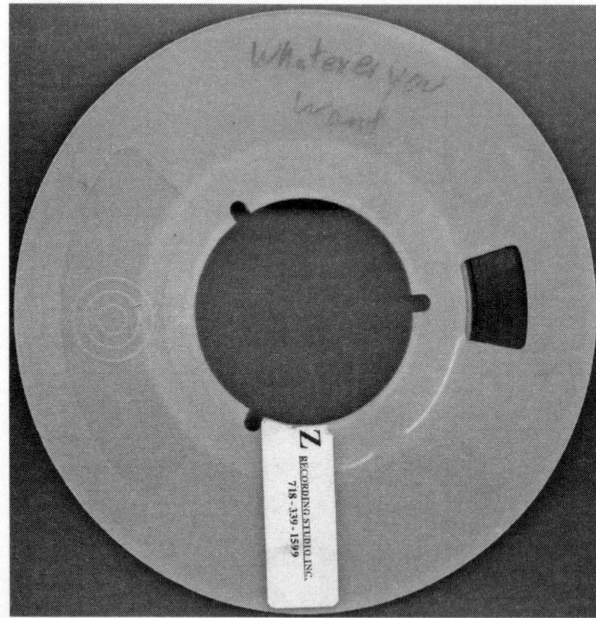

Multitrack tape of the 'Whatever You Want' demo.

The next and only time I saw her after that was in Paris during fashion week a few years later, at the legendary Queen disco. She was hanging in the VIP area with her fellow supermodels Claudia Schiffer and Elle Macpherson, while I was visiting my friend David

Stepanoff, who was the DJ there. Seeing me, she smiled and came over to say hello, and then introduced me to the other girls. It was a nice moment.

But after the Naomi session, we still had this amazing song, and no one to cut it. I heard that Sandra St. Victor was recording a solo album. She was the lead singer of the group Family Stand and had a killer voice. I was friendly with her bandmates Jeff Smith and Peter Lord, thanks to their work on Will Downing's debut album; also, Sandra had done backgrounds for me in the past. She was now signed to Elektra Records. After she heard our demo, she immediately wanted to cut it. She also asked me to produce another track, 'Love Is', which was to be the first single from her album, *Sanctuary*.

Starting from our demo template, Fred and I began to take 'Whatever You Want' further, working in my new studio, which was located in my apartment in Jersey City. We brought the track to life with some live guitars and bass. It rocked. We were all happy and excited about what we had. Only problem: Sylvia Rhone, the new president of Elektra, wasn't. Sandra got dropped from the label!

Back to the drawing board. We heard through the grapevine that Tina Turner was finally cutting an all-new album. That sounded very interesting, so I again sent the track over to Roger Davies. After a few weeks, I got a phone call. Tina was going to cut it, but with Trevor Horn!

The song was recorded at SARM West Studios in London, right around the corner from where I was living, having rented a flat on Westbourne Grove, near my new business investment, the Elbow Room. I wasn't invited to the sessions. There was really no reason why I should have been, as they had a great demo, and Trevor was one of the best producers out there. And in a bit of synchronicity, he had produced the Seal track that had first inspired me in the birth of 'Whatever', 'Crazy'.

When I finally heard their version of the song, I was blown away by Tina's performance, the sound of the record and the arrangement.

Well, the latter was pretty much the same as our demo, only with a full symphony orchestra playing our samples. It was amazing to hear, and it would be the first single from the album, so they needed some dance remixes. In a real turnaround, I was hired to do remixes for a song I had co-written! I decided to take it in a jungle/drum-and-bass direction, considering the slow tempo of the song, and did the mixing back at SARM West.

The sleeve of Tina Turner's single 'Whatever You Want'.

Next there was a video to shoot. In another coincidence, my good friend Stephanie Lang represented Stéphane Sednaoui, the director who was doing the video, so I attended the shoot as Steff's friend, not as the song's writer. The only other non-participant attendee was Stéphane's girlfriend, Kylie Minogue! We didn't really interact, but she smiled a lot and moved to the song.

The single was finally released on 23 March 1996, three years after we had started the process in Brooklyn. The record did well but wasn't the smash we had hoped for. But the most magical, mind-blowing moment was yet to come. I was invited by Tina's management to see her perform live at Radio City Music Hall on 30 July 1997, over a year after the song's release. I went with my Irish friend, singer-songwriter Simon Carmody, whom I was working with at the time. I had no expectations. The lights dimmed, and the first sounds I heard were those of the intro to 'Whatever You Want'! Then the orchestra joined in. There was literally a five-minute intro, before Tina appeared on stage to thunderous applause and started singing our song.

It was one of the most memorable moments of my entire career.

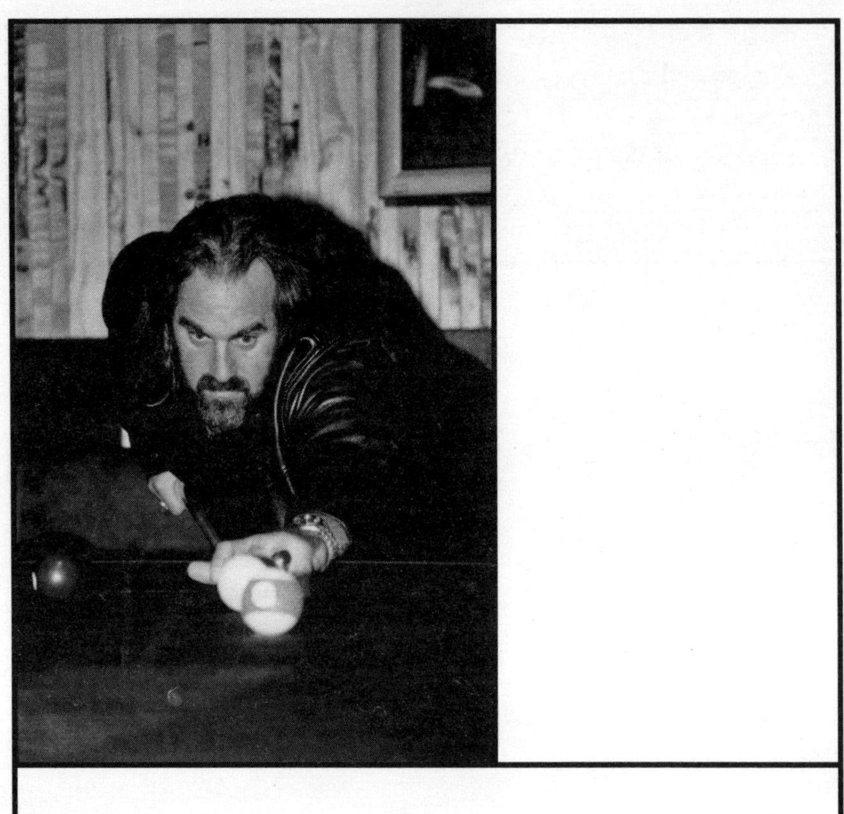

32.

GO WEST

1991–5

Looking back at the random paths that connect us can, ultimately, be surprising. How people find their ways into each other's lives is often unpredictable. The path to my involvement with the Elbow Room, and the friendships that were spawned there, leads back to one song. Not one of mine, by the way.

I was blown away the first time I heard 'Where Love Lives' by a new British singer named Alison Limerick. It was playing at the Sound Factory Bar in NYC, and I got its details from Frankie Knuckles, who had done the mix. I called my friend Mike Sefton, after noticing that the company he worked for, BMG, had a publishing credit on it. I thought the song, the message and the arrangement encapsulated something so strong. I was really interested in meeting the writer, not the singer. Mike mentioned that it was a Swedish producer/writer who was living in London, Lars 'Lati' Kronlund.

Lati was living close to Elephant and Castle, so I went to his flat and met him and his young girlfriend, N'daye, who was Swedish-African and a fledgling actress. They both spoke great English, Lati being a fan of NYC and the music originating there. He told me he was planning a move to Brooklyn shortly, at pretty much the same time as I was preparing to move to London.

Before that, though, we started hanging out. I connected with two of his good friends, Daniel 'Papa Dee' Wahlgren, a Swedish rapper, and their Irish friend Paul Daly, a designer and furniture-maker. He was from Dublin and was mates with the U2 crew, as was I. He had done some design work for the band's tour set-up. Before too long, we were all getting stoned and hitting Portobello and the Notting Hill Carnival. Lati and I started working on music together, to the extent that we co-wrote and produced Alison's next track, 'Come Back (for Real Love)', in 1991.

But Lati had made his mind up. He'd decided that New York was where he had to live, so he left N'daye and his flat and moved over to Brooklyn. By this point I was living two lives: my married life in New Jersey, where I had a beautiful new studio in Jersey City, and a whole other life in London, where things were starting to get real exciting, musically. I had plenty of projects to keep me busy, and for those I had to be where my studio was. I was working on a new Al Green album, the one I had signed a deal with BMG Germany to produce. I also had my new solo album, which I decided to put out under the name of Nation of Abel.

Lati Kronlund and me in my Jersey City loft, 1992.

I included Lati in all my musical undertakings, including a 12-inch we put together early in our collaboration. My friend Johnny Dynell hosted a weekly party night called Jackie 60 every Tuesday in the Meatpacking District. It was the most outrageous night out in NYC, offering gay, fetishist, straight, transvestite and poetic clubgoers a twisted variety show that included voguers and beautiful dancers of all persuasions. Everyone from the fashion and art worlds would attend. I remember often being jammed in the DJ booth and smoking joints with such luminaries as Alba Clemente, Debbie Harry and Marc Jacobs.

The two duelling MCs, Richard Move and Paul Alexander, would rule the room, speaking over Johnny's amazing music mix. They'd call out and introduce guests they'd spotted in the audience (there was no hiding in Jackie!) and were outrageously funny. I felt we should make a record to commemorate this moment in NYC's nightlife, so Lati, Johnny and I went in and threw a track together that was a bit reminiscent of Van McCoy's 'The Hustle', naming it 'The Jackie Hustle'. There was a hooky vocal sample I snagged from my archives that exclaimed, 'House, getting heavy on my head', so we incorporated that into the track.

I brought Richard and Paul over to the studio and let them 'speak' away. Paul Shapiro, a talented horn player whom we had just met, came in and blew some great sax and flute overdubs, and Johnny did a few mixes. I also let a DJ I had recently met try his hand at a couple of mixes – Danny Tenaglia. The results captured the unique Jackie 60 club vibe to a T and scored us a deal in the UK with Arista. We called the act Jackie 60 Presents the Jackie MCs. A UK tour proved influential, introducing NYC underground gay culture to Britain. I particularly remember one gig in Nottingham, where we had two up-and-coming opening acts: Jon Pleased Wimmin and Sasha. I pretty much played tour manager and just enjoyed proceedings from a distance.

Most of my collaborations with Lati in the States were in my Jersey City home studio, which housed all the equipment from Shakedown. My spectacularly designed, three-level loft had both a pool table and a regulation-size basketball hoop. (I regret having sold it during my eventual divorce from Joanie.) One night, while Lati and I were hanging out, getting stoned in the studio after a guitar overdub session had been cancelled, I threw on a track I had started with Maceo Parker a few years earlier that I had sitting in the can. This was just as the new acid-jazz scene that was percolating in London was making its way over to NYC via the Giant Step/Groove Collective parties. I figured I might be sitting on some gold with my Maceo solos, and that Lati's funky new jazz grooves might make a perfect bed for them. We started experimenting, throwing in some loops and samples, and were both very excited by the results. When we decided to take the project further, we went all in, cutting an album and creating a band.

I had released a few underground club cuts on Minimal Records as the Brooklyn Funk Essentials and had then let Victor Simonelli and Lenny Dee make some tracks under that moniker. But I figured Lati's and my new jazz-funk tracks fit the name much better, so I basically took it back for our project.

Also, a year or so earlier I had recorded a house remake of Pharoah Sanders's 'The Creator Has a Master Plan', a long-time favourite of mine. I figured it would be perfect for the Brooklyn Funk Essentials, so threw that idea in the pot. We recut it in more of a reggae/dancehall stylee, with Papa Dee on vocals. It sounded fairly commercial to us. We ended up signing the project to a new British label, Dorado, which was owned by Ollie Buckwell. Its offices were right in the middle of Soho, and the label had a great energy around it, putting out an eclectic brand of cutting-edge music, with a strong acid-jazz slant. Ollie had hired a young A&R man named Ross Allen, who was well into what we were doing. When I decided to relocate my Minimal label to London, I eventually locked in a distribution deal through Dorado, and Ross became my label manager/A&R man.

When 'The Creator' was finally released in 1994, it was a hit, making the pop charts all over Europe. With a second single, 'Big Apple Boogaloo', scheduled, Lati finally decided to put a NYC-based live band together and start gigging. Me and my bank account elected to get back into the remix business, and my manager, Stephen Budd, actively started looking for gigs. With my new production, 'Love Is a Beautiful Thing' with Al Green, getting great reviews, he was able to get me some decent remixes.

I was hired by Wet Wet Wet to do housy remixes of a few of their tracks. The band, who were produced by my friends Axel Kroell and Michael Baker, were successful in the UK but pretty much unknown in the States (I remembered the story Willie Mitchell had relayed to me re their Memphis sessions). I was happy with the outcome, and my mix of 'I Can Give You Everything (Soul Mix)' was scheduled to be a single. But at the last minute it ended up as the B-side of a song the group had just recorded for a new British film. The movie was *Notting Hill*, and the track was 'Love Is All Around', which ended up going to #1 in the UK chart and staying there for fifteen weeks. It went triple platinum in the UK, selling over two million copies.

So, for me, it was London where things were really heating up. There was the Atlantic, a new art deco bar/restaurant/club in Soho, which became *the* major hangout spot for the music industry. It was upscale and grown-up, located in the beautiful basement of a stately old hotel. Oliver Peyton, the proprietor, had stripped the place down and uncovered beautiful wooden walls and amazing marble floors. It was like going back in time. The Atlantic also had Dick's Bar, a cocktail bar helmed by Dick Bradsell, who was coincidentally an old friend of my engineer, Jay Burnett, who had also moved over to London. The line-up of DJs there included the Boilerhouse Boys and Tommy D.

Soho's Chinatown was great for really late-night eating. It was during one such meal at my favourite spot, the Lido (the late Steve Walsh had introduced it to me), that I happened to meet the chap who ended up being the lead singer on my next solo project. He was a Canadian named Romel Henry, who was a model and looked like a star. He also claimed he could sing, but I'd find out soon enough. He was sitting with Duggie Fields, a legendary British pop artist, and an intriguing woman named Ali Zapak, who was an aspiring singer.

Around this time I scored a gig through Kathy Nelson to produce some songs for the new *Flintstones* soundtrack. She wanted hip UK acts, so that's where she wanted me to be – in London. The timing was perfect: I felt I *had* to be in London – and my hotel was paid for! I got three cutting-edge acts involved in the project: the Stereo MC's, Big Audio Dynamite and Us3 featuring Def Jef. Lots of fun was had hanging with the bands and making their tracks. Getting to record with Mick Jones, of The Clash and Big Audio Dynamite, was a dream come true. I had been a major Clash fan, and BAD's 'The Globe' had been a favourite of mine. We cut two tracks, one for the soundtrack and one for the BAD album. Through Mick I was exposed to the bagel bars of East London's Brick Lane, which catered for our stoned-out late-night sessions. Not far from Brick Lane, in Hoxton Square, was a new club called the Blue Note, where the Acid Jazz label had started their own great weekly night. Lati's friend Paul Daly happened to have his design studio in the same square. We'd become good friends in Lati's absence and would often hit the Blue Note. Paul approached me about a new business venture that he was getting involved with: an American-style pool hall called the Elbow Room. I was intrigued. After meeting Justin Carter, the man behind the concept, and the other investors, I decided to take up the offer and become a partner. But opening the Elbow Room would take a while.

During the *Flintstones* project, I was staying at a hip boutique hotel, the Gore, in Knightsbridge (on MCA's dime). It was close to where the Elbow Room was planned in Notting Hill. Since I was booked in for a month, they had upgraded me to a duplex suite, so of course I had to throw a party there celebrating the completion of the soundtrack. Earlier in my stay, Snoop Dogg had had a suite party that had been broken up by the police, so I had been warned to keep the noise down. But how you gonna tell punk-rockers to be quiet? With BAD, the Stereos, members of ABC, Romel and various other funkers and rappers in the house, you just know the police made a return appearance.

I had tried to get Massive Attack for the *Flintstones* soundtrack, which didn't happen. But I did meet up with one of the group's members, Mushroom, through my part-time PA, Sara Dunn. I took a trip to Bristol to hang with Mush, who'd decided to call me Art. Now pretty much no one ever calls me Art, because I actually hate it. I dislike Artie too; only two people have called me that – Al Green and my late friend Owen. But Mushroom was like that. We went into his home studio, and he showed me the most amazing EQ I have ever – and I do mean *ever* – heard. An engineer friend of his (a proper engineer, not a music engineer) had developed an EQ that could pinpoint frequencies and notch them up like crazy. Mushroom took a drum loop we had sampled (don't ask me what or where it was from) and found a frequency that when pimped sounded like the most booming 808 I'd ever heard. We made a beat and added a hi-hat drum loop and a string/piano bit, and that was it.

I don't remember the specifics (must have been all the weed we smoked), but I eventually got our instrumental over to Billie Ray

Martin, the singer from Electribe 101. She wrote a killer song over it called 'Still Waters'. Mush and I didn't have much to do with the rest of the record-making process, but I did visit Billie at SARM West when she was mixing it. During a break, we had dinner, and I gave her a bit of engineering advice, which I don't think she took. In any case, it's still a favourite track of mine. (I actually recycled the song on my Nation of Abel album as a duet between Romel and Billie. Bad idea.)

Around the same time I was also approached by New Order, through their new manager, Rebecca Boulton. She asked me if was interested in remixing the track '1963' for a single and also finishing up 'Let's Go', which we had worked on years earlier for the *Salvation!* soundtrack. I had always loved '1963' and really wanted 'Let's Go' to get a release, and we'd have a proper budget, since the group was now with London Records, after the demise of Factory. So I was in.

I planned to go to Manchester to do overdubs with both Hooky and Barney and attend a party for the release of *The Best of New Order* compilation. Barney asked me to meet him at Johnny Marr's home studio to cut some new guitar parts and maybe some vocals. I took the train up from London, and it was good to get back to Manchester. Johnny's place was amazing, and he gave me a tour of his ridiculous collection of guitars. Which should have been impressive, but I have to admit I wasn't the right guy to really appreciate what he had there.

We were finally getting some work done. Barney and I completed the lyrics for the 'Let's Go' instrumental that we had started seven years earlier, plus some more guitar parts. When we were finishing up, I asked the guys if they were going to make it to the release party that night. Barney wasn't really interested in going, or at least that's what he said. But during our recording session he had been teasing me about the fact that I was abstaining from doing any of the lines that he was laying out. So I figured . . . well, I took the bait, basically. 'Hey, if you come to the party, I'll do a couple of lines with you!' I told Barney. I think that piqued his interest. I hadn't done any cocaine since the last time I had been in the studio with New Order, and that had been seven years ago. But I had made a pledge to him and stupidly didn't really think much about it.

That night I anxiously made it to the party before Barney. I spotted Hooky as I entered and somewhat excitedly asked if he had any charlie. He sort of did a double take, but handed me a full baggy, and off I went. Hit the loo and went for it. Not a good move. There's a reason people overdose after having been off drugs for ages. I did the amount I used to do when I was doing tons. Which was way too much.

My heart was pounding by the time Barney got there. He immediately said, 'Don't worry, you don't have to do a line.'

I gulped and said, 'Mmm, bit too late.' I think he felt somewhat bad about it, but we went on from there, drinking and partying like it was 1986.

Next day I woke up, and I was taken right back to the morning after the last time I'd done cocaine – totally fucked and wanting more. I knew right away it was a stupid, risky thing I had done. Also, I was meant to be in the studio with Hooky that morning. The only upside was that he'd gotten as high as I had the night before and would understand.

When I got to the studio, I was a mess, as was he. He told me that he and his wife Caroline would be in NYC in a few weeks, so we could record over there. I felt panicked and alone. I had taken this major risk after being clean for seven years, without really thinking it through at all. I decided to call Ali, the girl I had been seeing in London. We were having issues, and I knew the relationship wasn't going to last, but thankfully she hopped on a train when I asked her to come over and helped me not do cocaine that next day and night.

I haven't done any since.

I met up with Hooky a month or so later in NYC. He was with Caroline, and when I popped in to see my accountant for a few minutes, I left them getting a cocktail at the nearby Charley O's pub. By the time I made it back they were really going at it, two Mancs yelling at each other in Manhattan. Luckily, they didn't get arrested!

I felt like I'd never get the overdubs for the track done. But the next time I was back in London we made it into Mayfair Studios in Primrose Hill and got Hooky's bass parts down. I finally mixed both tracks back in Jersey City at the end of the year. (I used the fee I collected for the two remixes as my deposit on a condo at the South Bay Club in Miami.) The '1963'/'Let's Go (Nothing for Me)' single ushered in the new year, finally being released on 9 January 1995 and peaking at #21 on the UK pop chart.

I worked on the final mixes of my Nation of Abel project in Jersey City with Tchad Blake. Tchad had also engineered many mixes of my tracks on the Al Green album. He had originally come to my attention through his great work with Soul Coughing, whom I had seen live at Wetlands, in NYC, and for whom I had remixed their track 'Down to This'.

I was also writing quite a few songs with another new discovery, a British blue-eyed soul singer named Conner Reeves. We had taken a songwriting road trip from NYC to Miami and had come back with a slew of new songs, some of which ended up on my album. One of them, which we completed with my friend Axel Kroell, was called 'If You Only Let Me In'. It somehow found its way to a character named Denis Ingoldsby, a hot manager/producer who was working with the hit British girl group Eternal. Denis wanted the song for his new act, MN8, who were just coming off a #2 UK hit. We gave it up, and it was released in April 1995, peaking at #6. Conner and I were very optimistic after this, considering we thought we had written some much better songs for my Nation of Abel album.

It was an exciting time for me. We launched the first Elbow Room in Notting Hill in 1995. I more or less lived next door, renting a flat at 130 Westbourne Grove, while the Elbow Room was at number 103. Paul Daly handled the design, and I developed the music policy. My notoriety in the music business helped us get press, and I often acted as the Elbow Room spokesman. It opened around the same time as the first Soho House was launched, so it was really part of the new generation of cool bars and restaurants with American flair.

We had a fantastic, sloppy, West London opening throwdown. Barney and Johnny Marr showed up, along with local legends such as DJ Nicky Holloway, Finley Quaye, Blur's Alex James and Damon Albarn and Ash bassist Mark Hamilton, plus US stars like Snoop Dogg, all of whom immediately became customers. Customers dug the burgers, the pool and the cocktails. It became one of the prime Notting Hill hangouts of the day, limited only by size and legal opening hours.

Around this time I also put out a track with Ali Zapak, whom I was now in a relationship with. She was a unique talent and had attracted attention from Flavour Management. She had a meeting with Carl Flavour and his business partner Meg Mathews in Notting Hill, so I went over to their office to pick her up. When I got there, there was a quiet young guy sitting in the waiting room along with me. When Ali came out with Meg, I was introduced to the guy: Noel, from the new band Oasis.

I ended up connecting with Tim and Chris Abbott, two brothers who were working with Oasis and had offices out in East London, in Shoreditch. Tim was a marketing genius and would become managing director of Creation Records, whereas Chris was a music guy and loved his techno. They were fans of my music, and we ended up becoming friends. When they realised that I had rid myself of my drug issues, they decided they had a bit of a favour they needed from me.

They wanted me to talk to Robbie Williams.

'About what?' I asked.

Robbie had been part of the biggest boyband in UK history, Take That. But he had recently quit the group and taken up with Oasis, and being the good adopted Manc lad that he was (Robbie was originally from Stoke-on-Trent, but Take That were a Manchester band), had been getting wankered with them at the Glastonbury Festival. I think the Abbotts were thinking of managing the lad and thought that he needed a pep talk from me.

'Sure,' I said.

So Robbie, who had been hanging out in the Abbotts' offices, popped in, and they did the introductions. Robbie and I both lived in Notting Hill, so I offered him a ride home. We chatted about Manchester, New Order, Pulp (he was friends with Ant Genn, who worked with Pulp, and whom I knew a bit). I spoke of living in London, my hard-partying NYC days, and how I eventually stopped my wicked ways. I didn't come down hard on him at all. I actually thought he should have fun. Just that he shouldn't OD!

When Robbie eventually got his huge solo record deal, his first single was a cover of George Michael's 'Freedom! '90'. My old friend (and ex-A&R man) Chris Briggs, now fully sober, hired me to remix the single. I killed it. This gave my manager, Stephen Budd, some additional ammo to get me working, just as Britpop was running rampant across the UK. He always seemed to come up with random remix gigs with rockish acts who wanted to get a bit dancey.

One was a new act from the Midlands called Babylon Zoo, who were releasing a single. They were pretty off the grid, but Clive Black

Silver record for Robbie Williams's 'Freedom'.

was their A&R guy, so we knew that he'd make sure the song got some attention. The track was down-tempo, and time-stretching wasn't really a thing yet, but I thought the Bristol and drum-and-bass vibes might work.

I had discovered jungle/drum and bass during nights out at Speed, in London's Milk Bar, with Roni Size, and through Metalheadz with Goldie at the Blue Note. I loved the spatial sounds, the booming bass, and beats that were very reminiscent of the early electro I had been a part of. So I went in to work on the track with my keyboard programmer/ex-Backbeat Disciple Mac Quayle. He did some very trippy programming and added a bass line in the Bristol vein. I messed with the vocals and finished the remix.

I turned it in, got paid and then . . . nothing. It was like it didn't exist, until it was finally released and became the fastest-selling UK single of all time. I wasn't even in London when 'Spaceman' busted out in January 1996!

Jas Mann of Babylon Zoo and me at the mixing desk in a control room at ABS Recording Studios, New Jersey, 16 April 1996.

Clive had swapped labels and taken the Jas Mann/Babylon Zoo track with him. The song had got some radio play and had been sped up by the DJ, which was fine with me. I had tried it but hadn't bothered to do it on my final mix. Then it was used on a Levi's Christmas ad. Boom. Mr Budd had for some reason got me points for this particular remix. So, ka-ching!

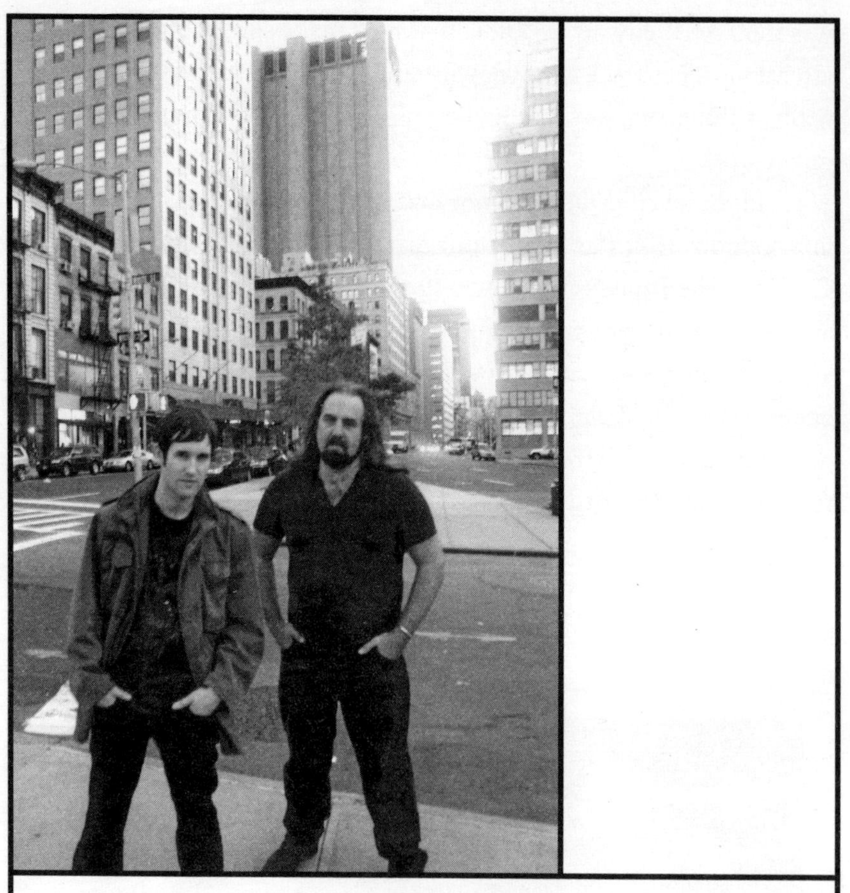

33.

TWISTED TENDERNESS

1998–9

The music scene seemed to be moving Camden way, so around this time I switched hills, leaving Notting Hill and moving to Primrose Hill. Stephen Budd's office was there, along with Creation Records, Mayfair Studios, Primal Scream's studios and my friends Neneh Cherry and Cameron McVey's mews house. This was the heyday of Britpop, of Blur vs Oasis. And lots of the action was going on in my new 'hood. The Primals' studio was like a clubhouse, and I'd hang with Bobby and Mani, Innes and Duffy, smoking spliffs and entertaining them with my 1980s NYC stories.

Noel and Meg lived around the corner in Belsize Park, in their house Supernova Heights, and I'd occasionally make it over for their infamous all-night parties, along with various Primrose Hillbillies, the Abbotts and the McGees. People were always a bit surprised when I passed the plate without partaking. Thing was, I was never even tempted after that last Haçienda party.

I had first worked at Mayfair Studios while doing additional production for my remix of New Order's '1963'. I remember sitting with Barney during an England vs Argentina football game, and him going on about the Argies. I guess it had something to do with the Falklands War. The studios were on the other side of the mews from my small one-bedroom, first-floor flat, which was next to a Baptist church (whose singers would wake me up on Sundays) and across the road from Neneh and Cam's.

In Primrose Hill, you might bump into Robert Plant or actors like Sadie Frost and Jude Law in the pub. And there was that beautiful hill, from which you could see the whole of London. I spent time hanging with photographer Jamie Morgan, It-girl Tara Palmer-Tomkinson and journalist Sean O'Hagan, drinking coffee, commiserating about our love lives and eating at the local Russian tea room.

I was now involved with a new film project, *Human Traffic*, investing a fairly large sum to help finish it. It sought to be the first movie to really capture rave/dance culture, and it also brought a good sense of humour to the scene. I thought it had big potential. I was originally

Poster for *Human Traffic*.

brought in to be the music supervisor, but when the project was pitched to Pete Tong at London Records, he insisted on taking that role as part of the deal. Pete and I had known each other since the 1980s, way before he became a club and BBC radio DJ, thanks to me bringing my Streetwise releases to London, so I didn't make a big issue out of it. I was more interested in ensuring the film was completed and getting my cash back, to be honest, and when a deal with Harvey Weinstein's

Miramax was signed, I actually doubled my investment (since I put the last money in, I got the first money out).

Still, the Elbow Room was my main focus. We opened up number two in Swiss Cottage, which was down the road from my flat. It was in an odd-shaped venue spread over three floors and ended up having too many staff and too few pool tables to turn a good profit. So I would make my way back to the first Elbow Room in Notting Hill for food, pool and drinks.

London nightlife was starting to explode, with the new hot spot being the Met Bar, in the Metropolitan Hotel by Hyde Park. It quickly became the Britpop place to be and acted as the *Top of the Pops* after-party joint. I'd regularly head there after the Elbow Room shut.

Our next Elbow move was out of London, when we opened a twelve-table venue in Leeds in early 1998. Leeds was on the up, with even a Harvey Nichols opening there. I also had a good friend who was considered to be pretty much the mayor of Leeds clubland: Dave Beer from Back to Basics. I suggested we hire him to manage the Elbow Room's nightlife and music bookings. He brought in many weekly club nights, the most successful being the Utah Saints' award-winning Sugarbeat, at which most of the major British-based DJs of the time, from DJ Zinc to Zane Lowe to Krafty Kuts, performed. I would finally play there in 2003, bringing my Return to New York party, with 2 Many DJs and I hitting the decks.

Around this time I was approached by Barney Sumner and Johnny Marr to see if I was interested in co-producing the next Electronic album. Johnny later told Tim Wheeler from Ash that Barney had loved their single 'A Life Less Ordinary' (which I had produced) and had played it obsessively for him. I had cut the track under the ultimate pressure of it being the lead single for the film of the same name, which would be released within a month. Ash had attempted to record it a few times, but without success. I met with the band in Dublin, right after their triumphant gig opening for U2 on the night of Princess Diana's car accident. We rushed to Rockfield Studios in

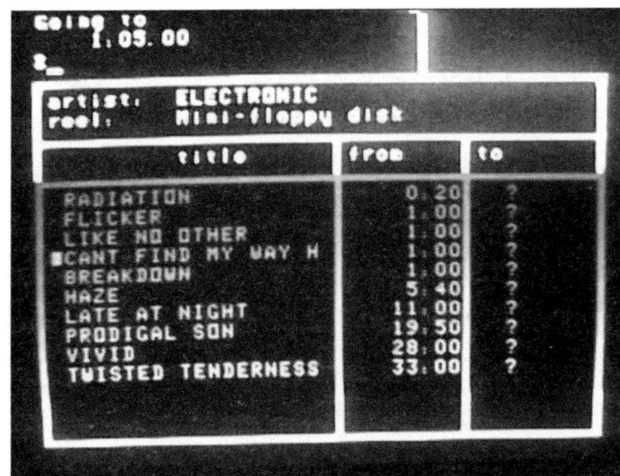

artist: ELECTRONIC
reel: Mini-floppy disk
title
from
to
RADIATION 0:20 ?
FLICKER 1:00 ?
LIKE NO OTHER 1:00 ?
CANT FIND MY WAY H 1:00 ?
BREAKDOWN 1:00 ?
HAZE 5:40 ?
LATE AT NIGHT 11:00 ?
PRODIGAL SON 19:50 ?
VIVID 28:00 ?
TWISTED TENDERNESS 33:00 ?

The *Twisted Tenderness* album on the computer screen.

Wales to record the track and had completed it by the day of Diana's funeral.

So I guess the song must have been what had piqued my old friends' interest in working with me again. I was excited by the prospect, so I went up to Manchester to discuss it with them. I took my friend/keyboardist Mac Quayle, who had worked with me on the Babylon Zoo remix and was anxious to get involved with the record.

Johnny and Barney got on well with Mac, and it was agreed that he'd be involved. On the train back, we were about to pull into Euston when an exotic girl appeared by the glass door, looking strangely at us. She started to turn away but accidentally triggered the door, so she decided to come towards us. She started a conversation, saying that we had met at the *Top of the Pops* Christmas party a year ago. I'd definitely been there, I told her. But I said (and this wasn't a line) that if we had met, 'I definitely would have remembered you.' Then it dawned on me. 'Did you have a different hair colour?' She admitted she had been blonde at the time. That was it. I had been with my now ex-girlfriend Ali at the party. We had had a fight, and I had taken her home. Then I went back to the party, sort of hoping to find the nice blonde I had spoken to. She had been an occasional presenter on *TOTP*.

We exchanged details on the train, as she was about to leave for the Christmas holidays, and agreed to meet up next year. Mac was impressed.

In January we met up. Her name was Bertje, but she went by the nickname of Bear. She was a Dutch TV presenter and was really into indie rock music, introducing me to some of her current faves, bands like Royal Trux and Tindersticks. I would go to gigs with her and her friends.

With Johnny and Barney deciding to commence recording in early April, I began to prepare and brainstorm. As I was somewhat immersed in this new indie sound, I decided that it might be an interesting idea to bring in a few of these young bands I had recently discovered. They had been influenced by Johnny's and Barney's music, so why not have them jam together? I thought it might give the record a more cutting-edge, fresh vibe.

There were two new acts who I thought would be perfect for the project. One was Fridge. They were a young London three-piece, led by a kid named Kieran Hebden. I had first heard them on XFM. I found out that they had an album on Trevor Jackson's Output label. I called Trev, he called Kieran, and it was all arranged.

The other band were Bear's favourite rockers, a strange, mostly instrumental Scottish band called Mogwai. I met them after a gig and spoke with their manager, a young Scot named Colin Hardie, who was excited by the idea. I was convinced that their energy might bring out something fresh from Electronic.

We booked into RAK Studios in St John's Wood, only a ten-minute walk from my flat. They were situated in an old school and were owned by the legendary producer Mickie Most, who had produced acts such as Donovan, the Jeff Beck Group, Suzi Quatro and Hot Chocolate. Many classic rock'n'roll acts had used them and all swore by their greatness. Occasionally, ol' Mickie would walk the halls.

We all set up in the live room and started jamming awkwardly. I remember some rocking grooves happening. I wish I still had those jam tapes, because I'm sure there are some gems that we didn't take full advantage of. I think working with the young musicians provided Johnny and Barney with a bit of energy, though they fell back into their more comfortable writing approach fairly quickly. But obviously the guys from Mogwai and Fridge ended up with memories that will last a lifetime. Kieran recently mentioned to me what a buzz it had been for him, that it was his first time in a proper studio. He remembers meeting Mickie and how chilled the guys all were. The plus for me was that I started collaborating with Kieran and guitarist Stuart Braithwaite of Mogwai on my own solo record project, and we are friends to this day.

Bernard Sumner at the Real World *Twisted Tenderness* sessions.

Early in our RAK stay we bumped into Chrissie Hynde in the studios' dining room. Johnny had somewhat famously walked out on a Pretenders tour (so the myth went), and Chrissy made a few somewhat veiled comments about that. I guess she was still a punk at heart and loved to fuck with people. When I mentioned I was from Boston, she immediately gave me a hard time, saying that Boston was a shit music town. After I'd defended my city with numerous examples of its greatness, I asked where she was from. When she said Ohio (she was from Akron), I started to list all the great funk acts that came from her home state. She was basically clueless about them.

My relationship with Bear began to teeter at exactly the wrong time – during the recording of this important project. I let the situation get the better – or should I say the worst – of me. I wasn't all in on the project because I was obsessed with my new girlfriend. The guys weren't happy at all but did show me some understanding, in between poking fun at me.

We moved the recording out of London to continue work at Peter Gabriel's studio, Real World, hoping that the move would get me more focused on the project. Real World was an amazing place to work. It was in the middle of the countryside near Bath. We had great rooms in a beautiful old mansion, with fields and meadows to roam in and a chef – everything you could want. It was like being on a retreat with your crew. Looking back, I should have really enjoyed it, but I didn't. I was in full obsession mode.

Then I was notified that *Human Traffic* would be screening at the Cannes Film Festival a few weeks later, and my production partners wanted me there. I planned to go for a few days, and the guys had no problem with that. For some reason, I called Bear to tell her. It turned out that she was attending too, doing some presenting for MTV. So what had been planned as a trip that would take my mind off her became another blast of obsession. And her ex was going too.

When I mentioned all of this, Johnny and Barney were a bit worried and actually warned me to be cool. They didn't want to have to bail me out of a French prison. Little did they know how close it came to that. The film company had booked me into a random condo. Was it my fault that it turned out that Bear was staying right next door? As I walked out to stroll down the Croisette, I almost physically bumped into her. It wasn't like I was stalking her. Really. We spoke, and I convinced her to hear me out. She invited me up to her room, which was a bad idea. It all escalated pretty quickly, and the gendarmes arrived, escorting me out of the building. Never touched her or even yelled, so they let me go. Then her ex showed up to pull the old saving-the-damsel-in-distress routine. He told me she would probably never see me again. I was devastated; I don't even remember the film screening.

I somehow made my way back to London, just for one night; I had to get back to work. The next day I returned to Bath, with my tail between my legs, pathetically telling Johnny and Barney my tale of woe. Don't know what they thought by this point, but I had to try to focus on the music. New Order had some big gigs coming up – a Manchester homecoming show in July and the Reading headliner in August – so the pressure was on to finish the album. I called my boys Merv de Peyer (a London keyboard whiz whom I had met in NYC) and Mac and got them to Bath to help with programming and finishing things up. We completed the record in time, thanks to their help.

I was welcomed back into the New Order fold at the homecoming gig. I filmed the entire concert with my arm on the shoulder of their manager, Rob Gretton. He would be dead in less than a year. When I saw Barney at the Reading Festival gig, he was still mad about how I had acted. A year or so later, after not speaking to me for over twelve months, he gave me a full reaming for my unprofessionalism. He did forgive me, though. Eventually.

Twisted Tenderness was released in April 1999, a year after it was first begun. It seemed like it had been a lot longer than that.

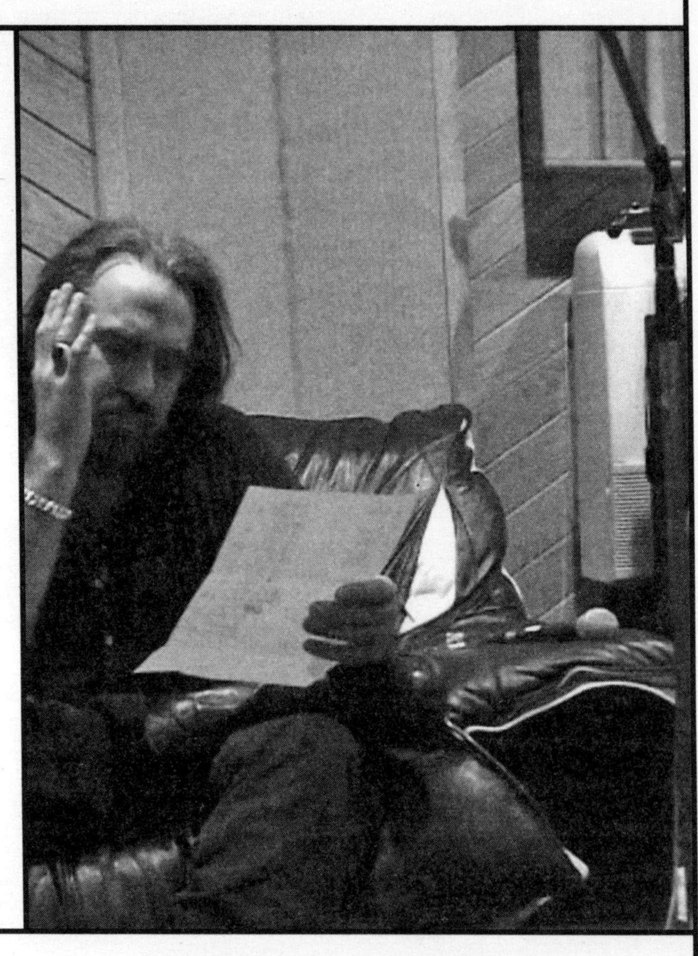

34.

'IT'S ONLY ROCK'N'ROLL'

1999

During my time living in London, a call from Stephen Budd usually meant work. Not always the best gigs, but over the years there were quite a few good ones. One of the great ones was when he called and asked if I'd be interested in producing a millennium children's record for the Prince's Trust. The project's producers had decided on a remake of the Stones' 'It's Only Rock'n'Roll', with a big cast of artists. I guess my work on 'Sun City' had put me in the running, along with Stephen's great sales skills. It sounded like it could be fun, and it was decently paid, which was a nice bonus. Then I remembered the stress of persuading artists to do a charity record. So I asked, 'Who's getting the acts?' Budd mentioned that I'd have to meet the executive producer of the project, a woman named Lorna Dickinson. She had worked on some Elton John music videos.

Lorna was fairly posh and confident, which you regularly find in England, but she seemed very nice and had connections. We obviously had a deadline: we were shooting for that magical UK Christmas #1, so it couldn't go on any later than November. It was also decided early on that we would travel to the artists, if necessary, and record wherever they were, guerrilla-style. We'd film the individual performances for the video too, at the same time as recording the vocals. Which meant compiling the vocals immediately for the singers to lip-sync to.

We were working with a young, first-time video director named Simon Rinkoff, who would be shooting a making-of documentary that would be screened on BBC1 to help promote the record's release. I'm not sure this had ever been done before for a multi-artist collaboration record. Recording and filming on the fly and going to the artists would have helped with both 'Sun City' and 'Listen Up', but the remote recording capabilities had amped up since those records were made (although they were still nothing like what we have today).

First, we needed a basic track for the singers to perform to, so I commenced recording 'It's Only Rock'n'Roll' at Mayfair Studios on 16 May 1999. I was able to tack the rhythm track recording onto the end of a session I had already booked for my now-in-full-swing solo project. I was cutting live drums for my new 'Real Fuckin' Noise' track with my crack rhythm duo, Si John and Robbie Merrill (of Roni Size's Reprazent). My Dublin buddy Simon Carmody, who was the ultimate Stones freak, also happened to be in town. My engineers, Teo Miller and Darren Nash, got things going, with Simon providing a strummy guitar part and a rough vocal, while Si and Rob rocked out a great version of the Stones classic.

At the time I was also working with Mark Owen from Take That on his solo project in Wales, at Rockfield. Mark had had a pretty successful debut album with RCA, but then Robbie Williams had blown all the other Take That side projects away, so the pressure to come up with something big was on even more. Mark and I shared a love of the recent Flaming Lips album, and we decided to go in that direction – pop tracks with huge, organic, overblown production. I brought in Si, Rob and Steve, from the indie band Voy, along with Merv and my buddy Gregg Sutton.

Mark later said:

> I went into Rockfield Studios in Wales and recorded six or seven tracks with Arthur. I've been very lucky and worked with some great people. Arthur's like a big lion. The Arthur stuff was sounding a little bit like a Flaming Lips kind of vibe, and we had the drummer who played with Roni Size, a band called Voy from Liverpool were doing guitars for us. It was quite an assortment of musicians, but the sound we were going for was quite a widescreen sound.

Listening back to it now, the music we created sounds very widescreen, ornate and beautiful, but I think it was too much of a statement for Mark at the time. We turned it in, but it was never released.

Mark, Bear, Gregg and I decided to make the trip from Rockfield to the Glastonbury Festival, renting a Winnebago. My old buddy, the Reverend Al Green, was performing a big gospel show on the Sunday morning, and I thought he might be into helping us out with the children's project. He slayed the crowd with an amazing old-school

Bear Van Beers and Gregg Sutton at Glastonbury, 1999.

church set in the sunshine, and good vibes were all around. After the set I talked my way backstage and had a quick reunion with the Rev. I mentioned the millennium children's project and asked if he'd be willing to give me an hour of his time while he was in the UK. He agreed! Luckily, he was staying at the Hyatt in Birmingham for a couple of days and asked if we could come there to record him.

This was very exciting to the team. Getting Al as the first voice would be a great coup. We were able to hook up with just the right tech person, Ian Duncan. He randomly got the gig through the rental company we called to set up the recording gear, but he had the skills and a calm demeanour, which would come in handy on a project like this. So we were ready to test out our new mobile recording system. Or we would have been, that is. We all made our way to Birmingham and waited for Al. And waited. We waited all day and spoke to his tour manager, but Al didn't come out of his room. Not a very auspicious start to the project.

Despite that, Lorna was not to be denied. When she called me the next day, she had somehow managed to nail down B. B. King, who was performing at the Royal Albert Hall. But this time we would be going to the venue to record, and B. B. wouldn't be able to escape! We went to his dressing room, Ian set up the system, and B. B. came in and sang a verse and a chorus. I was very satisfied with what we had, but Lorna asked if he could also play a bit of guitar. Which meant some more time spent setting that up. His road manager wasn't happy and said something about him playing just one chord. But as soon as B. B. had Lucille in his hands he was never gonna play just one chord, and he ended up jamming over the entire track. We were in business.

Herbie Hancock happened to be playing a few weeks later at the Barbican, so we made our way over there and hooked up a MIDI keyboard, and he did some jamming to the track. I hadn't seen him since 'Sun City', and we had a bit of a catch-up. He mentioned that Ray Barretto, the Puerto Rican percussionist who had also played on the anti-apartheid record, was in town, so we caught up with him, and he bashed down a great conga performance. We then took a bit of time off for the summer break.

I had gone over to Florida for my dad's birthday and a vacation, when I got a call from Lorna, saying that James Brown was in the UK for the V Festival, and we had an 'in' with him. After getting burnt by Al, I figured the Godfather probably wouldn't show up either and decided not to fly back on the off chance. But, having kept our crew waiting all day, the Godfather *did* eventually turn up and gave a great performance, even dancing with the kids. After seeing the footage and hearing his vocals, I regretted missing the session. But at least having him on the record got other folks to pay attention.

We then started rockin' and rollin' for real. It was a whirlwind tour. This was my third such multi-artist record, and I'd realised how difficult it was to bond with an artist, to get them to trust and perform for you, all within minutes of meeting. Our first big group recording session really tested those skills. It was late August; summer was done, and we were ready to focus on finishing the project. The record had a November release date, so we had only a couple of months in which to get it finished. We were booked into AIR Studios, on Hampstead Heath, very close to my Primrose Hill flat. It was one of the best studios in the world; things with full orchestras, like the James Bond soundtracks, were often recorded there. I had five acts to record in one action-packed session: Robin Williams (Robin the comic, not Robbie the singer); guitars from Status Quo; Womack and Womack (along with their numerous kids); and two duelling divas, Annie Lennox and Chrissie Hynde. Baptism by fire.

Let me state first that I love Annie's voice. Her early records with Dave Stewart are among my favourites of the 1980s; 'Sweet Dreams' and 'Here Comes the Rain' are classics. But we just didn't click. She wanted me to count her in, which usually was easy for me. I mean, hey, I had counted Diana Ross in. But somehow I didn't get into the flow quick enough for Annie, and she got a bit impatient. I had thought Chrissie, whom I had met with Johnny and Barney, might be the difficult one, but no. Maybe it was the cameras filming my every move for the making of the doc – I don't know. But Annie is the consummate pro, and we eventually got some great vocals.

The rest of the session went smoothly. Chrissie nailed the song; I think she mentioned she had sung it many times over the years. The genius of Robin Williams immediately showed through: he just jammed some comic ideas, riffing over the track, finally settling on his Jagger-meets-a-Frenchman vibe. Status Quo plugged in and rocked out over the track. Lastly, there was the joyousness of Womack and Womack and family, who added a gospel tinge to it. All in all, a great session.

Next up, Lorna had somehow scored Jon Bon Jovi to take part, so I travelled to NYC and my old stomping ground of Right Track to record him. Surprisingly, our paths had never crossed, so we had a bit of time to chat and reminisce about NYC in the 1980s. The session went smoothly, and Jon had a lot of interesting things to say for the making-of documentary.

I then made my way out to LA to meet the full team, led by Lorna. She had organised an action-packed couple of days: we were going into A&M Studios to record Dolores O'Riordan from The Cranberries, Huey Morgan from the Fun Lovin' Criminals, the madman Ozzy Osbourne and the comic genius Eric Idle. Huey agreed to come in as long as we had a table set up to make margaritas, which he proceeded to mix upon arrival (he made a great margarita, by the way). He had his posse with him, along with ideas on how his segment of the video should be shot.

He brought a bit of rap swagger to proceedings. In his interview, he told kids to stay away from drugs and to never be insurance agents. This was our first meet-up, but we would become future West London friends, and I'd regularly appear on his BBC Radio 6 Music show in the future. Dolores came in, quietly nailed her lines and was in and out without any time wasted. Eric didn't seem extremely happy to be there, but he quickly came up with a silly routine and his version of Jagger.

But where was Ozzy? He had forgotten about the session, of course, and was in the UK. We'd have to get him via telephone line later.

The next day we journeyed out to Santa Barbara to record my old friend Bonnie Raitt and Jackson Browne, who were on tour together. Both had been on 'Sun City', and I hadn't seen Bonnie in years, so it was great to catch up. We ended up recording on their tour bus, which was definitely a memorable session.

That was it for the US, and we quickly headed back to London, where we had a session booked at Abbey Road. We arrived at the studio the next morning, totally jet-lagged, to work with the singer Skin, from the band Skunk Anansie. Skin is known for her mad energy, and we were all dying. Somehow her vocal was recorded, and she ran up and down the halls while shooting her part of the video.

The next two sessions were among the easiest and most memorable: the duelling Detroit rockers Kid Rock and Iggy Pop. We made our way up to Manchester to meet up with Kid Rock, who was really blowing up at the time. He was there doing press. We recorded him at the Renaissance Hotel, the day before he headed down to London for a gig at the Astoria 2. He was excited to meet me, as he was a fan of my early electro tracks, which he said had really influenced him. To prove it, he sang me 'Play at Your Own Risk' a cappella, and I immediately offered to produce a version with him, should he ever want to cut one. For our version of 'It's Only Rock'n'Roll', I decided to have him focus on the line about the boy being insane, and he nailed it with his natural energy. He then went buck wild while shooting the video, running crazily round the big hall while lip-syncing for the video. The next night I went to his gig, which was really impressive. He played numerous instruments and had the crowd in his hands the entire show. I met up with him afterwards, and we walked the streets near Tottenham Court Road, with fans jumping all over him to get autographs. It's really sad how in recent years he's turned into a fully fledged Trumper.

A few days later, we met up with Iggy Pop. He too was playing at the Astoria 2, and I went to see the gig, which was, of course, explosive. Lorna had organised a session with him the next afternoon at the Halcyon hotel. She introduced a well-dressed, suited-up Iggy to me. He was familiar with my name and seemed happy to meet me but wanted to get down to business quickly. I gave him the line 'Suicide, right on the stage', and he got it in two takes. I think he got the lip-sync for the video on the second take, slicing his hand across his neck in a 'cut' gesture and exiting the room as the music continued playing, never stopping to say goodbye. Perfect.

We continued working through early October, with sessions at the Metropolitan Hotel with Gavin Rossdale from Bush, Ronan Keating, Mark Owen and The Corrs; at Mayfair Studios with Natalie Imbruglia and her cute Jagger strut, and Dina Carroll, who surprised me with her voice and her energy; and then . . . the Spice Girls!

They launched their Spice invasion at Whitfield Street Studios. The wave of energy they brought with them was pretty insane. They were at the top of their game at the time, and they knew it and how to play it. I had been introduced to them by my friend Rob Manley years earlier, just after they had been signed, at Bagley's nightclub in King's Cross, and they had jumped en masse into my lap. For the recording they all went into the live room together, each with their own microphone, and let the chorus rock. Tuning? To put it in their own words: 'Oh well, you can tune us up!' Which we did. But they offered their flavour, and the vibe they gave to the video was great.

I still had some great singers to record over the rest of the month. First, I got to record Joe Cocker at the Athenaeum hotel in London. The documentary cameras caught me singing Joe his parts, which he obviously sang a lot better than me. Then it was Lionel Richie at Rive Droite Studio, in glamorous Hampton Wick. We had a nice chat. I mentioned our meeting at the party in Quincy's house in LA, years earlier. As I was a big Commodores fan, I asked him for a couple of old-school 'yows' to accent his vocal. He humoured me and gave me a few.

Then we made two great trips to Paris. First, we recorded Mary J. Blige at the very ornate Le Royal Monceau hotel. Mary arrived with a small female posse. After a few niceties, she listened to the track intently and then got down to bizness. She sang in a laid-back,

Me and Joe Cocker recording at the Athenaeum Hotel in London, 1999.

Me and Mary J. Blige recording at Le Royal Monceau hotel in Paris.

nonchalant style. I thought, *That's nice*. But upon listening to playback, I was really hit by her beautifully restrained, powerful, emotional performance. It was one of the top moments for me, standing in a hotel bedroom with Mary J. while she sang. Her interview for the documentary was also one of the most insightful; she spoke of her childhood in a very intimate way.

Back in Paris days later, we grabbed Jamiroquai backstage before his gig at Palais Omnisorts de Paris-Bercy. He was very gracious with his time, considering he was getting ready for a huge sold-out show. His vocal went down quickly; he was a fan of the song and just went for it. His video section was shot just moments before the lights went down for the show, but he gave it his all, dancing around the huge backstage area.

For Ozzy's vocal (which he performed along with his daughter), I had chosen the line 'This dude is crazy' for him to sing, which I thought would really suit him. The session was over the phone line, with Ozzy at Capitol Studios in LA, and me in the studio in London, so when he asked me to count him in and point to him when he should sing, I had to explain, 'Sorry, that's sort of not possible, Ozzy. I'm in Brixton, mate!'

Now it was just down to the Glimmer Twins, Mick Jagger and Keith Richards. We recorded Keith from his home studio in Connecticut, with a big glass of whisky by his side. Besides playing his own song, we asked if he could play the Chuck Berry riff that I had sampled, since we weren't able to clear it. Which he answered by immediately jamming the riff.

So now we had only one artist left. From the beginning we'd been nervous about whether we'd be able to get Mick to sing on the track. I'd sent it to him as a work in progress, but I don't remember getting much feedback. I also didn't feel my past history with him would work in our favour, and I could tell he wasn't thrilled with the scenario of our conversation being recorded by the camera crew. After some catch-up chatter, with me mentioning my desire to re-release my 'Too

Much Blood' remix (he immediately shut that down), he listened to the track. He then requested to talk to me on the phone.

'Arrrrrrthur,' he slurred, 'there's really no room for me to do anything on the track. There's nothing left for me to sing.'

Which I guess was sort of true. I told him I'd make room and took some vocals out. I communicated that I'd find some great spots for him when I went to do the mix. He then performed a couple of takes, asked me if they were OK and was gone. Mick was the final piece of the jigsaw. 'It's Only Rock'n'Roll (But I Like It)' by our supergroup, Artists for Children's Promise, was released on 9 December 1999, peaking at #19.

Looking back and watching the video years later, it's impressive how I managed to find a place for each and every artist. The whole thing holds up as a true celebration of the joy of rock'n'roll, with musicians from so many genres and generations sharing their love for a good cause. It's too bad that these kinds of things don't really happen any more.

35.

SUNDAY JAMMING

2000–1

After finishing up 'It's Only Rock'n'Roll' and appearing as an expert judge on the BBC TV show *Get Your Act Together* (a predecessor of *Pop Idol*), hosted by Ronan Keating, I was ready for the end of the millennium and to move on into 2000.

First, I decided to fly to Florida to celebrate New Year's Eve with my dad and family in Boca, followed by a quick Southern road trip with Bear. We made it to Memphis (getting to Graceland and the Stax studio) and New Orleans and the House of Blues, where we were lucky enough to catch Dr. John and Gregg Allman on consecutive nights. We also ate great food at the Commodore and Mother's sandwich shop. But once we got back to London it looked like it was time to finish both the album and the relationship.

I had the Elbow Room in Chapel Market to help open. We had really nailed it with our fourth venue, having found a big, wide-open space on an old market road in Islington. This spot would prove to be the real jewel of the chain, and this time my involvement was key to its success from the start. Paul Daly outdid himself on the interior design, creating a real adult playground, with a dozen 'Prince' purple pool tables and a bespoke DJ booth, complete with computerised disco lighting and a large dancefloor that was bordered by a lit-up neon bar. It was created for good times and big parties.

From day one the vibe was all about the party. The launch event is still one of the most memorable nights of all my years in London. We organised the opening as a fundraiser for the Royal National Institute of Blind People. Sir George Martin, The Beatles' producer, was the institute's chair and gave an opening speech. I produced the event, getting my friends Jocelyn Brown and Alabama 3 in to perform live. We had an amazing guest list, with such greats as Damien Hirst, Joe Strummer of The Clash, Bobby Gillespie and Mani from the Scream, Bez from the Happy Mondays, bass player Guy Pratt of Pink Floyd, singer Kym Mazelle and actor Keith Allen all in the house. I was enlisted by the folks from the RNIB to interview them all on camera for future promotional use. Some of the stuff was useable, some not. Case in point:

my interview with legendary Clash leader Strummer. We were both pretty hammered at the time, so I'm not sure what I asked him, but he blurted out his opinion that he felt bad for blind people, because they weren't able 'to see the beauty of Pamela Anderson's breasts', which was hardly politically correct. But then, let's face it, a lot of the 1990s wasn't particularly politically correct by today's standards.

With free drinks all night, things got out of control quickly; it was like the debauchery of the Groucho Club meets Chapel Market and rock'n'roll. I was hanging in the booth with Bobby Gillespie as he was DJing. He was playing a variety of punk rock at a very loud volume when Sir George approached. He politely asked if Bobby could please lower the level just a bit. Bobby, without a pause, told him to 'Go fuck off, old man.' Not sure if he recognised the legendary Beatles producer. Sir George just walked off.

The other low point of the event was when John, our venue manager, didn't allow me to keep the venue open for a lock-in. The after-party ended up being held in hotel rooms in the area. I made my anger very clear, and this would be the last time something like that would happen to me there.

Around this time I finally bought a car, a used blue BMW, to get me around in comfort. This would lead me to a whole new world. The car had a radio, so I started to listen to the recently launched radio station XFM. One late-night show in particular, John Kennedy's *X-Posure*, caught my ear. John would play lots of new cutting-edge bands and artists. I contacted him to compliment him on his show and ended up being invited to be a guest on it. Through that, I made friends with some of the staff, including Charlotte Soussan, who oversaw the marketing. Charlotte and XFM ended up being great supporters of both me and the Elbow Room from the jump. She introduced me to this hot new mash-up DJ duo, 2 Many DJs, who also performed as the rock band Soulwax, bringing them over for an Elbow Room set. This started a great friendship between the Dewaele brothers and me; they would soon be resident DJs at my Return to New York parties.

I'd frequently discover new acts on the radio while driving and would usually stop and call the station to find out more information about the artist. That's how I first heard Peaches' 'Fuck the Pain Away'. Within a few hours I'd tracked her down and booked her for a late-night set at the Elbow Room. She brought her drum machine and her friend Gonzales for a legendary show that wasn't packed but is now one of those gigs everyone claims to have been at.

resident dj ARTHUR BAKER
with very special LIVE guests
Sun 15th Oct
South
Sun 22nd Oct
Beta Band
Sun 29th Oct
Kinobe headline the Silvertone 'Stone Roses Remix Album Day'
Sun 05th Nov
Cosmic Roughriders
Regular Fries DJ set
Sun 12th Nov
Fridge
Sun 17th Nov
Clint Boon DJ set
admission is FREE and doors are open from 12 noon - 10.30p.m with guests starting from 3.00p.m
American Pool Tables, American Style Brunch & Cocktail menu
Newspapers available all day & Waitress service
tel> 020 7278 3244 :: www.elbow-room.co.uk
89-91 Chapel Market, Islington, London N1
EXCESS

Flyer for the 'Sunday Jam' party at Elbow Room.

XFM collaborated with me on a weekly live Sunday session at Chapel Market that would feature the best of new British rock and dance. It was called 'Arthur Baker's Sunday Jam', and the acts that would pass through (whether hanging or performing) were a who's who of cutting-edge British music of the early 2000s. The Beta Band led it off in early October, with bands such as Ash, Elbow, Fridge, Mogwai and Alabama 3 following. I would end up collaborating with most of them on my album, along with old friends such as Alan Vega of Suicide and Peter Hook.

Ah yes, my album. Well, it had already received some great advance press from both *Melody Maker* and the *NME*, even though I still wasn't finished with it. Mogwai were in town for the *NME* Awards in February, and drummer Martin Bulloch mentioned our collaboration in his interview, saying it was amazing and would be released soon. I took advantage of both Stuart Braithwaite and Hooky being in town for the awards by booking time at my local studio, Mayfair, so that we could work on my track 'Love Hymn'. The song featured a transcendental saxophone performance by the late, great Pharoah Sanders, whom I had been able to persuade to play on two tracks, after I made him aware that I had co-produced a version of his 'The Creator Has a Master Plan' with the Brooklyn Funk Essentials, which had made the charts all over Europe. The Sanders session was unforgettable. He transformed my rough melodic ideas with his amazing skills, playing

Pharoah Sanders and me at Mayfair Studios.

four beautiful ten-minute solos, one after the other. It was quite emotional for all there to witness it, and I was sure I saw tears in his eyes after one take. The session ended with me handing him a brown paper bag filled with cash (his idea). We then added Stuart's and Hooky's guitars and bass, along with harp, tabla and other orchestral percussion, to the song. ('Love Hymn' would finally be released some twenty-five years later as part of the Red Hot Org's *Transa* project.) Hooky also asked me to remix the first single from his new Freebass project.

I had purchased a new computer program called ACID in the middle of 1999, which was a game-changer for me, enabling me to sample, loop and stretch audio to my liking. I started making loads of tracks for fun, quickly building an amazing variety of them using this program, from disco loopers to atmospheric rockers, hip-hop beats to electro-break grooves. I was able to sample some of my favourite old-school tracks and manipulate them to the point where they were unrecognisable, while keeping their vibe and essence. This control was very exciting to me, and I was creating tracks daily, some of which I wanted to complete for the album. One of the first I made with ACID was a nu-school breaks song called 'Like No Other', which featured vocals by Simon Carmody and myself. Rennie Pilgrem had done a mix that could be played at either 33 or 45 rpm, and the song busted out well on the jungle and breaks scenes.

Early on I came up with a track that sampled a favourite song by a west coast rock band that I had been obsessed with in the early 1970s, Little Feat. I flipped the intro of their classic 'Willin'' and built a song around it, with a thumping bass line and housey drums. It was unique and really good. I thought that Ash's Tim Wheeler might sound great singing over it, so I sent it to him, and he quickly composed lyrics and a melody that sounded like a fucking smash. The song was called 'Glow'.

I was now working with a new engineer in Shepherd's Bush, a mellow Israeli guy named Yoad Nevo. He was a great programmer and engineer who also worked with the team from Waves, the software company. He had access to all the cutting-edge music programs and was able to help me dump my ACID tracks over to a more complex music program called Logic and make sense of them. Tim met me in Yoad's room at Town House Studios and recorded his vocals and guitar over my electronic track. Once he'd finished, we both loved the results. It was very different from what he did with Ash, while maintaining their poppiness. And it inspired me to keep working towards getting the record finished.

And then came the exciting news that XFM were offering me my own weekly show, *Baker's Dozen*. My remit was to introduce new hip-hop and nu-school breaks to the station's listeners.

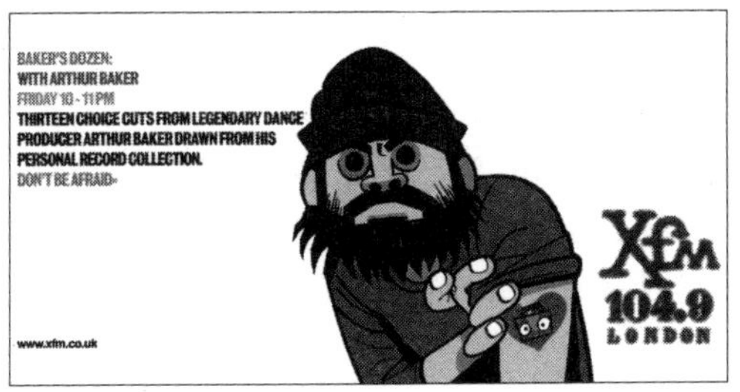

Ad for my *Baker's Dozen* XFM radio show.

I was now actually making music in two parallel universes, going from my solo rockier/indie stuff and shifting into breaks, both using the ACID software. I still wasn't releasing much, other than a couple of tracks for Rennie, which he put out on his TCR label.

I then reconnected with my old mate Paul Oakenfold. He was now *the* man in dance music, producing, remixing and opening for acts such as the Happy Mondays, U2 and Madonna. He also had a label called Perfecto, which was distributed through Mushroom Records. When I told Paul about my radio show and the nu-school breaks scene, he quickly offered me a deal for the release of a compilation of my 1980s hits. I agreed, with the proviso that it should be a double album, with a second disc of new material. He said yes, and that became the start of an entirely new project. So while I still had my solo album pretty much in the can, I started going through all the bits of music I had created in ACID and brainstormed some possible collaborations for this new album!

Another song I discovered through XFM provided me with two other future collaborators and long-time friends: Felix Da Housecat and Tommie Sunshine's great 'Silver Screen Shower Scene'. I played it on my first show, having initially heard it on John Kennedy's show earlier that week. When I reached out to Tommie, it turned out that he was a fan of mine and was keen to collaborate. It was June 2001; I was on my way out of town, and Tommie was on his way to London, so I offered to let him crash at my new flat in Camden. He brought Felix over with him, and later told me that when Felix saw my framed New Edition silver record on the wall, he freaked. He had no idea who the fuck I was!

When I got back, we all went into the studio late one night, had a laugh and threw together a mad electroclash track that we called 'Quiet Riot'. We named the band The Crazies, and the 12-inch release was backed with the track I did with DJ Face, 'Jamaica, C'Mon'. I still think the latter is vastly underrated.

Through my radio show, I connected with some interesting people at XFM. Zane Lowe was the early-evening DJ, and Ricky Gervais was the morning drive-time guy. Ricky's great sense of humour was evident even then, and team meetings with him were very reminiscent of *The Office*; I'm pretty convinced a lot of his ideas for the show were inspired by the odd things that XFM's station manager regularly did. Zane, meanwhile, was a big hip-hop head and loved my stories of the New York old school.

Soon after I started at the station, Tom Silverman asked me if I wanted to get on a Tommy Boy twentieth-anniversary tour with Afrika Bambaataa, Maseo from De La Soul and Dan the Automator. Sounded like a blast. I ended up bringing the Tommy Boy crew over to XFM for an on-air interview with Zane to coincide with the launch of the tour. We shot a few pics, adopting old-school hip-hop poses. Travelling with this crew was pretty heavyweight; I was actually physically the smallest! We launched in Paris, complete with a crew of breakdancers, and then hit Derry, Dublin, Bristol and London.

The number of records we were travelling with was insane. It was agreed we'd just play vinyl, no CDs allowed. Bambaataa had at least twenty flight cases full of records. He also had a thing about flying on propeller planes. 'I ain't gonna fly on no Tarzan planes,' he said, and we had to exchange the small prop plane that was meant to take us from Derry to Dublin for a few old vans. But soon flying of any type lost its appeal, following the terrorist attacks on the Twin Towers in NYC. It was a crazy time everywhere, and I was fine staying put in the UK, where I was in the process of opening a pop-up of my restaurant Harlem, which happened to launch on 11 September 2001!

Perfecto were excited by my project and got lots of press for it. One of those new 'lad' magazines asked me where I'd like to travel to that I'd never been, within reason. So I picked Russia. I flew over with the journalist and a photographer, meeting up with two local DJs that Paul knew who would act as our tour guides. Big mistake. After driving through Moscow at over 100 mph, complete with bottles of vodka in hand, we had a horrible meal and then pulled a drunk all-night tour of the clubs, complete with pissing on the walls around Red Square. The night ended with me on the bathroom floor, passed out, having puked my guts up for only the third time in my life! The next morning, I had an interview to do and a photo shoot to pose for. Ouch.

The album, *Breakin'*, was released on 15 October 2001. Didn't tear up the charts, but the new tracks we cut have stood the test of time fairly well.

And the Elbow Room in Chapel Market became the most successful in our chain. Many memorable days and nights were spent there. Unfortunately, right around the time we were planning to roll the brand out, there was a tragic occurrence. On New Year's Eve 2007 a near-fatal shooting happened on the dancefloor. An American footballer had hit on the wrong guy's girl, and almost died for it. While he survived, the incident had a lasting effect on the Elbow Room, and the entire business was sold a year later. The Elbow Room party was over.

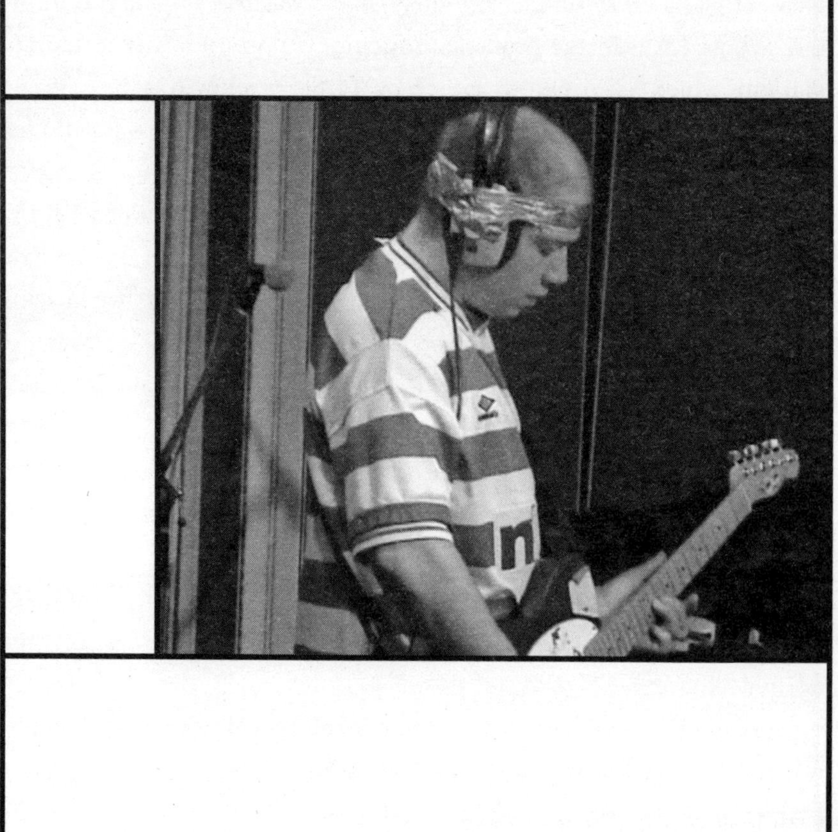

36.

‘MY FATHER, MY KING’

2000–1

My first-ever live musical experience occurred while attending temple with my family as a very young child during the Jewish high holidays. I remember being captivated by the majestic sounds of the cantor's voice, the organ and the choir singing ancient psalms. I was mesmerised by the most beautiful psalm of all, one sung exclusively during the Ten Days of Repentance, the holiest days of the Jewish calendar, from Rosh Hashanah to Yom Kippur.

That psalm, 'Avinu Malkeinu' ('Our Father, Our King'), was ingrained in my consciousness from day one, its beautiful, melodic call-and-response immediately unleashing a tidal wave of emotions in me and the entire congregation. Even as a young child, I could feel that connection and pride we were all feeling. The fact we were one people was evident and sealed through this melancholic piece of music.

Year after year I'd wait in anticipation of hearing it sung again. 'Avinu' was so captivatingly beautiful, with its haunting melody sung in an ancient round, that you'd immediately feel a responsibility to atone for your year's sins and indiscretions. While I would hear it only a few times a year, its melody would constantly be in my consciousness. I never thought to seek out a recording of it, because in my heart I knew that its place was in the temple. The idea of some day recording it myself? It would never, ever have entered my mind.

So when I first witnessed the band Mogwai, it wasn't obvious that they could perhaps do justice to the most important song of my childhood. But it wasn't long after experiencing them that the idea hit me. I just knew they could make further magic with it. I first heard Mogwai live, not on a record, and it was quite by chance, on a walk through a crowded Reading Festival in 1998. I had made it to the festival for two reasons: first, to see New Order play live and try to revive my friendship with Barney, having let him down a bit during the recording of *Twisted Tenderness*; and second, to take Bear to see her heroes, Page and Plant.

She was also a Mogwai fan and dragged me over to the tent where they were playing. We pushed inside and tried to get close to the stage. It was packed, which was impressive. The lights dimmed and an unassuming-looking group of guys got on stage, with two guitarists, a bassist and drummers. The music began very fragile and intimate, with the guitar parts reminding me of the old English folk group Pentangle.

After the gig, I made my way backstage to try and speak to the band. I had been blown away by their playing, their soft to loud, majestically explosive transitions and their melodic compositions. Strangely, they reminded me of the Mahavishnu Orchestra combined with the musicality and jamming power of the Allman Brothers. It was fairly chaotic backstage, and their Glaswegian accents didn't help. I'm not great with strong Scottish accents; I've been good friends with Irvine Welsh for decades and still have a problem understanding him. I approached their guitarist, Stuart, and introduced myself. I probably mentioned New Order and 'Planet Rock'; that usually got a decent response. He smiled, we shook hands, and he introduced me to the rest of the band. We had a few beers and hit it off. I also met their manager, Colin Hardie, who must have been all of twenty years old. I spoke to him about getting the guys to work with me on my record. I knew it would be great if I could get Stuart to play on some of the tracks I'd already started. He is an amazingly creative guitarist, going from almost folk-like arpeggiator lines to slamming heavy metal in seconds with a stomp on his effects pedal.

But late one night it dawned on me that Mogwai might be the only band who could record 'Avinu Malkeinu' and do it justice. If they nailed it, then it would fit perfectly into my solo project, as I was trying to do a selection of songs that would touch on spirituality.

I reached for my handy Steinberger bass, which I am eternally grateful to Tina Weymouth of Talking Heads/Tom Tom Club for introducing to me, found the notes and tried banging out the two major melodic sections of 'Avinu' as I imagined Mogwai might play them, with a helping of Peter Hook-style melodic rhythm bass on top. Only thing is, I can't really play bass, though I can fake it a bit. I recorded my ideas onto a cassette and listened back to them. Yeah, I figured that they'd be able to hear what I was going for. I gave Stuart a call and told him my plan. He was really curious, because he had never heard of 'Avinu

Malkeinu', none of the band being Jewish. Next morning, I walked the cassette over to a small post office at the back of a magazine shop in Primrose Hill and sent it up to Glasgow. Not sure what they thought about my bass-playing skills, but they must have got the idea, because Stuart hit me back to say they were keen and would give it a shot.

It took quite a while till they had a lull in their schedule and could try recording the track, but on a cold March day I arrived at Chem19 Studios in Hamilton, ten miles south of Glasgow, and found the group already absorbed in their work on the track. Mogwai looked pretty much the way New Order had early on (they could have been plumbers), but more cheerful. Also, Stuart had strapped his headphones to his head with electrical tape, which I've never seen anyone else do, but he acted like it was perfectly normal. They stopped jamming, and we all did our hellos.

I went into the control room and joined their engineer behind the board, as the boys launched into their arrangement of 'Avinu Malkeinu'. I listened intently as they slowly revealed how they had adapted the psalm, unfolding the song so delicately, introducing the initial melodic section with just Stuart's guitar and then building, with Dominic on bass, John and Barry (his first time in the studio with the band) on additional guitars and Martin on drums adding more intensity, until Stuart stepped on his distortion pedal and it all went apocalyptic. At this point my girlfriend, who had been sitting listening quietly on the couch, got up and started bouncing around with a big smile on her face, while the intensity kept growing.

Then, almost silence, and into the second section of 'Avinu', with Stuart again playing a delicate, almost acoustic fugue to a klezmer waltz-like beat. This brought back vivid memories of the temple as a child. Then the song again built its way back up to a climactic, anthemic, melodic symphony, before ending in amazement.

We were absolutely blown away. It was a moment of both pride and satisfaction in a random idea that had worked, and in how this magnificent rendition might help expose the beauty of my religious heritage to those who would otherwise never have experienced it.

While Mogwai were using the concept I had suggested on my cassette, they had obviously felt the power of those ancient melodies and taken the psalm way beyond anything I could ever have envisioned. I was ecstatic that my idea had worked.

Feeling uplifted, we took a break, and Martin took us for a meal at the Chinese restaurant where he worked in East Kilbride, a neighbouring town about five miles away. Afterwards, I took a wander around the area, and for some reason I looked up and my gaze fell on an old building bearing an inscription in Hebrew. I later found that it translated as 'Take his soul'. It must have been a temple many years ago. It was an unbelievably magical day.

Photo I took in Glasgow when I happened upon a building bearing the inscription 'Take his soul', March 1999.

I left with what I felt was a treasure: a digital copy of the amazing performance. A few days later, I brought it to London so that my engineer Merv and I could add a few arrangement elements and mix the track for my album. We got to work on 30 March 1999. My idea was to add some strings and a clarinet, playing off the melody in the second klezmer-like drop. Merv made some small fixes to the original performance, and eventually we got a mix we really liked. But while we were working on the track, Mogwai continued to rehearse it, developing additional ideas that came from playing it live numerous times. It was gaining more power as they performed it.

The next time I saw the band play it was just a month later, at a new festival, the Bowlie Weekender, curated by Belle & Sebastian. Mogwai weren't even in the line-up; they were unannounced surprise guests. The Flaming Lips, whom we all really liked, were appearing, along with a plethora of up-and-coming bands. It was also by the sea, at the Pontins holiday camp in Camber Sands, Sussex, which probably closed the deal for us.

It was the day after my birthday, so I was in good spirits. And the line-up was a great one, with acts like the Lips and Mercury Rev performing and Jarvis Cocker of Pulp DJing. It was mostly young indie kids, at the start of their search for new sounds, let loose in a typical English holiday camp with tons of beer and weed. What could go wrong? Actually, it seemed fairly calm when we arrived. The sand dunes were alluring, so I ran down them and dived into the freezing sea. The gigs were mostly in circus-type tents, as was often the way at British music festivals. I wanted to get a good spot for the Flaming Lips, and the tents were not that big, so we entered early, figuring we'd see whatever band was playing before them. There was an announced special guest on the schedule, so who knew what we were in store for?

It was Mogwai! And they played a blinding set, which I captured on my video camera. But they didn't play our track. Not that I expected them to. We spoke afterwards, and then they headed off on tour, playing all over the world.

The next month I went out on the road with New Order. They were playing the Fuji Rock Festival, and I had never been to Japan before, so I figured, why not? When I got there, I found out that Mogwai were on the bill too and was excited to catch up with them. They asked me to come up on stage and watch from the side. It was an amazing, magical set. It started right before sunset, and the crowd was mesmerised by the music, a sea of Japanese faces quietly staring up at the band. It was getting towards the end of the set, when Stuart looked at me with a smile on his face and said something into the mic. I thought I might have heard him say my name. Then Mogwai started playing 'My Father, My King'! (the name was a basic translation from the Hebrew). It was an unbelievable, unreal, surreal moment for me, hearing it live in front of this audience. It went on longer than any song I'd ever heard live, with all its peaks and valleys; there was no boredom at all. They had live strings, with Barry playing the flute, and it was sonically out of this world. It ended in explosions and looping feedback. The crowd were in shock, I think, frozen in their tracks. And I realised the band had taken the song another step further on from where we had gotten to. It was now their encore, and they'd typically play it for over twenty minutes!

So while I had somehow lost focus on this amazing song, at least I had unleashed something within the band that had spurred an important piece of music for them. I was proud of what my idea had birthed: a great band's encore song and a focal point of the end of their set.

They soon hired the legendary rock engineer/producer Steve Albini to oversee the recording and mix it at Mayfair Studios, a block away from where I lived when I first had the idea. By this time, they had been playing it live for so long that they knew exactly how it should sound, and Albini captured it perfectly. There was no production credit for me, but I did get one for the arrangement, along with the band, which I was very happy with.

The thing is, it was only recently, when I started going through my archive, that I found a lost video from the sessions in Glasgow. I now realise with hindsight that we had actually *nailed it* in that second session. The studio footage looks fucking amazing, as if they were again performing it as their encore in front of 10,000 people. A leaping Iggy Pop painting on the studio wall seems ready to crowd surf, as Stuart places his guitar on the floor and bangs on it.

Sadly, the one multitrack from that session has gone missing, so people will probably never get a chance to experience that full version.

37.

ON THE ROAD AGAIN WITH NEW ORDER

2001

Among the many things the year 2001 would bring, DJing for my friends New Order wasn't something I would have predicted. We reconnected when I made it up to Manchester for the *24 Hour Party People* shoot. The film-makers had recreated the Haçienda, so this was unmissable. The club had been knocked down a year or so earlier, and here they were, in true Factory fashion, having to rebuild it for the film. Seeing Steve Coogan lead the character he played, Tony Wilson, around the set, and Barney hanging with John Simm, who was playing him, was surreal. The recreation of the club was pretty exact; they'd certainly spent quite a bit of money on getting it right. We all went out afterwards and did a late-night basement-club and pub crawl. I remember eating Chinese with Hooky somewhere very late. It was quite a night.

In August they released a new album, *Get Ready*, with a lead track, 'Crystal', that was so good it made me jealous not to have been involved with it; my friend Lee Coombs killed it with his remix. So it seemed as if they'd be back on the road again. For my part, I set out on the Tommy Boy twentieth-anniversary tour. We gigged throughout Europe, ending up on 17 July in Derry. New Order had a warm-up gig at the Olympia in Liverpool the next night, which I somehow made.

Then – and I'm not sure how this happened – I ended up flying to Tokyo with the band on 27 July. I wasn't DJing at any of the band's upcoming gigs, and for the life of me I can't remember how or why I was on the flight, sitting comfortably in business class with them, but there I was. It would be my first time in Japan.

Phil Cunningham had recently joined the group, and this was his first luxury flight. As we relaxed in the British Airways lounge, it suddenly dawned on the new guitarist that everything there was free, including all drinks. So, of course, he started hammering them down. Quickly. Before boarding. I think Hooky may have been a bit of a bad influence, and by the time we boarded, Phil was truly fucked. He barely made it into the toilet, then there was silence. We were about to depart, but not with young Phil passed out. The stewardess made it clear that the plane would sit there until he was safely in his seat and buckled up. After much prodding by all of us, he finally emerged, spending the entire flight passed out in his seat.

Another new addition to the band was one Billy Corgan of the Smashing Pumpkins. According to him, New Order were his Beatles, so he wanted to play with them live, having appeared on their new album. When we arrived in Tokyo, Billy was followed everywhere. We went out to a few bars, and he had all these Japanese girls trailing behind him, pointing and looking up. We made it to the bullet train the next morning, only to find another rock star in our midst – Neil Young! He obviously knew Billy well, as they were chatting away; even though I'm pretty sure Barney was a fan of his guitar-playing, I'm not sure they spoke. We all packed into a carriage and rocketed up to the Fuji Rock Festival. I was really happy to be among them, but I would have loved to have had a reason to be there, like DJing or something.

I watched New Order introduce Corgan as part of the band for the first time. The set was great, and I think Billy enjoyed it hugely, though he doesn't really smile much. Then they did some press in Tokyo with my friend Mika, whom I had met in London when she lived there. She worked for Warners and had been assigned to work with the band. When I decided to stay in Tokyo an extra day, Mika and her husband showed me round the city.

New Order had a short UK tour lined up to promote *Get Ready*, and they asked me if I'd be into doing some opening DJ sets. I had to think about it as I was in the midst of planning my pop-up restaurant, Harlem, at the Saint restaurant off Tottenham Court Road in London, plus I had a bad knee, which had me hobbling and walking with a cane – a cool one, but still . . . But I figured I'd have time to do a few of their gigs in October, as Harlem would already be open by then. But 11 September happened, and the world changed.

The tour was still on, though, starting at Manchester Apollo on 4 and 5 October, less than a month after the terrorist attacks. Everyone was still on edge, but the home-town crowd loved the

Billy Corgan performing with New Order.

shows, obviously, and they both went smoothly. Then we headed to Glasgow for two gigs, starting on 7 October at Barrowland. Stuart and Colin from Mogwai were in the crowd, and before my set I tipped out to say hi. I remember sitting backstage with New Order, all of us glued to the TV, watching the breaking news, as the world was informed by President George W. Bush that an attack on Al-Qaeda and Osama bin Laden was in progress in Afghanistan. Barney wasn't happy. But the show must go on, and the band went out and played a great set, launching it with their new single, 'Crystal', which in my opinion is the last great New Order song (although I did like 'Be a Rebel' – especially the remix I did of it!).

The crowd went mental, as only a Glasgow crowd can, and when the set was over, they howled for more. I think the band played an encore, but not a long one. Once backstage, a disagreement occurred. Barney was done and wanted to get the fuck out; he was really nervous about the potential of some sort of home-grown terrorism there at the gig. I remember things getting trashed as the disagreement escalated. I hobbled back out into the hall to find Stuart and Colin. Things were getting somewhat nasty, and they looked worried. They didn't want me to show my face, since the crowd was really upset by the lack of a better encore. I went back to the band to tell them what was going on. They were definitely ready to roll out of there, so we somehow snuck out without the now extremely unruly audience spotting us. Colin and Stuart called me, saying that people were really tearing up the place. A week later, New Order got a message from Noel Gallagher. Oasis had played Barrowland the following week and had been very impressed by what a good job New Order had done of smashing up the place – they were still cleaning up!

We made it to London and a gig at the Brixton Academy. I was opening for the band and was excited by the prospect of playing there. I had lots of mates in the audience, a big crowd to play to, and I had my set planned out. DJing before a band's gig was different to playing in a club. First, no one was gonna dance. Second, they were there for New Order. No ego if you're warming up for a band; you are the appetiser. So I'd play stuff that would appeal to their crowd. At the time, the new thing was mash-ups, and I was making lots of them. One of my favourites was a clash between Peaches and The Kinks. Another was a mash-up of the Beach Boys' 'Good Vibrations', peppered with bits of Busta Rhymes and Missy Elliott. I called the artist the Beach Bustas. I played it at Barrowland, and it worked really well ending my set, so I planned to do the same in Brixton. As I started to play, I was told by Andy Robertson, New Order's manager, that I'd get a call from the band when they were close to the venue, but I had around an hour. So I played and I drank (probably vodka and cranberry). I was feeling good, and the crowd was into it. I was getting close to the forty-five-minute point when I got a call from Barney. He told me that they'd arrived and would be ready to go on in five minutes, so I threw on my 'Good Vibrations' mash-up. When people realised what song it was, and the Busta vocal busted through, they went off. Just like I thought they would. Mayhem. The track played through, and I then looked for the band.

No band, and no follow-up track cued up.

My phone rang. It was Barney. They'll actually be there in twenty minutes, he laughed.

Ha-ha. I rushed to find another track. Trust me, I was never fooled again.

Laminate from New Order's 2002 tour of Australia.

The band then asked me to join them in Australia for a couple of gigs at the Big Day Out festivals in January 2002. Since I had never been to Oz, I decided to do them, although my knee was still giving me major problems. I invited my new girlfriend, In-Sook Chappell (a writer/actress I had just started seeing), to come along. On the way over we stopped in Hong Kong, and I foolishly did lots of walking through its hills, which made my knee much worse. By the time we made it to Sydney, it was pretty fucked. I had to use crutches, navigate the huge festival grounds on a golf cart and sit on a stool while I DJed. And while In-Sook and the band had fun doing lots of touristy stuff, I was laid up in the hotel, in pain. Luckily, the girl from New Order's record label had a surgeon brother who was able to see me. It turned out it was my meniscus, and I needed surgery! I had it immediately, and as a result was finally able to get some strong painkillers. The doctor told me the best thing for my rehabilitation would be to start swimming, which would build up my calf. That was how I got into swimming laps, which I still do to this day.

In-Sook got a call to audition for a big film, so she went back to London without me. When I later returned to England, on orders from the doctor I had to break up the long flight back, so I stopped off in

Hong Kong for a few days. From my hotel bed, I watched my hometown football team, the Patriots, play and win the Super Bowl on TV, sharing the experience with my father over the hotel phone. Quite a phone bill, but it was well worth it.

Closer to home, New Order were headlining a festival in Finsbury Park that summer, and I got to open for them. I was also given a tent so I could promote my new label, Whacked – I needed a way to get my latest productions out. I launched the label with a mash-up of Argent's 'Hold Your Head Up', with 2 Many DJs providing a great remix. The guys came to check out the gig, along with Tommie Sunshine and Trash's DJ Erol Alkan. I remember it was raining on and off all day, but as New Order made their way out and I played my 'Good Vibrations' mash-up, the sun started shining.

Erol Alkan, me and Tommie Sunshine at New Order gig, Finsbury Park, 2001.

After the gig, the band, Tommie and I made it over to the Landmark Hotel. I was sitting next to Tommie; Barney, Hooky and some other folks were on the other side. Tommie was looking across the room, and he whispered to me, pointing, 'Look over there. Is that Entwistle?' I looked, and damned if it wasn't John Entwistle of The Who. I motioned to Hooky, who I knew must be a Who fan; if you listen closely to the intro of 'Love Will Tear Us Apart', you can hear a bit of The Who's 'Pinball Wizard' in there. I pointed out the Ox to the Hook, then we both motioned to Barney. The four of us walked over and introduced ourselves to Entwistle and his friend. Obviously, we gushed all over him, saying how we were big fans. I mentioned to him a Who gig I had gone to when I was in junior high school, and how long my ears had been ringing for afterwards. John seemed to brush his hair from his ears, then pulled out two hearing aids and said, 'Look what playing with Townshend for forty years did to me!' Barney then mentioned that he had reached out to Townshend re his tinnitus, which they both had, and how helpful Townshend had been.

I was tired and not far from home, so I said my goodbyes, caught a cab and went to bed. I later heard from the guys that they had ended up in Entwistle's room, staying up late partying. Two weeks later, Entwistle died in Las Vegas.

Barney and Hooky at the Fuji Rock Festival, Japan.

The next time Barney, Hooky and I would get together was when they agreed to DJ my second Return to New York party, in a battle against the Pet Shop Boys, on 22 February 2003. That was a pretty wild night; it might also have been the impetus for unleashing Hooky on the world as a DJ. The next evening we all went to have a meal at Harlem. I shared many bottles of red, and I remember Hooky and Phil running off into the night after the meal was done, off on a bender. Hooky has told me that this was his last major drinking session. I think it was also the final time I'd see Barney and Hooky together.

I booked Hooky for a few DJing gigs. One was particularly memorable: my first Return to New York party in Barcelona, at Razzmatazz. I had just started going out with Annette (who is now my wife) and took her on the trip. Hooky was on first, playing a mixed set made up of some New Order mash-ups and random techy stuff. Meanwhile, Annette and I had a drink and chilled out, in our own world. I went on next, playing for an hour or so. When I finished, I came back to my new girlfriend, who was now off her face. Hooky had got her smashed on vodka and cranberry. Annette and I then had our first big fight. I somehow managed to catch her as she ran down the road, and we sorted it out. Hooky quit drinking soon after.

A now-sober Hooky played with me and Blur's Alex James in Paris and at a RTNY party in Miami in 2005. Then his band split in 2007. Hooky had been on my friend Clint Boon's radio show and had said something about New Order being no more. Which set off a tidal wave of events that quickly split the band into two warring factions. One day I was on a train to Macclesfield to go to Barney's stag party, as he and Sarah, his long-term partner, were finally getting married. It was pouring down when I got off. Someone poked me on the shoulder, and it was Hooky. He looked somewhat down. 'You up here for Bernard's do?'

'Yeah,' I answered. 'Aren't you going?'

'No, I'm not invited,' he answered sadly. He went on to tell me that he had been to see Tony Wilson, who was pretty much on his deathbed.

I went to Barney's do and mentioned seeing Hooky. I prodded him to give Hooky a call.

'No way.'

That ended that.

A few weeks later, Tony passed away. I planned to go to Manchester for the funeral, but then Tony's son Ollie called me, saying that Tony had requested that I play at his wake. The funeral was attended by Hooky and many of the industry people who had known and loved Tony. I sat with my friend Seymour Stein, who was really distraught. It felt like the end of an era. It seemed like a funeral for not only Tony, but also Factory. And maybe New Order.

Since then my relationships with New Order's two warring factions have been complicated, but I've somehow stayed friends with both sides (I think Factory's legendary designer Peter Saville may be the only other person to have managed this). I've tried to get them back together. Even though I know how difficult it can be, I thought there might be a way with New Order.

I was in the process of starting to produce music docs and had been put in touch with a production and distribution outfit called Submarine. The company's David Koh expressed interest in a film about New Order. There had never been a proper one made, so I called my friend Don Letts and asked if it would be of interest to him. Don had made the great *Westway to the World*, about The Clash, and he could definitely handle anything a rock band in disarray might throw at him. He thought the New Order story might be the last rock'n'roll tale, and a documentary he'd love to make.

I mentioned it to New Order's management team and to Hooky. Both parties were excited; they all loved *Westway* and Don. We organised a trip to Macclesfield on 20 May 2013. First up, a pub lunch with the band. They were all very interested but a bit apprehensive about doing anything while involved in a lawsuit with Hooky. We tried to alleviate their concerns, telling them we could shoot the doc and not release it until there was a settlement. Don also promised that he would need them for just two days. So, lunch concluded, it was looking doable. Barney then asked the big question: 'So I guess you're gonna go see him?' We answered in the affirmative, so he offered to drive us over to the pub that Hooky was in, but he'd only drop us at the bottom of the driveway. When we got there, Hooky was busy with his ghost-writer, working on his new book. He was totally up for doing the film, no issues at all.

Don and I were pretty excited and confident on the train back to London. We got another UK film production company called Pulse interested. It all looked great. But then Steve and Gillian had an issue: they wanted to look forward, not back. OK . . . It's always gonna be something with New Order.

My last real attempt to get the ex-friends and former bandmates together came when I was in Manchester for Hooky's sixtieth-birthday do in February 2016. It was a great, intimate party with lots of his old friends; I think me and the DJ Graeme Park may have been the only other music people there. While I was over I called Andy, New Order's manager, and left a message, telling him I was in town.

Before leaving for the airport I sat with Hooky for breakfast. My phone was on the table, when it rang, with Andy's name showing up. Hooky saw it. I picked up the phone, tipped outside and had a few words with Andy, who offered to drive me to the airport. I went back in and asked Hooky if he wanted me to speak to Andy about sorting out their legal situation. He said, 'Go for it.'

By the end of the ride with Andy, we had seemingly worked out something I could go back to Hooky with. Which I did. Hooky seemed open to following up on the offer, but when my flight landed, I saw that I had a slew of messages from Andy. He had spoken to New Order's lawyers, and they had given him a real bollocking. The offer was off the table. And that was that.

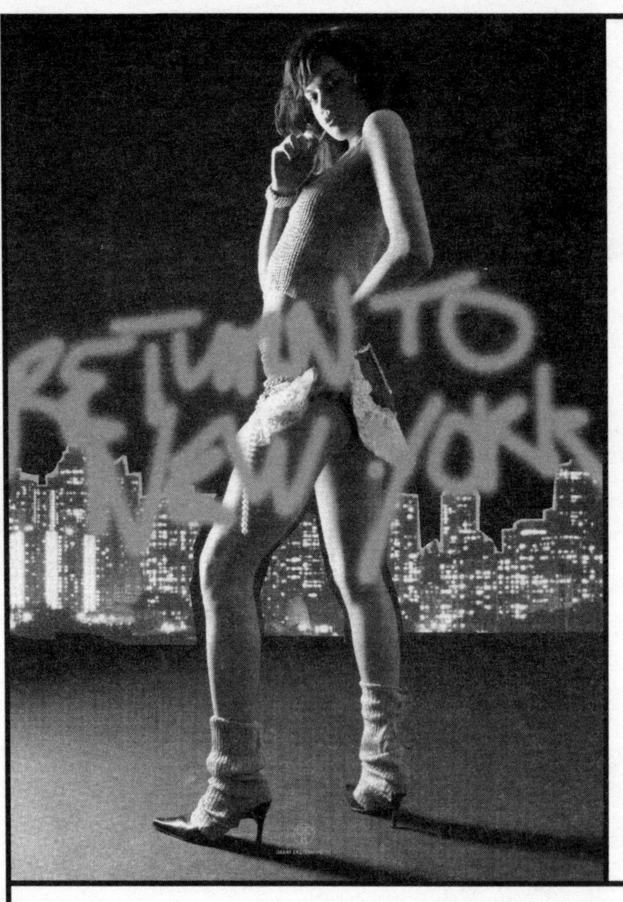
RETURN TO
NEW YORK

38.

RETURN TO NEW YORK

2002–18

In June 2002 I penned an article for *Fader* magazine's 'Electroclash' issue while lying hungover on a beach in Barcelona. It was my first trip to Spain, there to DJ at the Sónar festival, opening for the Pet Shop Boys. I wrote about my recent discovery of DJ Larry Tee and his Frankenstein-like electroclash creation, how it was re-energising and inspiring me, and how, after spinning at a party at Luxx in Brooklyn, I had felt a strange urge to go back to NYC. I ended the article by saying, '. . . maybe now I can return to New York'.

While I never returned to the city I called 'home' in the 1980s, I was inspired enough by these new vibes to launch a club night by the name of Return to New York in my new home town of London. Created on a whim, this party was an instant success and birthed many lifelong friendships, inspired a new sound and helped change the club scene worldwide. Its short shelf life was due to my lack of focus, along with too much partying by both me and my partners. After a three-year run, it was pretty much gone.

I had recently moved to Notting Hill. I had a weekly radio show on XFM, co-owned a chain of pool bars in all the hippest locations and was also in the process of opening my own soul-food restaurant, Harlem (more of that shortly). And I was still working on completing my solo album. Why the hell would I want to launch my own party? Good question!

Part of my reasoning was the lack of a good party in London, a place where I could DJ and test out my new music, and maybe just a bit of me wanting to be relevant at a time when my musical output was just a few remixes and productions. But, again, I didn't think it through. I jumped right in, trusting partners I didn't really know, thinking I could rely on them for business savvy, while I could be the creative force. Unfortunately, it just didn't work out like that for me.

This time I attempted to do things correctly. I met a promoter named Sean Mclusky through his American wife, Katy. Sean had been the drummer in the 1980s band Jo Boxers. He loved the idea of collaborating on an event that would bring together the hip 1980s DJs and bands with new-school electro talent for a night of debauched fun. While London was still vibrant, Britpop was no longer at its peak. Times were changing, and there was a thirst for something fresh. Sean and I schemed. He knew many of the venue owners, agents and new acts we'd need to connect with in order to make our dream party happen.

We immediately decided to focus on the Shoreditch/Hoxton/Liverpool Street area. I was opening an Elbow Room there and had been clubbing at the Blue Note in Hoxton for years. There were some good parties happening in the area, in particular the Electric Stew at the Great Eastern Hotel. The hotel was owned by Sir Terence Conran, the legendary architect, designer and restaurateur. We liked the Stew's approach but thought that with our musical concept and connections, we could take it a step further. We met with the Great Eastern's management and sold them on our concept, proposing a full takeover of the hotel. We would sell rooms in combination with tickets. Unbelievably, the hotel was empty at weekends, and they quickly gave us the green light to launch our party. Looking back, it does seem like we stole the Stew's venue, but that was never our intention.

I already had connections at the hip new radio station XFM, as my friend there, Charlotte Soussan, headed up its marketing department. She loved our Return to New York idea. We had collaborated on my Elbow Room 'Sunday Jam' parties, which already had a dedicated following. When I mentioned our idea of a UK tour to launch the brand, she jumped at the chance of XFM being involved. Besides having a show on the station, I was also a rabid listener, which is how I first came across LCD Soundsystem's 'Losing My Edge'. Upon first hearing it, I reached out to Trevor Jackson, the head of their UK label, Output. He connected me with the band's leader, James Murphy. I quickly offered James the headliner spot for the launch of Return to New York, only afterwards asking whether he had a live band. 'Sure,' he replied. He was sort of fibbing. I later found out they hadn't done a single fucking gig, a fact I only discovered when James admitted on stage that it was their first LCD gig. *Ever.*

Sight unseen, the band would be our headliner. Their record was a game-changer, tearing up the airwaves and clubs like Erol Alkan's Trash. I reached out to Erol with the news that we had booked LCD and offered him a gig. He was in. Then it was on to 2 Many DJs, who were also excited by the prospect. We finally added Trevor to the DJ line-up.

Me and James Murphy of LCD Soundsystem at a Return to New York party at the Elbow Room, Shoreditch, 2002.

Looking back, it was pretty amazing that my agents at International Talent Booking were able to book a Return to New York DJ tour of Britain pre our London launch. 2 Many DJs, Erol and I played the Glasgow School of Art, Liverpool's Chibuku, Birmingham's Medicine Bar, Manchester's Music Box and the Leeds Elbow Room before the London launch, with the Empire in Belfast, the Half Moon in Cork and Spirit in Dublin coming afterwards.

Back in London, things seemed to be coming together nicely. Sean searched for sponsors and locked in Pioneer. Then there was the old-school talent to book, so I called my long-time friends Jellybean Benitez, Kurtis Mantronik and Lady Miss Kier, who were all in. I added Princess Superstar (whose album I was producing) and her DJ partner, Alexander Technique. We now had an exciting, decade-spanning line-up. And it came together painlessly because we had booked the artists directly – without dealing with their agents! Those hassles would come later.

This being well before social media, we actually had to print and distribute fucking flyers (which Sean curated) around the city's record shops and clubs. Sean also commissioned innovative projections for the walls of the hotel's twenty-storey atrium; looking back at the videos, the visuals have held up really well. We had somehow navigated a complete takeover of this huge hotel. Amazingly, they had given us full run of the place. At 2 a.m. the partying could move into the suites and go on all night long.

By dawn the next morning, it was clear (through our hazy hangovers) that our 23 November party had been all we had hoped for and more. It had been a sell-out and an undeniable creative success. LCD Soundsystem, playing in what looked like a hotel function room (which it was), had blown everyone away. It was obvious to all that they were a band on the rise. We had launched them to a standing-room-only London audience – and, in reality, to the entire world. Both Erol and 2 Many DJs had killed it, playing their mash-ups and electro to a joyously out-of-control crowd; it had been a gig that helped to cement their legends. Erol had even hopped onto the drum kit and banged away, augmenting the Dewaele brothers' bombastic set. I hadn't got around to much DJing. I had been too busy running from room to room, checking on things and shooting video (and drinking red wine). I had been *so* in my element – proud and having fun hanging with friends both old and new. It had been reminiscent of those 1980s nights at the Funhouse.

Sean and I both got suites, relaxing there for the weekend and basking in the party's success. Unfortunately, amazing though it was, we made absolutely no money that night. This would be a running theme of these events, as, out of insecurity, we constantly booked way too many fucking DJs, as well as booking 2 Many DJs.

The next day was a bit of a hungover mess. Many of the artists and attendees had booked rooms in the hotel and partied through the night, but the word was out. When the next issue of *NME* hit, we got a great review for both the party and LCD's performance.

Sean and I realised that we'd need help with the production side of the parties. Being musicians/artists, neither of us was great at it. But since Sean had been producing events for quite a while, I figured he had it all covered. Also, I had unfortunately always been bad at realising how much drug-taking my partners did, until it was too late.

At this point I decided it might be a good idea to record an anthem for the party and for New York City (remember that the 11 September tragedy had happened only a year and a half earlier) entitled 'Return to New York'. Crazily, I decided to provide the lead vocal! Princess Superstar, whose album I had been working on, provided the rap and an appearance in the video.

Me and Princess Superstar on the Brooklyn Bridge, shooting our music video, 2003.

Since my article for *The Fader* had sort of been the start of RTNY, I approached Eddie Brannan, the magazine's creative director, to partner up for a RTNY party in Miami for the Winter Music Conference. It was typically a house-music-heavy event, but I thought we could make some noise by bringing in indie/electro heads to stir things up. *The Fader* crew loved the idea, and I got to calling up some friends to see if they wanted to get some sun and fun in Miami. We pulled out all the stops, with Adidas joining *The Fader* as sponsors. Looking at the list of acts we brought to the Winter Music Conference now, it seems insane: The Rapture, Peaches, LCD, 2 Many DJs, Junior Sanchez, Princess Superstar,

Electrocute and Kenny Dope! We found a spot called the Soho Lounge, in the then sketchy Design District, and our party rocked, although at some point the police shut down 2 Many DJs' outdoor set.

We again took the party on the road, this time to Ibiza in August 2003, which was my first visit to the white island. Our party there was a co-production with MTV Aqua Sonic and the Ibiza Zoo, where I played, along with 2 Many DJs. It was so hot that I ended up DJing shirtless; when you approached the DJ booth and could see me only from the waist up, it looked pretty strange. The Dewaele brothers still joke about how it looked like I was naked behind the decks!

David Dewaele, Stef Dewaele, Peaches and Gonzales at the Great Eastern Hotel for a Return to New York party, 2003.

Sean and I then played the back room at a Return to New York-branded MTV after-party at Privilege, which at the time was the biggest club in Ibiza and the home of Manumission. These gigs brought the new electro sound to the island for the first time, meaning we were on the map there. We also did a few more gigs that summer, including the Lovefields festival in Holland, again with 2 Many DJs and Erol, and Cafe Monde in Barcelona with Junior Sanchez.

Sean brought in a young guy named Robin Scott-Lawson to help with operations. He was very organised and quickly became our junior partner. But we soon realised that we had outgrown the Great Eastern Hotel. After some searching, Sean discovered the perfect spot: seOne, a huge venue made up of numerous railway arches, just south of the river, that would be perfect for a Return to the Rave extravaganza. This party would be our biggest swing for the fences, and we went for it with a cracking line-up. I put together the House Room, which was headlined by Todd Terry, playing his first UK gig in four years, Marshall Jefferson, Kurtis Mantronik and DJs Are Not Rock Stars. In the Electro Room, 2 Many DJs headlined, along with producer Richard X, Erol Alkan, me and Andy Fletcher of Depeche Mode. The Rap, Breaks & Hip-Hop Room featured the then up-and-coming DJ/producer Mark Ronson and Scratch Perverts. The live bands were my act the Loose Cannons, plus Whitey, Avenue D and Output.

After doing a promotional radio interview at KISS with Princess Superstar, I took Todd Terry and Mark Ronson to a pre-rave dinner at the just-opened Harlem. We dined on waffles and fried chicken, before taking a car over to seOne. As we drove over London Bridge and approached the club, I saw a huge line snaking around the block! When I realised that the doors weren't open, I freaked. I jumped out of the car to see Sean standing there. I calmly (not really) attempted to find out what the fuck was going on: something about one of the doors being stuck. I sort of remember pushing it open and making sure the impatient crowd were able to make their way in. Only very recently did a friend tell me that Sean typically did this to make it look like he had a crowd – only this time, we really did.

As it was a rave, most people were partaking in the drugs of that time and others. But not I, who was just sipping red wine. The music was full-on and awesome, each room blowing up. The House Room was like an old-school Chicago throwdown, with each DJ bringing it.

The Electro Room rocked. The visuals were amazing, with huge electronic landscapes projected above the DJs, which was something that was pretty new at the time. I was meant to spin, but there was never enough time for me at these parties. This took clubbing in London – maybe even worldwide – to a new level. We had around four thousand people coming through the door, the party was truly out of control, and at the end of the night, exhausted and somewhat wasted, Sean, Robin and I sat in the back room, divvying up boxes of cash. This would be *the* high point of our RTNY journey, both financially and artistically, and, unfortunately, the beginning of the end of a great thing.

A short while later, I was in back in NYC, visiting the new Soho House, relaxing, and having a drink. My thoughts were interrupted by a shout: 'Hey, Arthur!' It took me a second, but I realised that it was the Manumission crew from Ibiza. Brother Andy McKay, after a quick hello, wasted no time in informing me of his plans. 'Hey, man, that was an amazing Return to New York party at seOne. We're gonna rip it off in Ibiza. We're going to call them Ibiza Rocks!' Not sure what I said in response. Obviously, I was not happy, but what was I going to do? I had unleashed the genie from the bottle. I later heard from Eddy Temple-Morris, a DJ and friend at XFM, that he had come up with the name Ibiza Rocks, and Andy had shafted him too.

We decided to stick with seOne when we started planning our next party in London. The warehouse was a perfect venue, and we could fit in thousands of ravers. We planned a huge two-day celebration on 4 July. Big mistake. We hadn't factored in how much competition we'd have from the summer festival season. We put together a great line-up, tagging the party as a '4th of July Weekend Bash'. Saturday was '28 Hour Party People', with Mike Pickering, Graeme Park, Shaun Ryder, Mani and Bez. In the Electro Room, we had Erol Alkan, Headman, Tommie Sunshine and myself; in the Hip-Hop Party Room, it was Stretch Armstrong, Bristol DJs Krust and Die, and the Loose Cannons; and in the Live Room, a group I was currently producing for Mute Records, Pink Grease, and Mick Jones of The Clash's new band,

Carbon/Silicon. Sounds like an ace fuckin' party, and it was. We did well that first night.

Unfortunately, we bit off more than we could chew on the second night, which was aimed more at a gay audience. I brought Junior Vasquez, my old assistant and editor, over for his first UK set in seven years, and we did get lots of press in the run-up to the event. The fact he had not been in town for so long was a huge plus. Or it would have been, had he shown up at the venue. He never left his hotel room. No one had informed me that Junior had developed a bit of a substance issue. Word got out that he hadn't turned up, and the gay crowd went elsewhere. We had a great line-up, with Chromeo, Mark Moore, JoJo De Freq and an excellent Breaks Room, but the party was a flop. At one point, I called the venue where the gay crowd had gone that night to see if they'd like Junior to play a surprise set, as I still wanted him to have a crowd to play to. But even after I had worked it all out, he refused to leave his hotel room. I never saw him again, and when I didn't pay him the second half of his fee, he sued us. *Unbelievable*.

That was the last full-blown RTNY party that Sean and I promoted together. But I wasn't ready to give up on the brand, so Robin and I decided to take it on the road to Paris and the Rex Club. We planned

Pedro Winter, of Ed Banger Records, and Justice at the Rex Club, Paris, for a Return to New York party.

our first RTNY Paris event to coincide with Paris Fashion Week. My then girlfriend Annette's label, Felder Felder, was selling there, so we decided to throw a party to help bring visibility to the brand. The owner of the Rex loved the concept and agreed to pay the artists, Robin and me. A free trip to Paris, where we'd make some cash, keep RTNY alive and have some fun with friends? Hell, yeah!

Me, Hooky, Rowetta of the Happy Mondays and Barney at the Great Eastern Hotel for a Return to New York party, 2003.

Over the course of our run at the Rex, we had some amazing line-ups. Our first party featured Tiefschwarz, Erol Alkan, Trevor Jackson, Mu, Pedro Winter and myself. There were also these two young DJs hanging about, waiting for a chance to get on the decks. They were called Justice. Our next Rex event included Alex James from Blur vs Hooky on the decks, with me, Pedro and Justice DJing. Then we brought Soulwax Nite Versions Live to Paris, with Jarvis Cocker and Steve Mackey of Pulp, myself, Justice and Pedro all DJing – another excellent night. The friends of the Rex's owner had a great time, but the artists' costs ended up being exorbitant, considering the size of the room, and our Parisian experiment was over.

I had met a Canadian promoter named Mario Jukica through Junior Sanchez. He was one of the top club promoters in Toronto, so we discussed bringing RTNY over. Mario had a few venues available. First, we used a smaller one called the Mode Club, before eventually graduating to a huge club in an old department store called Circa, which had been opened by the legendary Peter Gatien, the man behind such infamous clubs as Limelight and Club USA in NYC. Mario was a great guy and really knew his music. Only thing is, his company was called AD/D! He was obviously open about his issues, but I should have known better.

Nonetheless, we were kindred spirits, and he really got things rolling in Toronto. He had a full schedule of gigs planned for 2005. I came over for the first few at the Mode. It was a cool club, almost like a little theatre, and was located on a small but busy street in Toronto. One night we were chilling outside, when Mario spotted someone and asked me, 'Hey, do you want to meet this local kid? He's in a soap opera, but he wants to be a rapper.' He motioned to this young guy walking down the street. I said, 'Sure,' and Mario introduced us. It was more like a quick 'Hello, good to meet you' than a long conversation. The kid's name? Drake.

The parties were becoming more successful, so Mario decided he wanted to book LCD Soundsystem to play a big 2,500-capacity venue called the Kool Haus. James agreed, and I came over to DJ the event and hang. LCD were great, and James, in a bit of a drunken speech, gave me a big shout-out for having promoted the very first LCD gig.

We then moved the party to Circa, where we hosted acts like Questlove and Lupe Fiasco. Things were going well between Mario and me, although I really wasn't seeing a lot of income, as was normal. Mario then had this idea for a residency in Ibiza, which I was totally up for. He had a great connection with a guy who could make it all happen: the son of the owner of Amnesia, who wanted to meet up with us. Being off-season, we both made our way to Barcelona to discuss the possibility.

Things sounded really good. The parties would be held on the same night as Amnesia's legendary foam bashes, and he asked us to book the type of acts that RTNY was known for. He wanted to bring electro to Ibiza. He agreed to have Mylo and Justice as our residents; both had big tracks out but were still up and coming and weren't ridiculously overpriced. We spoke with their agent, Martje at Decked Out, whom I knew, as she booked Erol. Fees were agreed and papers signed. It looked like we were actually going to bring RTNY to Ibiza for summer 2006!

Then things fell apart. First, Mylo now couldn't be the sole headliner on his night because he was also committed to doing a Cream party on the island. He could play ours, as long as he had a joint headliner. And, of course, he wasn't prepared to take any less of a fee. Next, my friends from Justice realised they'd have to catch connecting flights to get to the island for the Sunday parties we were proposing. They didn't want to have to sit in an airport for a few hours each week. Poof! Just like that, our Ibiza dreams were gone.

I still had a RTNY residency booked in Barcelona, at the great club Razzmatazz. These gigs at Razzmatazz have continued on and off for twenty years, with artists such as Stuart from Mogwai, Jarvis Cocker, Junior Sanchez, Ali Love, Princess Superstar and Alexander Technique all joining in. I helped pull off a massive Happy Mondays live gig there in March 2005, which was almost another disaster, as Javier, the promoter, paid Shaun Ryder some money upfront, before the show, and he and a few other band members just disappeared. Fortunately, they reappeared in time to perform a blinding set (and collect the outstanding fee). Afterwards, a young rave girl approached me while I was spinning at Lolita, the small club there, and offered me an E. I pointed to a grinning Bez, who was standing next to me. 'Give it to him,' I said, which she did, and Bez promptly went missing for a few days.

My last RTNY gig at Razz was on 24 August 2018, when I brought my band Rockers Revenge over to play there live. It was their first time in Europe and their first gig together in thirty years. The young crowd was very open to their music, and the band loved being there.

I then played the best set I have ever played at a RTNY party.

39.

MUNCHIE DREAMS OF A 'HIP RAP MOGUL'

2001–8

I really have no idea what got into me, trying to open a restaurant in London, and a soul-food restaurant at that. I really did love soul food – ribs, fried chicken and waffles – and definitely soul music. But did I need to actually open my own soul-food restaurant?

Absolutely not. I guess part of my motivation was that having invested in the Elbow Room and experienced its success, I thought it would be fun to do the same with a concept that was purely mine. But although I was involved with the Elbow Room and my Sunday sessions there were successful and fun, I never had to watch the till. Or do a rota. Or do anything but drink, eat, play music and have fun. I had no responsibilities there.

If anyone reading this is thinking about opening a restaurant, I strongly suggest you just hand me your money instead, and I'll hold it for you for safe keeping. You will thank me later. It's not a business for the faint-hearted, inexperienced or under-financed. One bad weekend or a broken piece of equipment or staff quitting at an inopportune time can kill your business. It's really that precarious.

There were problems with Harlem from day one. I actually found my first chef fairly quickly. That's where the real problems usually start – with the chef. Unless they are a partner in the biz, with a real stake in the restaurant, forget it. Chefs control most restaurants and often have the owners by the balls. I was hipped to a larger-than-life chef named Ashbell McElveen by my friend and BFE co-producer Lati Kronlund, who had taken a sommelier's course with him. Ashbell was a big dude, with an even bigger personality, who just loved his food. I went to his apartment in Harlem for a tasting, and it was the richest, drippiest soul food I had ever experienced. He was originally from Charlotte, North Carolina, and could cook shrimp and grits dosed with lots of garlic and chunks of butter like there was no tomorrow. He was also a total Anglophile, so didn't need much persuading to move over to London with me.

Early on, we had tastings for potential investors at my new house in Camden, with friends like Cameron McVey, Neneh Cherry and her best pal Andi Oliver (now one of the top TV chefs in the UK) in attendance. Everyone loved Ashbell, who was an entertaining chap with the gift of the gab, and his magnificent food. I couldn't believe my luck, but I decided I needed wider proof of concept to convince serious investors, so I approached my friend Eric Yu, who was a successful club, bar and restaurant owner in Soho, and told him about my idea. He offered to let me do a two-month pop-up at the Saint, and we could take it from there. Great idea. We randomly picked a date for the launch.

Ashbell was as excited as I was. He really needed a stage for his cooking; he lived for it and the attention it brought him. He started writing a menu for the opening, while I went through my contact book. It looked as if we'd have the most rocking pop-up restaurant opening ever in London. Eric got sponsorship from Buffalo Trace bourbon, I took care of the music, and Ashbell was ready to feed people. It was all feeling positive.

It was bright blue skies and sunny on the morning of our opening party. I was in my bedroom in Camden, getting ready to head into Soho to make sure everything was prepped and ready for the launch. CNN was turned on in the background, as it typically was back then. Out of the corner of my eye I seemed to see a plane hitting a skyscraper. I looked at my TV and realised that something really fucked was happening. Of all the days for our launch, we'd chosen 11 September

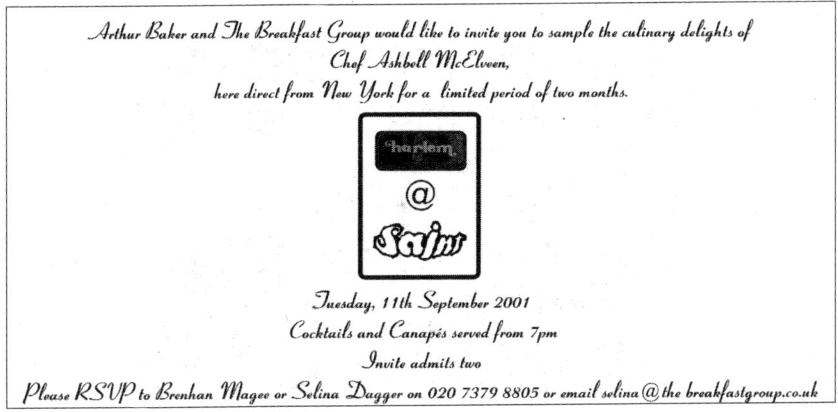

Arthur Baker and The Breakfast Group would like to invite you to sample the culinary delights of
Chef Ashbell McElveen,
here direct from New York for a limited period of two months.

harlem
@
Saint

Tuesday, 11th September 2001
Cocktails and Canapés served from 7pm
Invite admits two
Please RSVP to Brenhan Magee or Selina Dagger on 020 7379 8805 or email selina@thebreakfastgroup.co.uk

Invitation to the opening of the Harlem pop-up at the Saint, London.

2001. Within seconds my phone rang. It was Ashbell. He was freaking out, as he had friends and family who worked in the Twin Towers. He had already prepped quite a lot of the food the night before and wanted to know what we were going to do. I called Eric. We decided to just roll with it, so we all met at the Saint, continuing with our plans. Amazingly, quite a few people came. It was like an old Irish wake: everyone ate and drank and commiserated. Some of us found out that we had acquaintances in the building. It was a surreal night.

The next day Soho was shut down, in the fear that there'd be other attacks. We waited. As soon as London reopened, we were up and running, and Harlem actually did well. People enjoyed the food and the music. All in all, it was a success, and I should have called it a day right there and then. But, of course, I didn't. I started looking for a venue and investors.

When I finally found the perfect venue, it was right in front of my eyes, across the street from the Notting Hill Elbow Room. It was called Angelo's and was an infamous late-night, almost speakeasy-like den of iniquity, with less-than-average Greek food. I thought it could be a gold mine. Everybody in the music industry already knew of it, which was

Harlem, 78 Westbourne Grove, London.

a great start. I had been there many times in the past: after the Elbow Room closed we'd slide across the road and continue the drinking. It had the only late-night licence in Notting Hill, and I figured that if run properly, the bar alone could be extremely profitable. So I pursued it.

But my chef was getting antsy. He was desperate to be *the* star chef of London. In his mind, he already was, having done some catering and cooking for events and private meals. I kept him informed about our pursuit of Angelo's, and he was on board with that. So imagine my shock when I found out that he had made an offer on a venue less than a mile away. It was a small place on All Saints Road, which was historically a West Indian area. He was going to open it as Ashbell's, having been financed by an American hedge fund money man. This after I had paid for his trip over from NYC, loaned him money and helped him make a name for himself in London. I was fucking pissed off, and this incentivised me even more to open my spot and blow him out of the water.

He launched his place, and immediately the esteemed food critic A. A. Gill came by, loved the food and wrote a sterling review. That brought people there in droves. I went one night to check it out, and while the food was top notch, I knew that Ashbell would never be able to keep it up as a venue with that size and set-up. But it was proof of concept for me.

I still needed money – other people's, if possible – if I wanted to lock in Angelo's. There were many issues with the place. The owner had played fast and loose with his licence, and the council had whittled it down over the years, from all night to 4 a.m., and then to 3 a.m. They didn't really want it to be open late at all, so while he was in the process of trying to sell the place to me, the council was trying to take his licence from him. I had to prove to the council that I was an upstanding citizen, and I built my case through my being a partner in the Elbow Room, which was a well-run establishment. Eventually, I got a decent result. The council decided that we could stay open till 2.30 a.m., but no one was allowed admittance after 1 a.m. We'd also have to charge a membership fee. Eventually, having done all the checks and surveys, we exchanged papers. Angelo's was mine. But we still had neither chef nor investors.

Before we fell out, Ashbell had introduced me to Geoffrey Bullard, the owner of the Kalamazoo Grill Company in Michigan. He wanted to sell me a grill, *and* he knew a great chef he thought I should check out, Jon Fisher, who was a cousin of Narada Michael Walden, the record producer and drummer. I planned an eating trip to Kalamazoo, getting to Geoffrey's at close to midnight, hungry after travelling all day. I found chef Jon in the kitchen, smoking a joint. He smoked quite a few, Geoff and I joined in, and the clock ticked on. I think we ended up eating at 2 a.m. The food was amazing. Then he made some ice cream. We might have had that for breakfast – it's all a bit of a blur. I loved his food but was worried about his work ethic and the fact that he had never run a restaurant kitchen before. But he seemed intelligent, and Geoffrey vouched for him, and I agreed to bring him over to London so we could start developing the menu for Harlem.

But I was still under-financed, with no investors in sight. I got a message from my friend Melissa More, saying that she knew a restaurateur who might be interested in investing in and operating Harlem. Enter Stuart Hopson-Jones. Stuart was a partner in Smiths of Smithfield, a very successful steak restaurant right next to Fabric nightclub. This sounded very interesting, so we met up. He had just sold his shares in Smiths and had a quarter of a million quid to invest. He liked Harlem's concept and wanted to come in as managing director. I thought that if he was willing to invest that much, I'd be willing to let him run it. It had never been my intention to run Harlem anyway. But once I started to do some due diligence on Stuart, I had an uneasy feeling. I got his brother's number, and we met up at Martin Miller's hotel, right by my new restaurant. Stuart's brother relayed a few things to me about Stuart that made me feel even more queasy. At that point I had this intuition that I'd end up in court with Stuart some day. Which was right on the money. My main issue was, I didn't have the money to finish the restaurant. I talked to my partners, Paul Daly and Vijay Thakur, and we agreed that we needed his cash. They didn't have the same bad vibes that I had about Mr Hopson-Jones. In the end, I had no choice.

Things were coming together. We received our liquor licence, but any violation of its parameters and we'd be fucked and could lose it. Then Robin Scott-Lawson's sister mentioned that she had been at the opening of Zigfrid, the bar Paul was in the process of opening in Hoxton. She said the party had gone on very late. I got a bad feeling. Also, Paul hadn't even invited me. Suspicious, I called Robin, who was managing the bar. I asked him about the opening and how they were getting their late hours. He said, 'We're using Harlem's licence. Didn't Paul mention it to you?' No, he fucking didn't. Turned out my partner, who knew about all the difficulties I had gone through in order to get my liquor licence and the money I had spent, had decided to pull a fast one. Before Harlem was even open. I called him out on it, and he gave some ridiculous bullshit explanation. That was sort of the end of our friendship right there. He later pulled another scam on me that totally slammed the door on it.

But we finally opened Harlem. Jon was in the kitchen, his food was tasty and the buzz was picking up. I hired a great young restaurant PR person, Anouschka Menzies, and she started getting us on the press's radar. We did some friends-and-family events, and Stuart was behaving. Everything was looking pretty good.

After trading for a few weeks, we planned a grand opening party. I got my hot new act, the Loose Cannons, whom I'd just signed to Island Records, to DJ. I was co-managing them with their friend T, who was at the party too. Anouschka had a big guest list, as did Stuart. I invited friends from all over London and lots of locals, including a mortgage broker who lived on the block and had been dropping cash every night since we'd opened. He asked if he could bring a few of his clients. I said sure, without really thinking much about it.

Everything was going smoothly, and the cocktails were flowing. I was fairly buzzed and enjoying myself. It was turning into a great night – exactly what I had in mind when I decided to start this journey and open a restaurant.

Then this guy, one of the broker's guests – his friends were calling him Manc (he was from Manchester) – came up to me and said that his boss had ripped his suit in our bathroom. I asked who his boss was, and he pointed to this rather large guy in a fancy tracksuit. I was pretty wasted, so I said, 'Not to be funny, but maybe he ripped it because he's pretty large?'

Manc had a scared, shocked look in his eyes and said, 'You really don't want me to tell him that.'

I guessed his boss was out looking for me, since I was well known in Manchester for my work with New Order, so I said, 'Cool, let's go check out where the rip occurred.'

So me, Manc, his boss, the broker and T went down the very tight winding stairwell into an even tighter bathroom. My asshole partner had built a toilet with a curved wooden door that latched on to something that was meant to be a hook, but looked more like a fucking nail. It actually could have ripped the guy's pants.

'OK,' I said, 'I'll pay to have your pants tailored, no problem.'

But he said no, he wanted a grand for a new suit.

I said, 'What, really? For a tracksuit?' There was no way I'd pay that, and I felt confident that T, who was about six-foot-four and looked like a linebacker, had my back.

That really pissed the guy off. He turned around angrily and walked up the stairs and out the front door, followed by Manc and crew.

It was at that point that we were pulled aside and told by the broker that the boss was in fact the head of a London crime family. T went white when he heard that (T is black, by the way).

I immediately pulled the broker close, saying, 'What the fuck, man?'

He said he was sorry, but he was helping them obtain hard-to-get mortgages, because they didn't really like having to reveal their income, and he wanted to show them some fun. He said he'd work things out for me.

The next day I got a call. It was the man in the tracksuit. He asked, 'How about you come to my manor and we start over?' I declined. Who knew what he had planned?

Worried, I spoke to our Albanian door guys and the Albanian doorman godfather, who occasionally popped in to check up on his guys. He said they could handle any problem, but obviously I didn't want it to escalate into gang warfare.

Business went on. It was right before Christmas time, and Harlem was packed. My dad and stepmother were in town and were happily enjoying a meal and some drinks in the restaurant. I was standing by the bar, when this guy came up to me and poked his finger in my chest.

'Take care of this now and tell your boy T he's got to leave town!'

Then he was gone, just like that. He could have easily stabbed me, and no one would have noticed.

The next day I finally brought Stuart in and consulted with him. He said that we should send over a case of champagne and £500. That sorted it.

But Harlem was really starting to happen, and Anouschka was getting us a lot of press. We even got a review from the man A. A. Gill himself. It definitely wasn't as good as the one he gave Ashbell, and it was meant to be a diss, but I actually loved what he had written in *The Times*:

> Restaurants that are started as hobbies are rarely successful. Would you wear a suit made by an accountant who did tailoring on the weekends? But if you want to eat the munchie dreams of a hip rap mogul, then this is it.

Sounded good to me.

To be honest, our secret weapon was the late licence. That and the fact we served food till real late. At one point you could come to Harlem and get a steak at midnight, and we had a limited menu till 1 a.m. Which meant record labels started to make the restaurant their go-to spot, bringing travelling artists in late, after their gigs, especially black American acts, who they thought might be missing home cooking. For a time Grace Jones was a proper regular, holding court from her corner banquette. She particularly loved the special Harlem burger: a big fat American cheeseburger with fries, the type that wasn't

Annette, me, Grace Jones and Mark Jones attend a dinner to celebrate the release of Grace's album *Hurricane* at the Maddox Club, London, on 4 November 2008.

easy to get in London at the time. The Kills were late-night regulars, as were Ash, who did a photo shoot in the basement. Mark Hamilton from the band lived across the street, above the Elbow Room. Damon Albarn also lived down the road. He once called me late in the afternoon to see if the basement was available that night to do a gig with an African guitarist whom he was working with. That was a very memorable show. One night I came in to find Sam Moore, of Sam & Dave, sitting on a banquette. He was in town for a gig. He'd already finished his meal but was waiting around to tell me that he was the real Soul Man, after seeing a review in the window that called me 'a soul man'.

At one point, between all the Moroccan and Algerian chefs and kitchen staff, and the French waiters, waitresses and managers, my entire staff were 100 per cent fluent in French. This led to us becoming the weekend brunch spot for west London's French community, of which there were plenty. Where the French went, everyone else followed. We'd have lines out the door, and I'd be out there serving our mini-muffins to the ravenous waiting crowd. For a while the

Damon Albarn and his band perform at Harlem Notting Hill.

staff would automatically greet customers in French. One morning a familiar-looking guy came in with a crew. His name was taken and he joined the queue. After a moment I realised he was David Cameron, future prime minister. He had to wait like everyone else.

But the problems with Stuart started to become more frequent, as he liked his late-night sessions. Also, I was getting worried about his mental state. We had been thinking about taking on another space in Brixton, close to where he lived. Paul (whom I had to begrudgingly keep dealing with on Harlem business) and I had gained an option on a big old pub, the Prince of Wales. But since it was in Stuart's 'hood, he figured he should take the lead on the project. He did have some interesting, pretty ambitious plans for the venue. He had already hired a PA for himself and a full-time accountant for our 'head office', which was in his house. Paul and I thought this was premature. Though our first-year income bettered the projections in our business plan, we were still losing money because of the head-office costs.

But in the end we decided to take on Harlem Brixton, figuring it would make sense financially to spread the head-office expenses over two successful venues. While Stuart's state of mind worried us, his big concept of creating a rooftop club in the Brixton venue called DEX, which would feature DJs and hotel rooms, seemed to be a no-brainer.

The Prince of Wales was a sprawling pub, with an outdoor area that was great for eating and drinking, a separate building that was rented out for the time being but could potentially be a record shop, a first floor with offices and hotel rooms, and the rooftop club. Paul did a great job with fitting it out, mirroring the look and vibe of Westbourne Grove. I figured Harlem could be rolled out all over the country, and it could have been had it been run by the correct team, which we unfortunately weren't.

Again, we had to work hard getting the proper licence. For financial reasons, we would need to trade late into the night at weekends. While we were readying Brixton, I focused on west London and spent time watching the shop there. Our general manager, Michael Parker, was working between both spots. There were the typical food and staff issues. We went through chefs like water. I'd hire really good, soon-to-be-stars chefs like Richard Turner and Mark Broadbent, but couldn't find certain staff who could commit to the gig for the money we could pay. I lived a five-minute walk away and was spending much more time in Harlem than at home. I'd DJ at night, cash out at the restaurant after closing and then open up in the morning. Annette would tell me that Harlem was becoming my top relationship, and she wasn't happy.

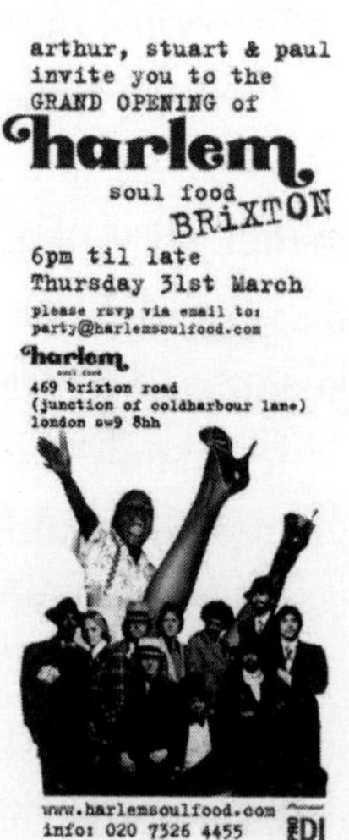

arthur, stuart & paul
invite you to the
GRAND OPENING of
harlem
soul food
BRiXTON
6pm til late
Thursday 31st March
please rsvp via email to:
party@harlemsoulfood.com
harlem
469 brixton road
(junction of coldharbour lane)
london sw9 8hh
www.harlemsoulfood.com
info: 020 7326 4455
DJ

Flyer for the Harlem Brixton opening party.

After a few false starts, we finally held our launch party for Harlem Brixton on 31 March 2005. It was rammed, drinks were flowing, the food was good and Stuart was in his element – his Brixton. Which was fine with me. Local heroes Basement Jaxx were in the house, along with Jocelyn Brown. More music people were on their way. There was a great vibe at the opening. I went upstairs to find Stuart so we could discuss something, and I interrupted a very troubling situation with a bunch of people in his office. I freaked out.

The next day I called a meeting with Vijay, Paul and my ex-wife Tina, who was also on the board of Harlem. We had to get him out. But it wouldn't be easy.

We ended up letting him leave his position. He still owned his shares, so we would have to come to a settlement. We hired an arbitrator and attempted to work things out. But while we were in negotiations, I was temporary managing director and running *both* sites, crossing town daily on the Tube from west to south in the heat of summer.

Things changed on 7 July 2005, the day of the London terrorist bombings. I regularly travelled on the Tube through King's Cross and was lucky not to have been involved. But the attacks obviously put a damper on summer fun in London. I remember sitting in arbitration, listening to Stuart accuse me of being a drug addict, when I had been clean since 1987. Eventually, we agreed to split the business, and very shortly after that I handed the keys to Brixton over to Stuart, while I kept the Notting Hill Harlem. I ended up paying close to £50,000 in legal fees.

Now I really needed help running the West London Harlem. My friend, the acclaimed restaurateur Jonathan Downey, came on board, and his team ended up managing it. I liquidated the original company at the end of 2008, and Jonathan bought the assets and kept it open. We would finally close the Harlem at 78 Westbourne Grove in 2010, with Jonathan relaunching that summer, right after my wedding, as Tiny Robot, an Italian bistro. The basement bar became the Starland Lounge members' club. Sadly, Tiny Robot didn't make it to 2012.

The Harlem West London site is now a Domus Nova estate agent's. Harlem Brixton is now the Prince of Wales pub, with the rooftop venue still trading as POW, a lively and very successful dance club, much like our plan for the original DEX.

I haven't seen Stuart or Paul in over fifteen years.

40.

FELDER FELDER

2008–18

I've often been asked which of my projects had me feeling the most pressure. Working with Dylan? *Beat Street*? The follow-up to 'Planet Rock'? The crazy deadline to finish 'Sun City' for the MTV premiere?

Nope.

None of these come even close to the stress and pressure you feel when preparing the music for a catwalk show. Prepping music for any fashion show can sometimes make Yom Kippur feel like a party. But doing it for a show held by my wife and her sister's label? Unbelievable.

Back story: I had grown up in the fashion business, at least the retail side of it. My dad had been the head buyer and merchandise man for women's coats at Filene's department store in Boston, before opening his own coat label. This job would regularly take him on buying trips to NYC when I was a kid, which seemed pretty exotic to me at the time. He was friends with a lot of the manufacturers he bought from, which translated into some nice big cheques from them for my bar mitzvah, and some of that cash ultimately helped finance my early music productions. As the buyer for the top retail store in Boston, my dad once hung out with Calvin Klein in Paris, before Calvin had his own clothing range. Dad was known in the industry as Mr Coats, and he launched a coat label by that name later in his career. My first paid DJing gig was for a Filene's fashion show at Sidney Hill Country Club in Boston that my dad put on.

I met my now-wife Annette at a fashion show after-party in London. I was single at the time, sort of playing the field, when my friend, make-up artist Georgina Graham, decided to take it upon herself to find me a girlfriend. She thought she knew the perfect girl, a model who would be at a Julien Macdonald party that night. So I went to a club off Carnaby Street. When she introduced me to said model, no sparks seemed to fly, and Georgina left me to my own devices. I was pretty hammered by the time I laid eyes on Annette from across the dancefloor. She was with two other statuesque blondes, one being her identical twin, Dani. I slid across the dancefloor and started chatting to her confidently. She was a tall, beautiful German, and intriguing. I seemed to remember having met her before, and I told her so. Not a line at all. We then figured out that it had been through our common friend, pop artist Duggie Fields, at Portobello Market a year earlier. Duggie had been accompanied by another German ex-model, Anita Pallenberg, that day. After chatting and getting a vibe from Annette, I tried to convince her to stay. I felt she wanted to, but the other two girls blocked that. Then, when we were about to leave, we ended up exchanging numbers, and things went from there. After some very long phone calls and a few memorable dinner dates, I realised that Annette was the one. She moved from her flat in Dalston to my place in Notting Hill soon after.

I was right in the midst of the hell that was my new restaurant Harlem, and Annette sort of got thrown right into it. After fine-tuning a few dishes that she and Dani liked to eat, I attempted to get the sisters to help me run the door for the downstairs club, which was Harlem's sole real cash cow. As admittance was cash-only, I really needed someone I could trust. After my convincing spiel finally won them over, they manned the door with their particularly selective, Studio 54 fashionista flourish. Eventually, we had the hottest crowd, and the cash would make it back to our safe without a hitch.

Annette had been a model but was now a fashion student at Central Saint Martins, with a desire to launch her own label with her sister. So, as a proud, doting new boyfriend, I invested my time (and money) in helping Annette and Dani to launch their label, Felder Felder. They had great ideas and a lot of potential. I also offered to make bespoke music mixes for their shows, with new remixes and productions for each and every one. I really didn't understand what I was getting myself into. That first Felder Felder catwalk show, for London Fashion Week's spring/summer 2008 collections, was a full-on shock to my system, sending me back to the drug-fuelled all-night mix sessions of the 1980s, only this time with no drugs and with duelling, stressed-out, twin rookie designers standing over me.

Me attempting to finish up the music for an upcoming – like in fifteen minutes – Felder Felder catwalk show.

To set the scene, there I was at the venue, on the floor, working through the night, dropping rough mix after rough mix, while praying for my dodgy old laptop not to crash and die. On finishing said mix, I'd run it down the hall to the auditorium and play it for one of the grandest damnedest dames of the fashion world, our stylist Patti Wilson. Oh, and Annette and Dani. Fortunately, Patti knew what she wanted and communicated it, down to the syllable of a gulp. Unlike the Felder sisters, who, although they had great taste in music, were definitely way less specific.

Our concept for the music for a Felder Felder show would be to take songs that were among the girls' favourites (after they'd decided on the theme of the show) and twist them through sampling or re-recording, often with great new female voices. Over the years we worked with some amazing vocalists, including Florence (of the Machine), Little Boots, Liela Moss (of the Duke Spirit), Anita Blay (the CocknBullKid), Eliot Sumner (I Blame Coco) and Kate Nash. I'd also pull in musician collaborators such as Stuart Braithwaite, Peter Hook, Johnny Turnbull, Lars Kronlund and Glen Nicholls to help me out. Moments before each show would start, I'd be sitting and sweating inside the venue. A

Dani and Annette on the catwalk, celebrating another successful show.

lot of interesting new music was made for just one grand play. Just like the fashion show itself, it required a huge amount of focus and investment for one very short performance.

Having a fashion label is much like opening a restaurant or starting a record label: the odds are stacked way against you from the start. Still, Felder Felder experienced creative success, dressing stars such as Florence, Rihanna and Kate Moss. The label was nominated in the prestigious Best Emerging Designer of the year category at the British Fashion Awards and gained NewGen/Topshop sponsorship for three consecutive seasons. We also did shows in Paris, NYC and Berlin, and collaborated with companies such as BMW and Baileys.

Thankfully, my relationship with Annette survived intact through all the fashion and restaurant traumas and music-business let-downs.

Models before the show.

So, after having been together for seven years, I finally shook off the fear of a third marriage and proposed to her. We were having a romantic, moonlit, ocean-side meal at Amante restaurant on the island of Ibiza when I popped the question. After calling her mother, she said yes! And, of course, we would get married on that island, our favourite place in the world.

I ended up taking total charge of proceedings, since Annette was deep in fashion craziness. At the time, she was still eating fish (she's now vegan), which made the menu choices a bit easier. I wanted to have our rehearsal dinner at my favourite restaurant on the island, Balafia, which had the best lamb chops, chips and tomato salad. Only problem was, it wasn't available for special events. They had never shut down for an event in the twenty-plus years they had been open. But I somehow convinced Miguel, the manager, to open on their one dark day (Sunday) and also to add grilled salmon to the menu for my soon-to-be wife and lots of her friends who didn't eat meat. They had never had fish on their menu and never have since. And as the rehearsal dinner had to be on a Sunday, our wedding was on the Monday, at Annette's favourite spot, El Chiringuito, a beautiful new beachfront restaurant. The celebrations were held on 4 and 5 July, which I thought was funny, seeing as the night before the ceremony was my last day of independence. Some friends were bothered by the wedding being on a Monday, but they all showed up and were very glad they did.

We had had to find a rabbi who would marry us. Annette planned to convert but hadn't done so yet, so most reputable rabbis wouldn't do it. We finally connected with Ibiza's infamous raving rabbi, a Chabad from Israel who would often be spotted partying at various Ibizan nightclubs. He was very well known at Pacha.

The night before the wedding I crashed out after the huge meal at Balafia. I had had more than my fair share of wine, lamb chops and after-dinner cocktails. We were staying in a big villa that our friend Stefano had rented, which ended up being party central that week. I woke up at around six to find a rave going on in the living room, with my friend Robert Levy DJing on his new portable mixer. And there was Annette dancing on the coffee table! To say I wasn't impressed is an understatement. I convinced her to come to bed, and the party ended soon after.

So our wedding day included a few hangovers. I was a bit nervous, so with a beer in my hand I decided to go swimming before the ceremony. After that, I sort of forgot my nerves and the fact that the clock was ticking. I was interrupted by one of Annette's girlfriends, who urgently communicated that Annette was waiting in the parking lot in a people carrier. She obviously wanted me there to see her arrival. So I dashed from the ocean to the bathroom by the beach, where I quickly donned my flashy Ozwald Boateng white suit. I actually got married with wet hair!

And it was a great wedding, even if I do say so myself. My dad and sister, along with Annette's parents and uncle, showed up to witness it. My dad was a real trouper; at eighty he was hanging hard with us all, and our friends really loved him. Annette looked beautiful in a

Me and Annette at our wedding dinner in El Chiringuito, Ibiza, 2010.

wedding gown designed by Dani. We got married right on the beach, under a traditional *chuppah*, after our friends first cleared out some nude sunbathers who were in our view! I had done a great job with the planning, but I hadn't thought about that.

The ceremony was a traditional Jewish service, until the rabbi segued into the current club smash, the Black Eyed Peas' 'I Gotta Feeling', keeping things light. My best man, John Robie, had decided at the last minute that he couldn't travel to Ibiza, so I had asked Tina to step in, which shows how strong our friendship has remained since our divorce! She gave a great speech, as did Annette's sister Dani and my dad. I regret being too shy (really!) to give one. I could do it now, though, and will give a great one at our next big anniversary celebration.

Most of our friends still claim it was their favourite wedding, that the food was second to none and the drinks flowed non-stop. It was just a great party. Lots of our friends pitched in, DJing and entertaining. And we even had an after-party! It was hosted by the great Sven Väth, a German DJ friend of ours. He gave Annette and I a plus-eighty list for his Cocoon party at Amnesia!

And the rabbi ruled the dancefloor there.

Both our marriage and the label are still alive and thriving. Annette and I are currently navigating lives as parents of the force that is Amarone, and Felder Felder has shifted its focus towards becoming a sustainable vegan fashion label – without those big, stressful fashion shows. However, looking back, part of me misses them. The label's catwalk shows consistently inspired me to come up with some of my most creative work in years. That music made up the majority of my musical output between 2008 and 2018. Unfortunately, it would all stay unreleased. Like so much of my later work.

41.

LIME LIFE

2007–14

I consider myself an ideas guy, although they're not always good ones. I often get bored if limiting my creative focus to just music, and there are no limits to my scope of brainstormed ideas or, I must admit, inability to finish what I have started. But popping between projects had always kept me more engaged, and the pressure excited me. Working on three separate things at once kept my ADHD in check.

Which leads us into my secondary career as a film-maker. Since high school, I'd always been intrigued by film production. I had been active in a video collective called Dog Dance Productions. We had somehow even made the cover of the *Boston Globe* with our early video experimentations. After my success with music, I'd been giving serious thought to making a movie, and the one I had in mind was an adaptation of the book *The Basketball Diaries*, which I had been obsessed with since high school.

I had one good connection in that world: my close friend Paula Harwood. We were mates from high school and had stayed in touch when we both moved to NYC in the 1980s. She had run a big commercial/music video production house, making the infamous Elizabeth Taylor diamond commercial and music videos such as Sir Mix-a-Lot's classic 'Baby Got Back'. She was married to the actor Peter Gallagher, who is an amazingly down-to-earth dude. Paula and Peter became my LA family. I watched their kids grow up, including their daughter Kathryn, whom I helped mentor early on in her musical career. She's now a Broadway star, having played the lead in *Jagged Little Pill*.

Back in the 1980s, Peter got a role in a film he thought was one of the best he'd ever been in. It was called *The Player*, directed by Robert Altman. There was a screening, and Peter asked me if I wanted to go. I loved Altman's films and jumped at the chance.

We got to the screening room at the Creative Artists Agency (CAA), and Peter introduced me to Altman, who was very charming. I was given a seat between the director and Paula. The room was filled with film-industry suits, who, I realised during the screening, were the target of a lot of the jokes in the movie. I loved the film. Peter was great, and I laughed a lot. I was the most animated person in the audience, and afterwards Altman grabbed my hand, shaking it sincerely and thanking me for laughing and being a great audience.

But I digress. I had always been a fan of cool indie films and had always loved the book *The Basketball Diaries*. When I approached Paula about developing it for a film, she was all in. I befriended the author, Jim Carroll, and almost got the option on the book, before losing out at the last minute. When the film was eventually released, with our choice, Leonardo DiCaprio, as the lead, I was pretty bummed out.

But making films never left my consciousness, considering how many of my Hampshire classmates had exploded in the business. There was Casey Silver, a poker- and b-ball-playing buddy who had become head of MCA; Robert Epstein, who had directed *The Times of Harvey Milk* and *Common Threads: Stories from the Quilt*; Michael Peyser, Woody Allen's right-hand man; Janet Perlberg, head of the SXSW film festival; and an unassuming guy who worked with Tina at the bookshop named Ken Burns.

Then there was my old friend from Everett Hafner's electronic-music class, Chris Hanley. We had reconnected in NYC in 1982, when he owned Intergalactic Studios. Then we were involved in a lawsuit. After that we had lost touch. A few years later, he started producing films, the most successful being the classic *American Psycho*.

Chris and I reconnected one night at London's legendary artist hangout, the Groucho Club. Chris was an art collector and good friends with Tracey Emin, who had been one of the so-called YBAs (Young British Artists) and would become one of the most influential artists in the UK. One day I bumped into Tracey while swimming in the rooftop pool at Shoreditch House. Knowing she was friends with Chris, I mentioned his name and jokingly said something rude about him. That turned our short talk into a long bonding conversation, as we swam in the pool and lounged by it. We quickly became friends, and she invited me to the opening of her *You Left Me Breathing* exhibition at the Gagosian gallery in LA soon after. Chris was going to host an after-party, which I ended up DJing at.

On arriving at the opening, I discovered Tracey and I had other friends in common. I bumped into my old friend Carole Siller, who had been my good buddy (and Pat Benatar's manager) Rick Newman's girlfriend in NYC in the 1980s. Her new boyfriend, Hamish McAlpine, a film producer, was quite a character, as were much of the art crew I was meeting.

Tracey Emin, photographer Richard Young and me at some posh do in London.

Tracey had taken over the bar and private dining room at the Beverly Hills Hotel, and it was quite an evening. I was now bitten by the art bug, and on returning to London, I decided that a dark comedy about the art world could do what Altman's *The Player* had done for the film world.

I dived right in and ended up spending the next few years consumed by writing a film script with a guy I randomly met sitting outside my flat on Alexander Street, Ron Johnstone. Amazingly, we put together a decent script for a film that I named *Paintbox*. It was decent enough for a new friend, Marcus Warren, an American living in London, to become interested in the concept and want to produce it. He had recently directed a great British political thriller/gangster flick, *The Heavy*, which was making some noise. I loved how it looked, so I tried to get him to direct *Paintbox*, but he claimed to have no sense of humour and wouldn't be able to do the script justice, because it was very funny. He didn't want to direct it, but he was all in on producing it. But try as we might, the project was never able to gain sufficient momentum to get a big enough director or lead actor on board, although we did get close.

At the same time, of course, I had another 'great' idea I'd started working on. I had produced Iggy Pop and Kid Rock on the 'It's Only Rock'n'Roll' project. Both sessions were comic and memorable, and they were both from Detroit. Two amazing characters – and their names, Rock and Pop. *Damn, there's something there,* I thought – The Pop & Rock Show! *How cool would it be to cast the two of them as father and son, maybe detectives, with sort of a* Rockford Files *vibe, but this time in Miami,* I thought. *And Iggy now resides there!* Even now, it still sounds like a winning formula to me.

I had spent lots of time travelling to Miami over the years, even purchasing a condo there back in 1991. I had witnessed it develop from a hub for retirees – a place to spend your golden years, in dilapidated hotels – to a burgeoning hipster destination for artists and musicians who wanted to escape the high prices and low temperatures of New York City. It had the sleaze of the East Village, right by the ocean, and was full of characters and graft, with venues such as the Sinatra Bar and Fat Black Pussy Cat – in other words, the perfect setting for our show.

Marcus and I slapped together a short treatment and tried to find a way to get it into Iggy's hands. I figured if Iggy was in, then Kid Rock would go for it – no-brainer. I had first met Iggy properly when I attended his gig at the Ritz, NYC, with Debbie Harry. She had introduced us after a set that saw Iggy climbing onto the suspended speakers and hurling himself from them. Then, for some reason, I let the project germinate for a couple of years. I guess I was busy with lots of other things. But when I saw that Iggy would be in London in July 2011 for the Hop Farm Music Festival in Kent, produced by my friend Vince Powers, I sprang into action. An excited Annette and I went to the gig. She was a big Stooges fan. I wanted to see if Iggy still had the moves. And he did; he killed it. He was all over the stage and diving into the audience.

Unfortunately, I didn't get a chance to meet him, but since I was now in Miami quite a bit, where Iggy resided, I figured we could hook up there. I had randomly spotted him in the city a few years earlier. I was walking down Collins Avenue leisurely when I spotted a cherry-red Eldorado with a beautiful Latino girl in the passenger seat. I then realised it was a shirtless Iggy who was driving. We locked eyes. He recognised me, stopped the car, hopped out, gave me a hug, got back in the car and drove off, without breaking sweat.

Before I made it back to Miami for new year 2012, I got a copy of our *Pop & Rock* treatment to Henry McGroggan, Iggy's manager. He responded positively, so Marcus got on to finishing up a pilot script in anticipation for a potential Iggy meet-up.

Somewhat coincidentally, right around the same time, I reconnected with an old friend who I was sure could take the project the next step further. Irvine Welsh, the Scottish author of *Trainspotting*, was now spending time in Miami too. He had name-checked Iggy and 'Lust for Life' in the book, and the song featured heavily in the *Trainspotting* film, which helped boost Iggy's career once again.

Irvine and I had made some music years earlier and had roamed the streets of Miami during a Winter Music Conference. It was great to meet up there again, and we spent New Year's Eve 2012 together at my friend's bar, Gramps in Wynwood. I mentioned the Iggy project, which we had by this time renamed *Lime Life*. He was interested, so I told him I'd send him the treatment script once it was done.

Things were moving. Henry then actually organised a lunch with Iggy, close to his home in Coconut Grove, at his favourite spot, the Greenstreet Cafe. It was a chill get-together, and we spoke a lot about music, the 1980s and NYC. I told him how much I had loved his set at Hop Farm and how Lou Reed's performance had been a bit disappointing. I also mentioned my past dealings with Lou, and how I been scheduled to produce his *New York* album, until he suddenly cut my fee down considerably. He also said it would be a closed session, with no drink or drugs, and no time limit, so the project could have gone on indefinitely. All of which made me lose interest in the project. Iggy asked what year that was, and when I told him 1988, he said, 'Well, he should have paid you around $50,000.' Which was exactly what the original deal was, until Reed tried to get me down to $30,000. When I asked Iggy how he knew, he said he had cut *Instinct* with producer Bill Laswell at the same time, and we were comparable, and that's what he paid Bill.

Iggy is extremely well read; he was very impressed by the new James Brown biography he had just finished. He was a big fan of the Godfather, and in later years would add horns to his solo band, which really gave the songs that funk and rock vibe that Mitch Ryder had used in Detroit in the 1960s. We eventually discussed my TV idea, and he seemed open to it. I left feeling very excited.

Marcus and I sent our script to Henry, who got it over to Iggy. They were still intrigued by its potential, and I met up with Iggy again, this time at his bungalow studio on the banks of Little River, very close to where I now live. But at the time the area felt rough, and Iggy entertained me with stories of the many times his place had been broken into. He had lots of Haitian art hanging on his walls that was worth something, but the crooks would leave it untouched and depart with big-screen TVs instead. As we sat in his garden overlooking the little river, two huge manatees popped their heads up, as if they had spotted two old kindred spirits, then went on their way as soon as we spotted them.

I also passed Irvine the rough script. He read it and liked the world it created. When I asked him if he wanted to get involved, he amazingly said yes, and that he'd get on to a script polish.

The last member of our *Lime Life* team would randomly come into the fold when I was invited to dinner at Casa Tua in Miami by a new friend, British film director Malcolm Venville. Malcolm mentioned that someone would be joining us: Jonas Åkerlund, a Swedish film, video and commercials director. Jonas and I bonded immediately. He had started out as a heavy-metal drummer and was now *the* number-one music video director. He also shot ads, one being a UK car insurance commercial starring Iggy Pop! He had convinced his client to use Iggy. How crazy was that?

I told him about the project, and he was interested. Irvine got me a revised script, which I gave to Henry, who was happy with the direction things were going in. I also sent it to Jonas, who thought it was brilliant. I then told him that Irvine Welsh was on board as writer/producer and that Iggy had a window in which he could shoot in Miami around the end of April 2012. Jonas was immediately in and gave me his manager's details. When I told Henry that Jonas would be shooting *Lime Life*, he was very happy, since Jonas had worked with Iggy numerous times. Things were moving really quickly now.

In the meantime, I was flying regularly between Miami and London. I met up with Jonas in London and saw a screening of his new film, *Small Apartments*. This got me even more hyped up on having him

Irvine Welsh, me and Iggy Pop at the Greenstreet Cafe, Coconut Grove, Florida.

direct the project, because I thought it was a great film, with clever casting, locations and direction.

Irvine travelled to the Cannes Film Festival in May, where he met up with my friend Robert Walak at the CAA party. A few days later, Marcus and I were back in London with Robert, pitching *Lime Life*. I then headed back to Miami with Irvine to meet Iggy at the Greenstreet Cafe. Irvine's recollection of our meet is: 'It was classic Iggy. He had some plot ideas and Miami scenarios, ran down a lot of crazy crime stories from the time he'd lived there and a lot of the local colour that he'd witnessed. He ended up saying that whatever the script, he will give it his full commitment.'

Now it was finally time for Irv, Jonas and I to meet up. We were all busy on numerous projects but somehow convened in LA in July. We had a great dinner at the Chateau Marmont, which was directly below Jonas's Hollywood Hills house, where he graciously let me stay. Irvine was close by, at his manager Trevor Engelson's house.

The rest of summer 2012 is pretty much a blur, as I travelled between Miami, London, NYC, Italy and Ibiza. Other than Jonas having lunch with Iggy in Stockholm and working on a *Lime Life* logo, we sort of put things on pause, before Irvine, Jonas and I had a dinner meet at the Chateau on 30 September to plan for our first meeting with CAA the next day, which went well. Both Irvine and Jonas worked with the agency, so there seemed to be some real in-house curiosity about the project.

Henry relayed that Iggy would be available in October to record his voice-over for the *Lime Life* teaser that Irvine and Jonas had written. I contacted my friend Joe Galdo (ex-drummer of the disco group Foxy) at South Beach Studios, where Iggy typically recorded while in Miami. The date ended up shifting, but we finally got Iggy in, and he recorded Irvine's dialogue as Jim Kaminski on 11 November.

Around new year, Annette and I travelled over to Miami for Art Basel and had our second, legal wedding on 2 January, which Irvine witnessed. Five weeks later, on 9 February, I finally got the full *Lime Life* team together – Iggy, Irvine, Jonas and myself – in Miami. Iggy drove up in his cherry-red Ferrari, which he parked right in front of Soho House. No one said anything about him moving it! We must have been quite the sight, the four of us scrunched into a corner banquette at Ceconni's. We probably looked like a weird old prog-rock band, with Jonas wearing a black witch's hat and Irvine in a white fisherman's cap. Iggy was wearing a shirt for a change, an old Stooges T, just in case anyone didn't recognise him.

We settled in to have a nice chat about how things were going. Iggy even had a mimosa to celebrate the occasion. Things seemed positive, until we discussed potential meetings with film people in LA. Iggy wasn't having it. He wanted no part of any meetings with suits. He told us the story of a meeting he had in Hollywood with the head of a film studio, which he had travelled across the country for. He had sat waiting for what seemed like an hour, before finally being led in. He sat down, only to be told by the guy that Iggy had once ghosted him at a party, hadn't come over to even say hello, so this was payback. That was all there was to that meeting – what an arsehole the guy was! Iggy said he wouldn't do a meeting unless there was a cheque involved, which seemed understandable to me. No dog and pony show for him.

I then sent Robert Walak the new updated script that Irvine had worked on. He loved it. He had just been hired for a new gig, heading up Harvey Weinstein's company in Europe, and he organised a meeting for us with David Glasser at Weinstein's head office in LA. Beforehand, Jonas, Irv and I met up at a coffee shop near the office and sort of psyched each other up. We were all veterans of these meetings, but somehow they were still a bit nerve-racking.

When we were led into Glasser's office, he was seemingly excited to meet us. He schmoozed us heavily, claiming to be very aware of and a fan of our individual work, telling us how much he loved the project and enthusiastically pitching the new Weinstein company to us and how they really wanted to get into the TV sphere. They were putting a TV department together and were interested in having us on board as part of the new company. When we were finished, he said that he'd be in London with Harvey and would meet with Robert on their way to the Cannes Film Festival.

When we walked out, we were high-fiving each other. I felt like we were getting close. It was another of those unforgettable moments. Unfortunately, that would be the high point of *Lime Life*.

A few weeks after the meeting I spoke to Robert, and he said, 'Rest assured we are extremely keen, and David has the US TV guys running a model.' It was an exciting time for Robert because the news of his hiring was going live right before Cannes. I did see him soon after the festival. We met at the Soho Hotel, and he was still very optimistic about the project.

Iggy came through London and played the Meltdown festival that June. I went backstage and said a quick hello, but it was too packed, with Peaches and Damien Hirst sharing the space.

Glasser had scheduled numerous calls with Jonas, Irvine and me. Typically, though, his assistant would come on and say, 'Sorry, he just got called in with Harvey.' We had no further contact with Glasser, other than me bumping into him at a BAFTA party at the Chiltern Firehouse a few years later. I said, 'Hey, David,' but when I tried to speak to him, he said he didn't recognise me or the project.

Iggy continued to be a fixture around Miami, appearing on Anthony Bourdain's *Parts Unknown* series, complete with his infamous 'Miami's a sunny place for shady people' tagline.

Jonas, Irvine and I continued to strategise on *Lime Life*, eventually concluding that it might be easier to pitch it as a film. Irvine rejigged the script, and we continued to hawk it around, but it would never again be our main focus. The momentum was lost.

I still feel bad about this one not happening because I truly believe it could have been great . . . and I feel that we somehow let Iggy down.

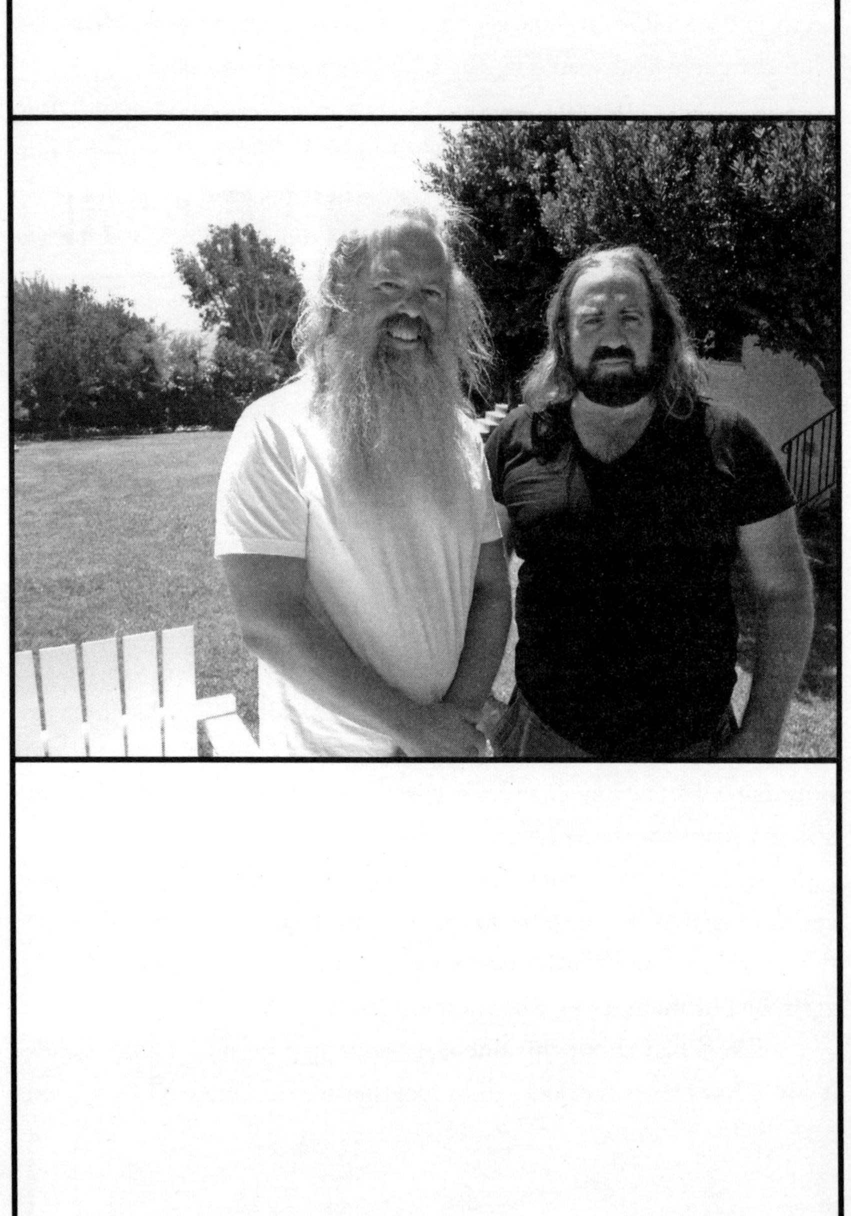

42.

808 THE MOVIE

2012–14

As a lover of history, I've always had a desire to document the music and the culture I've been involved with. Over the years I've attempted many music documentaries. There was *Slave to the Rhythm*, a history of dance music; *Sugar Hill*, the story of Joe and Sylvia Robinson (this one was also pitched as a biopic, with Beyoncé playing Sylvia); *The Last Rock & Roll Story*, about New Order, directed by Don Letts; and *DC10 Clubbed* (also directed by Don Letts). I put a lot of time and effort into these projects. They all sound interesting, correct? You'd want to see them, right?

None were made.

The thing is, to produce a music doc you need someone so passionate about the subject matter that they are totally irrational about the potential end result, and so throw caution to the wind and just go for it. Because music docs never really turn a profit. Sure, there's the odd exception, like *Searching for Sugar Man, 20 Feet from Stardom* and anything Ken Burns does. But how often does a doc turn a profit? Close to never. One of the main reasons for that is that a music doc inherently needs lots of music, which needs to be licensed from both the record labels (the actual records) and the publishers (the rights to the songs). In my experience, neither usually gives a shit about documenting their artists' music. All they care about is getting the largest advance they can. There are some exceptions, but I haven't found many. If you are attempting to use your own music, there's a way to make that happen. But even licensing a good friend's tunes becomes a bit of a slog. You can actually make the documentary in anticipation of people being mesmerised by your work, only to be left out in the cold, with very little of the music you speak about appearing in your final released version. There are so many music docs that never get released because they lack the financing to obtain any of the music they speak about. So beware of making one. Or, in my case, two. At the same time.

When I started producing *Finding the Funk*, a documentary on the history of funk, with my old friend, director Nelson George, for VH1, it was beyond exciting – finally, my first film. It was a real passion project of mine. We quickly got a large financial commitment from VH1 and a promise of an equal investment from Red Bull 420 Media House, so things were looking very promising. But when Red Bull backed out and I wasn't able to obtain another investor, I lost a lot of my focus. Although I helped procure Questlove Thompson to be the film's narrator and represented it at its premiere at the SXSW Film Festival (I was the moderator on a funk panel that included George Clinton, Bootsy Collins and Bernie Worrell (RIP)), Nelson and I ended up falling out over it. Which I still feel bad about. The film was eventually released, but it lacked lots of the original music, which we couldn't afford. As if that wasn't enough, I had started on *808* the movie. At basically the same time.

Director Nelson George, Bootsy Collins and me on the *Finding the Funk* shoot.

Now the other advice I'd give on making documentaries (or any other project) is to be extremely careful not to get into bed with the wrong partners. Being seduced by money can dissipate your natural instincts, as it's so hard to get the funds needed to complete a project (as you've read in my chapter on Harlem). *808* is a good case in point. I had a partner on the film, whom I had met through a friend, Max Niece. Max had started off as my intern and was a great kid and a joy to work with. If he had been my partner on *808*, I'm positive it would have been an amazing experience. But instead, it was a good friend of his, Alex Noyer. I don't remember Max ever vouching for Alex as a business partner, though I'm not sure it would have made a difference either way. And Alex wasn't a bad guy at all, just a control freak. Which you sort of need to be to get a film made. But I'm a control freak too, so there's the clash. Still, I'm fairly happy with how the film came out in the end, but getting there was a bit of a drain.

I first met up with Alex for lunch at the Groucho Club, to discuss working on some sort of music documentary. We ended up deciding that making a doc on the Roland TR-808 drum machine was a great idea. At the time I'd already been developing a book/documentary concept called *Looking for the Perfect Beat* with my friend, the journalist Luke Bainbridge, which would focus on the making of many of the 1980s electro classics, some of which I'd personally been involved with, with others made by my network of friends.

808 ended up following a similar narrative, only the focus would be on tracks made using the Roland TR-808 and on the open-minded producers who used the machine. When Alex claimed he had the ability to self-finance the movie and committed to me being an equal partner, it was music to my ears. I was all in (I know what I've said, but . . .). We hired Luke as the writer and researcher, and Alex brought in his friend, Alex Dunn, to direct.

Neither of the Alexes had much background in the music we were featuring, other than being fans, but I figured they'd rely on Luke and me to lead the way in the development of the doc. One thing we all agreed on was that it was my job to use my connections to bring in the talent for the film. No one else had the connections I had. Luke wrote a first draft of the script, and he and I put together a wish list of tracks we'd focus on and artists we'd involve.

We started with a few shoots in London at the end of 2012 and early in 2013. Two memorable interviews were shooting Goldie at his home art studio and Damon Albarn and Remi at Gorillaz's West London premises. Goldie's interview was as expected, supercharged and totally manic. My friends Damon and Remi, on the other hand, came to the interview very chilled out. I mean, *really* chilled out. Really quite stoned. Very mellow indeed, despite the fact that it was only 10 a.m.! Damon got into deep, spatial, quantum physics definitions of the Latin percussion sounds of the 808. Which made some sense to me. I'd always believed that the music-makers who used the 808 were a breed apart, and that would be what would make this doc interesting. It would be about the people.

We really got into full effect when we set up operations in Miami during the Winter Music Conference. I was convincing the multitude of DJs and producers there to be part of the project. Most people were excited and said yes, but the scheduling was left to the Alexes. We did get a lot done during that first trip to Miami, despite the fact that most of the people we were interviewing had been out all night getting stoned and doing drugs, etc. We did a full-on day of interviews at the Standard Hotel, as a bunch of the DJs were staying there, including Brodinski, Boys Noize, Tensnake, Toddla T, A-Trak, Soul Clap, the extremely hot Skrillex and, lastly, Diplo, who kept putting us off all day. Luckily, I was eventually able to drag him out of the pool for his interview. Luckily, because he was really the only one who provided much useable content. Skrillex was very hungover and shy on camera; he had seemingly not gotten his interview vibe together yet.

We did another group of interviews at Soho House, in the Snug lounge, scoring some better soundbites from the likes of the great talking head Questlove, Richie Hawtin and Tom 'Tommy Boy' Silverman. Questlove came up with a classic quote, calling the 808 'hip-hop's electric guitar'. Paul Oakenfold gave a somewhat lightweight interview, but to be fair, the 808 wasn't really his box. We finally got an interview with David Guetta, after my friends Caroline Prothero and Jean-Charles Carrere hooked me up. David was important to me because he had brought the 808 back into my consciousness when I met him in the DJ's booth at Pasha in Ibiza. He had been producing lots of smash-hit hip-hop dance tracks featuring those 808 sounds. I did the interview with David and think I did a decent job, as I knew his French hip-hop DJing history and was somewhat sympathetic. When the film was finally released, though, DJs in the audience would predictably boo David whenever he came on screen. I remember defending his right to speak about the 808 on more than one occasion.

We grabbed a few other big-name interviews in Miami, including Norman 'Fatboy Slim' Cook and Bernard and Stephen from New Order, before we made our way to NYC. Things were going well. In NYC, we kept jamming, scoring Afrika Bambaataa and the Soul Sonic Force, Strafe, Man Parrish, François K, T La Rock, DJ Mr. Mixx and drummer Chris Frantz from Talking Heads and Tom Tom Club.

I then ended up coming back to Miami to conduct a few interviews we had missed first time around. At Pharrell Williams's request, we booked Inner Circle's Circle House Studios for his shoot. He was working on a new Jennifer Hudson project there, and promised it would be the best way to get his interview done. We booked a few other interviews for that day, including two very important 1980s NYC producers: Chris Barbosa, who produced Shannon's 'Let the Music Play'; and Tony Carrasco, who produced Klein + M.B.O.'s 'Dirty Talk'. Jellybean brought Tony in, as they were lifelong Bronx friends.

Upon arrival at Circle House, I met the studio owner, who, it turned out, was the leader of Inner Circle, Ian Lewis. He had spent a lot of the 1980s in NYC and was a fan of the 808 and many of my tracks, so he laid out the red carpet for the crew. I did an interview with him that was a classic. Pharrell came by early on and checked in with us. He said he'd do the interview, but we should schedule him last. So we got to it and worked our way through our list of six interviews, until we were finally ready for Pharrell. His PA, John Rodriguez, came in. He didn't look happy. Pharrell followed him in. Basically, it went like this: 'Hey, man, sorry, but I'm in working with Jennifer and I can't just leave her alone to do the interview. If she was a rapper, I could leave her to write some rhymes. But she's not. Sorry . . .' Then he left.

I was really pissed off. We had travelled to him, booked the studio where he was working and just needed thirty minutes of his time. John could tell I was angry. He said that we could schedule something else and promised we'd get the interview in. He asked where we were shooting next. I said, 'LA,' and he said, 'Great, we will be out there at the same time.' I expressed my doubts, but he promised he'd make good on the interview.

The next week we got to LA. I had set up a tight schedule of interviews that were all important in telling our story. We travelled to the studio of platinum duo Jimmy Jam and Terry Lewis, who had scored huge with their productions of records by Janet Jackson and the SOS Band, among many others, all of which featured the 808 in a major way. They recalled hearing 'Planet Rock' for the first time, and I mentioned how freaked out I was when I first heard their 808-ladened 'Just Be Good to Me' by the SOS Band on the radio, like someone else had discovered my secret. Next we interviewed Lil Jon, Lady Tigra of L'Trimm and Public Enemy producer Hank Shocklee in a house we had rented in the Hollywood Hills where Luke and the Alexes were staying. All went smoothly. We then scored a big coup with another old friend, Rick Rubin, at his Shangri-La compound in Malibu.

Me and Lil Jon in LA, after rapping about him, Usher and the 808.

All the while I kept checking in with John regarding the Pharrell interview, which was scheduled for the next day. He said we were still on, but he didn't have any studio details yet, which was worrying. But then the night before I got a call: it was on, and he gave me the relevant information. We got up nice and early, packed up my rental car with all the gear and headed out to the Valley and another one of those out-of-the-way recording studios that I guess Pharrell likes to use. As we drove over to Burbank, we were hit with the sound of his voice on the just-released Daft Punk song 'Get Lucky', which sounded like a total smash and also featured my boy Nile Rodgers chugging away on it. I thought, *This is great. I'm sure Pharrell will be in a good mood.*

We arrived, and the studio staff knew we were coming, which was a good sign. We loaded the gear into the studio, and the team started setting it up. An interesting shaven-headed girl was hanging around in reception, listening to the radio. Finally, John and Pharrell arrived. Pharrell had shades on and greeted the girl, and they went into another room. John didn't look happy. 'Hey, Arthur, Pharrell had a bad night. He got food poisoning and . . .'

I cut in. 'John, unless he's dead, he's gonna do the interview! We've travelled to a studio of his choice *twice*, man.' John then told us that the bald chick was Miley Cyrus. Great, another singer Pharrell couldn't leave alone in the control room. I said, 'Let's get him in now and do the interview before anything else comes up.'

So John pleaded our case, and a less-than-eager Pharrell came into the studio. I immediately told him how much I loved 'Get Lucky' and what a smash I thought it was going to be, thanking him profusely for taking the time to do the interview. Luke then got right in and interviewed him. Pharrell wasn't the most animated, but at least we got him for the film, which felt like a big deal.

So filming was going well, and Alex Noyer and I hadn't had too many arguments. But that would soon change. I had been working on the Roland company, both its US and its UK offices, to help us secure an interview with the main man of the 808 and the father of Roland, Ikutaro Kakehashi, aka Mr K. We really needed to speak to him on camera and ask all the whys and hows in order to answer the mysteries of the 808.

As we finished up our interviews in LA, Jamie Franklin out of

Roland's UK office finally made the big Mr K interview happen. He would meet us in Tokyo. The only thing was, it was scheduled for my birthday, just a few days later, so we would fly to Tokyo from LA for just one day. Alex wanted me to fly economy. There was no way I would fly overnight to Tokyo, squished in economy, then fly straight back in economy. I also knew Alex would never do that. Cue a major impasse. I held my ground, and after a bit of back and forth, I flew business. But this definitely started the downward spiral in our relationship. Also, Alex didn't need my contacts any more because we had done most of the interviews I could score already.

The trip to Roland town in Japan was magical, with neither of the Alexes in attendance (they sent the film crew). I landed in Tokyo in the evening of 21 April, had a great meal, and then Jamie interviewed me for the Roland website. Next morning we were up early to catch the 9.03 a.m. train from Tokyo to Hamamatsu. I brought along my old friend Mika to be our translator. On arrival we had the run of the Roland Museum, and I was able to plug in any bit of gear they had on site, which was everything they had ever made. I slowly went through the history of all the gear Roland and Mr K had produced, even some of the pre-Roland things. I started banging out beats through a little amp. I was sure they had never let anyone else do that – I'm pretty sure no one had ever asked! Strangely, the 808 and 909 drum machines were missing from their spots.

Then we finally met Mr K at his residence, where he greeted us at the door. He was using a walker and had an oxygen hook-up too. He had a smile on his face. We shook hands, and I introduced him to Mika. He slowly led us down a narrow hallway, pointing out a few awards on the wall, one of which was from the mayor of LA. He laughed as he spoke, in fairly good English, about his time in LA as a young man, his early years as a salesman of electric organs and his love of cheeseburgers. We entered his office, a small room with a big desk. The team started setting up, and I sat down. Scanning the room, I noticed a table covered with a sheet of velvet. Curious.

We quickly got down to the interview. I heard the story of a man driven by his love of music. And of the organ. And how he originally just wanted to incorporate beats into the instrument, enabling the player to be a one-person band. Why the name Roland? He had picked it out of a telephone book! When we were finished speaking, Mr K got up and went towards the table, slowly pulling the velvet sheet off like a sorcerer. Underneath it was an 808. There was also a birthday cake, in the form of King Arthur and the Knights of the Turntable. He motioned towards the drum machine, as if to say, *Make me some beats*. I was really touched and threw down some crushing beats for the grandmaster.

Me and the legendary Mr K (Ikutaro Kakehashi), founder of Roland and the man behind the 808 drum machine, at his home in Japan.

It was the highlight of making *808*, and one of the high points of my career.

I'd continue working on the doc, conducting a few more interviews. I also introduced Alex Noyer to my old friend Craig Kallman at Atlantic, who would eventually release the *808* soundtrack and help with getting the movie distributed. But my relationship with Alex then broke down. Somehow, the deal he and I had signed no longer made sense to him. I had just found out that Annette was pregnant, and I really didn't need the stress of dealing with him any more, so the deal was renegotiated. I walked away and let the Alexes finish the film. Which took another year. They added a Phil Collins interview, which was much too long, along with a great one with the Beastie Boys (I had been trying to get Ad-Rock in as narrator originally).

Me interviewing David Guetta at Soho Beach House, Miami, for *808* the movie.

Having stepped away from working on the film, I now had plenty of time on my hands to look after my pregnant wife, taking to my dual jobs of being her full-time chef and messenger fairly well. I also started searching through piles of my unfinished music, looking for that golden sample. One song struck an immediate chord with me. It was a cut-up disco track that I had been working on, off and on, over the last ten years. It repurposed an unreleased song of mine from 1978, 'Can't Put No Price', with a filtered French touch (à la Daft Punk). I sent it to my friend Al-P, who was a great engineer/programmer with the Canadian group MSTRKRFT. He reinforced the music and quickly mixed it down. And just like that, it sounded like a hit. We then approached Dave 1 from the band Chromeo to add a lead vocal

Me, Dave 1 of Chromeo and A-Trak at Novikov, London.

that would augment the song's sampled background vocals, which had been recorded by Jocelyn Brown when we first met in 1978.

Everyone thought we had a hit on our hands. My guys at New State Distributors (who were distributing my Baked Recordings label) Tim Binn and Tom Parkinson had an idea. They'd call the record 'Disco Mystery' and get it over to BBC Radio 1, and into the hands of Annie Mac, the station's leading dance-music DJ. The plan worked – she loved it! Pretty quickly we had an old-school bidding war on our hands, and after lots of back and forth, my old mates Mike Pickering and Julian Palmer signed the track to Sony. We got them to cough up a rather large advance, which was uncommon at that time. It was all so perfectly timed, it felt like baby magic, helping us out financially just as Amarone was born (we had decided on her name after a drunken morning tasting wine in an Italian vineyard). Of course, I took time off to enjoy this blessed moment, and while being a father was something I had never really thought about, I was taking to it pretty well. Still, I couldn't drop the ball on the momentum of our potential smash – now called 'No Price' by Slam Dunk'd.

To back the release, I took Slam Dunk'd on the road live, complete with the rapper VAS, with me DJing and self-produced video projections for each of our songs. We opened for Fat Boy Slim in Manchester and at the Brixton Academy. Unfortunately, things went pear-shaped when, during the show in Manchester, the 'No Price' video started skipping, complete with loud audio feedback. After thinking that we had corrected the issue, it happened again at the Brixton gig, and this led to us not being booked for the rest of the tour. And on top of that, Sony messed up the song's release and gave the track back to me. What had started out as a certain hit ended up not seeing the light of day until many years later, on the Glitterbox label.

When the film was finally completed, I decided I'd get back in and be involved with its promotion. Although I was annoyed at how things had worked out, I was still executive producer of the project, and I wanted it to succeed. We did a great industry screening at the Winter

Music Conference, with lots of the interviewees in the house. The high point was a Q&A where Todd Terry explained that he had really liked the film, but it was a bit too long. I responded, 'Oh, OK then, we can cut a chunk of your interview!' to laughs from the crowd.

We premiered at South by Southwest in March 2015, followed by another Q&A and a party, with Hank Shocklee and I trading 808 beats and records for a packed crowd at the Soho House pop-up. Craig Kallman would end up helping us get a deal with Apple/Beats, and *808* would be the first film they released.

While I probably made only around $20,000 for all my time working on *808*, it documented a crucial part of our dance culture. And it was actually released, unlike many music docs that stay in limbo for years, often never seeing the light of day.

43.

'ON A MISSION'

2016–PRESENT

After our daughter, Amarone, was born in 2014, Annette and I started spending a lot more time in Miami as a family. I knew my father had thought I'd never give him a grandchild, so when she was born, I wanted him to really enjoy spending the time he had left with her. They had an amazing bond. She'd crawl or run to him immediately whenever we made it over to his house in Boca Raton.

Annette and I had already bought a condo in Miami right at the end of 2010. We found a nice spot up in North Miami, not far from the newly opened Soho Beach House, and started settling in. We continued to bounce back and forth between Miami and London, however, with Annette busy with Felder Felder, and me relaunching my DJing career, releasing music on my label Baked Recordings and playing gigs. One major live set stands out, at ACID FUTURE, where I jammed on my 808, while the Martinez Brothers worked the 303. We had earlier recorded a track together in Miami called 'Now Hand Clap', which I released on my label.

Me and the Martinez Brothers at Further Future, 2015.

But when the Brexit vote happened in 2016, and with my dad's age and health a concern, I decided that we should make the big move and live in Miami full-time. Annette, after some convincing, agreed. She loved my dad and thought we should do it for him.

So we left London and moved into our condo in Indian Creek. It was on the top floor and had an inspiring view of the ocean and the sunrise. I would sit at my laptop, whacking away at track after track. Being in Miami, I also rediscovered my love of Latin music. I reconnected with Oscar G of the local group Murk and started collaborating with him in the studio and DJing with him at his new Monday-night club residency.

Then, pretty much out of the blue, Dwight Hawkes from Rockers Revenge re-entered my life. We had been in contact only twice in the previous thirty years: a quick hello in 2010 and again in 2013, both via social media. I guess it was third time lucky when he reached out in July 2016. These kinds of reconnects started to happen regularly following the arrival of social media. It was always fifty–fifty whether you'd want to re-engage with or ghost the old friends who got in touch. But I definitely wanted to speak with Dwight. We had been real tight during an important time in my life and career, and he and his brother Donnie had recorded my first big UK hit, 'Walking on Sunshine', as Rockers Revenge. Dwight and I started catching up on the past thirty years via text. He had moved down to Georgia, living with his younger brother, Man, who had a great little recording studio in his house. He eventually suggested that we get back together and make some music. I thought, *Why the fuck not?*

I had one track in particular that had been kicking around for a few years and which I thought might work for Rockers Revenge. I had written 'On a Mission' during a trip to Ibiza in 2012, when it was born out of a night rocking at DC10. It had then resurfaced a few years later, when I played at a Soho Beach House/Art Basel party in 2014, DJing with Win Butler from Arcade Fire. So that was the song I decided to send Dwight, including some melody and chorus ideas I already had for it. I also sent him a few other instrumentals.

Me jamming with Win Butler's percussionists at the Soho House Miami/Art Basel event, 2016.

That first night Dwight worked on all the tracks I had sent, getting back to me the next day with MP3s. The other tracks he worked on didn't really kill me, but the verses he laid down for 'On a Mission' were spot-on. I thought he had nailed it, both lyrically and melodically. The only thing was, his singing didn't blow me away.

Dwight had not been the lead singer of Rockers Revenge; his brother Donnie had. He related to me that Donnie had given up music and stopped singing twenty-five years earlier. While Dwight had stuck with the music industry, producing singers and running record shops alongside his work with social action groups in Yonkers, NY, Donnie had ended up as an orderly in a big NYC hospital, which besides being a well-paid position also provided him and his family with great healthcare. He wanted nothing to do with the music biz. But I guess when Dwight approached him with the news that we were back in contact, he was curious about what we were working on, and when he heard the demo of 'Mission', he decided to at least give it one more college try.

Annette and I had already scheduled a trip to NYC around Christmas for a friend's birthday party, so I booked some time at my music publisher Downtown Music's studios. This would be my first recording session in New York in years. I was in a position that I never imagined I would be in: getting back in the studio with one of my old bands after three decades, working with a singer who hadn't set foot in one since 1989 and didn't really sing any more. Donnie showed up in his hospital scrubs, after a ten-hour shift. And following some hugs and a chat, he went in and killed it with an emotionally infused raw lead vocal. 'On a Mission' now sounded like an uplifting Rockers Revenge classic. After hearing Donnie sing and feeling Dwight's passion, I was inspired. All of a sudden, getting the band back together didn't feel like such a crazy idea. The fact that Annette had witnessed the session and seen Donnie and me in action made her supportive of the plan. *Maybe this could actually happen,* I thought.

Next, I needed a label that would believe in it too. After living with the track a bit, it dawned on me that there was one DJ/label owner who might get it enough to release it. I texted my friend Damian Lazarus, the owner of Crosstown Rebels. I'd known him since the early 2000s. We had partied together, DJed together and competed as party promoters when I was doing my Return to New York parties and he was running the City Rockers record label. I texted him, saying I had a new Rockers Revenge track. He thought it was magical that I had approached him with it. I sent the record over, and he liked it but thought the groove needed some work. He offered to help finish the track and release it, mentioning that Crosstown was coming up to its 200th release and that 'Mission' would make a great number 200. And it could be premiered at his next Get Lost party, at the Winter Music Conference in Miami. Damian wanted to know if Rockers Revenge were capable of performing live. Could I actually get the band back together? Of course, I said, 'Yes.'

The deal we were offered for the Winter Music Conference gig wasn't great, but when Damian kicked in some additional promotion money, we had just enough to pay for the three flights needed. I would put the band up at my house. I had an excited Dwight get in touch with the rest of the crew, and when both Adrienne and Tina agreed, it was happening. Get Lost would be the first time that the original Rockers performed together live since 1983. Or so I thought.

The day before the gig Donnie and Adrienne arrived in town from NYC; Tina was already in Miami. When Adrienne brought a random female background singer with her to rehearsals, it was a surprise to me, as I had been expecting Dwight. Then I got a call from him, saying he couldn't make the gig – he wasn't well enough. I was really surprised. The performance went great, though, and it was amazing to have Annette and Amarone there to witness it. To be able to hold my waving daughter while I was DJing was so special. Then I brought the group on and backed them up. Donnie was great, he immediately captured the crowd, and the girls were so happy as they performed. Overall, the vibes were amazing. It was a sunny day and the mostly young crowd sang along to the music, especially 'Sunshine'. I could see my friend Felix Da Housecat, who was on after us, smiling and grooving, as was Damian.

Following the gig a couple of guys from the Summit Conference approached me to see if Rockers would be available to play their event in Los Angeles at the end of the year. This was really exciting, as Summit was a big deal in the culture and tech sphere and could be a great vehicle in terms of relaunching the group for a young, hip audience.

When I was able to book us another Miami gig for the next month, it looked like momentum was starting to build. Or at least in my mind. True to his word, Damian helped A&R the project, providing some helpful ideas for 'Mission'. He suggested a certain percussion groove and sent me records to check out. I had Oba Frank Lords, a master percussionist, throw down lots of different rhythms on numerous drums, and that did the trick. Then Damian asked if I thought François K might be interested in doing a remix. When I got the track over to François, I think it surprised him. He couldn't believe it was new and was very impressed with Donnie's vocal. When he laid down a classic François K 1980s dub, which Damian loved, the track was ready to be released.

Our next gig was in Miami, at the Open Stage Club, so I decided to book my friend Andrew's studio and get some vocals down on a few songs that Dwight and I had been working on virtually. I also thought maybe I should start documenting things – as in filming them – for a potential documentary. I had sort of sworn off doing my own documentaries after two projects that I'd struggled to finish, and also Annette had made me promise that I would never, ever make one again. So do I try and start making one without financing? Using my own money? *No fucking way*. But I thought I could start small, so I hired my wife's good friend Mariela, a Cuban poet/actress/film-maker, to film the recording session.

When the group showed up, it was again without Dwight. He said he still wasn't well enough to travel and suggested our next session should be in Georgia, at his brother's house in Richmond Hills. The session at Andrew's studio went well; we got a few vocals finished, and the video footage and interviews were nice to have. I hired another guy to shoot the gig for $100, which was neither a big deal nor expense. I obviously should have stopped there.

I decided to go and see what was up with Dwight and flew to Richmond Hills from Miami. When I got there, I immediately discovered why Dwight wasn't travelling: he was in a wheelchair. I was shocked. Not shocked enough to forget about the documentary, though. Before I got the full story, I decided to film him revealing what the fuck had happened. We sat in the basement studio, just me and him, and he started to tell me his story, slowly, direct to camera. He had had cancer. The doctor had told him it was terminal and he had a few years to live. Which he hadn't accepted at all. Through his faith in God, family and music, he had beaten the disease. Then a separate procedure, unrelated to the cancer, had been screwed up, which had put him in the wheelchair. I was really blown away. I was also, by now, sold on telling his story, and the band's, in a documentary. We had a lead singer who had quit singing; a background singer, Adrienne, who ran a few day-care centres in Brooklyn; my ex-wife Tina, now a lawyer in London, who still had dreams of a singing career; the missed opportunity of turning down a gig on *Top of the Pops*; and Dwight.

I'll be honest, I thought it could be amazing – a human-interest story like *Searching for Sugar Man*! I was all in. When I told all this to Annette, she said, 'You *have* to do it.' Although if she had known the cost at the time, I'm sure she would have said, 'No fucking way!'

This would be the start of a four-year-plus odyssey, with the story of Rockers Revenge taking over my life.

I started to think of the band's journey. I realised that the most important moment, the pivotal point in their career and lives, was turning down a trip to London to play on *Top of the Pops.* At the time 'Sunshine' was in the top five in the British charts, and Tracy Bennett, the head of London Records, assured me that if they had performed on the show, the song would have gone to the top of the charts. Having a #1 record would mean an album, a tour and everything else associated with that. But they said no because they couldn't leave their day gig at the record store. That was their big mistake.

My first big mistake, this time round, was not hiring a director for the documentary, or at least a director of photography. What the fuck was I thinking? you might wonder. Well, I was thinking of the cost of paying people to travel around with me. So here I was, trying to direct a film about a band making an album, while also producing the record. On top of that, I was also trying to book gigs for the band, because I couldn't get us a fucking agent.

'Mission' was released at the end of June 2018, bringing Rockers new attention and getting a lot of club play. The band and I kept recording, mostly in Georgia. They had never made an album, so we started working towards that. The full reunion happened after Tina, myself, Annette, Amarone and Mariela, the cameraperson, all stuffed into my Hyundai and drove to Richmond Hills. It turned into an amazing bonding experience, which we captured while working in Man's basement studio. As we talked, I discovered that neither Donnie nor Dwight had ever been outside the States!

I had been booked to DJ at Razzmatazz in Barcelona that August, so I got on a call with my old friend Javier, the booker at Razz. I convinced him to let me bring Rockers Revenge for their first European gig. Success. Then I got on to my old friend (and Amarone's godfather) DJ Kaz James, convincing him to book us for his club Scorpios in Mykonos, Greece. Finally, the Mambo Brothers, Christian and Alan, agreed to let us do a set at Café Mambo in Ibiza. We had a European tour! Unfortunately, nothing came through in London. I really pushed for Dwight to come along, but he still wasn't well enough to travel. It was a very special experience for me, to be able to accompany my friend Donnie as he travelled and saw a part of the world he'd never witnessed. He, Adrienne and Tina had a magical time. Even though the audiences were really young, they reacted strongly, which surprised the group. We were in constant touch with Dwight over the phone, trying to make him feel part of the tour. Although I could tell that he wasn't well, he uplifted us with every call. He promised he'd make the Summit Conference gig.

But when it came time for our trip to LA, Dwight still wasn't well enough to take a cross-country flight. We were all pretty down after that news, since that had been our focus throughout the summer. Nonetheless, we decided to go. Upon arrival in LA we rehearsed in the hotel, and Dwight was on the phone with us the entire time. The gig, which I had built up too much in everyone's minds, including mine, would probably have been anticlimactic in any case, but we had to perform in the basement (of an otherwise amazing venue), right by the fucking toilets! I was royally pissed off and didn't hide it from the band or the Summit crew.

We then found out that Dwight really wasn't well and was very down. We still hadn't done a gig with all of us together. So, knowing that he might never be well enough to travel, I decided to bring the gig to him. I spoke to my friend DJ Pierre and his wife, who owned a recording studio and, just as importantly, the Wild Pitch club in Atlanta. We planned a recording session, a panel discussion and a gig right before Christmas. This would be the night the full Rockers Revenge line-up would finally hit the stage. We could all stay at Donnie and Dwight's sister Denise Armstrong's house.

The recording session went well, and the panel at the club was packed with curious fans. There was real interest from the young, mixed crowd. We spoke of the magic of NYC in the 1980s and received lots of interesting questions. But the mistake was, the promoter had left a few hours between the talk and the gig. It was a cold December night, and lots of the people who had attended the talk did not return for the gig. But those who were there loved the show.

It was a very emotional evening, Dwight, performing in his wheelchair, broke up as he gave a speech to thank the band and myself. Unfortunately, the lighting was pretty shit, so although we captured the magic moment on camera, the footage wasn't really useable. The next morning I got great interview footage of the band at Denise's house, with lots of Donnie and Dwight's family there.

Rockers Revenge live at the Fillmore, Miami, 18 January 2020.

But after that gig, not much happened for Rockers. We released a couple of other singles, 'What About the People?' and 'You Can Do It', which got club play, but nothing more. I had got Pulse Films to co-produce the documentary. My friend Michael Holman worked with me on developing the script and suggested I speak to his friend, filmmaker Shan Nicholson, about adding his direction and editing skills to the project. Shan started organising footage, with a plan to come to

Miami at the end of 2019 to do some linking filming and to interview me, in an attempt to frame the documentary a bit more. I decided to go back to Atlanta in November to get final interviews with Dwight and Donnie; that way I could get what we were missing in time for my sessions with Shan. The footage was well shot, and I thought I now had what I needed.

Shan came to stay in Miami and was super-professional, directing a great opening of me in my storage unit. Then he interviewed me, and the footage really worked, basically using me as the film's narrator. The problem was, the Atlanta gig footage was pretty bad, and we needed a finale for the film.

Then I got a call from New Order's manager, Andy Robinson. They were coming for another residency at the Fillmore Miami Beach and wanted me to open for them and help them book support bands. That was it – Rockers Revenge supporting New Order at the Fillmore! Andy and New Order were up for it. *Amazing.*

I planned to get the band in a few days before the first gig. Then I got a call from Dwight, saying that he doesn't want to put people out, he'll be a drain on us, and we should just do the gig without him. This time I refused to accept it. I booked a ticket for him and his son, and they made it to Miami. I got them a room at the Vagabond, the best local motel. After picking them up at the airport, we went directly to my rehearsal spot, where we were met by Donnie, Adrienne and Tina, along with Oba Frank Lords and his son, whom I got to play percussion for the shows. The next day Dwight was pretty exhausted, so we let him rest up until the big night. Barney from New Order came by to wish us a great set.

The gigs went off without a hitch, and it was an amazing few nights for everyone. The joy that I was able to bring to my old friends made it all worthwhile, and having Annette and Amarone right there on the stage to witness this triumphant first night was the icing on the cake. We shot everything, and it all looked great. Shan and I put it together, filming some new link pieces to make the story make sense. Now it seemed as if we were on the way to a finished doc, album . . . and onwards and upwards. We decided we could end the film with a coda of the band listening to the finished album and shots of each individual member having fun. We were all bursting with optimism.

Then Covid hit. Which was scary for all of us, especially at our ages. I had five friends in NYC lose their lives in those first months. And Donnie? He was working on the front line as an orderly in Maimonides Hospital in the Bronx! We started regular band Skype calls, with all of us pleading for him to quit his job. He was over seventy and could retire with full social security. But he was stubborn and wouldn't talk about it, even as he saw his co-workers dying in front of him. I recorded all these calls, not knowing what was going to happen and how the film would end now. I decided that when all this was over, I had to get Rockers to London. That was the only way to close this chapter.

Annette now thinks that making the Rockers Revenge film actually saved my life, as it was the one positive thing I focused on during Covid, while all around me there was the darkness of Trump, George Floyd and the pandemic. I'm not sure I totally agree, but I was definitely obsessed with the horrors of the world, and this was my one distraction.

When the vaccines became available, I started thinking about getting Rockers to London. I finally got an agent, Cris Hearn, a long-time acquaintance, to start looking for gigs for the group. He booked us in at the Jazz Cafe, just steps away from my old gaff in Camden. We all got the vaccine and went through the protocols we had to go through to make the trip happen. I met the band at Heathrow, and we cabbed it to Camden, stopping at a Covid test site on the way. We stayed in an Airbnb on the fringes of Camden Market. My film producer at Pulse, Alice Rhodes, helped me organise a shoot of the band at iconic London spots: Abbey Road Studios, the River Thames, London Bridge and, finally, Camden Market.

The gig that night was something none of us will ever forget. We rocked it. The Jazz Cafe was pretty full – of both love and people. Everyone was dancing and singing along. Rockers Revenge had finally

Rockers Revenge cross Abbey Road, London.

made it to London! During a fucking pandemic! At last I had the final footage.

I had yet to show the band the film, wanting to wait till I could tell them we had a distributor. When I realised that might not happen, I decided to send it as a surprise birthday present for Donnie. The three brothers watched it together. They loved it and said it was the best birthday present ever.

It was also the most expensive home movie ever. But it made some old friends happy. And possibly saved my life.

BEAT
STREET

44.

BEAT STREET THE MUSICAL

2016–PRESENT

Bringing a flawed, cult classic, 1980s hip-hop film to Broadway as a musical? It's a curveball, but it sounds like a good idea, right? I thought so too, but I didn't know when I started that I would have to put ten years of my life into the project.

There's no instant gratification in the world of film and television, as I've mentioned in earlier chapters. Broadway development can take even longer. It can take years, even decades to pull a project together and for it to come to fruition (or not). Then there's the financing, which is even trickier. So when you find a financier early on in a project, like we did, you can count yourself extremely lucky.

But I'm getting ahead of myself. My *Beat Street* musical journey started aboard a cruise ship in Miami in November 2016. The Summit at Sea cruise is a multidisciplinary event that brings together a diverse community of leaders and is designed to foster deep connections. My friend dream hampton is a founding member, and she proposed me and our buddy Fab 5 Freddy to moderate a panel on 'Hip-Hop and Street Art Culture'. The cruise was to depart from Miami the day after the Trump vs Clinton presidential election.

Months earlier, when Freddy and I had a conference call with the Summit's curators to plan our panel, I mentioned that as the election was the night before the cruise, maybe we should speak about hip-hop and politics, considering there was a chance (a good one, in my opinion) that Trump might win. The Summit folks weren't convinced, but after our call ended, I called Freddy back and made sure he brought the political hip-hop videos he had directed, and I'd bring my 'Sun City' one.

Unfortunately, I was right on point. Trump fucking won. That afternoon we were able to dive deep into the connection between hip-hop and politics, to a somewhat dazed crowd. The atmosphere on the ship was like a wake. I noticed Gina Belafonte at the talk. I knew her from *Beat Street* but hadn't seen her for years. She was a cast member in the film, while her father Harry had been its producer. With her was Raoul Roach (the son of the legendary jazz drummer Max), whom I knew from both college and the 1980s music business. After my talk, we spoke a bit about the election and *Beat Street*.

After that somewhat mentally rocky cruise, we reconnected at the Soho Beach House for some post-cruise decompression. Tina was there too, meeting her friend Gabbi Cahane, who had also been on board. Coincidentally, he was a big fan of *Beat Street*, having first seen it as a kid. Along with Gina and Raoul, we all started a big *Beat Street* love-in, reminiscing heavily about the film. Gina mentioned she was developing a *Beat Street* event at the SummerStage festival in Central Park that summer. This sounded real interesting to me, and I mentioned that I would love to be involved. I said I could try to get Craig Kallman at Atlantic to reissue the soundtrack. My wife Annette, on hearing all this *Beat Street* chatter, thought I should think about developing the film as a musical. That was a very timely idea, but maybe somewhat far-fetched, I thought. I knew the reality of a project like this and how many obstacles would be in our way. I mean, just convincing the film studio that owned the property to option the rights to us Broadway neophytes would be our first obstacle. Then finding the cash to pay for said licence would be a big hurdle; if we failed, we'd have to invest the money ourselves.

But it was an interesting idea, so I reached out to my old friend Michael Holman, who had also worked on the *Beat Street* film. He was second director on the iconic Roxy breakdance battle scene and had also directed and hosted the legendary *Graffiti Rocks* TV pilot, which my partners at Streetwise had financed. He was one of the first hip-hop impresarios, had big props, was still very connected in that world and was the person who back in the 1980s predicted that breakdancing would some day become an Olympic sport. He agreed that the idea of *Beat Street* the musical was a great one. As neither of us was a big fan of the final movie, we both thought we could fix the issues that had let down the film by making a grittier theatre piece.

The first step was connecting with Gina and getting involved with her SummerStage event. I also contacted Craig Kallman, whom I'd already collaborated with on my film *808*, and organised a meeting at Atlantic a few weeks later with him, myself, Gina and Raoul. We discussed Gina's social action group Sankofa, our ideas about the summer event and re-releasing the *Beat Street* soundtrack in box-set form with Craig and his team, who all seemed interested. Craig got back to me a few days later and was very excited about recreating the Roxy scene at SummerStage and reissuing the soundtrack record, which had been one of the first hip-hop gold albums when it was initially released on Atlantic. He even thought that organising a meeting between Len Blavatnik – the head of Warner Music, his boss and one of the main investors in the new musical *Hamilton* – and Harry Belafonte would be a great next step (unfortunately, that never happened).

After the holidays, Craig and a few of his team, Raoul, Gina, Michael and I reconvened at Atlantic. Everything still seemed very positive, with Craig wanting further concrete plans from us. So a few days later, I set up a creative call with Michael, Raoul and Gina, which didn't go at all well. Michael and Gina clashed over who should direct the event. Michael had directed a similar performance, the Tommy Boy twenty-fifth anniversary at Montreux Jazz Festival, very successfully, but I guess Gina had expected to direct this one. Then, when Michael asked about the fee, things went further downhill. Gina basically thought that he should just be happy to be asked to work on the project. At that point all discussions between me and Michael and the Sankofa two came to a halt. We decided to fuck the SummerStage project off and just sit down and start writing a treatment for a *Beat Street* musical.

Michael came down to Miami in June, and we started brainstorming and writing away. We did it at my condo, as I was trying to navigate taking care of Amarone, since Annette was away for a couple of days; my daughter had just turned three but was already getting herself involved in everything we were doing. Michael and I worked very well together, knocking out a story that had the original *Beat Street* essence but was way grittier and truer to the culture than the film. I decided to start looking for a way in at MGM, in order to attempt to option the

Broadway rights. Through Atlantic, I was able to contact Pam Reynolds, MGM's head of business affairs. I had an initial conversation with her, not knowing that we would be dealing with one another for another *three and a half years* before finally landing the option! She initially seemed sceptical about the seriousness of my query, so I tried to educate her on who Michael and I were, and on our involvement with the original film. This seemed to help, and at least I'd made first contact with the right person at MGM.

I got back to Craig, and he scheduled a meeting with Michael and me, his friend Randy Weiner, who had a theatre background and is owner of, and producer at, The Box, and Suzanna Lee, who handled that type of project at Warners. Randy also seemed sceptical about the concept of a hip-hop musical, and of Michael and I being able to pull it off. At the same time he mentioned he'd been in talks with Russell Simmons on developing one! Michael bigged up his *Widow Basquiat* project, which he'd co-written with Jean-Michel Basquiat's last girlfriend. Nothing much came from the meeting, but we were not deterred at all.

We continued developing our ideas, and I filled Tina in. She reconnected me with her friend Cahane, who she thought might be interested in investing in the project. When we finally spoke, he told me about a good friend of his, Richard Fearn, who just loved *Beat Street*, had been a b-boy himself as a kid and was a wealthy tech angel investor who might not be averse to getting involved. I called Richard and told him our plan. He listened and then ran through his b-boy creds and his love of all things *Beat Street*. We got together in London in late January, at the Shoreditch Club, my old home away from home. Our lunch meet went really well. He already knew a lot about Michael and myself – no sales job necessary. He was all in with bringing *Beat Street* to Broadway!

Michael and I were both excited. We finished the treatment and sent it to Richard, who was positive about it and arranged a meeting with us in NYC in April.

From then on there was lots of back and forth between Richard, Michael and me. At the same time, through my Pam connection, Patrick started negotiations with MGM. Optioning the *Beat Street* musical rights turned into a very complicated deal, and there were lots of hoops we were made to jump through by MGM. One of those was, we had to get the original writer of the film script, Steven Hager, to sign off on the deal. Michael and I, who had known Hager since before the film was even made, got together with him and explained what we were attempting to pull off. After schmoozing him a bit, he agreed and gave us some ideas he had for the musical.

There were never-ending conference calls with lawyers and MGM. I remember getting on one while in the VIP lounge at the Art Basel fair in Miami and having to find somewhere to charge my phone as the call dragged on into its second hour. Then, *a whole year later*, at the next Art Basel fair . . . another pretty similar conference call in that same lounge.

MGM put a consultant in place to coordinate between Lino Entertainment (us) and MGM. Her name was Lia Vollack, an ex-record company executive who was also in the midst of developing the Michael Jackson musical, *MJ*, which made her time pretty valuable. She was mostly a cog in us getting the deal done. We were neophytes in the business, and although she had started in another field herself, I felt she didn't really respect us. We didn't hold that secret magic Broadway potion. We had to pass every hiring through her on the way to MGM, including scriptwriter, director, music writer, etc. She had the potential to really screw with our decision-making process. We slogged along and played the game, but just as we were about to conclude our negotiations, Covid appeared. Which obviously threw a spanner in the works.

On 7 July 2020, after over two years of negotiations, Michael and I finally signed a deal with Richard that we were all happy with. The MGM deal still hadn't been inked, but after a few memorable Zoom calls, we finally got it signed at the end of December, right around the time when the first Covid vaccines were made available. By the end of January, Richard had paid the option money to MGM, and we were finally on the road to Broadway. Or so we thought.

We hit the ground running. Richard approached different New York-based theatrical management companies virtually, and we vetted them via Zoom. I decided to get back to Craig Kallman with the news that we actually had the option. He lined up a meeting with Riggs Morales, head of A&R at Atlantic, who worked directly with all things Lin-Manuel Miranda. He A&Red the *Hamilton* album and mix tape and was a good friend of Miranda. Michael and I had long been interested in getting Miranda involved with *Beat Street*. He has been quoted in the *New York Times* as saying how important the movie was in his early exposure to hip-hop.

Tina then hipped me to a movie called *The Forty-Year-Old Version*, starring Radha Blank, who had also written and directed it. I loved the film and suggested Radha to Michael and Richard as someone who might be perfect as our book writer. I then connected with Vivek Tiwary, who was the lead producer on the musical *Jagged Little Pill*. We tried to contact Radha, which proved difficult, as she wasn't repped by a big talent agency. When I finally got through to her office, we were told that she was not taking on any new projects. But we were convinced that if we could get Vivek on board, then Radha might reconsider.

Michael then connected us with a Broadway agent at CAA he knew, Olivier Sultan. He, Michael and I had dinner at Indochine, where we discussed the project. He recommended that we meet his client, Seth Rosenfeld, who was one of the writers on the TV series *The Get Down*. He also mentioned he was representing Nile Rodgers for Broadway gigs. Both Michael and I knew Nile and thought he could be a good call for *Beat Street*.

Michael and I had a positive meeting with Vivek, and Michael checked out *Jagged Little Pill*, which he liked. After we bigged up Vivek, Richard got on the bandwagon and spoke to Lia about him.

She and Vivek, who already knew one another, had a discussion about *Beat Street* in December 2021. Afterwards, Vivek asked to see our MGM paperwork, which Richard got over to him in January. Vivek's lawyer got back to us and said that unfortunately his client couldn't get involved because our deal with MGM didn't fit in with his typical licensing arrangements!

I then had a lunch meeting with Nile Rodgers in Miami, where he was living part-time. We approached Lia with our idea of potentially hiring him as composer/arranger. She thought it was an interesting possibility. Olivier told me to contact Nile's manager, Merck Mercuriadis, whom I already knew, to start moving things forward.

Then, out of nowhere, Radha Blank appeared, telling us she had been going through all her written correspondence, having been out of service because of Covid and personal issues, when she saw the words '*Beat Street*' and Michael's and my names on a call sheet. She claimed she freaked out when she saw the words and asked her manager, 'What's this?!' She explained that she was a real *Beat Street* fan and wanted to get together as soon as possible. This was, of course, very exciting!

I flew in from Miami, and Michael and I first met with Seth Rosenfeld, who I felt would work as a writer. We then met Radha at Ducked Up for dinner, with Michael launching an unabashed charm attack on her, telling her how great her film was and comparing her to Woody Allen. She fuckin' loved it. In return, Radha told us she was all about *Beat Street*, reassuring us, 'Look no further, guys. *I've got this!*'

After this great dinner – and a *Beat Street* screening with Radha the next night at Rafik editing rooms also went very well – we made our decision. But before we went all the way in, I contacted our guys at Atlantic. Riggs Morales said, 'She's a *bullseye*!' Michael contacted Olivier to tell him that although we really liked Seth, Radha had originally been our first choice, and now that we'd met with her, we had to see where that led. Olivier immediately attempted to push a director he repped, Camille Brown, on us.

Then, a few weeks later, in true Broadway tradition, he signed Radha up as a client, before our deal with her was in place!

I finally spoke to Merck, Nile's manager. He told me Nile was very busy, but we could make him an offer through CAA. At this point, I started feeling that we might be in danger of getting too locked in with one agency and one agent.

Michael Holman, Nas and me at the *Beat Street* after-party during the Tribeca Film Festival.

A while later, I got hit with a late-night text message from my friend Feh Tarty, with a mysterious link to *The Daily Show*. It was a clip of the rapper Nas telling Trevor Noah what his favourite movie was. 'You may not know it, but it's this old hip-hop movie . . . *Beat Street*!' Boom!

I immediately tracked down a contact for Nas through director Sacha Jenkins and Peter Bittenbender, CEO of Mass Appeal, which Nas is a partner in. Peter and Sacha had come to Miami for an Art

Basel/Hip Hop 50 event (a brand Mass Appeal owned), and we had a quick meeting. I pitched them on *Beat Street* and Nas, and Peter seemed interested.

At this point, inspired by Nas's Hip Hop 50 celebrations, I began to focus on plans to celebrate the upcoming *Beat Street* forty-year anniversary and the inclusion of breakdancing in the Paris Olympics. In my mind, this would include the release of the long-discussed *Beat Street* box set and a *Beat Street* 40 line with Puma, along with *Beat Street* 40 events. Fortunately, my friend, fashion designer Dao-Yi Chow, had worked with Puma and was interested in getting involved, as were Puma. Unfortunately, the people at MGM thought differently, and the head of merchandise there blew the deal by not responding to the Puma offer in time. Then the MGM film music department continued making a claim that they had been making for years: that while they owned the music rights to *Beat Street,* they had no contracts to back that up. Which made it difficult for Warners (who weren't interested in doing anything in celebration of the fortieth anniversary) to license it to a third party for a box set. So it looked as if all my *Beat Street* 40 plans would be for naught.

By the beginning of 2023, we still hadn't come to an agreement with Radha and were pretty much over Olivier. He had been condescending and rude, in the mode of Ari Gold (from *Entourage*). We made it clear to CAA that we had been negotiating with Radha since September, before she was their client, and that we needed to close these negotiations now.

I discovered that there was a Fotografiska exhibition, *Hip-Hop: Conscious, Unconscious,* in NYC at the end of January. Michael had a few pieces in the show, as did my friends, photographers Lisa Leone and Sophie Bramly. The exhibition was being curated in association with Mass Appeal, and rumour had it that Nas was going to perform. I contacted Peter and told him that Michael and I were attending and would love a quick meet-up. And to our surprise, Michael and I actually got a few minutes with Nas too, who was really positive about getting involved. So in March we started talks with Peter about bringing Nas in as creative producer on *Beat Street*.

After sparring with Olivier for what seemed like years, we finally got Radha to sign on the dotted line on 26 April 2023. Michael and I met her for a celebratory lunch at the Odeon a few days later.

In the third week of May I flew in to NYC from Miami and Richard flew in from London for meetings with press agencies about *Beat Street* the musical. We all got together at the Odeon again so that Richard and Radha could meet. We were all anxiously waiting for Radha to deliver her first draft treatment. When it finally arrived, we went through the treatment and notes process with her, which was when we finally realised that it wasn't going to work with her and let her go.

After a year of negotiations, Nas finally signed his creative producer contract on 16 February 2024. On 14 June we celebrated the fortieth anniversary of the release of the film with a screening at the Tribeca Film Festival, also announcing Nas's involvement with the musical and the release of an anniversary box set of the *Beat Street* soundtrack! I also released a *Breaker's Revenge* b-boy compilation on the Soul Jazz record label, in celebration of breakdancing appearing for the first time at the Paris Olympics. In the competition itself, the DJ played a remake of 'Breaker's Revenge' as the music for the event, which saw American b-boy Victor win the bronze medal. And as this book went to press, we signed Kristoffer Diaz, who wrote the book for the Tony-winning *Hell's Kitchen*, to write the book for *Beat Street* the musical.

Like Jimmy Castor, we've just begun!

OUTRO

The outro of a song is enormously important. It's how the artist leaves the listener; it's that one last audio view in the rear mirror. It's almost as crucial as the first bars of an intro. Is it insidious enough to make you want to put the needle back on the record? To obsessively hit repeat? If it's constructed correctly, yes. You need that perfect balance of just enough, but not too much. A great example is one of my favourite soul classics, 'Mighty Love' by The Spinners. The outro is perfect, a big symphonic groove that enables singer Philippé Wynne to take his time, teasingly stretching things out, giving it his all and taking us to church y'all. It's unforgettable, and I always play it again.

Do I want to hook the reader into reading this book again, rechecking a chapter or two? This was definitely not my intention, but I'd be more than happy if, after making it through my long journey, you're inspired enough to check out some of the music I've spoken about, whether it's mine, my friends' or one of the influences I've mentioned.

I can admit that I always feel proud when people compliment me on my music. It makes me smile when someone name-checks a random track or remix I've done. It amazes me that anyone remembers some of them. It gets me reminiscing about all the music I've finished and all the stuff I've left unreleased because I just couldn't finish it and let it go.

OK, so have I actually finished this book? Well . . . no, not yet. I'm sitting in Soho House, in my twenty-year home base of London, trying to tie the book up with a bow before a meeting with the publisher tomorrow. Will I succeed? Having read this far, you've probably realised that I've always had an issue with completing things, and won't be surprised that I didn't. But when is anything actually finished?

Writing this book, I've finally come to terms with all the time and energy I've put into music that was never released and projects that never came to fruition. I now realise it wasn't wasted time, at least in the case of the music, because that music still exists. The other day I was DJing at a sunset party and dropped some of my unreleased music:

a song called 'Sunrise' and a Pharoah Sanders track called 'Love Hymn', both of which were recorded at the end of the 1990s. Incredibly, they still sound fresh, and even better yet, people responded in a joyous way. That reaction was cathartic for me, and experiences like that and going through the process of writing this book have helped me let go of things I've held back on up till now.

Some people will assume this book was written during Covid. Although I started kicking around the concept of a memoir way back in 2010 with my friend Luke Bainbridge, I only started to focus on it after lockdown was over. During Covid, I was obsessed with the political disaster of the US, my own health and another project, my Rockers Revenge documentary. I lost many acquaintances and my uncle Arnie during those first few months of the pandemic. I really couldn't look back on my past until I felt that a brighter, happier future was possible.

Then I suddenly lost a very close young friend, Gabby Meijer, who passed away in Morocco. She was brilliant, beautiful inside and out, full of life, and her death hit me very hard. She had so many people who loved her, a vast worldwide network of friends whom she loved to connect with each other. One person she brought into my world was José Parlá, whom she had introduced me to years earlier in Miami. José had grown up in NYC as a graffiti artist/b-boy. We bonded through music and started making tracks during the run-up to the 2020 US election, until he was struck badly by Covid and intubated for months. We all expected the worst, and when I had to call friends of Gabby's to inform them of her unexpected passing, most people assumed I was calling about José. But he recovered and was able to attend Gabby's wake, which was the first time many of us had seen each other for a long time.

All the losses of the last few years have made me feel renewed gratitude for the life I've been able to lead through my music. When I took that first engineering course at the age of twenty-two, I never would have imagined that I would go on to have a half-century-long career in the music industry, remixing, producing, writing and DJing. Or that

I would get the chance to work with so many brilliant artists, including many of my heroes. My second-ever concert as a teenager was the Rolling Stones, Ike and Tina Turner and B. B. King; I later remixed the Stones, wrote a song for Tina and produced a session with B. B. King. As a kid, my favourite soul singer was Al Green; I later wrote, produced, travelled and argued with him! My favourite singer-songwriter was Bob Dylan, and I was lucky enough to work on one of his albums and get mentioned by him in his brilliant memoir, *Chronicles*.

I've had the good fortune of being able to travel the world and have incredible experiences through my music and film projects. Being able to document the history of the drum machine I helped bring attention to, the Roland TR-808, and interview its inventor, Ikutaro Kakehashi, in Japan was one of the high points. Working in the studio with Quincy Jones and Ray Charles and sharing a song credit with Arif Mardin during the making of the documentary *Listen Up* was another.

I'd have to say my work on 'Sun City' and the impact it had in terms of bringing an end to apartheid marked the apex of my career. Likewise being able to travel to South Africa many years later and work with many of the best African artists on a record in honour of the UN's '8 Goals for Africa' initiative. Using music to do good is something that should be done more often.

The opportunities I have been offered through music have been incredible. Some have worked out, others crashed and burnt. Music has opened doors, some of which should have remained closed.

In more recent years, I've been lucky enough to be able to share my successes with my wife, Annette, and daughter, Amarone. My daughter is so proud that I do what I do. She's at the age now that she's starting to get more curious and involved, and I want to have her experience things with me.

I could never have predicted what a roller-coaster ride life in the music industry is. Having such a meteoric rise early on had me presuming that my career would be one upward trajectory and that every success would lead to another. But you can't predict success, and my career, like that of most creatives, has been much more up and down. Still, I feel very privileged to have been able to make a living from my work. I still love working and recently started a weekly show on SiriusXM/Studio 54 radio, thanks to the help of my friend Steve Van Zandt. It is called *Baker's Revenge*, and I have free rein to play whatever I want, including much of my unreleased, never-heard-before music. It's been fantastic to have the ability to unleash material made years, sometime decades ago. I love people asking me where can they get the music, since they aren't able to find it on Shazam!

I'm still inspired to create, and I continue to make music every day, although it's now with no expectations, which in some ways allows me more freedom. I've actually come round full circle, and I'm back in the studio recording live for the first time in years. I'm working on a new rumba project with José . . . and no, it isn't finished!

Fifty years on, I'm still looking for that perfect beat.

ACKNOWLEDGEMENTS

Very special thanks and love to my wife Annette for keeping me sane through this journey; to Amarone for being all I could have hoped for in a daughter; to my sister Linda for her strength and love; my stepmother Elaine for the love and interest she has shown me and my family through the years; my sister-in-law Dani for her calmness; and Tina Baker for a lifetime of friendship, advice and collaboration.

Thanks to Paula Harwood and Carolina Mazzolari for being my sisters from another mister; Feh Tarty for *The Daily Show*; Kaz James for being Amarone's godfather; Sophie Bramly, Lisa Leone and Fiona Garden for being amazing friends and photographers; José Parlá for the poetry; Kelly Cutrone for being you; Robert Levy-Provencal for the pre-party; Lati Kronlund for the BFE journey; Ralph Robinson for the Celtics chat; dream hampton for the intro. To my London posse: Jonathan Downey for all the great meals and convo; Marcus Warren for irrational belief; Jake Nava for the hook-up; Ade; Vijay Thakur; Georgina Graham and Malachy McAnneny; Anouschka Menzies and Mathew Ducann; Charlotte Soussan; Kate Spicer; Sara Blonstein; Tracey Emin; Stephen and Assia Webster; Andre Shapps; Alex and Johnny Turnbull; Max Niepce; Vanessa Xuereb; Jonas Akerlund; Caroline Prothero; Tim Binns; Richard and Susan Young; Dave Lubin; Ron Rotholz; Mark Dale; Ali Love for the future; Robin Scott-Lawson and Sean and Katie Mclusky for the return; Mario Jukica; Eve Fiorillo; Ross Allen for all that; Tim Wheeler; Dave and Stef Dewahle; Cecille Fossheim (RIP); and Stuart Braithwaite for the encores. And to my Miami crew: Ben Wolkov; Jean-Charles Carré; Max Pierre; Adam Gersten; Aric Kurzman; Molly Birkholm; Esther Parks; Andrew Yeomanson for the digitising; James Quinlan; Jorge Moreno; Rene

Pereda; Charlie Levine and Natasha Tomchin; Ollie and Adel Buckwell for the sailing; and Eddy Grant, Dwight Hawkes, Donnie Calvin, Adrienne Johnson for the sunshine.

Thanks to Michael Holman and Richard Fearn for the perseverance; and to Nas, Peter Bittenbender and Kristopher Diaz for joining us in the future world of *Beat Street* the musical.

Thanks to Tony Higgins for the Faber intro; Irvine Welsh and Peter Hook for the blurbs and the friendship; Luke Bainbridge for always being on the other side of a DM; Ed and Debbie Cartwright for the advice; Andy Booth for the legals; Dan Papps for helping me through the journey; Rachael Williamson for getting it across the line; and Scott Pack for the chopping.

And to my partners in music, thank you for understanding me being me! To my Artists United Against Apartheid brothers: Steve Van Zandt; Danny Schecter (RIP); Owen Epstein (RIP); Rick Dutka (RIP); Hart Perry; and David N. Seelig.

To Michael Shamberg (RIP) for introducing me to my lifelong friends from Manchester: Bernard Sumner, Stephen Morris, Gillian Gilbert, Rob Gretton (RIP), Tony Wilson (RIP), Andy Robinson and Rebecca Boulton. To Steven Budd for the gigs; Chris Briggs, Jeff Young, Mike Sefton and Vickie Serene for A&M; and John Rocca for the voice.

To my Bean Town friends and collaborators: John Luongo, who showed me what was possible and helped me start the journey; Jo Bisso; Dan Cole; Danae Jacovidis (RIP); Cosmo Wyatt; Joey Carvello; Jimmy Stuard (RIP); Andrei Carriere; Maurice Starr; Michael Jonzun; Tony Carbone; Russell Presto (RIP); Larry Wedgeworth (RIP); Terry Gholson (RIP); Alan Schivek; Herb Jackson; Joey Lites (RIP); Rodney Butler; Michael Anthony Jones; Melvin B. Franklin (RIP); Michelle Wallace (RIP); Stu Kimball and Angelo (Face to Face).

To my NYC partners in crime: Howard Smiley; Joe Bataan for hipping me to hip-hop first; John Robie for your musical talents; Tom Silverman for the opportunity; Monica Lynch for the unique snaps; Ed Steinberg; Paul McCraven; Apache Ramos; Bobby Shaw; Joe Zynczak

(RIP); David Todd (RIP); Jellybean Benitez; Tee Scott (RIP); Fred Zarr; Shep Pettibone; Will Downing; David Cole (RIP); Richard Scheer; Lotti Golden; Steven Hager; Cindy Mizelle; Evan Rogers; Carl Sturken; Jocelyn Brown; Brenda K. Starr; Mac Quayle; Doug Wimbish; David Palmer; Keith Leblanc (RIP); Bashiri Johnson; Robbie Kilgore; Kennan Keating; Gavin Christopher (RIP); DJs Afrika Bambaataa, Jazzy Jay and the Soul Sonic Force (Mr Biggs, Pow Wow and MC G.L.O.B.E.); Tony Moran; Albert Cabrera (the Latin Rascals); Gail 'Sky' King (RIP); Victor Simonelli; Benji Candelario; Junior Vasquez; Adam 'MCA' Yauch (RIP); Elyse Klein; Brian Chin; Larry Flick; Nelson George; Bill Coleman; Junior Sanchez; Sean Mcgraw; and Cathy Williams.

To my engineers: Jay Burnett; Chris Lord-Alge; Tom Lord-Alge; Andy Wallace; Louis Scalise; Bob Rosa; Mark Plati; Frank Heller; Yoad Nevo; Jagz Kooner; Merv de Peyer; and Glen Nicholls for making me believe you were listening to me.

And, finally, apologies to all the bands and artists that I left hanging, and to all the songs that were never released and all the projects that were never completed.

PICTURE CREDITS

6 courtesy of AB collection; **9** courtesy of AB collection; **10** courtesy of AB collection; **11** courtesy of AB collection; **12** courtesy of AB collection; **15** courtesy of Pat Robinson; **17** courtesy of AB collection; **19** courtesy of AB collection; **20** courtesy of AB collection; **22** courtesy of AB collection; **24** courtesy of AB collection; **25** courtesy of AB collection; **28** courtesy of AB collection; **31** courtesy of AB collection; **32** courtesy of AB collection; **33** courtesy of AB collection; **34** courtesy of AB collection; **36** courtesy of AB collection; **42** courtesy of AB collection; **44** courtesy of AB collection; **45** courtesy of AB collection; **46** courtesy of AB collection; **48** courtesy of Jo Bisso; **51** courtesy of John Luongo; **53** courtesy of AB collection; **54** courtesy of AB collection; **55** Wikimedia Creative Commons; **58** courtesy of AB collection; **65** courtesy of AB collection; **68** courtesy of AB collection; **71** courtesy of the Zulu Nation; **73** courtesy of AB collection; **78** courtesy of AB collection; **82** courtesy of Monica Lynch; **85** courtesy of Planet Patrol; **86** courtesy of Monica Lynch; **88** courtesy of Ebet Roberts; **91** courtesy of AB collection; **93** courtesy of AB collection; **94** courtesy of Ebet Roberts **96** courtesy of AB collection; **98** courtesy of Chuck Pulin; **101** courtesy of Monica Lynch; **102** courtesy of Tommy Boy Records; **104** courtesy of Maurice Starr; **109** courtesy of AB collection; **110** courtesy of AB collection; **112** courtesy of AB collection; **115** courtesy of AB collection; **116** courtesy of AB collection; **120** courtesy of Rick Rubin; **124** courtesy of AB collection; **126** courtesy of Rick Rubin;

126 courtesy of Rick Rubin; **128** courtesy of David N. Seelig; **131** courtesy of AB collection; **138** courtesy of AB collection; **141** courtesy of AB collection; **143** courtesy of AB collection; **144** courtesy of Sophie Bramly; **146** courtesy of David Toop; **148** Album / Alamy Stock Photo; **150** courtesy of AB collection; **154** courtesy of AB collection; **155** courtesy of AB collection; **158** courtesy of AB collection; **161** courtesy of AB collection; **162** courtesy of AB collection; **164** courtesy of AB collection; **168** courtesy of Steven Marsel; **170** courtesy of David N. Seelig; **175** courtesy of AB collection; **182** courtesy of AB collection; **182** courtesy of AB collection; **184** courtesy of AB collection; **185** courtesy of AB collection; **186** courtesy of AB collection; **189** courtesy of AB collection; **192** courtesy of Deborah Feingold; **202** courtesy of AB collection; **203** courtesy of AB collection; **206** courtesy of David N. Seelig; **214** courtesy of Zoe Thrall; **217** courtesy of David N. Seelig; **210** courtesy of AB collection; **224** courtesy of AB collection; **226** courtesy of AB collection; **230** courtesy of AB collection; **232** courtesy of AB collection; **234** courtesy of AB collection; **236** courtesy of AB collection; **237** courtesy of Sophie Bramly; **242** courtesy of AB collection; **246** courtesy of AB collection; **248** courtesy of Sophie Bramly; **250** courtesy of AB collection; **256** courtesy of AB collection; **257** courtesy of AB collection; **258–9** courtesy of AB collection; **260** courtesy of AB collection; **264** courtesy of AB collection; **271** courtesy of AB collection; **274** Everett Collection, Inc. / Alamy Stock Photo; **283** courtesy of AB collection; **287** courtesy of AB collection; **290** courtesy of MCA Records; **294** courtesy of AB collection; **295** courtesy of AB collection; **300** courtesy of AB collection; **304** courtesy of AB collection; **306** courtesy of AB collection; **308** courtesy of AB collection; **311** courtesy of Andrea Kronlund; **320** courtesy of AB collection; **321** photo by David Corio/Redferns/Getty Images; **322** courtesy of AB collection; **325** courtesy of Alan Niblo; **327** courtesy of AB collection; **329** courtesy of AB collection; **332** courtesy of AB collection; **336** courtesy of AB collection; **341** courtesy of Lorna Dickinson; **341** courtesy of Lorna Dickinson; **344** courtesy of AB collection; **348** courtesy of AB collection; **349** courtesy of AB collection; **351** courtesy of XFM; **354** courtesy of AB collection; **359** courtesy of AB collection; **362** courtesy of AB collection; **366** courtesy of AB collection; **368** courtesy of AB collection; **369** courtesy of AB collection; **370** courtesy of AB collection; **374** courtesy of AB collection; **378** courtesy of AB collection; **380** courtesy of AB collection; **381** courtesy of AB collection; **384** courtesy of AB collection; **385** courtesy of AB collection; **388** courtesy of AB collection; **391** courtesy of AB collection; **392** courtesy of AB collection; **398** Dave M. Benett/Getty Images; **399** courtesy of Stephen Budd; **400** courtesy of AB collection; **402** courtesy of AB collection; **406** courtesy of Fiona Garden; **407** courtesy of AB collection; **408** courtesy of Fiona Garden; **410** courtesy of AB collection; **412** courtesy of Jonas Ackerlund; **416** courtesy of Hannah Harley Young; **420** courtesy of AB collection; **424** courtesy of AB collection; **427** courtesy of AB collection; **431** courtesy of *808* the movie; **434** courtesy of Jamie Franklin; **435** courtesy of *808* the movie; **435** courtesy of AB collection; **438** courtesy of Warren Jackson; **440** courtesy of Further Future; **442** courtesy of the Soho House; **448** courtesy of Warren Jackson; **451** courtesy of AB collection; **452** courtesy of *Beat Street: The Musical*; **461** courtesy of *Beat Street: The Musical*.

SHE BOP
TILL TUESDAY
SAM DEES SONGS
ALMO IRVING MUSIC
"A.E.I.O.U."
ROGER SANCHEZ
UNTIL YOU LET GO - M.HAMLISCH
2 SONGS BY GUY CHAMBERS.
UPFRONT 1 VARIOUS ARTISTS.
soundtrack
ongs for Al Green
TROUBLE" - Big Trouble
PETE WYLIE
"I WANT YOUR LOVE"
TURN Me loose
POLYGRAM RECORDS
MUSIC SEMINAR SAMPLER
FACE TO FACE
Confrontation
IVING IN A BOX"
NORTHEND DEMOS
STARR STUDIO
First song Rock motown
IOU
TDK SA60
BEAT ST
Nighttime Voc. Ideas
Beat St. Rap Ideas
Battle Cry Voc. Ideas
BILLIE RAY MARTIN
"STILLWATERS"
Date 27.7.95
JOHNNY DYNELL
BEATSTREET
The System.
PRINCE
4/3/84
DANGER ZONE (REMIX)
Roland
MICROCOMPOSER MC-202
DATA CASSETTE
"STOP AND THINK"
BACKING TRAK FOR WILL DOWNING
BAYYAN INT'L
LIVING IN A BOX
Walk away
WILL DOWNING
A LOVE SUPREME.
JEFF BECK
CHICAGO
BLACK EYED PEAS
ONLY FOR THE SEMINAR
ARTHUR BAKER
A&M RECORDS
"We Gonna Ride" - Krazy Horse
Sophie
DIANA ROSS
TINA BAKER
THE QUINC
TEVIN
Sister
TEAR
Jeff Bec
ARTIST.